Studies in French Cinema

Dedicated to the memory of Jill Forbes

Studies in French Cinema
UK perspectives, 1985-2010

Edited by Will Higbee and Sarah Leahy

intellect Bristol, UK / Chicago, USA

First published in the UK in 2011 by
Intellect, The Mill, Parnall Road, Fishponds, Bristol, BS16 3JG, UK

First published in the USA in 2011 by
Intellect, The University of Chicago Press, 1427 E. 60th Street,
Chicago, IL 60637, USA

A catalogue record for this book is available from the
British Library.

Cover designer: Holly Rose
Copy-editor: Rebecca Vaughan-Williams
Typesetting: Mac Style, Beverley, E. Yorkshire

978-1-84150-323-3

Printed and bound by Gutenberg Press, Malta.

Contents

Acknowledgements

We are grateful to the Intellect team for supporting this project from the outset, and in particular to the editorial and design staff for their careful attention to detail. We would also like to thank Intellect for the cover images, and the Association for Studies in French Cinema for generously financing the images in the book. We are grateful to Martin McKeand, Alex Nice and the French Department of Queen Mary University, London, in particular Sue Harris, for allowing us to publish Jill Forbes's keynote address, 'To the distant observer'. And of course, we would like to thank all our contributors for their enthusiasm for the project; we have thoroughly enjoyed collaborating with everyone involved.

All images are courtesy of the Bibliothèque du Film (BiFi), Paris, unless otherwise stated, and are reproduced with the kind permission of the authors, where known. Every effort has been made to contact the authors of the images used in this publication. Images from *Pierrot le fou* and *L'Année dernière à Marienbad* (Georges Pierre) are reproduced with the permission of Laurence Pierre de Geyer; *De battre mon cœur s'est arrêté* (Jean-Claude Lother and Why Not Productions); *Casque d'or* (Paris Films Coop [Paris] and Speva Films); *Mauvaise passe* (Pathé Cinéma and Etienne George); *Ma femme est une actrice* (Renn Productions [Paris] and Nathalie Eno); *La Graine et le mulet* (Pierre Collier); *La Femme du boulanger* (Roger Corbeau and Agence photographique de la RMN); *Gueule d'amour* (ACE Alliance Cinématographique Européenne); *Sous les toits de Paris* (Lazare Meerson). No information was available regarding the authors or copyright holders of images from *Les Enfants du paradis, Bel-ami, Les Misérables, La Bête humaine* or *L'Ennemi publique no 1*. The still from *Dans la vie* is reproduced courtesy of Pyramide Films, with the kind permission of Philippe Faucon.

Contributors

Jennie Cousins is a Lecturer in Critical, Contextual and Historical Studies at Plymouth College of Art, specializing in film and fashion studies. She also works as a freelance costume designer for film and theatre. She is the author of *Unstitching the film à costumes: Hidden Designers, Hidden Meanings* (VDM Verlag, 2009).

Ann Davies is Senior Lecturer in Spanish at Newcastle University. Her books include *Daniel Calparsoro* (Manchester University Press, 2009), *Pedro Almodóvar* (Grant and Cutler, 2007) and *Carmen on film: A Cultural History* (with Phil Powrie, Chris Perriam and Bruce Babington, Indiana University Press, 2007). She is also co-editor of *The Trouble with Men: Masculinities in European and Hollywood Cinema* (with Phil Powrie and Bruce Babington, Wallflower Press, 2004) and *Carmen: From Silent Film to MTV* (with Chris Perriam, Rodopi, 2005). She has also written various articles on Hispanic cinema.

Julia Dobson is Senior Lecturer in French at the University of Sheffield and has published widely on contemporary French cinema, including work on Kieslowski, first-person documentary and Jacques Audiard. A book on Cabrera, Lvovsky, Masson and Vernoux is forthcoming, to be published by Manchester University Press. She also publishes on contemporary French theatre, and her current research in this field focuses on 'performing objects'.

Jill Forbes (1947–2001) held academic posts at the universities of Paris (Ecole Normale Superiéure), Leicester, Loughborough, London South Bank, Strathclyde, Bristol and Queen Mary, University of London. She was a prolific author of work on French cinema and cultural studies, and major texts include *The Cinema in France: After the New Wave* (Macmillan, 1992) and *Les Enfants du paradis* (BFI, 1997). She was also a founder-editor of the journals *Paragraph* and *French Cultural Studies*. She died at the age of 54 following treatment for cancer.

Sue Harris is Reader in French Cinema Studies at Queen Mary, University of London. She is the author of *Bertrand Blier* (MUP, 2001), co-author of *Film Architecture and the*

Transnational Imagination: Set Design in 1930s European Cinema (AUP, 2007) and co-editor of *France in Focus: Film and National Identity* (with Elizabeth Ezra, Berg, 2000) and *From Perversion to Purity: The Stardom of Catherine Deneuve* (with Lisa Downing, MUP, 2007).

Susan Hayward is Professor of Cinema Studies at the University of Exeter. She has published widely on French cinema; her books include *French National Cinema* (Routledge, 1993; 2nd ed. 2005), *Luc Besson* (MUP, 1998), *Simone Signoret: The Star as Cultural Sign* (Continuum, 2004), *Les Diaboliques* (I.B. Tauris, 2005) and *French Costume Drama of the 1950s: Fashioning Politics in Film* (Intellect, forthcoming). She is also the author of *Cinema Studies: The Key Concepts* (Routledge, 1996; 3rd ed. 2006).

Will Higbee is Senior Lecturer in Film Studies at the University of Exeter and an assistant editor of the Intellect journal *Studies in French Cinema*. He is the author of *Mathieu Kassovitz* (MUP, 2007). He has published on Maghrebi-French and North African *émigré* film-making, contemporary French cinema and transnational cinemas in a variety of journals and edited collections. He is currently working on a monograph for Edinburgh University Press entitled *Cinemas of the North African Diaspora in France.*

Kate Ince is Reader in French Film and Gender Studies at the University of Birmingham. Her research in film studies includes the monograph *Georges Franju* (MUP, 2005), translated into French as *Georges Franju: au-delà du cinéma fantastique* (L'Harmattan/Les Presses universitaires de Laval, 2008). She is also editor of the volume *Five Directors: Auteurism from Assayas to Ozon* (MUP, 2008), as well as the author of essays on various contemporary film-makers. She is currently working on articles on women auteur directors, and planning a book in this area.

Sarah Leahy is Senior Lecturer in French and Film at Newcastle University and assistant editor of the Intellect journal *Studies in French Cinema*. She is the author of *Casque d'or* (I.B. Tauris, 2007), and has also published on stardom and femininity, Agnès Jaoui, Prévert and the Groupe Octobre, and cinema-going in Newcastle upon Tyne. She is currently researching screenwriters and classic French cinema.

Douglas Morrey is Senior Lecturer in French at the University of Warwick. He is the author of *Jean-Luc Godard* (MUP, 2005) and the co-author of *Jacques Rivette* (with Alison Smith, MUP, 2009).

Martin O'Shaughnessy is Professor of Film Studies at Nottingham Trent University. He is the author of *Jean Renoir* (MUP, 2000), *The New Face of Political Cinema: Commitment in French Film Since 1995* (Berghahn, 2007) and *La Grande Illusion* (I.B. Tauris, 2009). His main research interests are cinema and the political; classical French cinema, especially in the 1930s; Renoir; and the Dardenne brothers.

Alastair Phillips is Associate Professor in the Department of Film and Television Studies at the University of Warwick. His publications include *City of Darkness, City of Light. Emigre Filmmakers in Paris 1929–1939* (Amsterdam University Press, 2004), *Journeys of Desire: European Actors in Hollywood. A Critical Companion* (co-edited with Ginette Vincendeau, BFI, 2006) and *Rififi* (I.B. Tauris, 2009). His current projects include *The Blackwell Companion to Jean Renoir* (co-edited with Ginette Vincendeau).

Phil Powrie is Professor of Cinema Studies at the University of Sheffield. He has published a number of books on French cinema, including *French Cinema in the 1980s* (Clarendon Press, 1997), *French Cinema in the 1990s* (OUP, 1999), *Jean-Jacques Beineix* (MUP, 2001), *French Cinema: A Students' Guide* (Arnold, 2002), *The Cinema of France* (Wallflower, 2006), *Carmen on Film* (Indiana University Press, 2007), *The Films of Luc Besson* (MUP, 2007) and *Pierre Batcheff and Stardom in 1920s French Cinema* (EUP, 2009). He is currently working on a book about the French musical.

Keith Reader is Professor of Modern French Studies at Glasgow; he previously held chairs at Newcastle and Kingston Universities; he has published on Renoir, Bresson, Resnais and Godard among others and is currently working on a history of the Bastille/Faubourg-Saint-Antoine area of Paris.

Alison Smith is Lecturer in European Film Studies and French at the University of Liverpool. She has published books on the French cinema of the 1970s and on the films of Agnès Varda (*Agnès Varda*, MUP, 1998) and Jacques Rivette (*Jacques Rivette*, with Douglas Morrey, MUP, 2010).

Carrie Tarr is Visiting Professor of Film in the Faculty of Arts and Social Sciences, Kingston University, UK. She has published widely on ethnicity, gender and sexuality in French and Francophone cinema. Her publications include *Cinema and the Second Sex: Women's Filmmaking in France in the 1980s and 1990s* (with B. Rollet, Continuum, 2001) and *Reframing Difference: Beur and Banlieue Cinema in France* (MUP, 2005). She recently guest-edited a special issue of *Modern & Contemporary France* on 'French cinema: Transnational cinema?' (2007), and co-edited (with G. Rye) a special issue of *Nottingham French Studies* on 'Focalising the Body in Contemporary Women's Writing and Filmmaking in France' (2007) and (with R. Porton) a supplement to *Cineaste* entitled 'Beur is Beautiful' (2008). She is currently working on French women film-makers in the 2000s and on Franco-African cinematic connections.

Ginette Vincendeau is Professor of Film Studies and Head of the Film Studies Department at King's College, London. She has written widely on popular French and European cinema. She is the editor of *The Encyclopedia of European Cinema* (BFI/Cassell, 1995) and co-editor of *French Film: Texts and Contexts* (with Susan Hayward, Routledge, 1990; 2nd ed. 2000) and *Journeys of Desire, European Actors in Hollywood* (with Alastair Phillips, BFI, 2006). She is the author of *Pépé le Moko* (BFI, 1998), *Stars and Stardom in French Cinema* (Continuum, 2000; 2nd ed. 2004; published in French 2008), *Jean-Pierre Melville: An American in Paris* (BFI, 2003) and *La Haine* (I.B. Tauris, 2005). Her new book, *Popular French Cinema: From the Classical to the Transnational*, will be published by I.B. Tauris in 2011. She is currently working on a study of the representation of the South of France in international film and television, and co-editing *The Blackwell Companion to Jean Renoir*.

Emma Wilson is Reader in Contemporary French Literature and Film at the University of Cambridge and a Fellow of Corpus Christi College. Her recent publications include the monographs *Alain Resnais* (MUP, 2006) and *Atom Egoyan* (Illinois University Press, 2009).

Chapter 1

Introduction

Will Higbee and Sarah Leahy

For more than twenty years, UK-based academics have been making key and distinct contributions to the way French cinema (its history and theory) has been taught and researched in both English-language and French universities. Following on from pioneering work produced by academics in France and the United States during the late 1960s and 1970s, studies focusing on key film-makers and movements such as Godard and 1930s Poetic Realism had begun to emerge in English by the mid-1980s – see, for example, Colin MacCabe's work on Godard (1980), Roy Armes' monograph *French Cinema* (1985) and Keith Reader's (1981) analysis of French cinema in *Cultures on Celluloid*. In 1984, French cinema studies gained a certain visibility within the broader field of French studies, as the first-ever panel on French cinema at the Society for French Studies' conference was convened; as part of this panel, Keith Reader presented a paper on *La Règle du jeu/The Rules of the Game* (Renoir 1939), Russell Cousins on *La Bête humaine/The Human Beast* (Renoir 1938) and Jill Forbes on Jean-Louis Baudry and theory.

Perhaps one of the first events where the question of French cinema as a discipline was directly debated was at the pioneering conference on European Cinema convened by Susan Hayward at Aston University in 1982. The proceedings of that conference, published in 1985, contain a short piece by Hayward entitled 'Film Studies and Modern Languages', in which she argues for the importance of varying theoretical approaches according to what is made necessary by the 'filmic language' (Hayward 1985: 155), indicating a desire to avoid any methodological or epistemological *parti pris* – a concern that has characterized Hayward's work. The first PhD thesis on French Cinema was also completed in 1985. Submitted by Ginette Vincendeau to the University of East Anglia, this was entitled 'Social Text and Context of a Popular Entertainment Medium' (Vincendeau 1985).[1] It is this thesis – as Phil Powrie argues in Part III of this book – that, along with the intervention of academics such as Forbes, Hayward and Reader at the aforementioned conferences of the mid-1980s, marks the start of the UK strand of French cinema studies. Finally, 1985 was a key date in the sense that the end of the year also saw the publication of the first of a series of seminal articles by Ginette Vincendeau in *Screen* – the academic journal that was then, and remains now, arguably the most important and prestigious forum for academic debate in the discipline of film studies. The article was titled 'Community, Nostalgia and the Spectacle of Masculinity' (Vincendeau 1985a); though it was certainly not the first contribution on French cinema to be published in *Screen*, it was notable for the way that it identified multiple areas of inquiry – popular cinema of the 1930s, French stardom, gender representation – that would emerge as key concerns in UK French film studies. The mid-1980s was therefore a crucial period for the emergence and visibility of a nascent network of UK-based researchers whose contribution is being recognized by this volume, which considers UK perspectives on studies in French cinema from 1985 to the present.

Under the direction of Susan Hayward and Ginette Vincendeau, this early research, collaboration and ongoing intellectual exchange from the 1980s led to arguably two of the most important departures for French screen studies in the English language in the early 1990s. The first of these was the publication of *French Film: Texts and Contexts* (1990), a collection of new work on French cinema by French, UK and US academics, edited by Hayward and Vincendeau, which ranged from the early silent period to the mid-1980s. The second was Hayward's groundbreaking *French National Cinema* (1993), which established the Routledge National Cinemas Series and opened up discussions around the place and significance (ideological, political and economic) of the 'national' within a given national cinema or film culture, discussions that have had a broader impact in relation to national cinema studies in the fields of Film Studies and Modern Languages more generally.

What distinguished these two books was the way they considered French 'national' cinema in a context that combined research on the established key movements and moments (1920s Avant-garde, 1930s Poetic Realism, The Nouvelle Vague) in French cinema with apparently under-valued or overlooked films and film-makers who were seen as the antithesis of the art-house auteur that so characterized perceptions of French cinema from across the Channel.

Another significant achievement of *French Film: Texts and Contexts* was that it brought together for the first time leading academics from the United Kingdom, France and the United States who were working on French cinema. In much the same way that French national cinema must be seen in its transnational context – as part of a global network of cinematic relations – we recognize that scholarship is necessarily international in scope and in influence. Even a cursory glance at the bibliographical references in this volume reveals the centrality of international dialogue and exchange to the development of French cinema studies as a discipline. The focus on UK perspectives in this volume, then, is certainly not intended to exclude from the debate pioneering work on French cinema from France, the United States, Oceania, Canada and elsewhere. Rather, it is to take stock, after 25 years, of the evolution of the discipline with the UK university context and the impact of the emergence of French film as an object of study on the French studies curriculum, and to consider where the study of French cinema might be going from here. Inevitably, then, there is groundbreaking work – such as that of Bill Marshall (2009) on the French Atlantic, Mireille Rosello (1997, 2001) on postcolonial French film, Geneviève Sellier (2005) on gender in French cinema, Colin Crisp (1993) and Dudley Andrew (1995) on both the cinematic and cultural history of France, Laurent Creton (2004) on the economy of the French film industry, Michel Marie (1997) on the Nouvelle Vague and Raphaëlle Moine (2005a, 2005b) on genre, to cite just a few examples – which we have not been able to include directly, but whose major contribution to the field should be clear from the way this work has informed the scholarship presented here.

The focus of this volume also precludes the possibility of considering the important contribution of UK-based academics to the emerging field of postcolonial francophone French Studies – in particular, Murphy (2008), Thackway (2003) and Spass (2000), but above all the peerless contribution to studies of francophone North African and Sub-Saharan cinema produced by Roy Armes through numerous publications since the mid-1980s (see, for example, Armes 1987, 2005, 2007). The influence of such scholarship, its concern with colonial, postcolonial, diasporic and third cinema, and the ways in which diasporic film-makers from former French colonies destabilize or redefine our understanding of the boundaries of the nation in French national cinema is nonetheless present in this volume through the work of Carrie Tarr (Chapters 6 and 23) and Will Higbee (Chapter 16). Indeed, as the debates featured on the national and transnational of French cinema demonstrate (see in particular Hayward, Chapter 3 and Vincendeau, Chapter 24), these constantly shifting boundaries are particularly tricky to map.

Since the mid-1980s, then, drawing on a range of methodological approaches – from a focus on historical or textual analysis to cultural studies and feminist film theory – UK-based scholars of French cinema have published pioneering research in relation to French stardom, popular genre cinema, French women directors, representations of gender, French queer cinema and representations of sexuality, as well as postcolonial cinemas in France. These same scholars have also been attuned to developments in the wider field of film studies –in Chapter 7, for example, Vincendeau argues for a need to expand the work on stardom begun in the 1980s, which had been almost exclusively focused on Hollywood to the context of the 1930s French popular cinema and particularly the French star Jean Gabin. The choice here of a male star as the object of analysis also opened up questions of visual pleasure, the gaze and masculinity, thus bringing Vincendeau's work into dialogue with key figures in film studies such as Laura Mulvey (1975) and Steve Neale (1984). Similarly, Susan Hayward's seminal piece 'National Cinemas and the Body Politic' (republished here as Chapter 3) emanates from her own sustained engagement with questions of national cinema in the French context in order to offer an important contribution to a broader theorizing of the national in film studies. This chapter also prefigures, through Hayward's application of Grewal and Kaplan's (1994) concept of 'scattered hegemonies', a series of more recent debates around transnational, interstitial cinemas and cinemas of 'small nations' – see, for example, Ezra and Rowden (2006), Hjort and Petrie (2007) and Higbee and Lim (2010). Elsewhere, the work of Tarr, Forbes, Hayward, Reader and Powrie (including examples of their work found in this volume) has responded in various ways to what we might describe as the spatial turn that occurs in film studies during the 1990s, following on from the historical turn of the 1980s identified by Alastair Phillips in Chapter 19.

The United Kingdom's status as a pivotal site for new and original debate in the area of French Screen Studies was further confirmed in 2000 with the founding by Professor Susan Hayward and Professor Phil Powrie of *Studies in French Cinema* (Intellect), the only international refereed academic journal devoted exclusively to French cinema. *Studies in French Cinema* has played a key role in the way that its editorial policy, along with the annual conference linked to the journal, has consistently attempted to open up a forum for under-researched areas, moments, movements or histories of French cinema (e.g. French cinema of the 1950s and 1970s, popular genre cinema, French queer cinema). In this respect, the journal has reflected the contribution made by UK-based academics (again, in dialogue with colleagues based in US, French and Oceanic institutions) to an opening out of the multiplicity of voices, histories and trends within French cinema, beyond the established canonical moments and movements of the early silent period, 1930s Poetic Realism and the French New Wave.

What marks much of the scholarship on French cinema that has emerged from the United Kingdom since the mid-1980s is the unique perspective it offers on French cinema that is located both *within* and *outside* the culture – a position described by Forbes in Chapter 20 – borrowing from the title of Noël Burch's (1979) pioneering work on Japanese cinema – as that of the 'distant observer':

A 'distant observer' usefully describes the position of all those who study foreign cultures both because of the interpretative difficulties that distance throws up, and because of the privileges that distance confers and the capacity for totalization that it appears, perhaps dangerously, to offer to our gaze. The dialectic of closeness and distance, internality and externality, is one of the fascinating paradoxes of cultural studies – above all, perhaps, in the cinema, where the immediacy of perception tends to obscure the necessity for reflection.

Following Forbes' lead, we would argue that this position of the distant observer is an enriching rather than a limiting one. This is a critical perspective that comes with a considerable knowledge and understanding of the complex historical, social and cultural factors at play within French cinema – or, to borrow Hayward and Vincendeau's term, the texts and contexts of French cinema. However, it also offers an alternative view that repositions the focus of French cinema as an object of study at the same time as it seeks to shed light on previously obscured areas of French cinema via a plurality of perspectives (theoretical and historical) that challenge the homogenizing teleology of a French 'national' cinema. In a similar way, this positioning – which is both within and outside the culture it investigates – can afford productive encounters between French cinema history and theory via theoretical discourses that lie outside the realms/focus of French cinema, most obviously here the analysis of postcolonial and diasporic cinema that the work of Carrie Tarr has done so much to promote in the French context. Such work has been able to shed new light on the representation of France's postcolonial minorities within the context of a multicultural, postcolonial France by employing a set of critical and theoretical concepts (postcolonial cinema, third cinema) more familiar to Anglo-American than francophone academics. Similar arguments can be made for the application of queer theory, questions around the popular drawn from cultural studies and, of course, gender studies. Indeed, it is to this last area that the work of Keith Reader and Phil Powrie has made a considerable contribution.

Both scholars have, in their own ways, interrogated the power relations embedded in gender representation, notably revealing – through analyses of films ranging from René Clair's *Les Deux Timides/Two Timid Souls* (1928) to Resnais' *L'Année dernière à Marienbad/Last Year at Marienbad* (1961) and Eustache's *La Maman et la putain/The Mother and the Whore* (1973), from Bernard's *Les Misérables* (1934) to Besson's *Léon* (1994) – masculine identities that are most definitely positioned outside of a heteronormative, patriarchal paradigm (see, for example, Reader 1993, 2006, 2008; Powrie 1997, 2004, 2006a, 2006b, 2008, 2009). Indeed, this theme can be traced further in the work of Powrie. Drawing on Foucault's concept of heterotopia (Foucault 1986), Powrie considers the implications of contemporary French cinema's construction of space as 'other' not only for the films' protagonists but also for their spectators, who thus find themselves relating to something both familiar and yet distant – even irretrievable (see Chapter 4 of this book).

The notion of the outsider perspective thus emerges as a common theme across many chapters in this volume (see, for example, Chapters 3, 4, 11, 12, 13, 16, 20, 21, 22 and 23). Indeed, drawing on Bakhtin, Higbee (Chapter 16) emphasizes the 'mutually enriching' possibilities of such a dialogic encounter between two cultures, a point already emphasized by Carrie Tarr in her seminal article on beur film-making in the 1980s and 1990s that is reproduced as Chapter 6.

The second key concern of the scholarship on French cinema that has emerged from the United Kingdom since the mid-1980s has been a rigorous and multi-faceted interrogation of the uncertain status of the national in French national cinema in all its forms: theoretical, sociological, ideological, cultural, historical and economic. We might consider this preoccupation an inevitable by-product of studying French cinema – or indeed any national cinema. However, what is notable here is the extent to which UK-based scholars have wrestled with the slippery and uncertain concept of nation, employing a range of methodological approaches that incorporate the theorizing of nation as imagined community first proposed by Benedict Anderson (1983), the relationship between race, class and nationalism explored by Balibar and Wallerstein (1988) or the questioning of fixity of national history, memory and identity through a postcolonial or transnational optic. The most significant and sustained contribution to debates concerning the national of French national cinema has arguably been offered by Susan Hayward – and is reflected in this collection by the inclusion of her wide-ranging and thought-provoking article 'National Cinemas and the Body Politic' as Chapter 3. However, a variety of scholars have contributed to these debates on the form and function of French national cinema(s), challenging received and monolithic histories of French national cinema, exploring the place of 'other'-ness within the paradigm of the national, as well as the tensions between the continuity and difference that exists within a national film culture – to borrow from the title of Phil Powrie's (1999) landmark edited collection on French cinema of the 1990s. Reader's work, for example, as Morrey points out in Chapter 14, has consistently returned to – and overturned – received wisdom regarding the Frenchness of French cinema by deconstructing the myths surrounding such emblematic figures, movements or places as Renoir, the New Wave or Paris (see, for example, Chapters 5 and 22). Such concerns are, furthermore, addressed in a variety of ways across many of the chapters in this volume (see, for example, Chapters 3, 6, 11, 12, 13, 16, 17, 18, 20, 23 and 24).

In recent years, the intensive (some might say excessive) focus on the transnational in film studies has threatened to obscure or relegate the study of national cinema that was so prominent in the 1990s. The reality, however, is that the national and transnational should always be considered 'in relation', as conceptual terms that coexist within the same films. As the example of diasporic cinema shows us, the transnational can therefore exist within and beyond the boundaries of the national (Higbee 2007). In Chapter 24, Vincendeau thus argues for the need to reassess the 'quaintly retrograde' concept of the national and its continued relevance in understanding how cinema formulates and represents a given national identity, by analyzing the 'Frenchness of French cinema' through language. Despite offering a key indicator of collective and individual (national) difference, Vincendeau argues here that language ('surely the most overt marker of national identity since the coming of sound') has largely been sidelined in previous studies of French national cinema – a position that Vincendeau's chapter begins to redress.

The principal aims of this edited volume are threefold. The first is to reflect on the development of French cinema studies in the United Kingdom over the past three decades and the ways in which innovative scholarship in the United Kingdom has helped to shape the field in English and French speaking universities. Second, the volume is also meant as a *festschrift* of sorts, to acknowledge the contribution of six key figures within the field who have helped shape the direction of research and teaching of French cinema: Jill Forbes,[2] Susan Hayward, Phil Powrie, Keith Reader, Carrie Tarr and Ginette Vincendeau. Finally, the volume considers the potential 'futures' of French Cinema Studies by including brand new research from both established names within the field, as well as up and coming academics. As such, it is hoped that this volume testifies to the importance of discursive relations between scholars, with a view to mapping the dynamic and intricate networks integral to this field – as to many others in the arts and humanities. The above aims have thus influenced the structure of this book. Part I offers a selection of seminal articles from the six pioneering scholars honoured in this volume. Here we have selected a range of articles from across the past 25 years: from Vincendeau's 'Community, Nostalgia and the Spectacle of Masculinity: Jean Gabin', first published in *Screen* in 1985 (Chapter 7), to Phil Powrie's 'Unfamiliar Places, "Heterospection" and Recent French Films on Children', first published, again in *Screen*, in 2005 (Chapter 4). We have attempted to select a range of articles that we feel represent a series of key interventions in the field of French cinema studies offered by these six scholars, as well as reflecting the breadth of approaches offered to the subject in their respective work. In the interests of fidelity to the original publications, these chapters have been altered as little as possible at the copy-editing stage, even though this may give rise to some inconsistency of spelling with later chapters. (This also applies to Jill Forbes' Chapter 20, 'To the Distant Observer' in Part III.)

Part II offers a series of new pieces written by a subsequent generation of academics in the field. These chapters engage in a dialogue with earlier work by the six named academics. Sue

Harris and Julia Dobson respond to the work of Jill Forbes in Chapters 8 and 9 respectively. While Harris offers a very personal perspective on Jill's contribution to the development of French cinema as a discipline, Dobson engages with her work on *Pierrot le fou* (see Chapter 2) as a model for examining the text and intertexts of Jacques Audiard's *De Battre mon cœur s'est arrêté/The Beat That My Heart Skipped* (2005). Jennie Cousins (Chapter 10) and Sarah Leahy (Chapter 11) engage with Susan Hayward's pioneering work on the national of French cinema and her commitment to shedding light on under-researched areas. Cousins' chapter follows up on Hayward's current work on the 1950s costume drama, offering an analysis of the male characters' clothing in *Casque d'or/Golden Helmet* (Becker 1952). Leahy's chapter attempts to take up the challenge posed to readers at the end of Hayward's 'National Cinemas and the Body Politic' (see Chapter 3) to consider the role of cinema in representing the 'scattered hegemonies' of the nation to itself through the depiction of the sexed female body, with a consideration of the representation of the maternal in Claudel's *Il y a longtemps que je t'aime/I've Loved You So Long* (2008). Ann Davies (Chapter 12) and Alison Smith (Chapter 13) consider the contribution of Phil Powrie to French cinema studies. Davies, as a scholar of Spanish, Latin American and Basque cinema, explores Powrie's mapping of the field and engages with the questions surrounding national cinemas as disciplines to be studied. Smith, on the other hand, focuses on Powrie's ongoing work on masculine identities, considering two French films that cross the channel in order to explore particular aspects of masculinity: Michel Blanc's *Mauvaise Passe/The Escort* (1999) and Yvan Attal's *Ma femme est une actrice/ My Wife is an Actress* (2001).

Douglas Morrey (Chapter 14) offers an overview of Keith Reader's considerable contribution to French film studies in the United Kingdom (as well as to French Studies more generally), emphasizing his ability to render complex theory accessible to a wide readership, his constant concern for the physical availability of films and his thought-provoking analysis of the work of Bresson and Renoir, which has helped academics and students alike to consider these revered auteurs in new and original ways. Emma Wilson (Chapter 15) pays tribute to Reader's thinking on sexuality and gender in French cinema by explaining how his use of Deleuze's discussion of masochism to explore Resnais' *L'Année dernière à Marienbad* as a 'scenario of desire which rethinks (gendered) power relations' has allowed her to reassess her own position on the film. Will Higbee (Chapter 16) and Kate Ince (Chapter 17) reflect on the work of Carrie Tarr and her continuing influence on the analysis of representations of gender and ethnicity in French film. Higbee addresses Tarr's analysis of Maghrebi-French and North African *émigré* film-makers in France through one specific film, Abdellatif Kechiche's *La Graine et le mulet/Couscous* (2007), arguing that the film's treatment of space (location) in relation to diaspora, gender and class furthers Tarr's own ideas as to how difference is spatially coded in Maghrebi-French and North African *émigré* film-making. Ince considers the substantial contribution made by Tarr to our understanding of French women's film-making, which she describes as 'fundamental' to establishing it as an area of research for Anglophone studies of French cinema. Finally, Martin O'Shaughnessy (Chapter 18) and Alastair Phillips (Chapter 19) assess the formidable contribution made by Ginette Vincendeau to French film studies in the United Kingdom since the mid-1980s. O'Shaughnessy enters into a dialogue with Vincendeau's pioneering and wide-ranging work on French stardom to analyze the underlying tensions between the corporeal and the societal within a range of male star performances from Raimu to Delon. Phillips then positions Vincendeau's work as a theoretically informed film historian from two locations: first, the intersection between gender, class and performance; and second, questions of popular cinema, national identity and genre.

Part III includes new work from each of the six scholars featured in Part I. Some of these pieces take as their starting points specific considerations of under-researched films – for example, Hayward (Chapter 21) on Daquin's *Bel-Ami* (1954/57) and Reader (Chapter 22) on Bernard's *Les Misérables* (1934) – shedding new light on areas hitherto neglected by scholars (the tradition of quality costume drama and popular literary adaptations of the 1930s respectively). Others address wide-ranging issues for the consideration of French cinema as national cinema – see Vincendeau (Chapter 24) on the importance of language or Forbes (Chapter 20) on the role of the set designer) – while Tarr once again reveals the porosity of the boundaries of French cinema with an examination of Jewish–Arab relations in recent French and Maghrebi cinema. Finally, Powrie's piece offers an invaluable overview of the development of the discipline from its origins in the early 1980s up to the present day and, perhaps most importantly, considers where French cinema studies might go from here.

Notes

1. As Powrie points out in Chapter 25, there had in fact been two doctorates on French cinema awarded in the United Kingdom prior to Vincendeau's, but by individuals who were not to pursue a career in academic environments: see Jones (1978); Kwietniowski (1984).
2. Jill Forbes very sadly died in 2001, though her influence continues to be keenly felt in French film studies. We are delighted to be able to include in this collection a previously unpublished keynote address by Jill alongside the new research from Hayward, Powrie, Reader, Tarr and Vincendeau. The editors are extremely grateful to Martin McKeand and Alex Nice for their permission to publish her work in this edited collection.

References

Anderson, B. (1983), *Imagined Communities: Reflections on the Origin and Spread of Nationalism*, London and New York: Verso.

Andrew, D. (1995), *Mists of Regret: Culture and Sensibility in Classic French Film*, Princeton, NJ: Princeton University Press.

Armes, R. (1985), *French Cinema*, London: Secker & Warburg.

Armes, R. (1987), *Third World Filmmaking and the West*, Berkeley, CA: University of California Press.

Armes, R. (2006), *African Filmmaking: North and South of the Sahara*, Edinburgh: Edinburgh University Press.

Balibar, E. and Wallerstein, M. (1988), *Race, nation, classe: les identités ambiguës*, Paris: La Découverte.

Burch, N. (1979), *To the Distant Observer: Form and Meaning in the Japanese Film*, Berkeley: University of California Press.

Creton, L. (2004), *Histoire économique du cinéma français. Production et financement. 1940–1959*, Paris: CNRS.

Crisp, C. (1993), *The Classic French Cinema: 1930–1960*, Bloomington, IN: Indiana University Press.

Ezra, E. and Rowden, T. (eds) (2006), *Transnational Cinema: The Film Reader*, London: Routledge.

Grewal, I. and Kaplan, C. (eds) (1994), *Scattered Hegemonies: Postmodernity and Transnational Feminist Practice*, Minneapolis, MN: University of Minnesota Press.

Hayward, S. (1985), 'Film Studies in Modern Languages', in S. Hayward (ed.), *European Cinema Conference Papers*, Birmingham: AMLC, Aston University, pp. 154–57.

Hayward, S. (1993), *French National Cinema*, London: Routledge.

Hayward, S. and Vincendeau, G. (eds) (1990), *French Film: Texts and Contexts*, London: Routledge.

Higbee, W. (2007), 'Locating the Postcolonial in Transnational Cinema: The Place of Algerian Émigré Directors in Contemporary French Film', *Modern and Contemporary France*, 15(1), pp. 51–64.

Higbee, W. and Lim, S.H. (2010), 'Concepts of Transnational Cinema: Towards a Critical Transnationalism in Film Studies', *Transnational Cinemas*, 1(1), pp. 7–21.

Hjort, M. and Petrie, D. (eds) (2007), *The Cinema of Small Nations*, Edinburgh: Edinburgh University Press.

Jones, D.W. (1978), 'Jean Cocteau's Use of the Cinema to Express the Myth of the Poet', PhD thesis, Leeds.

Kwietniowski, R. (1984), 'Chantal Akerman and the Cinema of Stories', PhD thesis, Kent.

MacCabe, C. (1980), *Godard: Images, Sounds, Politics*, London: BFI.

Marie, M. (2000), *La Nouvelle Vague: une école artistique*, Paris: Nathan. Translated by Richard Neupert as *The French New Wave: An Artistic School*, Malden: Blackwell (2003).

Marshall, B. (2009), *The French Atlantic: Travels in Culture and History*, Liverpool: Liverpool University Press.

Moine, R. (2005a), *Les Genres du cinéma*, Paris: Armand Colin.

Moine, R. (ed.) (2005b), *Le Cinéma français face aux genres*, Paris: Association Française de Recherche sur l'Histoire du Cinéma.

Mulvey, L. (1975), 'Visual Pleasure and Narrative Cinema', *Screen* 16(3), pp. 6–18.

Murphy, D. and Williams, P. (2008), *Postcolonial African Cinema: Ten Directors*, Manchester: Manchester University Press.

Neale, S. (1984), 'Masculinity as Spectacle', *Screen*, 24(6), pp. 2–17.

Powrie, P. (1997), *French Cinema in the 1980s: Nostalgia and the Crisis of Masculinity*, Oxford: Clarendon Press.

Powrie, P. (ed.) (1999), *French Cinema in the 1990s: Continuity and Difference*, Oxford, Oxford University Press.

Powrie, P. (2004), 'The W/hole and the Abject', in P. Powrie, A. Davies and B. Babington (eds), *The Trouble with Men: Masculinities in European and Hollywood Cinema*, London: Wallflower Press, pp. 207–17.

Powrie, P. (2006a), '*Léon* and the Cloacal Labyrinth', in S. Hayward and P. Powrie (eds), *The Films of Luc Besson: Master of Spectacle*, Manchester: Manchester University Press, pp. 147–59

Powrie, P. (2006b), 'Of Suits and Men in the Films of Luc Besson', in S. Hayward and P. Powrie (eds), *The Films of Luc Besson: Master of Spectacle*, Manchester: Manchester University Press, pp. 75–89.

Powrie. P. with Rebillard, E. (2009), *Pierre Batcheff and Stardom in 1920s French Cinema*, Edinburgh: Edinburgh University Press.

Reader, K. (1993), '"Pratiquement plus rien d'intéressant ne se passe": Jean Eustache's *La Maman et la putain*', *Nottingham French Studies*, 32(1), pp. 91–98.

Reader, K. (2006), *The Abject Object: Avatars of the Phallus in Contemporary French Theory, Literature and Film*, Amsterdam: Rodopi.

Rosello, M. (1997), *Declining the Stereotype: Representation and Ethnicity in French Cultures*, Hanover, NH: New England University Press.

Rosello, M. (2001), *Postcolonial Hospitality: The Immigrant as Guest*, Stanford: Stanford University Press.

Sellier, G. (2005), *La Nouvelle Vague: un cinéma au masculin singulier*, Paris: CNRS. Translated by K. Ross as *Masculine Singular: French New Wave Cinema*, Durham, NC: Duke University Press.

Spass, L. (2000), *The Francophone Film: A Struggle for Identity*, Manchester: Manchester University Press.

Vincendeau, G. (1985a), 'French Cinema in the 1930s: Social Text and Context of a Popular Entertainment Medium', unpublished PhD Thesis, University of East Anglia.

Vincendeau, G. (1985b) 'Community, Nostalgia and the Spectacle of Masculinity', *Screen*, 26(6), pp. 18–39.

Part I

Chapter 2

Pierrot le fou and Post-New Wave French Cinema

Jill Forbes

Pierrot le fou marks a turning point in Godard's career and a challenge to the New Wave aesthetic. Although clearly a film of the 1960s, it is also the link between his major early films, *A bout de souffle/Breathless* (1959) and *Le Mépris/Contempt* (1963), and the seminal post-1968 works *Tout va bien* (1972), *Sauve qui peut (la vie)/Every Man for Himself* (1979) and *Passion* (1982). In its exploration of shifting attitudes toward the United States, it documents the decade of rapid change that rendered the France of 1964 unrecognizable to that of 1974, and in its investigation of conceptions of authorship, narrative and genre predicts the ruins of one aesthetic and the birth of another, signalling the visual and thematic changes that distinguish the '*après nouvelle vague*' from the *nouvelle vague*.[1]

The American challenge

The cinema embodied all the ambiguities of French attitudes toward the United States in the postwar period, portraying the US both as a vibrant source of social, economic, and cultural modernity, and as a ruthless colonial power bent on destroying France's cultural specificity. This accounts for the wry confrontation between old-fashioned French gangsters and new-fangled Americanized villains in French films of the 1950s, which often depicted, in thinly disguised fictional form, a fact of French life in the aftermath of the war, acutely experienced by Godard's generation as a colonial occupation.[2] By tracing the evolution of French attitudes towards America and the way these were inscribed in cinema, we can begin to understand some of the more elliptical moments of *Pierrot le fou* and what they signify in the context of Godard's *oeuvre*.

As a critic for *Cahiers du cinéma*, Godard had always attributed a world cultural role to Hollywood, claiming – somewhat provocatively – that its 'classicism' was analogous to the 'universalism' of French literature in the eighteenth century.[3] As a film-maker, he paid tribute to the seductive influence of Hollywood by reworking, in an obviously minor key, American genres such as the thriller and the musical and creating characters who imagine themselves to be actors in American films. The 'anxiety of influence', as Harold Bloom (1973) called it, was given full expression in New Wave films that saw Hollywood both as an agent for the destruction of the European tradition of high art *(Le Mépris, Tirez sur le pianiste/ Shoot the Piano Player* [François Truffaut 1960]) and as a model and a source. This explains why both Godard and Truffaut sought out American texts to adapt for the screen in *A bout de souffle* and *Tirez sur le pianiste*, but why both directors structured their films around the counterpoint of different, and often incompatible, narrative genres and voices.

Godard's early films also give a poignant expression to French cultural anxiety in overlaying or dressing the female body in the colours of the national flag, creating a metaphorical nexus that links the representation of women, the state of France and the prostitution of women in mass culture, underlining the idea that the cinema exploits the body politic at the same time, and in the same way, as the body female, and reinforcing the notion that the national question is a question of cinema (Leutrat 2000). We find instances of this in *Pierrot le fou*, where Anna Karina is called 'Marianne', the female figure who traditionally signifies the French Republic; where the colour scheme of her apartment and her clothes are *bleu-blanc-rouge* – blue bathrobe, white walls, red saucepan; and when, sitting in the boat, she is positioned against a French *tricolore*.

But the red and the blue also signify the blood and bruises of a fictionalized and aestheticized violence that, as Leutrat suggests, is now beginning to be real. It is clear that both Marianne and Ferdinand are inspired by popular culture – by slapstick routines, cartoon strips and pulp fiction. When they beat up a garage attendant, they use a gag derived from Laurel and Hardy; when hitching a ride, their *vade mecum* is the comic strip *La Bande des Pieds nickelés*; and when they are short of money they perform a 'mimo-drame', or comic sketch, for an improvised audience. Exaggeration, simplification, two-dimensionality and ellipsis, all of which are typical of the graphics and the narrative techniques of the comic strip, are brilliantly reworked in the film's use of flat planes of primary colours and highlighting of picaresque incident, so that the car accident is shown in all its gory detail and the dialogue also often imitates that of a cartoon strip – 'shit, there's another one'.[4]

Yet gradually these features take on a tragic dimension. Ferdinand's death is an absurd irony because at the last minute he cannot put out the touch paper of the dynamite, and his failure transmutes the pop art blue painted on his face into the somberly pessimistic shades of de Stael, Yves Klein or Picasso.[5] The Vietnam sketch cannot represent the reality of the war that erupts into the film in a news report heard by Marianne and Ferdinand just as they are embarking on their romantic adventure, and in a newsreel seen by Ferdinand recounting the atrocities committed by the American army at Danang, both of which bring home the point Godard was to make more emphatically in *Loin du Viêtnam/Far from Vietnam* (1967), namely that this war was not some far-off colonial conflict but a tragedy that deeply affected the lives of men and women in France and for which they bore some responsibility. For Godard, as for many French people of his generation who were deeply scarred by the Algerian crisis of the 1950s, the question of imperialism – American or Soviet – was often as important as French domestic politics. The international dimension continued to influence most of the political films created by the Dziga Vertov group in the wake of May 1968, which explore the link between imperialism and the activity of film-making, between the power to represent and the politics of the image. But at the same time *Pierrot le fou* tentatively begins the process of reorientation toward domestic concerns that was to become fully apparent in the ironically entitled *Tout va bien* – which is primarily about the state of France – as well as in all Godard's films of the 1970s.

[...]

Pierrot le fou – The Vietnam 'mimodrame' and the impossibility of representing the reality of war.

The death of the auteur

The process of disengagement from American culture is also achieved by questioning the role of the film-maker, of whom two appear in *Pierrot le fou*. The American director Samuel Fuller has a small role as one of the guests at Monsieur and Madame Espresso's cocktail party. Regarded by *Cahiers du cinéma* as an auteur, Fuller was known as a director of B movies that were inspired by his background as a crime reporter and war correspondent, and he had recently scored a critical success in France with *Shock Corridor* (1963). In his brief appearance, he defines cinema as a battleground consisting of the formulaic juxtaposition of primitive human actions and feelings: 'Love … Hate … Violence … Death'. Towards the end of the film, Jean Seberg appears in the fictional role of television reporter Patricia Leacock on location in Marrakech in a clip from Godard's short film *Le grand escroc* (1964). This pair typifies Godard's early style, the virtuoso combination of the B movie and the documentary to be found in his first film, *A bout de souffle*.[6] Fuller, in Europe to film *Les Fleurs du mal*, is like Fritz Lang in *Le Mépris* filming an adaptation of *The Odyssey* for a Hollywood producer. Patricia Leacock, in contrast, shares a name with the celebrated American documentary director Richard Leacock and states that her work is *cinéma vérité*, like that of Jean Rouch.[7] In both instances, the context provides an ironic challenge to the aesthetics of these film-makers. The cocktail party scene is suffused with the glow of the coloured filters that Godard had already used in *Le Mépris* and *Une Femme est une femme/A Woman is a Woman* (1961) and that he would later use in the commercials sequence of *Tout va bien*, to suggest the exploitation of women's bodies by the consumer society, advertising and Hollywood cinema. The Patricia Leacock sequence is positioned after the Vietnam newsreel, and what she says reminds the audience that Rouch's films show how the influence of Hollywood penetrates into the deepest corners of Africa, transforming the imaginative framework of the local people and changing documentary into spectacle.[8]

These are only two of the many occasions when fictional or real film-makers appear in Godard's films. *Pierrot le fou* belongs within the 1960s tradition that began to question authorship as a 'transcendental source and guarantee of meaning', and that was given new impetus by May 1968, seen as the supreme revolt against de Gaulle, the symbolic father of the nation.[9] After May 1968, it became impossible for the film-maker to remain an auteur in the sense that the New Wave had intended, and Godard was not alone in problematizing the notion in the aftermath of the Events. Like many other film-makers, including Truffaut who had perhaps been an even more persuasive polemicist for auteur theory, he began to re-examine the metaphor by reinserting familial structures into his post-1968 films.

[…] Godard always positions himself slightly obliquely in relation to familial structures, as the video watcher and manipulator in *Numéro deux*, the divorced father in *Sauve qui peut (la vie)*, the slightly ridiculous uncle in *Prénom Carmen/First Name Carmen* (1983). And, of course, he depicts paternity as problematic in *Je vous salue, Marie/Hail Mary* (1985). But he also gives the analogy a new twist by linking familial structures to questions of representation as well as to patriarchy.

[…] Godard's personal trajectory in the 1970s, his departure from Paris and creation of the Sonimage company, was an attempt to create a space in which he exercised sufficient control for the image to be as unmediated and unmanipulated by the forces of capitalism as it had been, hypothetically, in some utopian past. His video and television films of the 1970s, *Numéro deux* (1975), *Six fois deux/Sur et sous la communication* (1976) and *France/tour/détour/deux enfants* (1977–78) are, at first glance, very different from *Pierrot le fou* since they show an evident desire to engage with 'ordinary' people and to place on screen individuals and groups previously excluded from representation. They are a far cry from *Pierrot le fou*'s concern with theatricality and performance, and its occasional reminders to the spectator that it is a fiction film. Yet if we compare *Numéro deux* to its intertext, André Téchiné's *Souvenirs d'en France/ French Provincial* from the same year, we can see that although the former imitates the look of a television documentary, and the latter a 1940s melodrama, they both link subjectivity and representation to the family romance and the history of France. The auteur, as theorized by the New Wave, has become a nostalgic fantasy of patriarchal control, so that he is distanced from the real family matters in *Numéro deux* by the framing devices, and he is feminized or infantilized in *Souvenirs d'en France* by the powerful women whose subjectivity dominates the narrative and who take on the role of 'heroes' of the romance.

Tu peux pas dire Balzac? (Can't you say Balzac?)

But the legacy of realist fiction to the cinema was already at issue in *Pierrot le fou* – as it is, indirectly, in many of Godard's earlier films. His first feature, *A bout de souffle*, interweaves two fictional genres, the thriller and the love story, in such a way that each comments on and becomes imbricated with the other. *Le Mépris* is an encounter between a founding text of European literature, the Hollywood adaptation of it and a modern love story. *Pierrot le fou* provides an even more complex set of intertextual relations and an exploration of a whole range of fictional modes.[10] The issues are summed up in Ferdinand's ironic comment on the shift from telephone exchanges designated by names, such as 'Balzac', to exchanges designated by numbers – a comment repeated when he telephones home just before killing himself and says to the operator, 'Have *you* forgotten who Balzac is too?'[11]

For the proponents of the *nouveau roman*, the nineteenth century novelist served as an exemplar of classic realist fiction, the fictional mode they attempted to overcome in a different approach to realism, often based on a playful use of alternative narrative genres such as the detective story.[12] In the same way, *Pierrot le fou* forgets or ignores Balzac by mixing a range of different fictions and a range of narrative genres and modes – the thriller *(série noire)*, comic strip *(bande dessinée)*, *cinéroman*, journal, news clip *(faits divers)*, adventure story, autobiography, prose poem – which are often associated with different linguistic registers – advertising slogans, poetry, songs, journalism – to create a profoundly dialogic text.

[…]

Pierrot [...] draws strongly on the *bande dessinée*. We first see Ferdinand, whose literary tastes become an extremely important feature in the film, browsing in a bookshop next to the Jardin du Luxembourg in Paris. In another reference to eighteenth century literature, the shop is called *Le Meilleur des Mondes* (the best of all worlds), and he is holding a copy of *La Bande des Pieds nickelés* that recounts the picaresque and comic adventures of the gangsters Ribouldingue, Croquignol and Filochard in their travels across France.[13] From time to time, either Ferdinand or Marianne is seen reading this album, and occasionally an image from it is inserted as a close-up on screen. Later, when the couple has arrived on their improvised desert island, the paradisaical 'best of all worlds', Ferdinand reads from Céline's *Guignol's Band,* a picaresque and burlesque account of the First World War as a puppet show or extended comic strip. The film's many other sources of textual material, like these examples, initially stage an encounter between 'high' and 'low' culture that divides along gender lines, so that when Ferdinand and Marianne imagine what they might have done with the money, she says they could have gone to 'Chicago, Las Vegas, Monte Carlo'; he prefers 'Florence, Venice, Athens'. It is as though Ferdinand, the reader of Elie Faure's *Histoire de l'art* and of Defoe, Verne and Conrad [...], as well as Voltaire, Diderot and Prévost, had imitated Céline and chosen to rework the eighteenth century picaresque and the nineteenth century adventure tale in a twentieth century mode when he ran off with Marianne, living according to the morality and sexual politics of film noir in which the woman urges the more passive man – as in *Manon Lescaut* or in *Bonnie and Clyde* (Arthur Penn 1967) – to commit more and more atrocious and sexually exciting crimes.

These experiments with gender-based cultural preferences and assumptions bore fruit after 1968 in the strong French comic tradition led by Bertrand Blier and Josiane Balasko, whose films exploit the comic potential of actors or characters who do not behave according to physical type *(Tenue de soirée/Menage* [1986], *Trop belle pour toi/Too Beautiful for You* [1989], *Sac de nœuds/All Mixed Up* [1985]). They have also encouraged a critical tradition according to which this juxtaposition of textual sources is an examination of Ferdinand's subjectivity, exemplified in Ferdinand's remark, 'There's no unity. I should feel I am unique, I have the feeling of being many'. This has also meant that the narrative is viewed as 'discontinuous' or 'deconstructed', and that the film is usually described as a 'montage' or a 'collage' of disparate elements.[14]

Although the film is all these things, its structure is more accurately described as a palimpsest – that is to say, a work in which texts are written over other texts in such a way that glimpses of earlier texts interact with new ones. The characters therefore operate the kind of fictional 'world switch' that critics have identified in the writings of Raymond Queneau, whose *Pierrot mon ami* is a major intertext of the film.[15] The film creates the extraordinary sensation that Marianne and Ferdinand are observing themselves perform as fictional characters, that they are simultaneously the authors and narrators of, as well as characters in, particular kinds of fictions. It relies on verbal and visual indicators to designate such switches as well as innumerable references to the differences between life and fiction. Very early, when Ferdinand and Marianne have just decided to abscond, Marianne asks

Ferdinand and Marianne reading *La Bande des Pieds nickelés.*

whether their 'adventure'[16] can be as satisfying as that in a fiction: 'What makes me sad is that life and the novel are so very different ... I would like them to be the same ... clear, ... logical, ... organized, ... But they aren't like that at all', and it is immediately following this remark that she first calls Ferdinand by the fictional name of Pierrot she has invented for him. The characters attempt to impose a 'novelistic' structure on their adventure by a rational division of their experiences into 'chapters' that, as has frequently been pointed out, do not succeed one another in numerical order: 'next chapter', 'chapter eight', 'chapter seven'. Sometimes they give the chapter a title, as in 'a season in hell' ('*une saison en enfer*').[17] Frequently, the contents are spoken before they are shown, so that a world switch is usually accompanied by a voice or voices *off*: 'Marianne told ... a complicated story'. [...]

Many of their stories are not original, but are 'pinched from books' – like the stories of heroism, death and the macabre they recount to raise money in the cafe, stories about Aucassin and Nicolette or the aviation hero Guynemer. On other occasions, the switch is designated by visual effects, as when Ferdinand and Marianne disguise themselves as the nephew of Uncle Sam and the niece of Uncle Ho, or when visual inserts from *La Bande des Pieds nickelés* are used to suggest the kind of story world they happen to be in. The fragmentary nature of these stories, the mixture of genres and the complexity of the intertextual references all render *Pierrot le fou* a postmodern film before postmodernism was invented, but this does not make it inconsequential, as many of its first reviewers thought. Godard's text is a brilliantly controlled exploration of different narrative genres. On occasions, it appears playfully nostalgic for the satisfying narratives of classic realist fiction; at other times, it appears to experiment with autobiography in its depiction of the disintegration of the Karina/Godard marriage.

The palimpsest structure allows the film to be more than one thing at the same time and to superimpose different times and different moods by varying the tenses and mood of the verb and by using the voice *off*, which introduces a different time structure and disrupts or breaks into the continuous present of the film. In *A bout de souffle*, Godard had experimented, in a fairly restrained manner, with the dissociation of sound and image, using the possibilities of post-synchronization to achieve narrative ellipsis and a sense of rapidity. These experiments develop in *Pierrot le fou* into a thoroughgoing reflexion on narrative. Technical resources are linked to a play with grammatical structures, so that the voice *off* speaks a different tense, often the past historic, from the continuous present of the film; the infinitive is used to predict actions that will not be seen, and the present tense is used performatively to indicate an action that is not shown: 'I am placing my hand on your knee' ('*Je mets ma main sur ton genou*').[18]

Much of Godard's later work pursues these possibilities. *Numéro deux* and *Six fois deux*, for example, exploit the technological resources of video communication to this end. The film-maker in *Numéro deux* is able to mix images in the same way as sound is mixed so as to hold in view two images simultaneously and to create a third that synthesizes the two. In this way, the version of the Hegelian synthesis propounded by the central character Sandrine is also represented visually. In *Six fois deux*, he can overwrite the soundtrack using a character generator to print on the screen comments that reinforce or contradict what is being said. Film is less technically amenable to this kind of experimentation than video is. Nevertheless, in *Passion* Godard achieves extreme disjunctions of sound and image and gives the soundtrack a high degree of autonomy by, for example, interrupting lyrical musical sequences in mid-crescendo, leaving the viewer/listener profoundly dissatisfied, drowning speech in traffic noise or, in a radically de synchronizing move, showing a person speaking while playing a soundtrack that does not correspond to what is being said. Many independent film-makers in the 1970s experimented in this way with assonance and dissonance, anachrony and synchrony, but only Marguerite Duras most clearly perceived the radical possibilities of these ideas. In *Son Nom de Venise dans Calcutta désert* (1976), she reused the soundtrack of *India Song* (1975), but her images were of an empty landscape so she created long sequences of compelling beauty that have no narrative function like the shots of the sky in *Pierrot le fou* or *Passion*.

Poetry and painting

One of the most poignant scenes in *Pierrot le fou* takes place on the beach of the 'desert island' retreat. This is the moment when Marianne says 'of course' she will not leave Ferdinand, and we know that 'of course' she will. Their adventure disintegrates thereafter, the narrative becomes more difficult to follow, and it ends in the death of both parties, making sense of the film's frequent references to doomed romantic couples, especially those who encountered their nemesis in a distant paradise or a foreign land – Aucassin and Nicolette, Paul and Virginie, Ferdinand and Virginia (in *Guignol's Band)* or Verlaine and Rimbaud. This is the moment when sexual stereotyping is most obvious, and we realize that they have not 'reinvented love'. But it is also at this point that Ferdinand assumes an authorial role and begins writing his diary, like Robinson Crusoe. That text appears fragmentary because it is seen in close-up, but we can nevertheless just detect the quotation from Valery: 'poetic language rises from the ruins'. Ferdinand's diary, or journal, makes sense of the sequence of references to Rimbaud in the film. We are told that one of the 'chapters' is, as mentioned earlier, *une saison en enfer* after the title Rimbaud gave his great poem, itself a mixture of genres – some prose, some verse and a transposed account of his flight with Verlaine, 'la vierge folle'. The section entitled *L'Alchimie du verbe* ('Alchemy of the Word') sets out the kind of material, the 'ruins', from which Rimbaud created his poetic language. He writes that he 'found laughable the celebrated names of painting and modern poetry' and 'I liked stupid paintings, door panels, stage sets, backdrops for acrobats, signs, popular engravings, old-fashioned literature, church Latin, erotic books with bad spelling, novels of our grandmothers, books from childhood, old operas, ridiculous refrains, naive rhythms' (Rimbaud 1966: 192–3, author's translation).[19] From this very fragmentary, disparate and, above all, popular material came the 'alchemy' that allowed Rimbaud to invent a new poetic language using the 'synaesthesia' (correspondence of sensations), for which he – like Baudelaire – is celebrated:

I invented the color of the vowels – A black, E white, I red, 0 blue, U green – I regulated the form and movement of each consonant, and, with instinctive rhythms, I flattered myself that I had invented a poetic language accessible some day to all the senses.[20]

This passage, extraordinarily well known in the history of French literature as a manifesto of the new poetics, shows us the breadth of Godard's ambition in *Pierrot le fou* and allows us to consider the explosions of colour, when a custard pie is transformed into a fireworks display or when the lights from the road play on the windshield as Ferdinand and Marianne drive away from the cocktail party, as *mises-en-abyme* – miniature examples of the transformation of cinematic language into poetry.[21] The 'unity' Ferdinand seeks is one of art rather than subjectivity, a means to synthesize the multiple resonances of language and of colour.

The last words of the film are a quotation from Rimbaud's poem 'L'Eternité': 'It has been found again/ What has? – *Eternity*/ It is the sea gone off/ With the sun' (1966: 138–9; author's translation).[22] The first word spoken is the name of the great seventeenth century Spanish painter Velazquez. Ferdinand is reading aloud from Elie Faure's *Histoire de l'art,* in which Velazquez is described both as 'the painter of evenings, spaces and silence' and as the pitiless chronicler of the corruption and decadence of the Spanish court under Philip IV: 'The world he lived in was sad. A degenerate king, inbred infantas, idiots, dwarfs, cripples, a few deformed clowns clothed as princes'. Then Ferdinand emerges from the bathtub in which he was reading and reluctantly accompanies his wife to a cocktail party thrown by her parents, peopled by figures as grotesque as those at the Spanish court and, disgusted with this charade, he takes off with the baby-sitter Marianne to embark on the adventures that form the action of the film and lead, ultimately, to his suicide.

Godard's films are studded with visual and verbal references to the arts, especially to painting, and his films often 'quote' portraits of women, or 'represent' women, such as Joan of Arc, Mary or Carmen, as well as film stars who have become icons as a result of a long figurative or cinematic tradition. Frequently, the reproduction of a well-known painting, pinned to the wall, is compared to the filmic 'portrait' of the actress starring in the film. This is evident in the comparisons established in *A bout de souffle* between Jean Seberg and portraits by Renoir and Modigliani, and in *Vivre sa vie/My Life to Live* (1962) in which a shot of Anna Karina's head is juxtaposed with a clip of that of Falconetti playing Saint Joan in Carl Dreyer's *La Passion de Jeanne d'Arc/The Passion of Joan of Arc* (1928) and with a photograph of Elizabeth Taylor while Godard's voice reads from Poe's story *The Oval Portrait.*

Nevertheless, the reference to Velazquez signals a new departure. Hitherto Godard's preferred artists have been masters of the modern tradition in painting, such as Renoir, Picasso or Modigliani – painters whose attention is concentrated on the surface of the canvas and planes of colour, as with Renoir and the fauves, or on the exploration of form, as with Picasso and the cubists. In *Pierrot le fou,* these artists are no longer interpreted as modernists but as representatives of a national tradition, evident in the association of the name of Renoir with that of Marianne. It is Picasso's Spanish origins and nationalist sentiments that are evoked, rather than his contribution to modernism, and the quotation of his painting

Pierrot au masque links Ferdinand to the project of reinventing an identity and compares him to the *pitres* (clowns) of Velazquez. More generally, the reference to Velazquez signals a shift in interest from Italy to Spain. In *A bout de souffle* and *Le Mépris,* Italy represented the mythical locus of late 1950s modernity: Rome was the city to which Michel wished to transport Patricia, and the home of Cinecittà Studios where much of *Le Mépris* takes place. In *Pierrot le fou,* Ferdinand and Marianne also contemplate fleeing to Italy – although, like Michel and Patricia, they never get there. By contrast, Spain represents the weight of history and perhaps the failure of the modern (Franco did not die until 1975), and Ferdinand, whose name echoes that of so many of the kings of Spain and who is a former teacher of Spanish at the Lycée St Louis, abandons his Italian wife and her parents for an imaginary return to the sources of a different kind of art, away from a modern world that has become corrupt.

The reference to Velazquez sets the tone for the entire film and indicates that *Pierrot le fou* marks the start of a move from an aesthetic of surfaces to one of depth, from planes to spaces. Gilles Deleuze demonstrated how, very frequently, *nouvelle vague* protagonists appear physically – and perhaps psychologically – as two-dimensional, positioned against flat surfaces rather than located in space.[23] This is especially true of Godard, whose films up to and including *Tout va bien* contain a series of flamboyant and justly famous lateral pans, which, given their context, must be interpreted as critiques of the 'lack of depth' of modern society: *Vivre sa vie* shows the prostitutes lined up against a graffiti-covered wall, *Week-end* (1967) shows an immensely long traffic jam, *Tout va bien* shows both the cross-section of the factory and the raid on the supermarket. Not surprisingly, in *Pierrot le fou* it is the cocktail party that is filmed in this manner, with the camera following Ferdinand laterally as he passes from group to group, catching snatches of conversations almost entirely made up of advertising slogans delivered deadpan.

Pierrot le fou begins the critique of the visual regime that Godard had helped to create, and uses Velazquez to bring into play a different tradition and a different view of corruption. Instead of the harsh, artificial lighting of the coloured filters, he paints twilights and evenings; instead of the noisy chatter of advertising executives, he paints silence; and above all, instead of the surfaces of the modernists, he attempts to represent depth.[24] The lateral pan disappears as the film progresses to make way for the majestic, slowly rising shot of the sky to the accompaniment of lyrical music.

[...]

Past historic

The first encounter between Ferdinand and Marianne is said to have taken place four or five years before the action of the film, and an unspecified period of time elapses between their flight from Paris and the final sequences when they part and meet up again. Even so, like many New Wave films, *Pierrot le fou* almost entirely lacks a historical dimension or a strong teleological movement. In a manner typical of the 1960s, the action takes place in some unspecified present with only the intermittent references to Vietnam to remind us of the world outside that of the diegesis. There is no future tense: the love between Ferdinand and Marianne is 'without a future' and their actions a series of superimposed presents. This has remained true of Godard's cinema, so that although he is extraordinarily attentive to current trends and fashions – particularly those of a cultural kind – he did not participate in the desire to rediscover or rewrite history that was so critical in the wake of 1968. The revisionism that became possible after the death of de Gaulle transformed documentary film-making, as seen in Marcel Ophuls' *Le Chagrin et la pitié/The Sorrow and the Pity* (1970), as well as fiction films, such as Louis Malle's *Lacombe Lucien* (1974), but it did not engage Godard. Instead, the key text in *Pierrot le fou*, with respect to Godard's later cinema, is Elie Faure's *Histoire de l'art* because, for Godard, art is history. He has explained this by saying, 'When you get older, you become more interested in decisive moments' (Albéra 1989: 89, author's translation). The palimpsest narrative developed in *Pierrot le fou* enables Godard to view history not as the 'total resurrection of the past', which is the ambition of the heritage film with its investment in authenticity, but as a continuous present kept alive by iconography, a kind of *musée imaginaire*.

Pierrot le fou directly prefigures two films of the 1980s. The first is *Prénom Carmen* (1983), which, as Laura Mulvey has pointed out, is similarly a story of a doomed romantic couple (1996: 90). The other is *Passion*, whose title manifestly takes up Samuel Fuller's definition of the cinema as 'emotion'. There are various narratives in *Passion*, but the most spectacular concerns the film-maker Jerzy's attempts to stage and film history paintings by Rembrandt, Goya, and Delacroix to the accompaniment of snatches of Mozart's *Requiem*. These extraordinary tableaux are like the frozen frames of *Sauve qui peut (la vie)* or the inserts of *La Bande des Pieds nickelés* in *Pierrot le fou*, moments when, thanks to the cinema, the present is overlaid by the past historic.[25]

Notes

1. Terminology developed by Gilles Deleuze (1986, 1989).
2. Jacques Becker's tale of rival gangs in *Touchez pas au grisbi/Grisbi* (1954) is a good example of the way cinema addressed the question of 'Americanization', a topic discussed in Pascal Quignard's novel, significantly entitled *L'Occupation américaine*. (Paris: Editions du Seuil, 1994). The history of French attitudes toward America is usefully traced by Winock (1982: 50–76).
3. See, for example, his 'Défense et illustration du découpage classique' (Godard 1985: 80–4; Godard 1972: 26–30).
4. This is brilliantly discussed by Barthélémy Amengual in Estève and Amengual (1967, especially pp. 149 and 153).
5. The suicide of Nicolas de Stael in 1955 transformed him into a contemporary art legend; Yves Klein, known for his body art, painted blues exclusively around the end of the 1950s; Picasso's 'blue period' was marked by deep social pessimism.
6. The film was dedicated to Monogram Pictures and starred Jean Seberg.

7. See *L'Avant-Scene Cinema*, 46 (1965): 39: 'Inspector: You make documentary films like Mr Rouch? Patricia: That's right. It's truth motion picture [sic] le *cinéma vérité*.'

8. 'Carefully looking for … that moment when one abandons the fictional character in order to discover the true one … if such a thing exists.' This recalls the scenes in Rouch's *Les Maitres fous/The Mad Masters* (1955) when the Africans become performers who interact in the roles of Hollywood film stars like Dorothy Lamour.

9. The 'death of the author' is usefully discussed by Michael Worton in Forbes and Kelly (1995: 191–3).

10. Many of these are explored in T. Jefferson Kline's fascinating essay, 'The ABC of Godard's Quotations' (Kline 1992: 184–221).

11. So called after the Rue de Balzac, and designating the area near the Champs-Elysées where film production companies usually had their offices.

12. Alain Robbe-Grillet published his *Pour un nouveau roman* in 1963 (translated into English as *For a New Novel* in 1965). In it he attacks 'the only conception of the novel to have currency today … that of Balzac' (1965: 15).

13. This long-running cartoon series, first published in 1908, was drawn by René Pellos in the period 1948 to 1979.

14. Amengual was the best exponent of the 'discontinuity' thesis in the 1960s; Kline of the 'deconstructed narrative' in the 1990s.

15. I am indebted to Teresa Bridgeman for this terminology. Amengual (1967) discusses Godard's debt to Queneau without identifying this process.

16. The term *aventure* is ambiguous in French, meaning both adventure and love affair.

17. This title is, of course, borrowed from Arthur Rimbaud's great poem *Une Saison en enfer*. I return to this matter later.

18. This is particularly true of the early flight sequences.

19. Recall that both Jean Eustache, *Mes Petites amoureuses/My Little Loves* (1975), and Leos Carax, *Mauvais sang/Bad Blood* (1986) use references to *Une Saison en enfer* in the titles of their films.

20. Rimbaud (1966: 121): 'Voyelles', translation modified. ('J'inventai la couleur des voyelles A noir, E blanc, I rouge, O bleu, U vert Je réglai la forme et le mouvement de chaque consonne, et, avec des rythmes instinctifs, je me flattai d'inventer un verbe poétique accessible, un jour ou l'autre, à tous les sens).

21. In retrospect, Michel's facial contortions, imitated by Patricia in *A bout de souffle*, look like a practice run for articulating Rimbaud's vowels, while the carefully orchestrated exclamations of 'pleasure' in the orgy sequence of *Sauve qui peut (la vie)* might be read as a parody of 'Voyelles'.

22. Rimbaud uses or re-uses these two lines in *Une Saison en enfer* in a slightly different version: 'It's the sea mixed/ with the sun' (1966: 198–9; editors' translation). I am grateful to Michael Freeman for pointing this out.

23. See for example, Deleuze (1989: 189–203).

24. It is interesting that Michel Foucault's *Les Mots et les choses* (Paris: Gallimard, 1966) (*The Order of Things* [New York: Random House, 1970]), which begins with an analysis of the use of space in Velazquez's famous painting of the Infanta at the Spanish court, *Las Meninas,* was published a year after *Pierrot le fou* was first released. See Conley 2000.

25. This chapter was originally published as 'Pierrot le fou and Post-NewWave French Cinema', in D. Wills (ed) (2000) *Jean-Luc Godard's Pierrot le fou*, Cambridge University Press, Cambridge, pp. 108–32. The version reprinted here has been abridged for reasons of space. The editors are grateful to Cambridge University Press and to Alex Nice, Martin McKeand and the French Department at Queen Mary University of London for their permission to reprint the chapter as part of this collection.

Chapter 3

National Cinemas and the Body Politic

Susan Hayward

C inema is not a pure product. It is inherently a cross-fertilization (a hybrid) of many cultures, be they economic, discursive, ethnic, sexed, and more besides. It exists as a cultural miscegenation – and is, therefore, a deeply uncertain product as to its heritage. In its hybridity it cannot help but challenge modernist (binary) thought, however implicitly. Cinema is a product whose makers are widely scattered. It is not a single, unified voice, nor is it the product of a single patriarchal discourse. Thus, whilst some cinema may reproduce the myth of a unified nation (obviously propaganda films, films produced at times of national emergency), the greater bulk of its production will not be able to do so, however hard it may strive to conceal this fact. To 'frame' national cinema, to read it against the grain, is to delimit the structures of power and knowledge that work behind the scenes to assemble its scattered and dissembling identities, its fractured subjectivities and fragmented hegemonies, which in their plurality stage the myth of a singular and unified national identity. What follows is an attempt to address the multiplicity of questions that embody, both literally and figuratively, the idea of 'national cinema'. This questioning of concepts of national cinema is composed of two parts. The first will look at national cinema through the historical optic of capitalism, which will provide a backdrop to the second part, which will look at the politics of the (necessarily gendered) subject and its relation to cinematic expressions of nationhood; what I shall term, by way of shorthand, the corporealism of national cinemas.

Capital goes to the movies

Cinema is an industrial invention. It is a product of the nineteenth century, invented to make capital. The huge 'rivalry' between France and the United States as to who first invented the *cinématographe* and who could hold down patents to it started as early as 1896 (a year after cinema's invention). [...] This struggle for dominance so soon after the cinematograph's creation attests to the fact that economic and nationalist considerations were foremost, and were closely aligned with cultural concerns. Although the first *cinématographe* was conceived by the Lumière brothers as having primarily scientific applications, as public screenings increased, film proved to be a big attraction to the general public. From that point on, in order to attract a variety of audiences, cinema expanded by means of product differentiation.

Within capitalism – whose guiding motor is the principle that 'more is more' – not only products, but processes are commodified. This means that industries are vertically integrated (controlling investment, exchange, production, distribution) so that they can maximize market outlets and consumption. In the Western world, only a few nations' film industries have practised vertical integration – including, most famously, the United States and what has come to stand as *the* American film industry, Hollywood. Curiously, however, Hollywood's system of vertical integration did not survive, lasting approximately thirty to forty years (falling away in the 1950s after the effects of the anti-trust laws passed in 1948 against the studios' monopolistic practices).

[...]

Immanuel Wallerstein informs us (1983: 29) that vertical integration and historical capitalism date back to the sixteenth century. Thus Hollywood's model should not surprise us. What should surprise us is why other national cinemas never truly managed to adopt it. If we look at the historical contexts closely and take Europe as our example, we can find clues to this mystery. When, by 1920, Hollywood was fully established as a vertically integrated industry, it became extremely aggressive in its export strategy. Europe attempted to fight back –but rather ineffectually. It sought to seal alliances between countries and to create a pan-European cinema that could stand up against the United States and its drive to conquer foreign markets. However, the various efforts to establish a coherent international trade organization failed because of a lack of true cooperation. European Film Congresses may well have met and hoped that, by bringing European film-practitioners and producers together, some policies would be implemented. But this was never to be, for the simple reason of the uneven development, in capitalist terms, of the various nations' film industries.

[...]

In capitalism, the producer seeks to accumulate. So it is not only markets that will be of concern, but also the cost of labour (and its availability). Major companies of all kinds have long gone outside their own countries to seek cheaper labour costs, moving on to yet other countries once the cost of labour becomes 'too high' (see the examples of Nike and Reebok). Within the film industry, too, the search is always on for lowering costs. Thus increasingly, films in part or in their entirety are being made outside the country that produces them. The labour force involved in a film product is often international. Financing is increasingly multinational. And yet the final product will most likely be identified as emanating from one country – primarily by association either with the director, the stars or, in the case of literary adaptations, the original text. The case of *The English Patient* (Anthony Minghella 1996) is a good illustration in this context. Although it smacks of 'Britishness' (author, director, some of the stars), it is in fact an American-financed product. The profit made from this film will fill American coffers first, with smaller amounts going to the other parties concerned. What this tells us is that America is willing to back a winner (no matter its provenance) and to exploit talent outside its own borders. And once it has made that commitment, it will back it all the way from pre-production to distribution and exhibition. Hollywood/USA, therefore, does still practise a form of vertical integration, only not within a single studio complex as before, but by means of a kind of horizontal, or multinational, integration. If we compare this kind of cross-national success with European co-productions and their less-than-successful outcomes, we can see how poor investment at pre-production level first and subsequently at the distribution level, dooms these so-called Euro-puddings to sink without a trace.

What this also helps us to understand is how national cinemas expose the contradictions of capitalism, starting with the fact that the product value of a film is often less than the expenditure of making it. Most national cinemas run at a loss, yet they survive. They forge alliances with their own indigenous television companies, they attempt co-productions; they look to national and international financing to back their products – but even with all this mixed economy, they still manage to run at a loss. Capitalism cannot function if it does not find a market. But these cinemas do survive, even if they lack a strong enough market to make a profit. How is this possible? There are three possible answers to this question, all interlinked. First, within capitalism, selling and buying are always based in unequal exchange. Thus supply and demand will work both for and against the product (for example, a film may flop at the box office, but its pre-sale rights to television may help it recoup most of the loss). Second, and still within this notion of supply and demand, Hollywood's/the USA's monopolistic drive is always going to be to some degree at odds with the push for product differentiation. Hollywood likes to capitalize on a known formulaic success, but there is a limit to how many *Aliens* or *Rambos* audiences will want to consume. It therefore has to search for something new, and it may not be different enough to attract audiences – or it may be too different. Looking for the new product costs money; it may be necessary to search for cheaper production venues. Getting the new product right takes time; during these gaps, indigenous cinemas have some breathing space and their own products are able to attract audiences for a time. Conversely, the decision may be to play safe and not go forward, which can lead to stagnation and the opening of the market once again for indigenous products to flourish. Third, even though Hollywood seeks to dominate through monopolistic practices (by decreasing demand for foreign films and by invoking strong legal and state mechanisms), total domination is not sought. Competition, however uneven, is necessary. Without it, there are no markets and therefore no profit. In the first two answers proposed, we can see how cinema is about product and market instability, not only for the minority non-monopolistic cinemas, but for Hollywood's own. Cinema, all national cinemas, makes visible the very thing capitalism seeks to eradicate: economic instability within its own practice. In the third answer, other gaps open up and challenge capitalism differently. The dyad of dominant/non-dominant cinema cracks open and, simultaneously, the idea of a singular national cinema with it.

We are talking here of the permeability of borders – national borders, clearly, but also intra-national borders. Thus, on an intra-national level, differently structured economies – such as those pulled together by an independent producer – can bleed through the borders of a nation's dominant cinema, practising an economism that defies the workings of capitalism.

This cinema often gets referred to as 'artisanal' cinema (particularly within France), or art cinema, or independent cinema. Or again, minority groups of radical film-makers can attack monopolistic practices in a 'big' way at certain moments in the indigenous industry's history (think of the *cinema nôvo* movement in Brazil, for example). These practices – of economics and aesthetics – leave indelible traces and are always already co-present with the dominant national cinema. Whatever their label, their presence forces a pluralism within national cinema. Thus, by the very nature of their co-presence, these alternative cinemas (such as, for example, women's cinema, or the black cinemas emerging from France, the United Kingdom and the United States) become national cinemas – scattered hegemonies – in their own right. These cinemas, too, are performing the nation. But, significantly, they perform it differently. On an international level, we note also how 'minority' national cinemas can seep effectively into markets controlled by the dominant monopolistic one (as in the West, Hollywood), either because they play them at their own game and 'win' (for example, the French film-maker Luc Besson), or they break through via the film festival circuit (Turkish and Iranian cinemas are recent examples, including films made by 'dissident' film-makers or films that have not passed censorship at home).

[...]

No national cinema can be an autarky, although Hollywood comes the closest. While it has no need of imports in terms of keeping its own market buoyant, in economic terms it has to call on other nations to help finance its industry (either through international conglomerates, co-productions or partnerships). It uses content to bleed through into other nations' representations of their own history. Its economy finances another nation's narcissism (again, *The English Patient* is an excellent example of this). The reverse, however, does not occur. Thus, in this respect, economism shows us how disparate the concept of national cinema is. Some national cinemas, including France's, are 'forced' into a kind of nationalistic Malthusianism because of the monopolistic practices of others (in this context, we can think of Indian cinema as well as Hollywood; and, to a lesser degree, Egyptian cinema can be seen in this light). A number of national cinemas – particularly France's – depend on the interpenetration of the state in terms of policy and economism to sustain a viable level of revenue and production, Or, because they are nationalized (as is the case of, say, China), interpenetration brings with it an obligation to represent the nation according to specific laws of censorship. Other cinemas (primarily Hollywood) aim at the capitalist practice of autarky mixed with free trade (but only if it favours their market). [...]

So even if we wanted to wish national cinema away as an idea, it simply – if only for economic reasons – will not disappear. But what the above analysis also makes clear is that national identity is an integral component of cinema, necessary to its survival. The relationship between national identity and cinema is more symbiotic than we might at first believe (America/Hollywood needs competitors). The monopoly effects do not in the end drown out resistances. Indeed, they may even provoke them. These resistances in turn generate other models of production that challenge and break boundaries. Crucially, this suggests that these borders are permeable. As the next section will suggest, this permeability is an essential key to our questioning, and our problematizing, of the notion of national cinemas.

Corporealism of national cinemas

Elsewhere (Hayward 2000), I have discussed in some depth how the nation, through its nationalist discourses, cannot be conceived of without reference to the body, in particular the female body and even more specifically the maternal body (for example, the 'Mother-Nation' that we fight and die for, the 'Mother-Country' to which the colonized referred, the 'Mother-Land' that is violated/raped when invaded by the enemy, etc.). I am aware, of course, that certain nations refer to the 'Fatherland' and yet would argue that a similar desire for bonding – although this time with the father (the 'Symbolic Other') – is at play here. I now want to broaden these earlier considerations, using as part of my framework, first, the concept of Mother-Nation (although I will make one or two points about the Fatherland, a context for which there is more work to be done); and second, Lacan's psychoanalytic concepts of the Imaginary and the Symbolic. As soon as we speak of the body, we are immediately also speaking of the subject; and once we are speaking about the subject then we are in the realm of identity, subjectivity and, ultimately, the sexed subject and, of course, desire – and this necessarily brings us into considerations of the interrelationship between the key psychoanalytic concepts of the Imaginary and the Symbolic. If, when we speak of the nation, we refer also to the body (as we have argued we do), then we are immediately within this same context of issues concerning subjectivity. Let us take this a stage further and think about nation and desire, and what it might mean. We know that the nation (in its discursive mode of nationalism) dreams of itself as a unified entity. Its desired image of itself is as a unified subject of history. If we were practising a Lacanian analysis here, we might tentatively propose that the nation is in denial, lying as it does in a false sense of the pre-Symbolic – that is, in the first two stages of the Imaginary.

For the nation to possess a discursivity about itself (let alone anything else), it has to enter the realm of the Symbolic, in the Lacanian sense. Thus the nationalist discourses that it generates have also to be read as the subject-nation's attempt to enter into and maintain the social order of things. But to do so, the subject-nation must repress desire – in short, the libidinal drives experienced during the Imaginary phase. It can be repressed but not lost. And this repression, as we know, founds the unconscious. Thus the subject-nation, which within the Imaginary is both the idealized image and the desiring subject, is now also, within the Symbolic, a split subject (between the conscious and the unconscious) – and this has consequences. The subject-nation is a divided subject because, as it seeks to represent itself in the world (in the Symbolic order of things, in language), it does so at the expense of coming after the word. In other words, when the subject-nation (as the conscious subject) seeks to represent itself – gives itself a discursive form – by the time it has done so, the subject-nation (as the unconscious subject) has already moved on and is becoming something else. Thus there is a gap that opens up between the two states (between the conscious and unconscious subject). This, in turn, means that any notion of the wholeness of the representation (image, text, etc.) is false. What is left as the image, is that of a fading subject because the original subject has moved on, leaving behind an utterance (an enunciation) that is no longer representing the true self. It is this gap that interests us here. It shows us perhaps what the subject-nation is trying to hide (to answer our earlier questions of motivation): its split subjectivity. It tells us that it is deeply troubled by the lack of an idealized image or sense of unity. And it helps to explain why it would spend so much energy repressing difference (as in, for example, differently desiring bodies, such as the queer body). In repressing difference, it denies the gap; it attempts to meld (or merge) the two subjects (conscious and unconscious) together, erasing its own dividedness and implicitly the fading subject. This opens up a huge arena for investigation for us, in which image-constructions of the subject-nation can be taken to task (including, in this context, ideological representations of the nation-state).

Bearing this outline in mind, what now follows is a three-part examination of this question of nation and representation, which attempts, through a series of problematizations, to open up the complexities of writing about national cinema.

Nation and representation (1)

Cinema is one of a nation's many means of representing itself to itself. Clearly the mirroring is not a one-to-one relationship (however much certain nations at certain periods in their histories would like it to be); the mirroring offers a set of images of the nation unto itself. Nationalism (as a discursive strategy of the nation – *a* Symbolic Order) may well be about belief in the nation as a unitary-totality in and of itself but, as we know, it is not the only ideology floating around within a nation-state. What I am proposing here is that the concepts of nation, nationhood and nationalism need to be considered in a dialogic fashion. As the above made clear, the nation is not a unified subject. It is a sum of scattered subjectivities, therefore of scattered identities, therefore of scattered bodies. Implicitly, concepts/principles of nationhood and nationalism are equally scattered. This helps us to look towards creating our dialogic model. For, as Radhakrishnan (1992) argues, if we try to establish a model to articulate the multiple determinations (of 'a nation') that is based in relationality, we would get into serious representational problems. It would become impossible to establish 'boundaries and limits to a relational field' (1992: 81). Relational politics lead us into a chain (or domino) effect, one set of categories generating another, which in turn generates another, so that it becomes massive, dispersed and unmeaningful. 'Scattered hegemonies' is a better term (the term is from Grewal and Kaplan 1994). Better, because it points to a number of useful possibilities. First, there is a limit to the scatteredness of these multiple voices/hegemonies/ideologies; second, there may or may not be links between them; third, there is no presence of the concept of 'other'; fourth, it does not exclude an overlapping with other scattered hegemonies; finally, it does not oblige us into all-embracing but ultimately unuseful terms such as heterogeneity, hybridity, and so on. This term 'scattered hegemonies' helps us to offer a way forward from Bhabha's (1990: 4) for the discussion of a national culture whose 'locality' cannot be seen as unified or unitary in relation to itself, and whose cultural product cannot be seen simply as 'other' in relation to what is outside or beyond it.

To think in terms of the subject-nation as scattered hegemonies means that binary or bi-polar constructions of the nation evaporate (centre/margin; included/excluded). It means also that the subject-nation can be differently desiring, not singly desiring. As the next two sections go on to argue, cinema, national cinema(s) are a forceful function in exposing, in just this way, the subject-nation's masquerade as an idealized image or unified subject.

Nation and representation (2)

In considering nations and representation, we cannot help but observe that ideology is used to construct the nation-state. If we accept this premise that ideology is a political-cultural manifestation of a nation-state, then we cannot fail to note that ideology serves to enforce a certain set of priorities, all of which have at their heart the suppression of constructions that challenge that of the nation-state. Thus, in China since the Revolution, in Pakistan since Partition, or more closely to hand, in France until the 1960s, and in the Soviet Union from 1920 to 1990, cinema has functioned as an integral part of nation-building. This has occurred at the level of the industry as well as that of production (through a centralizing of industrial practice and of textual discourses that valorize cultural hegemony). Nations that repress difference and contradictions cannot in the end suppress the pathological cultural artefacts this repression produces. Thus other constructions emerge and make visible the contradictions inherent in the prevailing conceptualization of the nation-state. Difference in the end seeps through, and does so through images (be they televisual, filmic, digital, etc.) expressing the desire of other bodies.

What we do not understand – no matter what location we are looking or desiring from – we simplify. We reduce to stereotypes. We conflate other nations. For example, we still see Europe as two separate entities, even though it is one continent. We speak of Asia, or the Orient, or Latin America, or Africa. We do this so we do not have to see them. The ideology of mainstream cinema works in a similar fashion. Comedy and gangster films – which are the two top generic types of films produced by the French film industry – are redolent with stereotypes and expose difference as either amusing or threatening. The comfort of such genres is 'we are not like that'. What goes on, of course, is a form of comfort in denial (of difference). Do straight people ever ask themselves how gay people respond to the often foolish stereotypes (of camp) to which they are reduced? Do white people wonder at the dominant images of black people (often focused around their sexualness)?

Elsewhere, I have explained how the ideology of nation-states functions to create a homogeneous society (Hayward 2000). As such, it excludes (or denies) concepts of gender. It also, since it represses gender and therefore the sexed body, necessarily represses desire. This results in a first set of repressions of difference. In certain nation-states, it 'eliminates' class. In other nation-states – as history shows – it erases other embodiments of difference (Jews, communists, homosexuals, political dissidents). It gets rid of what it considers contradictions or flaws. And yet – as we might suspect – the nation falls into its own trap. It does this because it is in contradiction with itself (as we explained above). That is, its ideology – in the form of nationalist discourses – has repressed its own knowledge of itself as a subject-nation. How can a nation remain gender-blind if we know and see all around us example after example of the interpenetration of sexuality and the nation-state? [...] Politics is ineluctably about sex and gender – the term itself refers to the civil function of government, while the etymology of the word confirms that the 'civil' refers to the citizens of the *polis* (originally the city, but also the body politic – that is, the complex aggregation of people in society). Politics, then, is about administering (controlling) the subjects of the nation; and all subjects are sexed and, in one way or another, gendered. But the politics of gender have got swept away and [...] thanks to the ideological discourses of control, have been re-appropriated into a politics of repression. Because if nation (as an ideology) did recognize gender, then it would be obliged to recognize the sexed subject. It would mean that the nation stopped mis-recognizing itself and recognized itself as a subject-nation – a diverse, multiple set of subjectivities (something it constantly represses). To recognize the sexed subject would be to 'let all hell break loose' in the form of (recognition of) excreting bodies, disseminating bodies, fluids moving untamed from bodies, and so on.

Thus gender, and more precisely the sexual subject (because, of course, it does exist despite the subject-nation's lies to itself), has to be controlled, repressed. The split subject we spoke of earlier offers the subject-nation an unacceptable, un-idealized image to itself. The gap in between profoundly destabilizes the homogenized unified nation-body. And this brings me back to my comments on the erotics of nationhood. If, as I argued above, the subject-nation can be located in the pre-Symbolic (particularly at times of great stress), then it is occupying a doubly desiring position (it is libidinally motivated towards itself and towards its mother). To a lesser and greater degree, these are taboo positions: they are positions of mis-recognition; the target for libidinal expression is 'wrong'; finally, and crucially, in desiring the mother, the subject-nation invites the wrath of the castrating father. Thus the subject-nation is torn between desire for unity and denial of difference. Which is why, when a nation invades another nation, it does so in a way that forefronts the erotics of a nation. The terms are rape, pillage, plunder, genocide, ethnic cleansing. If we don't believe this analysis, then my question would be: why do women get raped by invading soldiers? Why is mass rape an integral part of a militia campaign of genocide (or ethnic cleansing)? Why, to take only one example – that of Rwanda – did Tutsi women get raped by Hutu soldiers who deliberately infected them with the AIDS virus? The newspaper reports tell us that 'propaganda pouring out from government radio stations in the months leading up to the (planned) genocide taunted Hutus with the mythology of the Tutsi women: they were taller, more beautiful and arrogant. They had to be tasted and humiliated before they were killed' (*Guardian*, 14 September 1999: 6). Hutu soldiers assailed, violated and infected the 'enemy' in the embodied form of Tutsi womanhood to bring down the Tutsis (that is, the entire Tutsi minority ethnic group) from their haughty ways and ensure (should any women survive their ordeal) that any new generations of Tutsis would be infected.

Gender-blindness, linguistic homogeneity, repression of difference, mythologizing or banishing to the boundaries bodies that threaten – recouping (through stereotype and trivialization) or denying the presence of bodies that hegemony wants not to matter – this is the generic cultural practice of mainstream Western cinema. What is the thriller or the Western about if not the fear of (white) phallic inadequacy? What is the sci-fi film addressing if not the relationship between national space and ideas of race (the invasion of the healthy body politic by aliens)? In Westerns and sci-fi movies, difference is written on the body (Indians in the former, aliens in the latter). These bodies threaten the national fibre of a country either by raping the white woman and pillaging the white man's land (Westerns) or by spreading disease and terror into the civilized state (sci-fi movies). Sci-fis are about the fear of the corruption of the body politic by impure and imperfect bodies. Westerns are about the fear of miscegenation, of a nation's ethnic purity (read whiteness), of its bloodline (its own bodily fluids therefore) being sullied and infected by another's impure fluids.

Nation and representation (3)

The question now becomes (since repression inexorably leads to pathological representation), when does cinema problematize the nation? And a *first* and primary answer (the only one this chapter has space to focus on) has to be in its performance of gender issues – in other words, when cinema challenges the short-sighted economy of nationalism. This has to be read as a first example of when cinema can get away with 'it' (which it does more often than we might at first suspect). What has to interest us here is that if national cinemas perform the nation, then this performance is ineluctably linked to the concept of masquerade. The concept of masquerade in film studies is closely aligned to the representation of the female body. It is a useful concept that might help elucidate how cinema can problematize the nation. This concept has a double value in that it is differently inscribed according to practice and effect. By that I mean masquerade has been identified within feminist film theory as a strategy practised by the male viewer/voyeur in relation to the female body (it is also, of course, a practice of mainstream cinema in terms of its construction of femininity). But, secondly, feminist theory has pointed out that there is an effect of this construction when it comes to reading the image (by reading against the grain as it were), for if the woman is masquerade, masked (as in: to conceal her true identity), then there must be another place behind the mask where the woman might be (Gledhill 1980: 17). The concept of femininity and masquerade is closely attached to the concept of fetishism. The purpose of fetishism is to contain woman, to make her safe. It is a strategy of disavowal of difference (sexual difference). The male seeks to find the hidden phallus in the woman. Thus he fragments off parts of the body (or clothing) and over-invests them with meaning, perceiving those parts as perfection themselves, making those parts figure as the missing phallus. The effect is a peculiar form of transvestism. Woman as a constructed image of femininity performs, masquerades in excess of and in denial of her own sexuality. But – and this is the crucial point – behind this mask there is another woman at work. Added to which, there is also a gap in meaning between the mask and the woman. What is being argued here is that woman performs the very contradictions that the nation tries to conceal – that is, the nation as a sexed subject and non-hegemonic entity. She also problematizes the nation in that the image construction of her femininity seeks to contain her but can only do so at the price of 'agreeing' to her being double-gendered performatively speaking (as feminine and as phallic). Once that is 'agreed', gender is on the table for all to see – but so too is the mask and what lies behind it (and the 'lies' behind the construction) as well as the space in between. This fissuring makes it possible to occupy three locations when peering upon the cinematic artefact before us. The politics of location become scattered, which in turn suggests a scattering of hegemonies.

This example of femininity and masquerade is not an isolated one. Far from it. As soon as we consider examples of masculinity, we can find similar practices in which a play with masquerade can also be unravelled. The male body is differently aestheticized to the woman's, but only to a degree, and often through lighting. The camera roves across the muscularity of the male in not dissimilar ways to its fetishizing effects upon the female body. The body bulges rather than voluptuates. It is hard rather than soft. But the camera is certain that the phallus is present – unlike with the female body, which it voyeuristically investigates and fetishistically attempts to contain as phallic. These hard bodies are as much in excess as their female counterparts, and so they too threaten. Thus they must be 'softened' (by having a weak point in their character, or by the effect of love), or they must perish, or if they survive they have to have gained some inner wisdom to balance out (atone for) the outer shell of masculine muscularity (Korben Dallas in Besson's *Le Cinquième element/The Fifth Element* [1997] is a recent example). The difference, of course, is that the male is not transvestisized, as is the female. The masculinity perdures through and through (both masquerade and behind the mask). Arguably, this is true even within films that represent male homosexuality, but where the representation is not inscribed within a queer discourse (e.g. Cyril Collard's *Les Nuits fauves/Savage Nights* [1991]). The in between (masquerade and mask) is not about disjunction or gaps in meaning in the way that it is with the female body as constructed by cinema. Nor is the excess about over-determination. Genderically, the male in this context is constructed as very secure (a unified subject of knowledge and history) and deeply embedded within the Symbolic order of things. He *is* the Symbolic order. Thus, in this instance, not a lot changes in our peering. The Phallic Law remains intact. But, the crucial point here is that, by raising the question of masculine representation in this manner, we can find new ways to suggest there is more to the image than pure surface would lead us to believe. If, at first, the kind of viewing/ reception analysis of masculine representation does not appear to help us problematize the nation, because in this context the male does not threaten to drop the mask, we still recall that there are gaps in between the mask/masquerade and the masculine body (in the same way that the split subject experiences gaps). Thus it does allow us to query (queery) the hermetics of the masculine body and the hermeneutics of dominant ideology. It is another first step to locating the nation (the subject-nation) within a politics of gender. It shows us how, on the surface, the politics of the nation-state occupy a single phallic location and will do anything to preserve that location against threats and that is a start. We are aware of how the artefact is at work for the cultural construction of the nation.

But what happens when the performance *is* based in transvestism? When we have men playing/performing women's parts – let's think about this in both senses of the term 'parts': the role and the ascriptions of femininity. Man performs both being a woman and the woman's bodily being – including her bodily parts, namely, her breasts and genitalia. Or at least he does so at the point of simulacrum. His body as her body is (as simulacrum) a hyper-real body and therefore a hyper-real sex. More real than real. Small wonder transvestites disturb. Performatively speaking, the transvestite's body is doubly gendered. It is, as Marjorie Garber says, 'a sign of overdetermination'. As an over-determined body, the transvestite's body comes close to the feminine body as described above. But, and here is the twist, and I am grateful to Marjorie Garber's excellent analysis of transvestism for this point, 'the transvestite marks the existence of the Symbolic' (1992: 125). How so? Because the transvestite is doubly gendered, s/he 'embodies' the Imaginary (as she) and the Symbolic (as he). Thus the transvestite marks the Symbolic order of things: s/he embodies the co-presence of the Imaginary and the Symbolic, and too the dialectics of the true body politic (as s/he).

If we return to our considerations of nation and representation within Western cinema and come back to what we were saying in relation to the representation of femininity as masquerade, then we can begin to understand why it suits patriarchy to confine woman to the Imaginary – to a speechless, silent space. If, as Judith Butler explains (1993), the only time that a woman's body 'matters' (counts as matter) is when she is the reproducer of life (as mother), then we can perceive why nations valorize the female body in distinct discourses that represent her as reproducer of the nation. It does not release her from her imprisonment within the Imaginary, however. Yet, paradoxically, cinematic discourses will also construct her as phallic woman, and thus as transvestite. As phallic woman she 'must' assume a position in which she becomes a s/he, a marker (as with the male transvestite) of the existence of the Symbolic. But as we explained above, more happens when s/he has transvestite qualities. We showed how she masquerades as one thing but is different underneath *and* in-between. And she always carries the threat of exposing all of this by dropping the mask. Surely, in her practices of gender and sexual border crossing, she transgresses national boundaries, challenges them just as much as (if not more than) the transvestite male or indeed the queered body? Do these three bodies perhaps occupy a third space – an in-between hyper-real space ironizing (to the extent of possibly shattering and scattering) the nation's simulacrum back to itself? Here I must leave the reader to ponder.[1]

Note

1. This chapter was originally published as 'National Cinemas and the Body Politic' in E. Ezra and S. Harris (eds), *France in Focus: Film and National Identity*, Oxford: Berg, 2000, pp. 97–113. The version reprinted here has been abridged for reasons of space. The editors are grateful to Berg and to Susan Hayward for their permission to reprint the chapter as part of this collection.

Chapter 4

Unfamiliar Places: 'Heterospection' and Recent French Films on Children

Phil Powrie

In 2002, two French films about children were released within two weeks of each other. Although *Être et avoir/To Be and To Have* (Philibert, released 28 August) was a documentary focusing on a village school and *Les Diables/The Devils* (Ruggia, released 11 September) was a drama about two institutionalized children on the run, they had in common the fact that they focused on pre-adolescent children. While there are plenty of films about adolescents in most national cinemas, there are proportionately fewer that focus on pre-adolescent children (Spanish cinema being a notable exception). These films therefore exemplify a trend: since the 1990s, there has been an unusually large number of films in French cinema whose protagonists are young children. The chapter will start by placing such films within a production context. Subsequently, it will be less concerned with explaining why there may have been a surge in such films during the last decade than in theorizing their effect on spectators, with specific reference to *Être et avoir* and *Les Diables*. It will do so by working with concepts of space, as used by Michel Foucault and Henri Lefebvre, familiar to theorists of the postmodern working in architecture, but not as yet particularly developed by theorists working in film studies. Using Foucault's spatially focused 'heterotopia', the chapter will develop a nexus of arguments focusing on the viewing position established by films with child protagonists. I shall argue that the pre-adolescent child's view brings together time past and an alternative space, first considering retrospection, linked with the familiar idea of nostalgia, before moving on to what will be called 'heterospection', a coinage which attempts to bring together issues of time and space in these films. Heterospection, I shall argue, involves a different way of seeing, and of conceiving the spectator's reaction to a film. In that respect, the chapter returns to 'screen theory', but from a different perspective, as well as illuminating how the child film functions.

Context

The group of French films focusing on pre-adolescent protagonists since 1990 show changes of focus relative to similar films which preceded them. There is a new focus on abuse, at its clearest in the controversial *L'Ombre du doute/Shadow of a Doubt* (Issermann 1993), which deals with an eleven-year-old girl's abuse by her father, but also found in *La Classe de neige/Class Trip* (Miller 1998), in which the over-protective father of a boy who goes on a school trip turns out to be a child abuser and murderer. There is a related emphasis on death in *Ponette* (Doillon 1996), which is about a four-year-old's attempts to come to terms with the death of her mother. There are also a number of films which improbably show their protagonists as drifters, homeless children seeking the parental affection which they have never been given, either because their parents abused them, as with *Victor ... pendant qu'il est trop tard* (Veysset 1998), about a young boy who runs away and forms a friendship with fairground workers, or because they have no parents and are trying to escape from institutions. The latter is the case for *Le Fils du requin/The Son of the Shark* (Merlet 1993), a film which refers directly to Truffaut's *Les 400 coups/The 400 Blows* (1959) as it follows two socially marginalized young brothers. It is also the case with *Les Diables*, a film in which two disturbed children, a brother and his mentally retarded sister, repeatedly break out of the institutions in which they are kept in an attempt to find the mother who gave them up. Despite this search, the film is less about the importance of the mother than the need for place, counter to the displacement which forms the narrative as they travel south in search of the family home. A recurrent scene is the sister's speeded-up assemblage of broken pieces of coloured glass in the form of their fantasized home.

Les 400 coups is also gestured at in *Être et avoir*, a film which, unlike *Les Diables*, was one of the most successful films of 2002, with 1.8 million spectators and 200,000 DVDs sold subsequently. *Être et avoir* is part of a small sub-set of such films set in educational institutions. It is a sensitive study of a year in the life of a small rural primary school in the Auvergne, with emphasis on the seasons which structure the school year. In this respect, it is the more utopian version of the considerably darker and more Loachian social-realist *Ça commence aujourd'hui/It All Starts Today* (Tavernier 1999), in which a socially conscious primary school head teacher in a northern French town, where unemployment is rife, gets involved in the lives of his pupils. In *Être et avoir*, we also focus on a male schoolteacher, who has a single class of pupils of all ages, and who comes across as a warm and sensitive mother-figure – cuddling the children when they are hurt, for example, similar to the protagonist of the big success of 2004, *Les Choristes/The Choir* (Barratier).

While *Être et avoir* and *Les Diables* are logical developments in the work of both directors,[1] they also suggest a broader interest in the intersection between state institutions and the role of the family, with children as potential victims of the failure of both, as can be seen in popularizing books such as the psychoanalyst Elizabeth Roudinesco's recent work, published in the same year as the two films.[2] It is not difficult to see why the French might be preoccupied by children in a socio-demographic and political perspective: on the one hand, France is the European country with the greatest increase in and number of births in recent years;[3] but on the other, divorce rates have increased,[4] as has the number of single mothers.[5] While these social shifts undoubtedly have their part to play in explaining why there has been a sudden increase in films focusing on children since 1990, I am not concerned here with pinpointing the causes so much as the effects. The films mentioned above, with the exception of *Être et avoir,* are clearly not intended for 'family viewing'; their intended audience is adults. This raises the question of how the use of child protagonists may create different meanings than the use of adolescent or adult protagonists.

Retrospection

Film representations of children look nostalgically backwards at childhood as a moment of purity and freedom from the materialistic constraints of the adult world, either explicitly in the case of a utopian film such as *Être et avoir*, or implicitly and liminally in more dystopian films such as *Les Diables*, in which the boy dies. This corresponds to the standard Romantic view of the child as one of almost pre-lapsarian innocence. Richard Coe, in his study of autobiography, writes that the Romantics 'were unable to make the distinction between the reality of their child selves and the sentimentalized-idealized image of childhood innocence' (Coe 1984: 40). Freud's polymorphously perverse child notwithstanding, it is a fantasy that has endured. This liminal nostalgia is present even in films where child-killers are the focus, as is the case with another film from 2002, the Brazilian *Cidade de Deus/City of God* (Meirelles/Lund, Brazil/France/United States). The sub-text in the first type is 'I wish I could find that state of innocence again' (nostalgia tinged with self-pity); the sub-text in the latter is 'thank God my childhood was not like that' (nostalgia tinged with pity).

The mention of child-killers is far from irrelevant, as it helps to unravel what 'innocence' might mean in these circumstances. The word is etymologically linked to the idea of death. Connected to the Indo-European root *nek-* (to bring about death), it gives us the Ancient Greek *nekros* (meaning dead), the Latin *nex* (violent death) and various derivations, including *nocere* (to harm) and *nocens* (guilty), leading to the antonym *innocens* (innocent), the one who is not guilty of harming. The child-killer is a contradiction, which accounts for the shock we may experience when such characters are encountered: in the Romantic view of childhood, children are supposed to be incapable of inflicting harm. The utopian child's point of view is therefore one in which violence does not exist, or is transformed into something else, a fantasy of immortality, as exemplified in *Ponette*, where the four-year-old girl fantasizes the return of her dead mother as she waits in the cemetery.

That cemetery is located very firmly in the countryside. In both *Les Diables* and *Être et avoir*, too, non-urban space and place are key, corresponding again to the Romantic association of the child with the natural world. In *Être et avoir*, there are frequent shots of the countryside going through the cycle of the seasons. These shots give the film a structure, embedding the cameos of schoolroom events, but also embedding the nurturing provided by the schoolteacher in a nostalgic framework. In *Les Diables*, the children are at their most free when in the countryside, away from institutions and ordered urban spaces. We see the children hiding in woods where Chloé reconstructs her fantasized home with coloured shards of glass. But whereas we might, more stereotypically, expect such a representation to be drawn with coloured pencils on white paper, Chloé's mosaic emerges elementally and 'magically' (these are the only fast-motion shots in the film) from the soil in the woods. The soil can be discerned through the coloured glass, underlining the link between 'natural' space, the fantasized home and the feminine.

This is in keeping with Henri Lefebvre's point that 'nature' is commonly perceived as origin: 'Natural space was – and it remains – the common point of departure: the origin, and the original model, of the social process – perhaps even the basis of all "originality"' (Lefebvre 1991: 30). He comments that social and political fragmentation leads to ideological appeals to the organic as mythified origin: 'The idea of an organic space … is … an appeal to a unity, and beyond that unity (or short of it) to an *origin* deemed to be known with absolute certainty, identified beyond any possible doubt -an origin that legitimates and justifies' (1991: 274–75). Against this mythified origin, he contrasts what he calls genital space, associated with property and the family, which is the arena in which capitalist societies retain some sense of order as social bonds are undermined (1991: 232–33).

Both films under consideration exemplify these ideologically determined representations. Both incorporate appeals to the countryside, and in both cases the status of the family is in question. In *Être et avoir*, we rarely see the families of the children, as if the school – which has children of all ages in a single class – provides a surrogate family closer to what Roudinesco calls the 'tribe' than the bourgeois family of modern times. In *Les Diables*, similarly, institutional carers act as surrogate family and the mother is presented to us as a psychologically fragile person, who abandons the children a second time after revealing to her son that the child he considers his sister is not related to him by blood at all, thus destroying his personal myth of himself as carer and nurturer. By contrast with what we might consider to signal the failing family, shots of the countryside are imbued with nostalgia. In *Les Diables*, the children not only travel through woods, potentially dangerous spaces familiar in fairytales, but also across the rather more idyllic lavender fields. These are associated with Provence in the French imaginary, which is itself associated with certain types of heritage film, such as Pagnol adaptations, whether those of the 1980s (*Jean de Florette/Manon des Sources*, Claude Berri, 1986) or the films directed by Pagnol in the 1930s and 1940s, to which these two films gesture (Powrie 1997: 50–61).

As I have explained in the context of British 'alternative heritage' films, the location of these films in provincial locations is an important component of spectatorial identification, which can be called *metastasis*, given the importance of displacement and the way in which displacement generates nostalgia:

> The regional factor localises pastness geographically, making the general more specific. Spectators need that specificity because it gives a strong sense of place, and the evocation of the past requires that we be displaced from the present by the pull of a past place, the unrecoverable home. Spectatorial response can therefore be defined as a kind of *metastasis*: we are displaced from the present into a very abstract place, a utopia – literally, a no-place – but we are attracted there by a very specific place, a place whose regional specificity is precisely what makes it attractive. The spectators of a film that generates nostalgia are thus invited to relocate the past place, and relocate themselves within it: 'I wish to be that boy in that place, because I was once (like) that boy in that place. I once also inhabited a very specific place.' We are thus invited to desire sameness while maintaining difference ('I could have been that boy in Liverpool, although in fact I was that/this boy in London') (Powrie 2000: 323–24).

This oddly fractured spectatorial position is characteristic of the child film, and I shall develop it by considering another aspect.

There is a crucial difference between the two films under consideration. *Être et avoir*, with its seasonal structure and gently maternal male schoolteacher, is a utopia predicated on circularity and stability. *Les Diables*, on the other hand, is a dystopian road movie, where certainties are gradually demolished in linear fashion, signalling the destruction of fantasized organicity and the maternally structured feminine, and the advent of Lefebvre's genital economy of space. It is precisely this difference allows us to pinpoint a second major issue relating to innocence, after that of nostalgia: desexualization.

The presence of a pre-pubescent child desexualizes relationships, in the sense that relationships are not represented as part of a genital economy. Part of the pleasure in *Être et avoir* is to see the male schoolteacher being as much a mother as a father to his charges, as is emphasized when the teacher holds up a piece of paper on which one of his pupils has written the word 'mother'. When this is linked to the rhythm of the seasons and shots of the countryside, with few shots of families, it is easy to see how a different, although sentimental and nostalgic, space is constructed, fantasized as pre-oedipal. The narrative structure of *Les Diables* is somewhat different. There is certainly retrospection, in the sense that the children are trying to return to the home they have never had; but by the same token, they must leave to do so and project themselves into the world, looking forward in prospection. The film is a road movie, and adopts the kind of linearity, quite unlike the circularity of *Être et avoir*, which such prospection into the future requires.

Projecting their desires into the future leads to sexualization for the children: the desire for home, as the fantasy is destroyed, gradually gives way to oedipal and sexual desire, as well as death. The brother, who has been told by his mother that his 'sister' is not his sister at all, becomes sexually excited as they play in an underground pool, which functions as a version of the swimming pool they have imagined as part of the fantasized home in the south of the country. Sex brings closure to the journey. The boy has a night of passion with his pseudo-sister, but is then, significantly, shot by a policeman he attacks when roaming the streets. The film thus stresses the reimposition of the Law, in its widest sense, including death as the law of desire. The brother-who-is-not-a-brother (and therefore no one he can recognize, since the film has insisted on his self-identity as a carer) slowly dies from his gunshot wound in the garden of the bourgeois couple the children have terrorized. The ending of *Les Diables* shows us then how desexualization and the evacuation of sexual desire are important for the child film. *Les Diables* shows, when contrasted with *Être et avoir*, how loss of desire for the other halts forward motion, halts projection and prospection. Lack of desire, lack of forward motion and lack of the narratively articulated fantasy of home, as in *Les Diables*, are the prerequisites for the circularity and stability we find as narrative structure in *Être et avoir*.

There is a further difference between the two films in this respect, demonstrating the in-between zone into which such films place us. It is the role of language. In *Être et avoir*, the children are constantly learning language, learning with difficulty how to articulate their position in the world. A similar situation occurs in *Les Choristes,* in which Clément Mathieu teaches the unruly boys to express themselves through song. In *Les Diables,* by contrast, although Joseph, the brother, also has difficulty expressing his desires without being aggressive, he is very articulate, and never seems to stop talking, as befits the protagonist of an oedipalized narrative whose entry into language and into desire is coterminous; his logorrhoea is an excess of language, paralleling the excessive nature of his desires for the fantasized home and for his 'sister'.

Children in the films I am concerned with are located between the advent of language (so after the infant stage – *infans* meaning deprived of language) and the onset of sexuality and death (desire and the death drive). The defining feature of representations of pre-adolescent children is that they are poised on a threshold, an in-between space – neither no-man's land, nor no-child's land – where fantasy and reality are jumbled. Adult spectators, to the extent that they may be identifying themselves with the child protagonists, are looking both backwards nostalgically in retrospection to a period of innocence, and forward in prospection to the entry into the 'guilt' constituted by desire and its violence. The child provides a threshold, or cusp, where desire can be configured as virtual, as a developmental horizon, in sight but out of reach, allowing the fantasy of pre-oedipal innocence to infect spectatorial affect. It is appropriate to remind ourselves that nostalgia is formed from the Greek words meaning home and suffering, in that order. In this optic, nostalgia is less a superficial phenomenon of postmodernity, associated with the visible, and history-free depthlessness, as Jameson (1991) might have it, than a deeply embodied affect, where meaning is invaded by emotion – accounting, no doubt, for the profound effect it can have on spectators.

In this section, I have shown how innocence and nostalgia are linked in films with pre-adolescent protagonists. Such films construct a fantasized pastness for spectators, an *illud tempus* or mythical time (the term frequently used by the historian of religions Mircea Eliade) prior to the atomization of the social into 'genitalized' family units by capitalism, as Lefebvre (1991: 382) would have it. They do so more easily precisely because the child protagonist invites the reading of space and time as pre-oedipal, as being *on the threshold.* This places the spectator in the position of looking back ('I was once that child'), while at the same time looking forward ('that child will be what I am now'). In the next section I shall consider how the threshold is not so much a binary structured on the retrospective and the prospective, or on the pre-oedipal/oedipal, as has been suggested so far, than a different type of space – a heterotopic space of difference – which the spectator is invited to inhabit.

Heterospection

What is heterotopia? Lefebvre occasionally uses this term purely functionally as part of a typology of spatial distinction (isotopias, utopias, heterotopias), where he defines heterotopias as 'contrasting spaces' or 'mutually repellent spaces' (Lefebvre 1991: 294, 366). Foucault had previously developed the idea in a 1967 lecture (Foucault 1986: 22–27).

Heterotopic spaces for him are 'counter-sites, a kind of effectively enacted utopia in which the real sites, all the other real sites that can be found within the culture – are simultaneously represented, contested and inverted'. There are clearly problems with such contestatory spaces, not least the perennial problem of any radical discourse, whereby the naming of such a space immediately reduces its radical potential (Soja 1995: 13–34; Genocchio 1995: 35–46). Notwithstanding such issues, we can, by analogy, suggest that the young child film constructs a heterotopic view. Amongst Foucault's examples are spaces where deviants are placed, such as psychiatric hospitals and prisons (the case with the children of *Les Diables,* as well as many other child films); spaces of juxtaposed spaces (cinemas, gardens); sacred spaces (cemeteries – *Ponette* configures a heterotopic child's view within a rural cemetery); spaces of accumulated time (museums, libraries); spaces of transitory time (festivals, fairgrounds, holiday cottages); spaces of illusion which critique quotidian space (brothels); spaces of attempted perfection (the colonies).

The spaces of which Foucault talks are real physical spaces, whereas the threshold space discussed here in relation to the child film is a more abstract space. Nonetheless, Foucault's notion is useful, for three reasons. First, heterotopic spaces combine incompatible spaces: 'The heterotopia is capable of juxtaposing in a single real place several spaces, several sites that are in themselves incompatible.' Foucault explains, for example, how one such space, the cinema, 'is a very odd rectangular room, at the end of which, on a two-dimensional screen, one sees the projection of a three-dimensional space'. A second reason is that watching a film is potentially to inhabit a heterotopic space in more than just the physical sense suggested by Foucault in the previous paragraph. He discusses the way in which the mirror is both a utopia but also a heterotopia, in terms which recall the Lacanian formulation of viewing familiar in film studies. It is instructive to replace the word 'mirror' by the word 'screen' in the following passage:

The mirror is, after all, a utopia, since it is a placeless place. In the mirror [screen], I see myself there where I am not, in an unreal, virtual space that opens up behind the surface; I am over there, there where I am not, a sort of shadow that gives my own visibility to myself, that enables me to see myself there where I am absent: such is the utopia of the mirror [screen]. But it is also a heterotopia in so far as the mirror [screen] does exist in reality, where it exerts a sort of counteraction on the position that I occupy. From the standpoint of the mirror [screen] I discover my absence from the place where I am since I see myself over there. Starting from this gaze that is, as it were, directed toward me, from the ground of this virtual space that is on the other side of the glass [screen], I come back toward myself; I begin again to direct my eyes toward myself and to reconstitute myself there where I am. The mirror [screen] functions as a heterotopia in this respect: it makes this place that I occupy at the moment when I look at myself in the glass [screen] at once absolutely real, connected with all the space that surrounds it, and absolutely unreal, since in order to be perceived it has to pass through this virtual point which is over there.

Identifying with a child protagonist is likely, I might argue, to increase this feeling of being 'over there' in a different space-time, identifying ourselves with the 'ideal ego' of psychoanalysis.

The third reason is that the word heterotopia is linked to a medical condition, although this is not something discussed by Foucault. The word heterotopia is attested in 1870. It is therefore clearly a phenomenon of modernity, broadly contemporaneous with the advent of film.[6] In medicine it is used to refer to a displacement, when a tumour occurs in the body which is composed of parts not normally found in that location. We can relate this sense of displacement to the loss and anxiety that form nostalgia, itself originally conceived in the mid-eighteenth century as a medical condition (Starobinski 1966: 81–103).

Bringing these three points together, we can hypothesize that heterotopic space, where viewing a film is concerned, is the abstract spectatorial space (conditioned by the physical experience of being in a physically determined heterotopic space, that of the cinema), which constitutes a combination of dislocation in time and space, experienced as loss and anxiety. This space is more likely to be experienced in films where spectators are asked to adopt the point of view of the child, because this displaces them from the present space-time of the viewing experience to the past. The difference between seeing the past articulated around a child rather than a former adult self is the *child's body*. Lefebvre writes about the radical potential of the body in relation to ordered genital space, saying that the body behaves 'as a *differential field* … as a *total* body, breaking out of the temporal and spatial shell' (Lefebvre 1991: 384). The child's body actualizes that differential more immediately, by calling attention to past time and the development of experience. The space is heterotopic in the medical sense of a space formed from spatial and/or temporal elements not normally found in the spectator's present; nor indeed is this space specific to individual spectators, except in the most generic sense that they might map their experiences on to those of the child protagonist.

Returning to the relationship between utopia and heterotopia, utopia is the space of imagined organic unity (similar to the 'ideal ego' of psychoanalysis). It precedes dystopia, which is the perception that we inhabit spaces that have lost the connection to the organic. Broadly, this is the difference between the vanished or vanishing social and communitarian on the one hand, and the fragmented genital spaces of the family on the other. It would be tempting to see heterotopia conceptually as a development along this linear axis: utopia-past, dystopia-present, heterotopia-future. But heterotopias coexist with the other two spaces; they constitute alternatives which combine the utopian and the dystopian, but which cannot be reduced to them. This is why we could describe *Être et avoir* as a utopian film and *Les Diables* as a dystopian film, while positing that both engage us in a heterotopic space. Heterotopic space is a different space. Its relationship to oedipal structures is one of differential; it is both within the male–female binary, and displaced within it, as a space which contests that binary. The difference suggested here is not just one of differential; there are two further issues related to it: defamiliarization and deviation.

The child's view defamiliarizes the world. We have seen, using Foucault, how the heterotopic space is both 'here' and 'there', combining the recognizable, and the recognizable displaced into a heterotopic elsewhere so that it becomes unrecognizable. The world, in other words, in the child film, becomes *unfamiliar in its familiarity*. This is Freud's definition of the uncanny, with its complex shuttling between the *heimlich* and the *unheimlich*, the homely and the unhomely, shading off into each other perplexingly. And what is *familiarity* if it is not the construction of the family? In other words, the child's view both questions the family and reconstructs it differently for the spectator. That reconstruction is itself a question, a double-edged question: is the family a place of protection or is it a place of death? *Les Diables* brings this issue into focus, with the recurrent use of Chloé's glass home: the shards have the colour and shape of an innocent child's construction of a safe space, but the pieces are made of glass, which can be partially seen through, in both the concrete and figurative sense, and are dangerous because they are sharp.

Finally, heterotopic spaces are spaces of deviation, Foucault suggests, citing as examples psychiatric hospitals, prisons and retirement homes – the reason for the last being that 'old age is a crisis, but is also a deviation since in our society where leisure is the rule, idleness is a sort of deviation'. He connects adolescents to 'heterotopias of crisis', but curiously does not mention the spaces inhabited by children. We could extrapolate from what he says of old age to characterize the social position occupied by children as one of idleness (rather than leisure), and to propose that their spaces, whether real or abstract, are *deviant heterotopias*. They are, to use a term employed by Mairé Messenger Davies (2005), 'crazy spaces'. In such spaces, a Bakhtinian contestation of order flourishes. However, crucially, this occurs without the adults who are in charge of that order being aware of it. In that respect, the world is not made topsy-turvy in a recognized moment of renewal through excess, but a moment of radical otherness, an unrecognized tumour within the visible body, but which creates pain (of nostalgia, of loss, of dispersal) nonetheless. It is less a case of the child's viewpoint being privileged, either consciously or unconsciously, over the adult viewpoint, than an issue of a different space, which, like the medical definition of the word heterotopia, uses elements taken from elsewhere to construct a defamiliarized space-time.

The word 'family' is based on a pre-Roman word, *famel*, meaning 'servant'. When it came to be used in Latin, *familia* originally referred to the household as constituted by a group of servants attached to a dwelling. Whatever else it may have meant subsequently in terms of blood-relatives gathered together as a group subordinated to patriarchal laws, originally the family was a *bond to a specific place* (the home, as demonstrated so well in *Les Diables*), as well as a more general bond to a space ('being a family together'). It therefore functioned, we might wish to argue, as both a place of servitude and servitude itself. Both *Être et avoir* and *Les Diables* demonstrate the attachment to that bond, as well as, paradoxically, the desire to escape from it – even if they do so very differently. *Être et avoir* appeals to a surrogate family structure (the school) and the rhythm of the seasons to construct a nostalgic framework. *Les Diables*, by contrast, shows its protagonists escaping from similar institutional structures (the home for disturbed children)' so as to rediscover the maternal home for which they nostalgically yearn.

What makes these films so interesting is that the child's view allows spectators to inhabit both space-times. As spectators, we are, like the children themselves – on a threshold, looking back to our past and looking forwards to the present of our viewing from the place to which we are looking back. In that sense, we are temporally (and temporarily) 'differentialized'. We are also desexualized, relating to oedipal structures tangentially, asymptotically. We are defamiliarized in the sense that the familiar (what we know, our social and conceptual structures) is made unfamiliar.

That spectatorial position can be defined as heterospection, in that it is not simply retrospectively (and potentially regressively) nostalgic; but nor is it entirely prospectively (and potentially progressively) 'futured'. Heterospection is a moment which, to quote Foucault again, 'simultaneously represents, contests, and inverts'. It looks backwards and forwards, but also sideways, outwards, escaping centrifugally into multiplicities, while at the same time coalescing in a specific moment, a specific place. It is a view which paradoxically captures a moment made of shifting refractions, where time and space collapse, rather like the coloured glass 'home' of *Les Diables,* emerging like a fast-motion kaleidoscope, only to be destroyed again.

Put more simply, heterospection is being-adult while also being-child, inhabiting two different but complementary space-times. The effect is to allow us *simultaneously* to experience innocence, not just to view it, and to escape from the inevitable pain of innocence experienced, but also lost.[7]

Notes

1. Philibert's major documentaries have combined an interest in institutions, and in how people communicate: the deaf in *Le Pays des sourds/Land of the Deaf* (1992); the Natural History Museum in *Un animal, des animaux* (1994); a psychiatric hospital where the inmates are working to put on a play in *La Moindre des choses* (1997); drama students trying to create a play around a theme in *Qui sait?* (1998); the Louvre in *La Ville Louvre* (1999). Ruggia's films focus on child protagonists: the short *L'Enfance égarée* (1993) and the adaptation of the well-known novel, *La Gone du chaâba (1998),* about the son of an Algerian immigrant in 1980s France.
2. Roudinesco (2002), *La Famille en désodre*, whose title translates as 'the family in chaos'.
3. The total was 779 000 in 2000, or 189 births for 100 women (in other words, 1.89 children per woman), compared with 164 in the United Kingdom and 134 in Germany. See Doisneau (2002: 12).
4. Four out of ten, or 39 per cent, in 1999 as opposed to 33 per cent in 1991 and 24 per cent in 1981. See Doisneau (2002: 15).
5. Whereas 10 per cent of women between the ages of 40 and 45 were single mothers in 1990, in 1999 the age-range for this percentage has dramatically increased to between 35 and 50. See Labarthe (2002: 30).
6. The concept of utopia originated in 1551 with the publication of Sir Thomas Moore's book. The word dystopia, interestingly, is contemporaneous with heterotopia, being first attested in 1868 according to the *Oxford English Dictionary*.
7. Author's note: I am grateful to Kate Chedgzoy and Ann Davies for their comments on an earlier draft of this chapter. Editors' note: The chapter was originally published in 2005 as 'Unfamiliar places, "heterospection" and recent French films on children', *Screen*, 46: 3, pp. 341–52. The editors are grateful to Oxford University Press and to Phil Powrie for their permission to reprint the article as part of this collection.

Chapter 5

The Circular Ruins? Frontiers, Exile and the Nation in Renoir's
Le Crime de Monsieur Lange

Keith Reader

There was a moment when the French people really believed that they were going to love each other. (Renoir 1974: 114)

Democracy is always tied to the 'pathological' fact of a nation-state. (Žižek 1991: 165)

Jean Renoir's 1936 film *Le Crime de Monsieur Lange/The Crime of Monsieur Lange* is generally numbered among its director's most important works, as well as being one of the key films of the Popular Front period in France. That reputation rests to a great extent upon the well-documented community spirit that pervaded its making, largely the result of the participation of many members of the leftist theatre Groupe Octobre, which was run on lines not dissimilar to the cooperative that forms the centre of the film's action. Three years later, just before his defining masterpiece *La Règle du jeu/The Rules of the Game* (1939) was released, Renoir was to confide in a letter to his partner Camille François his ambition to expand the communal film-making style of *Lange* into 'a sort of United Artists, that is to say a much larger and more disinterested enterprise than one which is solely about distribution' (Renoir 1998: 71; editors' translation). That dream was to come to nought, in a manner that we shall see suggests intriguing parallels between the ambiguous fate of *Lange*'s cooperative and Renoir's subsequent, particularly post-war career.

One of the Groupe Octobre's moving spirits was the film's scriptwriter, Jacques Prévert. Prévert is best known cinematically for the screenplays he wrote for Marcel Carné (such as *Le Jour se lève/Daybreak* of 1939 and *Les Enfants du paradis/Children of Paradise* of 1943); *Lange*, despite a couple of further projects that never progressed beyond the discussion stage,[1] was his only collaboration with Renoir.

Neither Renoir nor Prévert was ever a member of the French Communist Party, for reasons which were almost diametrically opposed. Renoir wrote a regular Wednesday column in the PCF's cultural daily *Ce soir* in 1937 and 1938,[2] but this was not to prevent him from going to Mussolini's Rome in 1939 and 1940 in an abortive attempt to make a film of *La Tosca*, of which only five sequences were ever shot – an undertaking which cost him the friendship of Aragon, among others. His first return from Italy in September 1939, when France declared a general mobilisation, all but coincided with the signing of the Hitler–Stalin Pact, by which he – unlike, presumably, Aragon – was scandalized ('Such an alliance seemed unimaginable. He thought about the hope of the Groupe Octobre gang while they were filming *Le Crime de Monsieur Lange*' [Bertin 1994: 215]). All this, like the remark quoted as an epigraph, helps to suggest why Renoir's sympathies for the Popular Front very rapidly turned into nostalgia for the good old days of Groupe Octobre *copinage*. For François Poulle, to speak of a 'sell-out' on Renoir's part would be to make a category mistake. His communist sympathies were precisely that: sympathies, shared 'emotionally, instinctively, without reasoning, without harsh personal necessity', so that in the 'disintegrating fraternity of pals … [h]e didn't look any further than the bread they ate together' (Poulle 1969: 134).

Renoir's genially communitarian version of socialism may now seem to have worn rather better than the Stalinist asperities of the PCF or even Prévert's maverick amalgam of anarchism and Trotskyism, which made him a forerunner of what 30 or so years later was to become known as *gauchisme*. It is unsurprising that, along with Sartre, he was among the first of his generation to express sympathy with those events of May 1968 initially so reviled by the Communist Party. If the Groupe Octobre, founded in 1932, lasted barely more than a month after the Popular Front's election victory, that was largely because of its and Prévert's hostility to certain Communist Party policies:

> The anticlerical couplets did not go with the policy of the outstretched hand; the hostility to the army and the police, shared by *L'Humanité* in the days of the 'Gueules de Vaches' column, became incompatible with the 'Long live the republican army' slogan, and in fact has been untimely since the Laval-Stalin agreements'. (Leroy and Roche 1986: 181)

Renoir's French Revolution fresco *La Marseillaise* (1937), largely scripted by the director, vividly illustrates the divergence between Prévert and himself. An early scene depicts poverty-stricken peasants and workers, on the run from the feudal law, hiding out in the hills near Marseille. Here they are succoured by a priest who explicitly identifies his situation with that of sergeants in the army – exploited, poorly paid and without hope of advancement under the current system. A clearer example of the *'politique de la main tendue'*, recruiting rank-and-file representatives of two hated institutions on to the side of progress, it would be difficult to find. Prévert's priest in *Lange*, by contrast, is a fatuous bumbler who is killed in a railway accident and whose garb is then opportunistically donned by the rascally employer Batala – a masquerade whose anti-clerical implication is evident.

On a visit to a theatre festival in Moscow in 1933, Prévert, along with Marcel Duhamel and Yves Allégret, refused to sign a book of congratulations to Stalin, which suggests that he would have been deeply suspicious of the Stalinist attempt to build socialism in one country, figured in microcosm in *Lange* by the cooperative's fragile, albeit exhilarating setting-up of a kind of 'socialism in one courtyard'. The film's construction and deployment of space, narrative and topographical alike counterposes to its warm sense of community an acute, possibly even tragic, irony – an irony intimately linked with the relationship between the Popular Front as a national phenomenon (*'les Français crurent vraiment qu'ils allaient s'aimer les uns les autres'*) and the internationalism of Prévert's perspective. The '"pathological" fact of a nation-state' alluded to by Žižek, and extensively developed in his work, is the point at which the coherence of *Lange*'s argument calls itself into question. Depending on which version of Lacan we adopt, that 'national fact' is either the signifying absence at the heart of the text or the 'Thing', the *objet a*, the 'real' which renders any self-sufficient closed totality impossible.

Le Crime de Monsieur Lange tells of a group of people living and working around a courtyard in the Marais area of Paris (the film's original working title was *Sur la cour*). That neighbourhood underwent spectacular renovation and gentrification in the 1960s, under the aegis of André Malraux's Culture Ministry, but at the time of the film it was still largely working class, with the vertical relations of community and kinship characteristic of the Parisian tenement. The printing works owned by the camp and repellent Batala (Jules Berry) is in severe financial difficulties as a result of his mismanagement. When he stages his disappearance and death in a rail accident, the workers take over and run the print firm on a cooperative basis, achieving immense success thanks to the 'Arizona Jim' Western stories written by the unworldly Amédée Lange (René Lefèvre). Batala, however, is still the firm's legal owner; disguised as a priest, he returns to claim his legal if not moral due at the height of a celebratory banquet held by the cooperative, and Lange, in a daze, shoots him dead, securing the cooperative's future at the potential cost of his own life. Lange and his lover, the laundress Valentine (Florelle), are driven to the frontier by the benevolent capitalist supporter of the cooperative, Meunier. Recognized as fugitives in a café, they are able to reach safety after Valentine has told their story to the people in the bar. The final shot shows them walking along a flat, and fairly gloomy, beach towards safety, turning to wave farewell to their allies and to the camera.

With *Le Crime de Monsieur Lange*, to quote Alexander Sesonske, 'Jean Renoir undoubtedly became the film director of the Left' (Sesonske 1980: 186). This commitment may not have lasted long, but its strength and the extraordinary results it produced certainly made him a marked man once France had fallen, and thus helped to provoke his departure for the United States at the very end of 1940. The film's celebration of community, its denunciation of Batala's sexual exploitation of his female employees, its condoning of what Dudley Andrew has pointed out is effectively a political assassination (Andrew 1995: 287) retain immense force to this day – a force that resides as much in the visual organisation of the film as in its narrative. The courtyard, at once home and workplace, a microcosm of *le Paris populaire* and a latter-day avatar of the Pension Vauquer in Balzac's *Le Père Goriot*, is at the centre of that visual organisation, which André Bazin has memorably shown has implications that go well beyond its boundaries.

Bazin's analysis hinges on what is usually described as 'the 360° pan' (it is actually nearer 270°) around the courtyard immediately before Lange kills Batala – an infringement of classic cinema's so-called '180° rule', which prescribes that the camera should not normally move through more than a semi-circle, for fear of disrupting the spectator's position. This shot was thought by Roger Leenhardt, normally a most incisive critic, to be the result of a blunder or shortage of money (Bazin 1971: 39) – a judgement nowadays easy to mock, but we should perhaps recall that audiences found the flashback structure of Carné's *Le Jour se lève* difficult to follow on the film's release in 1939. The 360° pan, on its rare appearances in the cinema, tends to evoke a precarious sense of community, as in the shot before the cattle drive moves off in Hawks' *Red River* of 1948, and that is certainly the case here.[3] For Bazin, Renoir's 360° shot functions as 'the pure spatial expression of the whole *mise-en-scène*' (Bazin 1971: 42), a *mise-en-scène* which the seeming circularity of the courtyard's cobblestones and the drunken *concierge*'s reeling round it as he struggles to put out the dustbins go to reinforce. It also, of course, calls the very title of the film into question, twice over. The shot's evocation of community – a community threatened by Batala's emergence from the shadows with legal if not ethical right on his side – acts to legitimize the shooting (is it really a 'crime'?), and at the same time to locate responsibility for it away from Lange himself (is it 'Monsieur Lange's crime'?). If ever a camera movement has performed a political action, it is surely here.

This reading – which my subsequent comments will I hope inflect rather than undercut – gains added force from the circular structure of the film's narrative. This is told in flashback by Valentine to the customers in the café who have recognized Lange from his description, and who at the end of her story – and thus of the film – allow the couple to go free. Daniel Serceau has observed how 'Valentine's story becomes image for us spectators just as it is a mental image for the customers in the café' so that 'our positioning is both less and more than that of our café correspondents. Less, because we don't have the right to set free or imprison which they (fictionally) do. More because we substitute the mental images they produce with the real images of a fiction' (Serceau 1981: 61; editors' translation).

To the circularity of the courtyard, the 360° shot and the narration, then, corresponds a concentric arrangement of two sets of 'jurors' who sit in judgement, not only on Lange's action but on Valentine's narration. There are indeed quite literally two 'courts' within the film – the courtyard in Paris and the impromptu bar-room *tribunal populaire*, as the Maoists would have called it, which sits in judgement not only on Lange but by implication on the whole Parisian cooperative endeavour. The one dissenter from the verdict in the café is the owner's son, denounced as an imbecile by everybody including his own father, which seems to confirm the widespread view that dissident or recalcitrant elements in *Le Crime de Monsieur Lange*'s view of community can safely be marginalized as buffoons. The *concierge*, M. Beznard – in the published script Baisenard (!) – with his sly boasting about his experiences with Tonkinois women and old-soldier racism – 'Indians, Tonkinese, they're all the same, Negroes … No mentality … and lazy with it … underhand' (Prévert 1990: 74; editors' translation) – is the best example of this, even though for Alexander Sesonske he is partially 'redeemed' by his drunken performance at the party, where he 'becomes the source for the rhythm on which the scene is built' (Sesonske 1980: 211). With the bar owner's son contemptuously neutralized and Beznard transformed from obnoxious into entertaining buffoon, it is tempting to read the film as an allegory of the triumph of class solidarity.

Tempting, but in many ways simplistic. The role of the 'good' capitalist Meunier is too crucial to be passed over, and Christopher Faulkner's description of him as 'the reservation to the complete socialization of the means of production of the printshop' (Faulkner 1986: 65) is a point well taken. Batala fails so calamitously, after all, because he is an inefficient capitalist, not because he is a repulsive one, and Meunier's twofold intervention – as financial saviour and as chauffeur to safety – can easily be read as figuring the necessity of the right kind of capitalist, in a way that brings the film closer to Richard Branson (or even Bernard Tapie) than to Karl Marx. Often commented on, too, has been the elegiac quality of the film's ending. To quote Sesonske once more:

> Lange and Valentine are free, 'so they say', but exiled from the court that held their lives, and, after the shock of his real encounter with death, we are not sure Lange will ever again write with the same careless delight, 'Arizona Jim killed one or two of them'. Hence the final image of these two lonely figures receding on the windswept dunes conveys as much of sadness as of joy. (Sesonske 1980: 196)

That sadness, only a few years before refugees in flight were once again to become a familiar sight on the roads of Europe, is intensified by Lange and Valentine's utter lack of possessions – not even a suitcase between them – and by the soundtrack's repetition of 'Au jour le jour', the song Valentine has earlier sung to Lange, which suggests that she may once have had to resort to prostitution and closes on the line 'It's a sad life'. It is difficult to view the final sequence now without reading back into it ending of Renoir's First War-set *La Grande Illusion/The Great Illusion* (1937), in which Rosenthal and Maréchal (Marcel Dalio and Jean Gabin) make their escape across the snow-covered frontier between Germany and Switzerland. As they cross into neutral territory, the commander of the pursuing German troops orders his men to lower their weapons, attesting to the performative effectiveness of the border despite, or perhaps because of, its invisibility. Such respect for the conventions of 'civilized' warfare – part of the 'great illusion' of the film's title – was not, of course, to survive into the post-1939 world, which gives the ending an ironic quality that brings it closer to that of *Lange* than may at first appear.

The importance of the frontier is the key to understanding how the irony with which *Le Crime de Monsieur Lange*'s 'triumph' is tempered, quite as much as that of *La Grande Illusion*, is closely connected with the '"pathological" fact of a nation-state' referred to by Žižek, and thus with the broader (and some would say still unresolved) political debates surrounding the time of the film's making. Lyall Bush states that, at the end of the film, Lange and Valentine cross 'the border into Spain' (Bush 1989: 55) – an assertion belied by the bottle of home-made *genever* prominent in the bar, which would seem to place it near the Belgian frontier. The reference to Spain may well have been influenced by the importance of the Spanish border as an escape route for refugees in the Second War, and before that in the opposite direction during the Spanish Civil War. Christopher Faulkner has drawn attention to the influence of the Spanish Catalan Joan Castanyer/Jean Castagnier on *Lange*, further pointing out that an early version of the screenplay actually sets the opening sequence on the Spanish border (Faulkner 1990: 58). Yet it is scarcely plausible that Meunier would have run the risk of driving so far south. Plausibility, however, goes on to raise the mildly disconcerting question of why the fleeing couple stop for the night on the French – 'unsafe' – side of the border. Meunier tells them that 'At first light you'll be able to cross the border', (Prévert 1990: 29) which might suggest the availability of a *passeur* to guide them across once it becomes light; but no such figure is seen in the final sequence, and by morning presumably their description will have been communicated to the border police. The obvious answer to my question is, of course, that there would otherwise have been no film – or at any rate no framing narrative and thus no possibility of putting class solidarity to the test. Beyond this, however, it seems to me that the film's difficulty in escaping the confines of France is emblematic of what Žižek calls 'the eruption of the national Thing in all its violence [which] has always taken the devotees of international solidarity by surprise' (Žižek 1991: 65).

Five years after *Le Crime de Monsieur Lange* was made, the Popular Front-dominated Chambre des Députés was to confer full state powers upon Marshal Pétain, thus effectively voting for its own destitution. The 'socialism in one courtyard' of the film's community, which acts as a microcosm at once of Paris (itself a metonym for France) and of the French working class, has already been shown to be dependent upon the good grace of capitalist benignity and to potentially be threatened from within by xenophobic feelings, however comically expressed. If Prévert's internationalist perspective reinscribes itself at the end of the film, it is only after a draining, potentially fatal struggle. Lyall Bush's view is that the border represents 'a trope for the futility of "escape" from ideology, or the gaze, or the hailing camera. The last crossing as a retreat much more than a transgressive act' (Bush 1989: 67), is certainly reinforced by the spatial construction of the final shot, the direct negation of the Paris-set 360° pan and the circularities that have led up to it. The shot is bleakly horizontal, depicting windswept dunes with no human habitation; the 180° rule is flouted, to be sure, when Lange and Valentine turn to wave to the camera, but by way of farewell rather than of greeting. They are, after all, as we have seen being forced into exile.

That exile offers striking parallels not only with Renoir's later work, such as *La Grande Illusion*, but with his life and development after the outbreak of war. *La Règle du jeu* was such a spectacular failure on its release in 1939 that Renoir felt tempted to leave France altogether well before 1941, when he finally arrived in Hollywood. The savage public and critical response to the film now appears a triumphant endorsement of its extraordinary innovativeness and vicious social criticism, but at the time it spelt doom for Renoir's 'United Artists *à la française*', even before the war destroyed such dreams once and for all. The Occupation's restructuring of the French industry, we should recall, placed it on a far more sophisticated industrial footing than before, which can be seen as having brought about major changes in the type of films made. For Alan Williams:

> It is most obviously the freewheeling, heterogeneous approach to filmic form and content taken by Jean Renoir, Jean Vigo, and others before the war – the improvisational feel and the sense of openness to a world which extends beyond the boundaries of the cinema screen – which was conspicuously absent in the new approach to film-making. (Williams 1992: 263)

The contrast between the static, nostalgic narrative quality and subject-matter of such Occupation films as Carné's *Les Visiteurs du soir/The Devil's Envoys* (1942) and Becker's

Goupi-mains rouges/It Happened at the Inn (1943) and Renoir's great works of the 1930s, explicable as much by the threat of censorship as by industrial reorganisation, is certainly a striking one.[4] In this respect, it is certainly possible to see the ending of *Lange* as a pre-emptive elegy for Renoir's shattered dreams of a cooperative industry, and more generally as foreshadowing the direction of his post-war career. For Janet Bergstrom, as for the vast majority of writers on Renoir, his post-war films, whether shot in Hollywood or in Europe, are markedly inferior to the 1930s masterworks. Bergstrom is particularly severe on *French Can-Can* (1955), his first post-war French film, deeming it 'a betrayal of the intelligent, socially evocative film-making Renoir had excelled in before the war' (Bergstrom 1998: 186). For Bergstrom, Renoir's long-delayed return to France had estranged him definitively from his '1930s realist mode' (Bergstrom 1998: 206), so that *French Can-Can* 'would qualify as a perfectly respectable Hollywood film' (Bergstrom 1998: 216). Not only that, its regression to the place (Montmartre) and very nearly the time of Renoir's own childhood, along with its comparatively conventional plot and dubious gender politics, place it for her with those tendencies in post-war French cinema that carried on where the films of the Occupation years left off. It is not necessary to share all the strictures of Bergstrom's view of the film (I, for one, do not) to appreciate the more general validity of her argument. Renoir's view of France in *French Can-Can* is primarily one constructed for an American audience, which may well have been the only way for him to have made a 'French' film in the 1950s. Yet for Poulle and Bergstrom alike, that meant that he had, as Žižek might put it, lost his 'national Thing', metonymically represented by the values triumphantly realized on both sides of the camera in *Le Crime de Monsieur Lange*. In that context, Lange and Florelle as they wave farewell are doing so in a manner more far-reaching than they, or Renoir, could have imagined at the time.

Is *Le Crime de Monsieur Lange*'s buoyant vision of community and solidarity, then, destroyed by its ending? Does 'the national Thing' in all its horizontal inescapability and nearly suicidal hesitation short of the border nullify the collective sweep of the 360° shot, reducing it to what my title (drawn from a Borges short story) calls 'circular ruins'? To answer 'yes', quite apart from retroactively invalidating years of teaching the film, would be to disregard the importance, the positive value, for Renoir of that very 'national Thing' that at the same time menaces the dreams and lives of his two central characters. It would also be to fall into the error of supposing *Le Crime de Monsieur Lange* to be an entirely realistic, prosaic, even didactic work. Yet Lange himself is constantly referred to as an inveterate dreamer throughout the film, whose flashback structure, along with the fact that Valentine and especially Lange are exhausted and in a state of shock as the story is told, intensifies this dreamlike feeling. The framing narrative itself is extremely brief (some seven minutes out of the film's 85 minutes, most of those at the beginning), so that when we return abruptly to it just before the ending the effect may well resemble that of waking from a dream, back into a reality the dreamwork had veiled from us – that reality in which Lange is effectively on trial for his life, accounting for the sadness evoked by Sesonske.

What now needs to be called into question is the opposition between 'dream' and 'reality' – and, more pertinently, the Real in a Lacanian sense – implicit in what I have just said.

Žižek's analysis in *The Sublime Object of Ideology* constructs 'fantasy as a support of reality' rather than as its converse or negation. This means, to over-simplify, that:

> When we awaken into reality after a dream, we usually say to ourselves 'it was just a dream', thereby blinding ourselves to the fact that in our everyday, wakening reality we are *nothing but a consciousness of this dream*. It was only in the dream that we approached the fantasy-framework which determines our activity, our mode of acting in reality itself. (Žižek 1989: 47)

This 'mode of acting in reality itself', which is among other things a description of the political, far from being the antithesis of fantasy is actually dependent on it. Fantasy here bears a close relationship to that 'function of ideology [which] is not to offer us a point of escape from our reality but to offer us the social reality itself as an escape from some traumatic, real kernel' (Žižek 1989: 45). That 'real kernel' is traumatic because it is at once inescapable and not directly representable, or representable only through the Lacanian *objet petit a*, 'the original lost object which in a way coincides with its own loss' (Žižek 1989: 158). Valentine's retelling of the cooperative's life – now clearly a 'lost object' for her and Lange other than through the surrogate process of narration – in its circular framing of the action of the film coincides precisely with its own loss, which is the direct effect of Lange's 'mode of acting in reality itself' through his shooting of Batala. That shooting destroys one dream – that of Utopia, of a community without tension or contradiction – in favour of another – Lange's unconscious desire to be the Arizona Jim whose adventures he has merely invented. It also signals the renewed eruption, *'la main tendue'* (the outstretched hand) notwithstanding, of class struggle – a term somewhat more in favour at the time of the Popular Front than it is now, and one that Žižek, political activist as well as thinker and writer in first Yugoslavia, now Slovenia, is one of the few cultural theorists to have continued to use. Lange's identification with Arizona Jim is clearly a dream, although/because it is never acknowledged as such, but unless we bear in mind the curiously oblique relationship Žižek postulates between dream and social reality, it may be hard to see why this is also true of the eruption of class struggle. An answer may be suggested by Žižek's assertion that 'the ultimate paradox of the notion of 'class struggle' is that society is 'held together' by the very antagonism, splitting, that for ever prevents its closure in a harmonious, transparent, rational Whole' (Žižek in Wright and Wright 1999: 74). That moment of closure in a Whole, cognate with the imaginary in its Lacanian sense, may appear to have arrived for the cooperative with the disappearance of Batala and the utopian revels that ensue. Beznard's racism – 'tied to the "pathological" fact of a nation-state' if anything is – seems to have disappeared, mellowed into drunken buffoonery; yet even this is the occasion of 'antagonism [and] splitting', evidenced by his wife's growing irritation and the bearded man who appears at a window angrily demanding that the noise stop because he has to get up for work in the morning. Antagonism and splitting have not been foreclosed or overcome, merely transposed from an (absent) ethnic to a (present) class 'other'. Batala's recrudescence – in the most classic sense, a return of the repressed – is thus foreshadowed even as the merriment reaches its height, and his shooting surely puts paid to any harmonious closure of the kind ironically evoked by Žižek. On this reading, the 360° pan operates less as the agent of such a closure than as a 'holding together' that incorporates antagonism and splitting into itself rather than seeking to deny or transcend them. The opposition between its circular dream and the harsh linear reality of the concluding shot is thus not a simple one of 'nice' Utopia and 'nasty' *realpolitik* (which is precisely what a Stalinist or even Popular Frontist reading would give us, masochistically privileging the latter), for Utopia and *realpolitik* are ultimately indissociable like the 'fantasy' and 'reality' of which they are manifestations. Visually, indeed, the final shot can be described as more truly 'Utopian', for Lange and Florelle as they walk towards the horizon seem bound precisely for no-man's land or 'no place'.

This analysis has, I hope, shown that Dudley Andrew is quite right to say that *Le Crime de Monsieur Lange*, sometimes compared to Duvivier's 1936 *La Belle Équipe* which acts out its analogous problem by way of two alternative endings, often 'dances through the other disturbing issues it raises' (Andrew 1995: 288). That is not so pejorative a judgement as it may appear, for if the film's politics work on the level of agit-dream rather than agitprop, that is because 'politics needs its imaginary, but also needs to know, precisely, that it *is* imaginary' (Reader 1986: 58). Thus it is that we may feel justified, with Borges and perhaps also along with Žižek, in concluding that, as Lange crosses the border, 'in relief, in humiliation, in terror, he understood that he, too, was an appearance, that someone else was dreaming him' (Borges 1973: 42).

Notes

1. Details of these are to be found in André Heinrich's introduction to the screenplays of *Le Crime de Monsieur Lange/Les Portes de la nuit* (Paris, Folio, 1990: 21).
2. Many of these are reproduced in Renoir (1974a).
3. Godard – author of the notorious axiom 'tracking shots are a matter of morality' – also makes use of a 360° pan in *Weekend*, there to illustrate the tedium with which a Mozart piano recital in a Normandy farmyard is received.
4. The view taken, for example, by Jean-Pierre Jeancolas (Jeancolas 1983) that there was a fundamental continuity between pre-war and Occupation cinema also has a great deal to be said for it, but in the particular case of Renoir it seems considerably less relevant.

Chapter 6

Beurz n the Hood: The Articulation of Beur and French Identities in *Le Thé au harem d'Archimède* and *Hexagone*

Carrie Tarr

Beur cinema

John Singleton's film, *Boyz n the Hood* (1991), was one of a number of popular black independent films to emerge from the United States at the end of the 1980s, and I am borrowing from its title as a starting point for examining the ways in which beur-authored cinema in France challenges dominant gendered understandings of ethnicity and identity through its representations of beurs in the *banlieues* of France. I shall begin with a brief overview of beur-authored film production in France and then move on to analyze the recent film *Hexagone* (1994), written and directed by Malik Chibane (who appears to be the first of a new generation of beur film-makers), comparing it with Mehdi Charef's earlier success *Le Thé au harem d'Archimède/Tea in the Harem* (1985). As film-makers of the periphery, working on the borderlines where – according to Paul Willeman (1989: 28) – the most intense and productive life of the culture takes place, both Charef and Chibane attempt to bring to the centre of French culture a concern with the hybrid identities of the beurs. In so doing, they are also exploring the question of what it means to be French, testing out the permeability of French national identity and culture. As Chibane said in an interview with *Libération*: 'I would say that, overall, the *banlieue* has not changed since 1978 and the arrival of drugs. The only key difference is that we are French.' It is this understated difference, this involuntary recognition that beur identities have to be articulated in relation to French identities, which informs both *Le Thé* and *Hexagone*. In comparing the two films, each produced at a significant moment in the history of postcolonial France, I shall be seeking to highlight shifts in the ways beur cinema addresses its audiences and can or cannot problematize the articulation of beur and French national identity in French cinema.

Beur cinema was defined by Christian Bosséno (1992: 47–48) as referring to films which were not only directed by film-makers of North African/Maghrebi origin born and/or brought up in France, but which also took the experiences of the beurs as their topic. The term embraces both the militant-activist films produced as shorts and documentaries within community associations and exhibited on alternative distribution circuits, and a handful of commercial feature films which are the topic of this chapter. *Le Thé à la menthe /Mint Tea* (1984), directed by Abdelkrim Bahloul, is considered to herald the genre (though in fact Bahloul was/is an Algerian working in Paris, and his young hero is an Algerian immigrant). It was followed by *Le Thé au harem d'Archimède* (1985) and *Miss Mona* (1987), directed by Mehdi Charef, and *Bâton Rouge* (1986) and *Cheb* (1991), directed by Rachid Bouchareb. The success of Charef and Bouchareb's first features has been attributed to their combination of realism of setting (the grim suburban housing estates and crime-ridden city streets) and the construction of attractive, streetwise, young beur/immigrant characters who are able to shrug off the victim status characteristic of films about immigration made in the 1970s, and demonstrate the possibilities of integration in a multicultural if marginalized working-class/ underclass melting pot. References to racism and anti-racism, political activism or Islam – if present at all – are oblique, and such structuring absences enabled French critics, with a collective sigh of relief, to praise beur film-makers for their refusal of 'miserabilism'.

The concept of beur cinema as a genre might initially seem to be an empowering one. The adoption of the word beur, coined by the beurs themselves (originating in Parisian backslang for 'arabe'), signalled the beurs' active presence in the Parisian working-class suburbs, if not in France as a whole, and challenged the (continuing) dominant French misnaming of second- (and now third-) generation Maghrebis as 'Arabs' and 'immigrants'. Beur cinema similarly suggests both agency in the production of representations by this particular ethnic minority and a challenge to dominant representations of 'Frenchness' and 'otherness'. However, the term inevitably draws attention to the difficulties facing oppressed groups involved in identity politics. For how can beur cinema be empowering if it is grounded in an essentialist understanding of ethnic difference? Not only does it risk confining beur film-makers to a cinematic ghetto, whose filmic expressions are largely understood as something different from – and inferior to – the cultural practices of Franco-French directors; it also risks constructing an audience who will respond to the film in terms of their positive or negative images of specific ethnic groups, rather than their potential opening up and problematizing of the question of difference itself. While it may be of strategic importance at any given time to mobilize politically around particular definitions of identity, a fixed label leaves little space for understanding beur cinema, like the rest of French cinema, as the site of multiple and contradictory constructions of subjectivity and identity.

The interventions of beur film-makers in the French cultural arena need to be seen in the wider context of discourses on ethnicity and national identity in French cinema as a whole. However, French film culture – like dominant French culture in general – lacks the will and the vocabulary for addressing identity politics. In the United States, the designation 'black' has now been replaced by the preferred term 'African-American', which at least recognizes both the hybridity and the American-ness of those concerned, even if the 'whiteness' of the dominant film industry remains unnamed. In France, apart from the 'black-blanc-beur' movement, which implicitly recognizes the 'whiteness' of the dominant culture, the Eurocentric discourses of Franco-French cultural production are similarly ignored, and a term that fully recognizes the hybrid Frenchness of the beurs without conflating the meaning of the word beur with either Arab, immigrant or Muslim – Maghrebi-French, for example – has yet to become acceptable. In French film culture, the problematic articulation of beur and French national identity has been displaced by the focus first on beur cinema and more recently on *cinémas de la banlieue*, which allows Franco-French-authored and beur-authored representations of the multi-ethnic working-class suburbs to be grouped together without regard for the different discursive positions which they might be mobilizing in relation to national identity. It is not insignificant that in the *Cahiers de la Cinémathèque's* recent special issue on 'Cinémas et banlieues', Michel Cadé's article on 'Des immigrés dans les banlieues' (Cadé 1994: 125–27) fails to distinguish between the national identities of immigrants and beurs. In this chapter, given the current lack of alternative terminology, I shall be using the opposing terms beur/beurette and Franco-French, not in any essentialist sense, but in order to leave the notion of an unqualified Frenchness open to a plurality of meanings.

Clearly the combination of Franco-French anti-Arab racism (fuelled by Islamic fundamentalism and terrorism in Algeria) and the dominance of national French discourses favouring integration based on assimilation rather than multiculturalism (a debate raised to fever pitch by the ongoing *affaire des foulards*), circumscribe the ways in which beur film-makers can address wider French audiences. Both beur-authored films and recent African-American films, like Singleton's *Boyz*, seek to give cultural visibility to oppressed ethnic minorities and claim authenticity for their films' representations of everyday life. But whereas Singleton (and others) have been able to use 'tougher, abrasive and quintessentially black elements' (Biskend 1991: 6) in their representations of under-privileged African-American communities, beur film-makers have been obliged to tread more carefully in the exploration of their hybrid identities. Their films use the medium not just to promote the visibility of the beurs in an address to what is, after all, a relatively small beur audience, but also to counter the negative stereotyping that informs mainstream media representations in their address to the wider Franco-French audience. In so doing, they tend to support the dominant model of assimilation (and thereby the suppression of differences) rather than investigating multiculturalism (and the recognition and acceptance of differences) as an alternative way forward for French notions of national identity.

The production and success of Charef and Bouchareb's first films can be linked to the historical moment of the early years of Mitterrand's presidency, at the time of the growing visibility and media hyping of the beur generation following the 'March Against Racism and for Equality' in March 1983. The slogans of the period, '*J'y suis, j'y reste*' (in response to the deportations of young offenders) and '*Touche pas à mon pote*' (launched by SOS Racisme) touch on two fundamental issues for the period: the beurs' claim to rights of residency in France, and the need to combat the growth of racism and the Front National. However, they also indicate the contradictions between a self-assertive beur-organized movement ('*J'y suis, j'y reste*') and the potential recuperation of the movement by wider interests (both speaker and addressee of '*Touche pas à mon pote*' could be assumed to be white and male, while the notion of '*mon pote*' neatly evacuates the question of difference in favour of an unproblematic concept of youthful fraternity). The suppression or marginalizing of differences, and the desire for and belief in the possibility of integration through assimilation, inform Charef and Bouchareb's first films, which each construct narratives based upon friendships between beur and white youths with remarkably similar looks, desires and experiences. At the same time, the unquestioned privileging of a hetero/sexist version of masculinity in these films specifically prevents a consideration of gendered (and other) forms of oppression.

Charef's and Bouchareb's second films are notably more pessimistic in respect of the fortunes of their main characters: the immigrant/beur protagonist remains fundamentally isolated, while the sympathetic young white French males of the first films constitute a significant new structuring absence. However, a more complex approach to questions of gender and sexuality is to be found: *Miss Mona* tackles the topic of homosexuality, transvestism and prostitution, while *Cheb* gives space to a young beurette's crisis of identity and need for independence. In each case, the male immigrant/beur protagonist (and the spectator, too) is required to rethink accepted categories of gender as part of the film's narrative trajectory. These second films are decidedly less conciliatory towards a potential white crossover market and draw attention to the particularities of immigrant/beur experience and culture, and to the power of the state to make life intolerable for illegal immigrants, beur offenders or sequestrated beurettes. They can be read as signs of beur disillusionment with the anti-racist alliances of the mid- to late 1980s, but at the same time their relative lack of popularity at the box office indicates that audiences were reluctant to confront the question of immigrant/ beur identities from an uncompromisingly beur-centred perspective.

The situation facing beur cultural activists in 1995 is arguably even more problematic. The return of the right to power in 1993, with its policy of curbing immigrant rights to French nationality and citizenship, its introduction of racist identity controls as a measure against fundamentalist terrorism and its provocative directive allowing head teachers to ban the wearing of the *hijab* in French state schools, means that Arabs, immigrants and Muslims – and, given the interchangeability of the terms, by implication the beurs too – are constantly constructed by the media as 'other' to French national identity. Furthermore, the beurs are still scapegoats for Franco-French fears about unemployment, delinquency and drugs, as well as being potential scapegoats for fears about AIDS. It would not be surprising, then, if representations of the beurs at this time were to return to a rhetorical bid for integration through assimilation, by suppressing signs of difference. In fact, both Charef and Bouchareb have turned away from making films specifically about the beurs. Charef's subsequent films, *Camomille* (1987) and *Au pays des Juliets/In the Country of Juliets* (1992), focus on other forms of marginality in France, while Bouchareb's third feature, *Poussières de vie/Dust of Life* (1994), addresses the topic of Amerasian children abandoned in Vietnam after the American withdrawal, and (like *Bâton Rouge*) is aimed at an international American audience. Both film-makers are still exercised by issues relating to marginalized identities, but have chosen not to pursue directly the representation of relations between whites and beurs in France. However, in 1994 two younger beur film-makers emerged to take up the challenge: Malik Chibane, whose first film will be discussed shortly and who is currently working on a second feature *Panne des sens* centred on three beur/Algerian women; and Karim Dridi, whose first feature, *Pigalle* (1994), focuses on white rather than beur marginality, but who has announced that his second film will be about racism in France.[1] It looks as though the mid-1990s will see a second wave of beur-authored films marking a new preoccupation with questions of ethnicity and national identity in France.[2] Furthermore, Abdelkrim Bahloul (director of *Le Thé à la menthe*) is currently making a film about Muslims in Marseille, while

Thomas Gilou, director of *Black mic mac* (1986) (and adviser to Chibane on the making of *Hexagone)* is in the process of shooting *Raï* on location in Garges-lès-Gonesse, north of Paris.[3] What remains to be seen is the extent to which these films will continue to work within the generic constraints of beur realism and promote or challenge the possibility of integration through assimilation. Certainly, Bahloul departs from the genre in his second feature, *Un Vampire au paradis/A Vampire in Paradise* (1992). In this film, Nosfer Arbi, a would-be vampire, is a Maghrebi immigrant anxious to return to his native land, whose story is interwoven with a distinctly BCBG family's convoluted attempts to diagnose and cure their daughter's inexplicable outbursts of speech in Arabic. The film incorporates elements of fantasy, comedy, satire and romance, ending with the young French girl and her Maghrebi male counterpart staring at each other in mutual fascination. But it fails to deliver on its comic or satirical potential, perhaps because of the producer's insistence on highlighting the film's fantasy elements.[4] To date, it remains unrepresentative of 'beur cinema' in its attempt to explore representations of ethnicity and identity through the use of popular genres.

Hexagone and *Le Thé au harem d'Archimède*

Hexagone by Malik Chibane returns to the realism of earlier beur cinema but, because of its unusual production context, it has been described as 'the first film to be made by the beurs for the beurs'. Like Mehdi Charef's *Le Thé au harem d'Archimède,* an adaptation of the director's semi-autobiographical novel *Le Thé au harem d'Archi Ahmed* (Charef 1983), *Hexagone* draws on first-hand knowledge and experience of life in the Parisian *banlieue* and specifically addresses the problems facing unemployed youths. However, Chibane was concerned less with telling his own personal story than with documenting the lives of the beur generation. One of four young people who created the community association IDRISS[5] in 1985 to promote self-help among young unemployed beurs in Goussainville, he turned to film-making after the death of a friend who had contracted AIDS from an infected needle: 'Immortalizing the generation to whom we belong has become increasingly urgent as this cultural invisibility [on the part of the beurs] becomes, for me, more and more intolerable.'[6] Like Charef, Chibane had no prior training in film, having a CAP d'électricien and four years of unemployment behind him. But whereas Charef was sponsored by Costa Gavras, Chibane set up his own production company and took six years to make *Hexagone*, facing problems in raising funding at every stage. The original script failed to get the *avance sur recettes,* and in the end the shooting of the film was financed through support from the local community, thanks also to technicians and a local amateur cast who were willing to work for free. The editing of the film was eventually funded by the FEMIS (Fondation européenne des métiers de l'image et du son), and post-production costs were secured by Bernard Tapie who, just two weeks before the Socialist Party lost power, pushed grants through from various ministries. This film, then, was made outside the normal structures of the French film industry.

The lack of finance, as well as Chibane's lack of experience, are factors leave their traces in the finished product. *Le Thé* is a much more professionally finished film, more self-conscious and assured in its direction of the actors, its camera and editing techniques and its use of colour, music and sound. In contrast, *Hexagone*'s camera and editing techniques make it look and sound more like a home movie, and the film opts for a more low-key 'authentic' realism in its use of an amateur cast, its refusal of an extra-diegetic 'ethnic' music track and its restricted range of depressingly recognizable locations in Goussainville. The look and sound of the film are obviously important in determining its commercial appeal, especially if it is to attract a wide crossover audience. To date, *Hexagone* has enjoyed a critical success and a reasonably successful first run for such a low-budget film (1.2 million francs). It has been screened in 80 towns in France thanks to the ACID,[7] and has been released on video. However, Chibane has so far been too immersed in his next project to get it subtitled for international distribution.

There are differences between the two films, which are attributable to differences of funding and experience. But on the more fundamental issue of the representation of beur identities in France, a comparison of the narrative and audio-visual strategies used by the two films reveals both significant differences and significant similarities of approach. In the rest of this chapter I shall address these differences and similarities, in order to assess whether independent beur film production in the 1990s is more able to problematize the notion of French national identity than was possible in the 1980s.

Both *Le Thé* and *Hexagone* document the life of a working-class suburban community through an episodic narrative structure which interweaves the lives of a variety of characters. Various elements of *mise-en-scène* and plot are common to both: visually, the films give priority to the exteriors and interiors of the blocks of flats and the other spaces frequented by the young people – streets, cafes, discos, trains and cars; narratively, both films include scenes foregrounding the effects of having no money or jobs, the tensions between beurs and their parents, and young people's attitudes to crime, drugs and sex.

In *Le Thé*, the narrative focuses primarily on the (mis)adventures of the duo formed by Madjid, a young beur, and his mate Pat, a young white youth, which lead straight into the hands of the police; but *Le Thé* also engages with a variety of white characters, like Josette, the single mother who attempts suicide, and the vicious Frenchmen living on the estate. In contrast, *Hexagone*'s fragmented multi-stranded narrative centres almost entirely on the thoughts and activities of a group of (mostly) unemployed beur youths and three beurettes. The narrative, which is loosely organized around the older generation's preparations for the festival of Aïd, cuts between the lives of Slimane, his sister Nora and brother Samy, drug-dealer Karim and Samy's fellow drug-addict Paco, Slimane's friends Ali and Staf, and Staf's two sisters, one of whom, Nacera, is secretly Slimane's girlfriend. Although ostensibly dealing with similar basic situations and narrative structures, then, there is a fundamental shift between *Le Thé* and *Hexagone* in the latter's focus on an almost exclusively non-white community and its incorporation of beurette voices. Chibane specifically refused advice to cut down on the number of beur roles, or create a role for a star actor like Smaïn, and was criticized for the absence of white roles. His uncompromising beur-centred perspective was intended as a form of 'provocation'.[8] The centring on beur characters does affect the way in which the film addresses its audience, as a comparison of the opening sequence of each film reveals. In *Le Thé*, the credit sequence introduces the spectator into Madjid's home via the character of Josette, who brings her son to Madjid's mother to be looked after, while the following sequence introduces the local gang via the character of Pat. So Madjid is initially perceived, as it were, through white French eyes: first in bed, reluctant to get up, and then unsuccessfully attempting to repair his motorbike. In contrast, *Hexagone* opens with a striking establishing shot which pans from a view of the open countryside to the sight of what appears to be a small town until the frame takes in the blocks of flats dominating the skyline. It is a shot which boldly displaces the cornfields and birdsong of '*la France profonde*', placing the blocks of flats and the noise of aircraft at the centre, rather than the periphery, of the hexagon which is contemporary France. The film then cuts between children at play and a group of young beurs hanging about in the street outside the *Maison du développement social du quartier*, an economical strategy for contrasting images of carefree childhood with the representation of the beur youths' problems of insertion into French society.

The opening sequence of *Hexagone* is accompanied by a voice-over (later identified with the character Slimane), voicing the speaker's feelings of emptiness and despair. The use of the voice-over was criticized in several reviews of the film – perhaps because the sound quality and intelligibility of the speech leave something to be desired, perhaps because of the fact that it is not initially attributable to a specific character. What the voice-over does, however, is to establish a discursive position emanating from the beurs themselves, which directly addresses the spectator as someone sympathetic to the beur predicament – 'Don't you find?' asks Slim – opening up the possibility of dialogue between spectator and speaker. Whereas Madjid is relatively passive and silent (and ends up in a virtually catatonic state), Slimane asserts his subjectivity through his appropriation of the soundtrack and his ability to comment on and express his feelings about the apparently hopeless situation he and his friends find themselves in. In *Le Thé*, language is a source of conflict and misunderstanding which disadvantages the beurs – Balou did not understand what was meant by '*le théorème d'Archimède*' and, like the white audience, Madjid cannot (or will not) understand his mother when she rages at him in (unsubtitled) Arabic. However, in *Hexagone* the beurs express themselves and communicate in a mixture of French, *argot*, *verlan* and Arabic, positioning the audience to accept such speech as the norm (even if the press release included a glossary).

The films' titles indicate a similar shift in self-awareness. *Le Thé au harem d'Archimède* still references the beur as 'other', even if the title is a joke at the expense of native French speakers. But *Hexagone* can be read as a claim for the beurs in the *banlieue* to be recognized as central to any conceptualization of contemporary France. The film is not just an exotic representation of an under-privileged working-class ethnic ghetto, outside mainstream French experience, but rather an assertion of beur claims to citizenship, *à part entière*, regardless of ethnic difference.

This assertiveness reveals itself in a comparison of scenes in *Hexagone* which parallel scenes in *Le Thé*. For example, at the unemployment office (ANPE), Madjid passively accepts that as the target of racial prejudice he will never get a place on a *stage* (work placement), whereas Slim and Staf devise strategies to overcome the disadvantages they face, getting Ali to forge them false diplomas and chatting up the girls working in the ANPE office. If Staf just makes a fool of himself, Slim persuades the beurette employee to take an interest in his case, and his prospect of a place on a *stage* at the end of the film arouses some hope for his future. Conversely, in parallel disco scenes, Madjid flirts with a white French girl apparently without any fear of racial discrimination, whereas Staf feels obliged to hide his ethnic origins from Annick, and is criticized by Slim for denying his identity. When Staf eventually opts to reveal the 'truth', he is rewarded with Annick's shamefaced smile. *Hexagone* is potentially more empowering than *Le Thé* in its assumption that openness, and the recognition and acceptance of difference, is a better route to overcoming racial prejudice than dissimulation.

In fact, the debate around integration and assimilation is explicitly raised in *Hexagone* in a scene in which Chibane himself plays an uncredited cameo role. In the course of a night out in Paris, Slim, Ali and Karim decide to prepare themselves for racist hostility by acting not as '*des Rebeus complexés, paranos*' ('mixed up, paranoid beurs') but rather as '*des Rebeus qui assurent … de beaux gosses*' ('good looking, confident beurs').[9] They still get turned away from their chosen nightclub because they are identified as '*arabes*', and spend the evening instead at a disco on the outskirts of Paris where, as a couple of beurs point out, the only 'Français' (*sic*) are on television! In a discussion with Thierry (Chibane), who sees no reason for the beurs not to be successfully assimilated into French culture like so many other immigrants before them, Ali argues that the beurs are still the victims of racism and need to assume their cultural difference and colonial past; and Thierry eventually concedes the point. However, if Ali asserts the importance of assuming beur history, culture and experience, Chibane as director takes care to confine the film's construction of beur identities within clear, acceptable limits. Both *Le Thé* and *Hexagone* avoid dealing with really contentious issues and work to keep open the possibilities of assimilation through three principal strategies: they stress the ways in which beur lifestyles are similar to other young French people's lifestyles; they construct a sympathetic understanding of the role played by drugs and delinquency in the lives of the under-privileged; and they confine the representation of Islamic beliefs and Maghrebi culture to the older generation.

Both *Le Thé* and *Hexagone* are primarily male-centred youth films, concerned with the effects of mass unemployment on young men and exploring their strategies for survival. *Le Thé,* however, foregrounds the shared macho sensibility of its male protagonists and constructs misogynist representations of most of its (white) female characters, while *Hexagone* works to problematize unreconstructed male heterosexuality and constructs a relatively progressive representation of the beurettes, making the film much more enjoyable for a female audience. True, it is Annick – the white girl – who is made to bear the brunt of representing white racism (and Chibane has admitted that this may be a weak point in the film's structure). But the film explores the economic constraints and personal problems of the beurettes as well as beur youths, including a scene in which Nora, Nacera and Nacera's older sister Yasmina (a single parent) meet to chat about men, sex and marriage in ways which would be recognizable to most other young women. Nevertheless, it is noticeable that their assumptions about the desirability (or otherwise) of virginity, arranged marriages and inter-racial sex, for example, are articulated in a context which suppresses more explosive and divisive issues like unwanted pregnancies or the wearing of the *foulard*. And there is nothing in the street fashions adopted by the beurettes which distinguishes them from other young French women.

Nacera's relationship with Slim provides an opportunity for suggesting that the beur generation is freeing itself both from the strict Islamic moral codes of their parents' generation *and* from the casual misogyny which informs *Le Thé*. Slim is forced to reflect on his behaviour towards Nacera, and Nacera herself – despite the fact that she does not appear visually in the opening or closing sequences of the film – emerges as a forceful and independent-minded young woman. Unusually, their relationship is seen from Nacera's point of view as well as Slim's: it is she who takes the initiative in arranging their rendezvous and she who criticizes the moral hypocrisy of the beurs in not taking issue with their parents and voices the need to make an open commitment. Furthermore, in a love-making scene which has no equivalent in *Le Thé*, *Hexagone* shows Slim not only being attentive to Nacera's needs, but also using a condom! A more vulnerable beur masculinity is represented, too, in parallel bed scenes, for whereas Madjid in *Le Thé* simply loses interest when he discovers that his partner has got her period, poor Staf finds himself unable to make love to Annick for fear that his circumcision will give away his identity. Despite its apparent liberalism and honesty in sexual matters, however, as a realist film (and one which is therefore bound to be read as representative of the community which it purports to represent), *Hexagone* could be criticized for shying away from addressing controversial and contentious issues like prostitution, homosexuality or AIDS among beurs. It chooses to foreground a normative and unthreatening image of beur sexuality which wider French audiences can relate to unproblematically: Nacera even says that it is Slim's '*côté françaouais*' ('French side') which she finds attractive!

A similar sort of wariness can be seen in *Hexagone*'s construction of delinquency. Both films take care to represent drug abuse as self-destructive and drug dealing as reprehensible, but Chibane does not evoke the death from AIDS that originally inspired *Hexagone*. Instead, Samy quietly dies of what is presumably an accidental overdose, and Karim, the dealer, is picked up by the police. *Hexagone*'s stylistic and ideological refusal to foreground images of crime and violence makes it a very different film from the African-American films epitomized by *Boyz n the Hood*, or indeed from *Le Thé*. *Le Thé* is structured through a series of petty crimes, and Madjid and Pat are constantly involved in acts of violence of one sort or another – they steal from a racist slob, pimp for a local prostitute, mug a gay man and burgle a tennis club changing-room in a wealthy suburb. Their crimes are justified by their economic plight (which is not of their own making), by the questionable morality of their victims and by their own sympathetic nature (demonstrated by their inter-racial male camaraderie and their protection of the estate from drug dealers). So when they are finally picked up by the police for a crime they have not actually committed, the spectator is still positioned to feel sympathetic towards them. In *Hexagone*, in contrast, the principal characters display little signs of violence and the images of crime are toned down and even verge on the comic. Samy steals odd shoes and watches to pay for his drug habit, while Slim and Staf use Ali's false papers to try to get jobs. When Samy is caught shoplifting, the spectator is positioned to applaud both the way Slim rescues him and, after an awkwardly shot chase sequence, his own escape from the police (who in both films have an extremely low profile). But crime and violence are not represented as such a pervasive part of life in the suburbs as in *Le Thé* or *Boyz n the Hood*. Whereas the aggressivity of *Boyz* can perhaps be read paradoxically as a measure of the director's sense of security about the African-American male presence in American society, *Hexagone*'s reluctance to tackle drugs and violence outside of a conventional moral framework suggests that the beurs' presence in *their* Hood is one that still has to be very carefully negotiated.

In both *Le Thé* and *Hexagone*, the representation of the parents' generation provides an opportunity for the beurs to distance themselves from the religious beliefs and cultural expectations of their parents. In *Le Thé*, Madjid's mother may be the emotional heart of the community but she is also a devout Muslim who strongly identifies with Algerian culture and is unable to understand Madjid's problematic hybrid status. In *Hexagone*, the representation of Islam is relegated to the older generation's preparations for the festival of Aïd and the religious rituals accompanying Samy's death, and the film partially reverses the challenge to the traditional composition of the immigrant family constructed in *Le Thé*. The mother figure (Slim's mother) is a superstitious woman, heavily dependent on her *marabout* and unable to comprehend what is happening to her family, while the father figure, who is marginalized or absent in the early beur films (here Staf's father, played by Algerian film director Mahmoud Zemmouri) is constructed as relatively tolerant and understanding in his relationship with his younger daughter. Such a shift in the representation of the family call be read as a sign of the film's desire to reassure French audiences both that the father's position has been normalized *and* that authoritarian relationships are giving way to more progressive ideas about women's roles. However, by clearly signalling that certain traditional elements of Maghrebi culture (belief in Islam, female virginity or arranged marriages, for example) have no significance for the younger generation, both *Le Thé* and *Hexagone* are also signalling that, despite their hybridity, the beurs are really not very different from other young people in the audience they are addressing.

The endings of *Le Thé* and *Hexagone* are indicative of their different emphases. In *Le Thé*, when Pat opts to join Madjid in police custody, their inter-racial friendship – however problematic and limiting – is the only flicker of hope to emerge from an otherwise pessimistic narrative closure. *Hexagone*'s ending is apparently more open. Slim alone, suffering from a terrible headache, contemplates his current situation. His voice-over accompanies a fragmented montage sequence showing how his friends are now going their separate ways:

Samy is dead, Karim is arrested, but Staf renews his relationship with Annick, Ali seems to have found a job, and Slim himself has a place on a *stage* and the opportunity to embark on a more honest relationship with Nacera. Arguably, *Hexagone*'s disjointed multi-stranded structure productively replaces *Le Thé*'s closed narrative of despair with a recognition that, however limited and negative to date, the beur narrative can be a pluralized and individuated one. However, the film actually ends on a blank screen while Slim, still alone, having concluded that Nacera is the best thing in his life, delivers the final line: 'In the end, woman is a man's future.' Rather than a positive and empowering assertion of the beurs' active place in the hood, this question suggests a rather uncertain retreat into an unproblematized and depoliticized private sphere.

Hexagone does more than *Le Thé* to foreground male and female beur subjectivities, and so engage pleasurably with a beur audience. It moves away from the rather naïve embracing of integration characteristic of the early beur films, and shifts the grounds of the debate on to a beur-constructed terrain. Nevertheless, the particular representation of beur identities foregrounded in *Hexagone*, despite or perhaps because of the film's evacuation of Franco-French male voices, works even harder than *Le Thé* to construct an image of the beurs that is culturally acceptable to a wider French audience, and that requires little or no shift in the dominant construction of 'Frenchness' beyond an acceptance of the visibility of beur faces and beur variants of the French language. The film suggests that the problems and aspirations of the beurs (male and female) arc basically little different from the problems and aspirations of French working-class youth in general, merely exacerbated by racism, their parents' cultural expectations and confinement to the ethnic ghetto. By making the case for assimilation rather than constructing beur subjectivities and identities as diverse and contradictory, *Hexagone* fails to problematize the dominant culture's construction of French national identity and its continuing marginalization of those who wish to exercise alternative sexual, cultural or religious practices.[10]

Notes

1. Regrettably, no Beurette film-maker has yet made a commercial feature film. Feminist activist Farida Belghoul has made two short fiction films, *C'est Madame la France que tu préfères?* (1981) and *Le Départ du père* (1983). Moufida Tlatli's successful first film, *Les Silences du palais/The Silences of the Palace* (Tunisia, 1994), offers a model of contemporary Maghrebi women's film-making.
2. *Panne de sens* was released under the title of *Douce France* (Chibane, 1995), while Dridi's second film was entitled *Bye-bye* (1995).
3. According to *Libération* (10 December 1994), during the shooting of *Raï*, several drunken amateur actors dressed as CRS set up a roadblock on the motorway north of Paris and forced white French drivers to submit to an identity control: '*On a inversé le délit de sale gueule*'. The actors were described as '*tous arabes*' (and not Beurs).
4. Author's interview with Abdelkrim Bahloul, 15 September 1994.

5. IDRISS is a youth association in Goussainville.
6. Malik Chibane, quoted in press release for *Hexagone*.
7. ACID stands for l'Agence du cinéma indépendant pour sa diffusion.
8. Author's interview with Malik Chibane, 12 September 1994.
9. In the original dialogue, Chibane uses the term 'Rebeus' (i.e. *verlan* or backslang for Beur). The implication for the use of the term Beur and its appropriation by the mainstream – a fact which compels Chibane to use Rebeu as a term to describe his Maghrebi-French characters – has been discussed earlier in this chapter. For consistency, however, the term Beur has been used in the translation.
10. This chapter was originally published as 'Beurz n the Hood: The Articulation of Beur and French Identities in *Le Thé au harem d 'Archimède* and *Hexagone*', in *Modern and Contemporary France*, 3: 4 (1995), pp. 415–25. The editors are grateful to Taylor and Francis and to Carrie Tarr for their permission to reprint the article as part of this collection.

Chapter 7

Community, Nostalgia and the Spectacle of Masculinity: Jean Gabin

Ginette Vincendeau

In terms of economic power and authorial status, Jean Gabin is the only 'real' star of French cinema of the 1930s. The so-called Gabin 'myth' is effectively an intricate intertextual construction which radiates through not only the films themselves, but also an array of other texts such as memoirs and testimonies (his and others), fan magazines, newspaper reports, plays, music-hall shows and songs. From these has emerged the familiar image of the 'strong, silent and often deeply human hero, and more often, anti-hero, of such milestones of the French cinema as Duvivier's *Pépé le Moko*, Renoir's *La Grande Illusion* and Carné's *Quai des Brumes*' (Katz 1982: 459). Both Gabin the proletarian hero *par excellence* and 'a screen symbol the world over of the tough but tender Frenchman' (Powell 1976) have been widely analyzed, and although the literature on the subject would benefit from a reappraisal, it is not my purpose here. My present concern, rather, stems from an awareness that an important component of the Gabin screen representations, and hence 'myth' – namely masculinity – has been overlooked or, if not overlooked, at any rate taken as a self-evident, transparent factor.

Since the interest in sexual difference in relation to film has come primarily under the impulse of feminism, the concentration has been on images of women and on the relation between female sexuality and textual systems. The debate on masculinity, in this respect, has only just begun. Moreover, where writers and scholars (Richard Dyer, Paul Willemen, Steve Neale, Andrew Britton) have shown an interest in this area, it has been overwhelmingly related to American cinema – as, indeed, have been the studies of femininity and female stars. Looking at how a male *European* star functions in films which are part of French film history as well as being 'classic narrative' films in the Hollywood sense of the term opens up several levels of enquiry. Furthermore as the characters portrayed by Jean Gabin in his mid- and late 1930s films were all proletarians, the question of sexual difference also intersects with that of the representation of class in, and the historical inscription of, films made in the crucial period of the Popular Front, Munich and the approach of the Second World War.

This chapter concentrates on *La Belle Equipe/They Were Five* (Duvivier 1936) and *Pépé le Moko* (Duvivier 1937) as popular entertainments within the mainstream French film industry of the period. The latter was a triumph both in France and internationally, while the former had a more modest, though 'honourable' box-office career (it ranked fifty-ninth of the 75 films deemed successes in 1936, out of the 450-odd shown that year). Both were designed to accommodate the Gabin persona, which had emerged fully in Duvivier's *La Bandera/Escape from Yesterday* (1935) – the story of Spanish legionnaires in Morocco – also a box-office hit.

Intertexts: Populism and proletarian heroes

The success of *Pépé le Moko* prompted an immediate Hollywood remake, *Algiers* (Cromwell 1938), made with stars of equal if not higher international status, Charles Boyer and Hedy Lamarr. Contemporary reviews, though complimentary about the competence of the remake as a whole, often stress the 'miscasting' of Boyer as Pépé, while recognizing his impeccable credentials as an actor. Boyer's relative failure was one of register: he could not embody a convincing criminal who was also a proletarian hero. Gabin, on the other hand, represented *the* proletarian hero. That was first a function of his screen persona, able to accommodate dichotomies (e.g. honest/dishonest) for the successful resolution of the narratives of his films. But Gabin's equation with the proletarian hero was also over-determined by powerful intertexts specific to France in the 1930s. Particularly relevant here are the dominant populism of the period present in all popular art forms, the importance of performance in French films of the 1930s (Gabin started his career as a music-hall performer) and the dominance of narratives involving all-male groups spread across a variety of genres (army melodramas, military vaudevilles, populist melodramas).

Duvivier, like Clair and Genina, like Carné, Renoir, Chenal and others, was working against the background of populist literature prominent in the 1920s and 1930s, and used it. Populist writers such as Pierre Mac Orlan, Marcel Aymé, Francis Carco and Georges Simenon were adapted for the screen, but the influence of populism went beyond direct adaptations. What these writers (and many others) had in common was their fascination with the working-class milieu and the underworld – an interest they shared with many others involved in the popular arts of the time: singers, graphic artists, photographers and film-makers. It is a fascination which in effect dates back to the late nineteenth century, to Dumas, Zola and Maupassant, and had been transmitted to the tradition of the 'realist' singers typified by Fréhel (who appears in *Pépé le Moko*), Damia and later Edith Piaf.

The populist interest in the 'lower classes' should not, however, be confused with socially committed art. *La Belle Equipe* may start off as a film 'about' a workers' co-op, but the subject of the film is quickly displaced from the workers' endeavours to make the co-op succeed to the sexual rivalries that eventually destroy it. The social referential world in the film thus becomes a background for a melodramatic intrigue rather than the substance of the film itself, a point Duvivier explicitly acknowledged when he said: 'The Popular Front may have been taking shape while I was making the second half of the film, but *La Belle Equipe* is not political – unless you count all films with workers in them as left-wing' (Duvivier 1959: 14).

What interests populist art is the *spectacle* of the 'lower classes'. Writers, film-makers or photographers in the 1930s express a common fascination for the *petit peuple* (usually of Paris), shopkeepers, concierges, artisans, and also the more marginal fringes of that class, right down to the underworld. The same preoccupation with *looking at*, with 'knowing', this stratum of French urban society is echoed in a wide range of texts all the way through from Léon Lemonnier's *Manifeste du roman populiste*[1] to Marcel Carné's (1930) exhortation to 'describe the simple life of the people, to render the atmosphere of its labouring humanity' and the work of Brassai, who specialized in taking night photographs of Paris, choosing as his subjects workers, pimps, prostitutes and mobsters.

What Brassai's pictures have in common with Mac Orlan's novels, Carné and Duvivier's films, or Fréhel's songs is an iconography which gives prominence to a *décor*, that of the popular areas of Paris, usually at night and often shiny with rain, with highly contrasted lighting. The Parisian tall building is a key element, with its staircase a strong focal point and its rooftops perhaps the most recognizable motif. André Bazin has underlined the importance of the building in Carné's *Le Jour se Lève/Daybreak* (1939) (Bazin 1963), and Henri Jeanson, scriptwriter of his *Hôtel du Nord* (1938), described the latter as 'a love story between HIM: the canal, and HER: the hotel' (Jeanson 1956). Even in *Pépé le Moko*, where the Parisian decor is physically absent, it is still the desired object and point of reference; this is made explicit in the famous scene where Pépé and Gaby find a way of communicating by reciting the names of *métro* stations, ending together on *Place Blanche*, an emblematic choice since it is the point where the working-class areas of Montmartre meet the seedy underworld of Pigalle. Paris, its popular areas and its underworld, are also at the centre of the world brought to life by the 'realist' song, or *chanson vécue*. Beyond this, the populist iconography concentrates on a number of privileged *loci*, notably the cafés in town and on river banks in the country (themselves rendered familiar by late nineteenth century Impressionist paintings).

But whether in songs, photographs, posters, novels or films, the most powerful iconographic motif of all is that of the proletarian hero himself, who focuses all the representations of the proletariat and the underworld at the same neuralgic point. The (populist) proletarian hero oscillates between the good-natured worker and the sinister criminal (or pimp), but often includes elements of both in varying proportions. What unifies these different values are the clothes, the language and the accents. The example of one simple piece of clothing, the cap, shows this condensing effect. The right-wing activists in Renoir's *La Vie est à nous/Life is Ours* (1936) chose caps, as symbols of the working classes (which they called *salopards*), on the cardboard cut-outs they used as targets in their shooting practice.

Populist films, being fascinated by the *spectacle* of the working classes and the underworld, significantly feature actors who are also performers. Gabin, as well as Albert Préjean (star of many populist films)[2] and less prominent actors in the populist vein such as Andrex, had a music-hall background and sang. Recordings of their songs (often from the films) contributed to their fame. This emphasis on performance has, as we shall see, important implications in terms of the representation of the male proletarian hero and of his community.

The individual and the community: Nostalgia and spectacle

Towards the beginning of *La Belle Equipe*, there is a sequence which employs the long take and complex camera movement in the characteristic style of director Julien Duvivier: here a crane shot with a zig-zag movement describes the shape of the open staircase and the descending movement of two characters (Jean and the hotel owner). The shot is very long (one minute, 35 seconds) and draws us by its movement to the central character. At the same time, it powerfully links him with his environment: the staircase in the seedy hotel.

The next scene takes place in a café, the group's displaced home, a surrogate home for the uprooted urban worker, and a motif common to many French populist films of the 1930s (a particularly apt example is *Hôtel du Nord*). In *La Belle Equipe*, it is in the country café (the *guinguette*) that the group of friends will build their new 'home'. This café scene further establishes the centrality of the Gabin character, through camera angles (the only low-angle shots are for him) and movements. A typical shot of the friends is a pan across the group, panning back to frame Gabin at the centre. A similar strategy operates in *Pépé le Moko* in the scenes set among Pépé and his acolytes.

In addition to camera movement, lighting is used to establish Gabin's place in the narrative. The precise technique is that of a thin band of light on his eyes, offset by semi-darkness in the rest of the frame (legend has it that Gabin's eyes were severely burnt while shooting *Pépé le Moko* as a result of Duvivier's over-indulgence in the technique). The emphasis on Gabin's eyes by way of spot lighting is a constant feature in his late 1930s films. This 'expressionist' type of lighting is used to signal particular states of mind: deep thought (*Le Jour se Lève*, where it also marks the beginning of flashbacks), moments of intense decision-making or even madness (*La Bête humaine/The Human Beast* [Renoir, 1938]). In any case, the effect always signals *difference*.

While both *La Belle Equipe* and *Pépé le Moko* focus on small groups of male friends, and ultimately on their central hero, in both films these groups are set among (or against) wider communities. *La Belle Equipe* exhibits the women in the workshop making flowers, the hotel population, the customers of the country café. In *Pépé le Moko*, apart from the gangsters on the one hand (of whom Pépé's gang is the hard core) and the police on the other, the largest community represented is the Casbah, characterized mostly by its women. As befits the populist atmosphere in both films, these communities are presented as essentially composed of simple working people, even though there is a slippage, from 'honest' in *La Belle Equipe* to 'dishonest' in *Pépé le Moko*: the women making flowers in Paris are replaced by the prostitutes of the Casbah, the workers by criminals. But in neither film are the communities actually defined by their occupations. These are presented as a *given* in the films, and not explored in either case (the prostitutes are not seen at work with clients, the criminals are not seen performing their exploits). At the same time, it is clear that the communities are not simply decor and that they stand as the embodiment of certain values.

The first striking element in both films is the ambiguity in the relationship between the hero and the community. It is particularly explicit in *Pépé le Moko*, where the Casbah population is both a liberating presence (it is comforting, supportive and protects Pépé from the police) and a repressive one: it is, in effect, a prison, hence Pépé's overwhelming desire to leave Algiers. The strong identification of the Casbah with its women designates this structure as the classic oedipal dilemma of the (male) child's relation to the mother. In displaying the Casbah as both immediate (joyful, desirable) and yet already *passée*, the film, moreover, inscribes the representation of the community as fundamentally nostalgic. This nostalgia frames other types of nostalgia (notably for Paris) which reflect each other. In *La Belle Equipe*, the hotel population plays a similar role to the Casbah in *Pépé le Moko*. Whereas it represents something Jean and his friends want to leave behind, it also evokes, in the scene where they celebrate winning the lottery, a supportive community, thematically reminiscent of other populist films (*Le Million/The Million* [Clair 1931], *Quatorze Juillet/ Bastille Day* [Clair 1933], *Hôtel du Nord*, etc.) and which the group of friends try (in vain) to recreate in their country café. The communities evoked by the two films are neither the latter's subjects nor a mere decor. The films navigate between these two poles, making the communities both central and peripheral, active and passive, by transforming them into audiences. Thus it is through their common look at a spectacle that the communities are constructed as important structures within the films: passive in the sense that they are not themselves performing, and active through their gaze at, and therefore construction of, the performer, Jean Gabin.

In *La Belle Equipe*, the scene where Gabin goes down the open staircase anticipates another scene on the same staircase, itself a rehearsal for the song in the country café in the second half of the film. The second staircase episode follows the news that the group of friends has won a million francs in a lottery. In the general confusion which ensues, the staircase, open to the courtyard, acts as a stage for the display of the community spirit. Gabin, already identified with the staircase where he vented his anger against the hotel owner, is seen again 'performing', this time his joy, and with the community as witness. The zig-zag movement of the crane shot following the shape of the stairs also serves to link the members of the community together, pausing slightly at both ends of each landing, where people are seen coming out of their rooms at the sound of Gabin's voice. He is here both our figure of identification and the object of attention of the diegetic audience. At the end of the scene, the camera tracks back, revealing the whole staircase full of people – the effect of the long shot being to bind all the characters and the environment together, to present them as a unified whole in that space. The same phenomenon operates when Gabin performs elsewhere in the film in a more classic sense, singing '*Quand on s'promène au bord de l'eau*'. The lyrics of '*Quand on s'promène au bord de l'eau*' echo what the scene is showing through the *mise-en-scène*: the community bound together, not by work but by the pursuit of pleasure and leisure. Thus the representation of performance and audience within the film reflects what the cinema itself does outside it: that is, restructure a community through spectatorship.

In *Pépé le Moko*, the emphasis in the lyrics of the song performed by Gabin is more on individual pleasure. However, the scene where the song occurs also elicits a sense of community bound by its look at the performer. Throughout most of the song, Gabin is not seen though his voice is heard. What we see on screen is a quick montage of a wide range of Casbah inhabitants – an old woman sifting grain, a young woman delousing her son, prostitutes, a young girl also sifting grain, a (male) shoe-mender beating a shoe to the rhythm of the song, women dancing likewise to the rhythm of the song. The scene therefore acts both as the expression of Pépé's state of mind and as the construction of a community through its common look at the performer and attention to his song (even incorporating his rhythm). Spectatorship is established both on an aural and a visual register. Through their *mise-en-scènes*, as well as thematically, both *La Belle Equipe* and *Pépé le Moko* thus structurally construct a community in its pursuit of pleasure and spectatorship. It is now time to turn to the nature of the spectacle which binds the communities together, and by extension the spectators of the films themselves.

Jean Gabin: The male hero as object of the look

Whereas it is now generally accepted that classic (Hollywood) cinema constructs women as privileged objects of a gaze which is primarily male, it is also necessary to problematize this position in terms of the female spectator on the one hand and of central male characters on the other. The films of Jean Gabin are a particularly interesting example of the latter. While *La Belle Equipe* and *Pépé le Moko* have narratives overtly concerned with different problems, their apparent themes are to some extent contradicted by the manner in which the *mise-en-scène* singles out the star as the object of the look. Gabin's status as performer makes him the spectacle within both films, but both films also construct him as such in other ways, proceeding further to a fetishization of his image, which in effect becomes 'feminized' in the process.

It is significant that Gabin does not make his entrance at the beginning of either film, but is the structuring absence and the subject of the dialogue in both cases. In *La Belle Equipe*, Mario tells Huguette that only Jean can resolve his dangerous situation. In *Pépé le Moko*, the process is more marked, as Pépé is the sole subject of conversation between the members of the Algiers and Paris police. His identity, exploits, but above all 'charm', are exposed. The delay in Gabin's entrance in both films is of course part of standard industry practice (raising audiences' expectations of the presence of the star in the film), it also works on another level, that of the impact of the star discourse on the film text itself. Being delayed, Gabin's entrance is made more *spectacular*.

In both *La Belle Equipe* and *Pépé le Moko*, there is a beautiful woman whom Gabin desires (and obtains) – Gina and Gaby – and who might be expected to fulfill the classic role of object of the gaze, with Gabin's look playing the part of relay for the (male) spectator. This classic scenario, however, is contradicted by the fact that both women, on meeting him for the first time, also express their desire for him. In *La Belle Equipe*, Gina's status as 'model' (prostitute) allows her to express her desire by her provocative behaviour towards Jean – literally by her look when she meets him, but also by the flaunting of her own sexuality in the naked photographs on the walls of her bedroom, and in the deliberate removal of her stockings, a classic motif for the 'loose' woman.

In *Pépé le Moko*, Gaby's desire and fascination for Pépé are made more explicit. She herself stages a second visit to the Casbah, abetted by Inspector Slimane, especially in order to *see*

Pépé and to *show* him to her friends. Her first encounter with him is remarkably revealing in its organization of looks.

Gaby and her friends are visiting the Casbah when the police raid takes place. Slimane takes her into a young Arab woman's house for shelter. As Gaby is being told about Pépé's exploits, he himself enters the room, followed by Jimmy and Max. The scene then displays to a remarkable degree the fetishization of Gabin's image that operates generally in the two films. Pépé's entrance, off frame, is represented through the gaze of Slimane and Gaby. When he appears on screen, it is as a fragmented body (his legs, a recurrent motif throughout the film, culminating in the famous scene of his final escape from the Casbah). When Pépé finally notices Gaby, their interaction follows the classic organization of looks, which is then effectively countered by two factors. Firstly, Pépé is looking at her jewels, thereby initiating an identification between the two which will run throughout the film. The second reason why the scene does not follow the classic male looking/female looked at pattern is that Gaby looks with equal fascination at Pépé, whose face is lit in the same way as hers. However, although Gaby can assert her desire for Pépé, this desire is strictly circumscribed by the narrative because of her gender positioning. Although she tries to assert her independence by walking out on her 'sugar daddy' with the jewels, the combined patriarchal forces of her protector and the police stop her. She is ultimately condemned to a role of exchange currency in the games played by men.

Before the arrival of Gaby, Pépé is qualified as wanted by all women. But Pépé's status as erotic object is expressed most forcefully through Inspector Slimane's look. His fascination and desire for Pépé take overt voyeuristic forms in his obsession with Pépé's erotic exchanges with Gaby. Slimane's diegetic role as policeman makes it his duty to keep watch over Pépé's activities; however, the exchanges between the two men are overtly erotic and hence make Slimane's look at Pépé go beyond the call of professional duty. His repeated motto, that he wants to capture Pépé 'slowly, slowly', thus incurring his superiors' disapproval, also suggests the ritualistic pleasure of courtship in postponing the moment of conquest. Finally, always kept in the background and at the periphery of the frame are Pépé's accomplices, silently watching him, following him, emulating him. Similarly, in *La Belle Equipe*, the members of the team, though they have more separate identity, follow Jean's every gesture.

The intense fetishization of Pépé, in his centrality as object of the look and in the representation of his body as (erotic) spectacle, is often in excess of the requirements of classic narrative cinema. This in turn has important implications for the position allocated to the spectator in relation to the hero and the community represented by both films, and for the notion of masculinity represented.

Identification and spectator positioning

While everything in *Pépé le Moko* combines to make Pépé the undisputed centre of attention, he is also constantly surrounded by groups of people. Thus the spectators' look could be said to be mediated by the other characters who, in this respect, may become secondary figures of identification. The spectator's look is relentlessly directed at Pépé, and the moments when he sings do not provide significant breaks from the narrative (the 1937 audience was also well aware of Gabin's training and experience as a music hall singer). Thus, here the code of the star works towards bridging the possible hiatus between narrative and spectacle, assisted by the ritualistic nature of some aspects of Gabin's acting. His famous explosions of violence, anticipated by the spectator, act as mini-spectacles in their own right, regardless of their narrative value. Pépé, in other words, is *constant spectacle* to the diegetic as well as cinema audience who, as a result, enjoy a secure subject position, reinforcing the identification with Pépé and the spectacle he gives, and thus the spectacle of the whole film.

It could be argued that the very secure spectator position afforded by *Pépé le Moko* goes some way towards explaining its success. By contrast, the near box-office 'failure' of *La Belle Equipe* could be ascribed, at least partially, to a less complete cohesion of the conflicting demands of narrative and spectacle, despite the unifying presence of the star. This has to do with the different representation of community in the two films. In *Pépé le Moko*, the Casbah has a relation to Pépé which is purely that of spectatorship; otherwise, it is literally foreign to him and to the French spectator, radically 'other' in cultural and ethnic terms. In *La Belle Equipe*, on the contrary, there is empathy between Jean, his group of friends and the community at large, each inserted in and at the same time reflecting the larger group. This has the effect of splitting spectator identification between Jean, his friends and the community. Moreover, the moments in *La Belle Equipe* given over to spectacle and performance (the scene on the stairs, the song, the dance) emphasize the sense of solidarity between the hero and his milieu, whereas the narrative parts of the film work towards conflict and division. Whereas the spectacle scenes involve the spectator in the community *as well as* with the performing hero, the melodramatic narrative involves the spectator with the internal conflicts of the hero which precisely divide the community. The too apparent conflict between narrative and spectacle unsettles the spectator in his/her position of identification, producing a less happy resolution and thus, arguably, a less 'successful' film.

The Gabin hero as 'degree zero' of masculinity

Duvivier (1959) has declared in interviews that his films were always 'men's stories', a point substantiated by their concern with groups of men and their treatment of women. Summarily dismissed in *Pépé le Moko* by repeated exhortations to 'go home', the women attached to members of Pépé's gang are treated as appendages, even brutalized. If Gaby materially fares better, her economic subjection to her protector is made very clear. This attitude to women finds its most eloquent manifestation in the extraordinary scene in *La Belle Equipe* where Jean and Charles (lover and husband) go arm in arm to tell Gina that she has become redundant. The dialogues of both films abound in hostile and contemptuous remarks directed at women. But *La Belle Equipe* and *Pépé le Moko* are 'men's stories' beyond what might at first glance be interpreted simply as misogyny – they tell the story of masculinity – or rather of one of its possible paths under a patriarchal regime and, in this respect, the films carry their historical and social inscription.

If, as has been argued by Neale (1983: 16), masculinity in films is tested, not investigated, this testing nevertheless provides a definition. In both *La Belle Equipe* and *Pépé le Moko*, the hero portrayed by Gabin is surrounded by a group of men. Compared to the complexity of his character, his friends or accomplices are one-dimensional, each the carrier of one of several characteristics which could be listed as follows. In *La Belle Equipe*, these include weakness (notably in front of women), irresponsibility, excessive sexuality (the 'Latin lover'), extreme sensibility, alcoholism and homosexuality. In *Pépé le Moko*, these characteristics range across brutality, infantilism, desexualized age, deviousness and the values traditionally associated with virility (in French culture at the time): physical strength, comradeship, attractiveness to women, the capacity to consume large amounts of alcohol. Each of the men surrounding the hero demonstrates one of these attributes, but crucially, *to excess*. In *Pépé le Moko*, Carlos takes toughness to the point of brutality; in *La Belle Equipe*, Tintin's excessive drinking indirectly kills him. At the same time, all these values are portrayed as essentially masculine and positive: wine is part of communal celebrations in *La Belle Equipe*, violence is 'necessary' in *Pépé le Moko* – that is, generically justified.

The purpose of this configuration is, I would argue, twofold. First, it allows for the least acceptable male values to be endorsed by characters other than the hero. Thus complete empathy and identification with Jean/Pépé are made possible by the splitting of the positive and negative aspects of each value between characters. Secondly, and more importantly, the configuration I have outlined allows the film to present a definition of ideal masculinity *en creux*, by default. In *La Belle Equipe* and *Pépé le Moko*, masculinity is tested against its own excesses, its own caricatures. Thus the paradigm is male/excess male rather than male/female (or, to be precise, male/non-male) (see Johnson 1973: 26). Against the excessive values embodied by his friends and accomplices, the Gabin hero stands as the norm. Whereas they are one-dimensional and therefore incomplete, he is complex and complete, but the ideal masculinity he represents – being the result of a comparison to extremes rather than the positive affirmation of particular attributes – is strangely lacking in substance, the effect achieved being more that of a 'degree zero' or a neutral point than of an ultimate. It is a definition of masculinity which is more passive than active, more negative than positive.

La Belle Equipe and *Pepé le Moko*, by almost eliminating women, elicit a definition through a relation of comparison with other men, a structure that operates in practically all pre-war 'classic' Gabin films. The feminine, banished from the centre of the narrative, returns in different ways into the group of men, but most forcefully in its central hero. The ideal of masculinity embodied by Gabin, which results from a comparison with all the possible and excessive positions granted to men under patriarchy, itself includes in significant proportion values traditionally ascribed to femininity. Hence Jean and Pépé are both ideal hero to their friends, and the object of their desire. By allowing a different male/female division to cut across its central hero, whose masculinity is thus truly at a 'degree zero', the films also allow him to be a powerful figure of identification for both male and female spectators. And, as far as the male spectator is concerned, the anxieties that might have been aroused by an all-powerful hero are mitigated by the weaknesses and hesitations of his 'feminine' aspects.

It should not be assumed from the preceding analysis that Duvivier's films are 'progressive' in their representation of sexuality and their admission of the erotic value of male heroes not only for female spectators but also male ones. Both *Pépé le Moko* and *La Belle Equipe* find ways to channel their view of masculinity – despite its inclusion of the feminine – into more conventional routes, although in so doing they only partially eradicate contradictions.

Ideal masculinity in its conventional sense finds its testing ground in *Pépé le Moko* in a variety of 'devious' characters, whose deviance is punished according to its degree. Régis, the informer, is executed; l'Arbi, 'half-informer', is only knocked out. These outsiders also show how the attributes of masculinity can shift among the characters in the group: faced with a really deviant character, even an internally disunited group is then unified in its reassertion of virility. Hence, the striking scene in which Regis is killed by the whole group – including the already dead Pierrot. The phenomenon is even more marked when there is a hint of the greatest 'threat' to the notion of virility as represented, namely homosexuality. No doubt this shows the force of disavowal at work, since homosexuality is the logical extension of the predominantly male world of the films. This is evident in the ambiguous relation between Pépé and Slimane, where their physical closeness, evidenced by the image, is violently contradicted by their narrative antagonism and expressed in their repeated vows of mutual hostility.

With regard to *La Belle Equipe* and *Pépé le Moko*, there is a clearly observable paradox: the hero's masculinity on the one hand, overtly displayed with its traditional connotations of strength, courage and superiority to women, is accompanied by passivity and a distinct lack of maturity on the other. This paradox is underlined and echoed in the contradiction between the place of the Gabin hero *within* his group (where he reigns supreme) and his place *outside* it, where he is variously an outcast, a deviant or a solitary 'anti-hero'.

The all-male group: Regression and class identity

Contrary to films in which the existence of an exclusively male group could be ascribed to war or the demands of an all-male institution, the narratives of *La Belle Equipe* and *Pépé le Moko* are set within a recognizable framework of everyday routine. Yet in these films, especially in *La Belle Equipe*, the male group tries to recreate a community cut off from real social relations and without women. Moreover, these male groups display the regressive features which are also characteristic of popular French comic genres of the 1930s, such as the military vaudeville.

In the early café scene of *La Belle Equipe*, the group's team spirit is affirmed in finding Huguette's birthday present. The necessity for finding her a present arises out of guilt at forgetting and fear of disappointing her, a representation of the classic son–mother relationship (Huguette's maternal role will be reinforced later in the film by the short-lived part she takes in the team's work as their meal provider). As none of the friends has any money, they steal the contents of a slot machine in which cheap objects can be captured with the help of a remotely controlled arm. The operation has to be performed while trying to avert the eye of a father figure – the *patron* of the café. The men play at cheating the machine (and hence its owner); play at giving presents which are toys rather than real objects; Mario and Huguette play at getting married when the Wedding March comes out of the radio. These occurrences are part of a recurring motif of games and play that runs throughout *La Belle Equipe* – including, of course, the lottery which provides the initial motivation for the narrative. The doomed fate of the co-operative which the friends set up is already inscribed in the café scene: Tintin's card trick fails and Charles announces that he is unlucky at cards.

But the fate of the co-op (and of Jean), like that of Pépé, cannot be so easily ascribed to bad luck. The regressive nature of the exclusively male group points all too clearly to its social inadequacy. Thus, if the Gabin films are at variance with the dominant form of oedipal narrative common to many French films of the 1930s, in that their hero is not a father figure, they can be seen as the reverse side of the coin: in not wanting to grow up and assume fathers' positions in a patriarchal society, these heroes are indeed doomed, having locked themselves in the untenable position of an unresolved oedipal complex.

Within this framework, women are not excluded from the male group because they are inferior but, on the contrary, because in standing for the world of adult social relations – marriage, jobs, responsibilities – they represent a threat to the men's regressive desire for play. Having fun has to be divorced from women – as the heroes of René Clair's *À Nous la Liberté/ Freedom for Us* (1931), walking away from the 'civilized' world, sing, 'those who, like us want to take to the roads must renounce marriage'. This refusal of women informs many Gabin films, and indeed may be more widespread in French cinema of the 1930s than is usually recognized because it is often overlaid by different discourses. In choosing to belong to an all-male group, the Gabin hero is positioned in a double bind, where women are marginalized (or rejected) to make room for relations between men, but where the classic patriarchal avenues are obstructed and the hero is therefore exposed to the threat of castration – a position which, in effect, echoes the dual nature of the classic oedipal configuration.

What mediates the contradiction between the hero's assumed position of power within the group and his powerlessness outside it is the notion of *performance*. In *Pépé le Moko*, Pépé's superiority within his group of accomplices is constantly reaffirmed through rituals or in narcissistic reaffirmations of his power by asking all his men in turn to confirm the correctness of his opinion. In *La Belle Equipe*, the confirmation of his power takes the more direct form of actual performance (on the staircase, in the country café). In a larger sense, Gabin's acting, which is itself ritualistic (the explosion of violence), sustains this definition of working-class masculinity. His own performance, compared with that of his group of friends, produces an effect of under-statement. This is, of course, the mark of the star, as opposed to character actors or actors belonging to different traditions, but the characteristics of Gabin's acting style also contribute to his definition of masculinity. Within the male/excess male paradigm that his films articulate, his performance always tends towards the 'degree zero' of masculinity present in the narrative: he is laconic where they are talkative, restrained in bodily movements where they gesticulate. The very moderation of his movements, magnified by close-ups and lighting, becomes the sign of its own restraint, the emblem of a self-contained, powerful masculinity, carrying the hint of its own violence, confirmed by the occasional outburst. But this display of masculinity remains just this, a *show* for the diegetic as well as the cinema audience. Gabin's verbal and physical restraint become easily akin to paralysis: Pépé trapped in the Casbah, Jean sitting in the country café mourning Tintin, like François in his bedroom in *Le Jour se Lève,* are emblematic of the ultimate powerlessness of the Gabin hero *vis-à-vis* patriarchal forces.

Through their display of virile behaviour, the Gabin heroes and his groups of male friends in *La Belle Equipe* and *Pépé le Moko* embody the very contradictions of working-class masculinity in a patriarchal capitalist society. If women in these two films are the first victims of this system of values, in being punished, rejected or marginalized, the heroes are themselves trapped by their own absurd system. The tragic ending of these two films is, in the end, the tragedy of working-class masculinity, and the only logical narrative resolution within a patriarchal economy. Both films are, in this sense, classic narratives, in that the patriarchal order is restored by the death of the 'anti-hero' – who refuses to, or cannot, enter the symbolic order of the father or, on a more sociological level, the realities of class struggle. On the other hand, the self-generated need for the affirmation of virile values means that the comforting world of the feminine has to be rejected, while physical closeness with other males must be heavily disavowed. Denied (denying himself) both the comforts of the feminine and the rewards of patriarchy, there is no solution left for the Gabin hero but destruction.[3]

Notes

1. 'We believe that the *peuple* offers a very rich novelistic subject-matter, one which is almost entirely unexplored' (Lemonnier 1929: 23).
2. Préjean is mainly remembered as the hero of Clair's *Sous les Toits de Paris/Beneath the Rooftops of Paris* (1930), but his 1930s filmography includes some of the most notable populist French films: *Un Soir de Rafle/Dragnet Night* (Gallone 1931), *Le Paquebot Tenacity/S.S. Tenacity* (Duvivier 1934), *L'Or dans la Rue* (Bernhardt 1934), *Dédé* (Guissart 1934), *Un Mauvais Garçon/Counsel for Romance* (Boyer 1936), *L'Alibi/The Alibi* (Chenal 1937), *Mollenard/Hatred* (Siodmak 1937), *La Rue sans Joie/Street Without Joy* (Hugon 1938), *Métropolitan* (Cam 1938) and *Dédé la Musique* (Berthomieu 1939).
3. This chapter was originally published in 1985 as 'Community, Nostalgia and the Spectacle of Masculinity: Jean Gabin' in *Screen* 26: 6, pp. 1839. The version reprinted here has been abridged for reasons of space. The editors are grateful to Oxford University Press and to Ginette Vincendeau for their permission to include the chapter as part of this collection.

References to Part I

Albéra, F. (1989), 'Cultivons notre jardin: Entretien avec Jean-Luc Godard', in R. Prédal (ed.), 'Le Cinéma selon Godard', *CinémAction*, 52, pp. 81–89.

Amengual, B. (1967), 'Pierrot le fou', in M. Estève and B. Amengual (eds), 'Jean-Luc Godard au-delà du récit', *Etudes cinématographiques*, 57–61, pp. 146–73.

Andrew, D. (1995), *Mists of Regret: Culture and Sensibility in Classic French Film*, Princeton, NJ: Princeton University Press.

Balio, T. (1996), 'Adjusting to the New Global Economy: Hollywood in the 1990s', in A. Moran (ed.), *Film Policy: International, National and Regional Perspectives*, London: Routledge, pp. 21–35.

Bazin, A. (1963), '*Le Jour se Lève* (1947)', in J. Chevallier and M. Egly (eds), *Regards Neufs sur le Cinéma*, Paris: Editions du Seuil, pp. 146–63.

Bazin, A. (1971), *Jean Renoir*, Paris: Champ Libre.

Bergstrom, J. (1998), 'Jean Renoir's Return to France', in S.R. Suleiman (ed.), *Exile and Creativity: Signposts, Travellers, Outsiders, Backward Glances*, Durham, NC: Duke University Press, pp. 180–219.

Bertin, C. (1994), *Jean Renoir*, Paris: Editions du Rocher.

Bhabha, H.K. (1990), *Nation and Narration*, London: Routledge.

Biskend, P. (1991), 'The Colour of Money', *Sight and Sound*, August, p. 6.

Bloom, H. (1973), *The Anxiety of Influence: A Theory of Poetry*, New York: Oxford University Press.

Borges, J.L. (1973), *The Aleph and Other Stories*, London: Picador.

Bosséno, C. (1992), 'Immigrant Cinema: National Cinema. The Case of Beur Cinema', in G. Vincendeau and R. Dyer (eds), *Popular European Cinema*, London: Routledge, pp. 47–57.

Bush, L. (1989) 'Female Narrative and the Law in Renoir's *Le Crime de Monsieur Lange*', *Cinema Journal*, 29(1), pp. 54–70.

Butler, J. (1993), *Bodies That Matter*, London: Routledge.

Cadé, M. (1994), 'Des immigrés dans les banlieues', *Cahiers de la Cinémathèque*, 59/60, pp. 125–27.

Carné, M. (1930), interview, *Cinémonde*, 85, n.p.

Charef, M. (1983), *Le Thé au harem d'Archi Ahmed*, Paris: Mercure de France.

Coe, R. (1984), *When the Grass was Taller*, New Haven, CT: Yale University Press.

Conley, T. (2000), 'Language Gone Mad', in D. Wills (ed.), *Jean-Luc Godard's* Pierrot le fou, Cambridge: Cambridge University Press, pp. 81–107.

Deleuze, G. (1986), *Cinema 1: The Movement-Image*, trans. Hugh Tomlinson and Barbara Habberjam, Minneapolis, MN: University of Minnesota Press.

Deleuze, G. (1989), *Cinema 2: The Time-Image*, trans. Hugh Tomlinson and Robert Galeta, Minneapolis, MN: University of Minnesota Press.

Doisneau, L. (2002) 'Panorama démographique de la France en 2000', *Données sociales: la société française*, Paris: INSEE.

Duvivier, J. (1959), interview, *Cinémonde*, 15 September.

Ezra, E. and Harris, S. (eds) (2000), *France in Focus: Film and National Identity*, Oxford: Berg.

Faulkner, C. (1986), *The Social Cinema of Jean Renoir*, Princeton, NJ: Princeton University Press.

Faulkner, C. (2000), 'Paris, Arizona on the Redemption of Difference: Jean Renoir's *Le Crime de Monsieur Lange*', in S. Hayward and G. Vincendeau (eds), *French Film: Texts and Contexts*, 2nd ed., London: Routledge, pp. 27–41.

Fofi, G. (1972), 'The Cinema of the Popular Front in France (1934–1938)', *Screen*, 13(4), pp. 5–57.

Forbes, J. and Kelly, M. (eds) (1995), *French Cultural Studies*, Oxford: Oxford University Press.

Foucault, M. (1966), *Les Mots et les choses*, Paris: Gallimard.

Foucault, M. (1986), 'Of Other Spaces', *Diacritics*, 16: 1, pp. 22–27, trans. J. Miskowiec, accessed 7 May 2005 from <http://foucault.info/documents/heteroTopia/foucault.heteroTopia.en.html> ['Des Espaces Autres. Hétérotopies', lecture to the Cercle d'études architecturales, 14 mars 1967; originally published in *Architecture, Mouvement, Continuité*, 5 (1984) pp. 46–49].

Garber, M. (1992), 'The Occidental Tourist: *M. Butterfly* and the Scandal of Transvestism', in *Nationalisms and Sexualities*, London: Routledge, pp. 121–46.

Genocchio, B. (1995), 'Discourse, Discontinuity, Difference', in S. Watson and K. Gibson (eds), *Postmodern Cities and Spaces*, Cambridge: Blackwell, pp. 35–46.

Gledhill, C. (1980), '*Klute* I: A Contemporary Film Noir and Feminist Criticism', in E.A. Kaplan (ed.), *Women in Film Noir*, London: British Film Institute Publishing, pp. 20–34.

Godard, J.-L. (1972), *Godard on Godard*, eds J. Narboni and T. Milne, New York: Viking.

Godard, J.-L. (1985), *Jean-Luc Godard par Jean-Luc Godard*, ed. A. Bergala, Paris: Cahiers du cinéma/ Editions de l'Etoile.

Grewal, I. and Kaplan, C. (eds) (1994), *Scattered Hegemonies: Postmodernity and Transnational Feminist Practises*, Minneapolis, MN: University of Minnesota Press.

Hayward, S. (2000), 'Framing National Cinemas', in M. Hjort and S. MacKenzie (eds), *Cinema and Nation*, London: Routledge, pp. 88–102.

Jameson, F. (1991), *Postmodernism or, The Cultural Logic of Late Capitalism*, Durham, NC: Duke University Press.

Jeancolas, J.-P. (1983), *Quinze ans d'années trente: le cinéma des Français 1929–1944*, Paris: Stock.

Jeanson, H. (1956), 'Le métier de scénariste', *Cinéma 56*, 11(10), n.p.

Johnson, C. (1973), 'Women's Cinema as Counter-cinema', in C. Johnson (ed.), *Notes on Women's Cinema*, London: Society for Education in Film and Television, pp. 24–31.

Katz, E. (1982), *The International Film Encyclopedia*, London: Macmillan.

Kline, T.J. (1992), *Screening the Text: Intertextuality in New Wave French Cinema*, Baltimore, MD: Johns Hopkins University Press.

Labarthe, G. (2002), 'Les Structures familiales', in *Données sociales: la société française*, Paris: INSEE, pp. 31–38.

Lefebvre, H. (1991), *The Production of Space*, trans. D Nicholson-Smith, Cambridge, MA: Blackwell. First published in 1974 as *La production de l'espace*.

Lemonnier, L. (1929), *Manifeste du Roman Populiste*, Paris: Jacques Bernard.

Leroy, G. and Roche, A. (1986), *Les Écrivains et le Front populaire*, Paris: Presses de la Fondation Nationale des Sciences Politiques.

Leutrat, J.-L. (2000), 'Godard's Tricolor', in D. Wills (ed.), *Jean-Luc Godard's* Pierrot le fou, Cambridge: Cambridge University Press, pp. 64–80.

Messenger Davies, M. (2005), '"Crazyspace": the politics of children's screen drama', *Screen*, 46: 3, pp. 389–99.

Mulvey, L. (1996), *Fetishism and Curiosity*, London: BFI.

Neale, S. (1983), 'Masculinity as Spectacle, Reflections on Men and Mainstream Cinema', *Screen*, 24(6), pp. 2–16.

O'Regan, T. (1996), *Australian National Cinema*, London: Routledge.

Poulle, F. (1969), *Renoir 1938 ou Jean Renoir pour rien? – enquête sur un cinéaste*, Paris: Éditions du Cerf.

Powell, D. (1976), untitled article, *The Sunday Times*, 21 November.

Powrie, P. (1997), *French Cinema in the 1980s: Nostalgia and the Crisis of Masculinity*, Oxford: Clarendon Press.

Powrie, P. (2000), 'On the Threshold Between Past and Present: "Alternative Heritage"', in A. Higson and J. Ashby (eds), *British Cinema: Past and Present*, London: Routledge, pp. 316–26.

Prévert, J. (1990) *Le Crime de Monsieur Lange/Les Portes de la nuit*, Paris: Gallimard.

Quignard, P. (1994), *L'Occupation américaine*, Paris: Editions du Seuil.

Radhakrishnan, R. (1992), 'Nationalism, Gender, and the Narrative of Identity', in A. Parker, M. Russo, D. Sommer and P. Yaeger (eds), *Nationalisms and Sexualities*, London: Routledge, pp. 77–95.

Reader, K. (1986), 'Renoir's Popular Front films: Texts in Context', in G. Vincendeau and K. Reader (eds), *La Vie est à nous!: French Cinema of the Popular Front, 1935–1938*, London: BFI, pp. 37–59.

Renoir, J. (1974a), *Écrits 1926–1971*, Paris: Belfond.

Renoir, J. (1974b), *Ma vie et mes films*, Paris: Flammarion.

Renoir, J. (1998), *Correspondance, 1913–1978*, eds David Thompson and Lorraine LoBianco, Paris: Plon.

Rimbaud, A. (1966), *Rimbaud, Complete Works, Selected Letters*, trans. W. Fowlie, Chicago: University of Chicago Press.

Robbe-Grillet, A. (1965). *For a New Novel*, trans. R. Howard, New York: Grove Press. Roudinesco, E. (2002), *La Famille en désodre*, Paris: Arthème Fayard.

Serceau, D. (1981), *Jean Renoir l'insurgé*, Paris: Sycomore.

Sesonske, A. (1980), *Jean Renoir: The French Films, 1934–1939*, Cambridge, MA: Harvard University Press.

Soja, E.W. (1995), 'Heterologies: A Remembrance of Other Spaces in the Citadel-LA', in S. Watson and K. Gibson (eds), *Postmodem Cities and Spaces*, Cambridge: Blackwell, pp. 13–34.

Starobinski, J. (1966), 'The idea of nostalgia', *Diogenes*, 54, pp. 81–103.

Wallerstein, I. (1983), *Historical Capitalism*, London: Verso.

Willemen, P. (1989), 'The Third Cinema Question: Notes and Reflections', in J. Pines and P. Willemen (eds), *Questions of Third Cinema*, London: BFI, pp. 1–30.

Williams, A. (1992), *Republic of Images : A History of French Film-Making*, Cambridge, MA: Harvard University Press.

Wills, D. (ed.) (2000), *Jean-Luc Godard's* Pierrot le fou, Cambridge: Cambridge University Press.

Winock, M. (1982), *Nationalisme, antisémitisme et fascisme en France*, Paris: Editions du Seuil.

Zhang, Y. (1994), 'From "Minority Film" to "Minority Discourse": The Questions of Nationhood and Ethnicity in Chinese Cinema', paper delivered at the East Asian Colloquium at Indiana University, September.

Žižek, S. (1989), *The Sublime Object of Ideology*, London: Verso.

Žižek, S. (1991), *Looking Awry: An Introduction to Jacques Lacan Through Popular Culture*, London: MIT Press.

Žižek, S. (1999), *The Žižek Reader*, eds E. Wright and E. Wright, Oxford: Blackwell.

Part II

Chapter 8

Asserting Text, Context and Intertext: Jill Forbes and French Film Studies

Julia Dobson

Jill Forbes' early death from lung cancer in 2001 created incalculable professional and personal losses to which others have borne better and more appropriate witness elsewhere (see Edgar 2001; Harris 2001; Marshall 2003a, 2003b; Reader 2001c).[1] Even in the limited scope of this chapter, which focuses predominantly on her contribution to establishment and development of French cinema studies in the United Kingdom, the scholarly losses are felt in the tension between the exhilarating legacy that continues across the wide range of her completed projects and its haunting by the projected trajectories of her future works. This text will, however, refrain from such hypotheses and present an introduction to the key issues addressed in Forbes' work followed by a detailed, central engagement with one article: 'Pierrot le fou and Post-New Wave French Cinema' (Forbes 2000).[2] I aim to exploit this single and singular piece to highlight the insistence, central to all of Forbes' work, on the simultaneous breaking down of traditional barriers and the building of wider connections in order to place a film within its widest constellations of cultural and socio-political signification and to contextualize the blind spots created by canon formation and a predominantly auteurist approach. I conclude with a discussion of the continuing importance of the central tropes of the article in the form of a response that engages with the cinema of Jacques Audiard. This link originates in Forbes' (1999) article on Audiard's second feature film, Un Héros très discret/A Self-Made Hero (1996), which addresses the performative reinventions of the Resistance past and is reflected in my work on Audiard that foregrounds the relationships between genre, realism and performance (Dobson 2007, 2008).

An overview of Jill Forbes' contribution to French film studies would not be complete without its wider contextualization within the range of commitments that she made to the development of learning, teaching and research in this field across universities and non-academic institutions. She undertook a series of professional appointments that included membership of the Council for National Academic Awards (1986–92), the UK Council for Graduate Education and the Inner London Education Authority (1986–90), posts that reveal her involvement with the future direction of education across sector boundaries. A selection of her public appointments, from Fellow of the Royal Society for the Arts (elected in 1991) and Governor of the British Film Institute (1978–82) to contributions towards the national evaluation of academic research and teaching produced by universities in England provides a fuller picture of her investment in the status and development of her chosen disciplines. Such lists, however, cannot accommodate an accurate picture of one of the primary drives of Forbes' work, which was markedly consistent in its insistence on transgressing boundaries of academic and disciplinary division at all levels of engagement. Her pioneering activities, through teaching and research, as Head of Department, and as co-founder of the journal *French Cultural Studies*, remained emphatic in their assertion of the rightful presence and importance of cultural studies within the parameters of modern language studies. Such a presence was encouraged and maintained through groundbreaking publications in which Forbes was involved as co-editor and major contributor. *Contemporary France: Essays and Texts on Politics, Economics and Society* (Forbes and Hewlett 1994, 2nd ed. 2000), through its challenge to conventional views of the history of post-war France as a linear drive towards 'modernity' and its inclusion of illustrative French language texts, encouraged students to engage with the antagonisms and tensions of contemporary French politics, economics and society in a dynamic and inclusive mode. Witness to both the powerful impact of Forbes' work and to the extraordinary range of her interventions in cinematic and cultural analysis is borne by the special issue of *French Cultural Studies*, published in her honour in 2003.[3] *French Cultural Studies: An Introduction* (Forbes and Kelly 1995) remains a pioneering work, which provides a wholly integrated discussion of culture as 'the visible territory on which the struggle continues to define and defend a certain idea of France' (Forbes and Kelly 1995: 290). The volume's important definition of cultural studies as 'not just the study of the constructed rather than the given world, but also of the ways in which, over time, cultural objects and the relations between them … have become ideologically eloquent' (Forbes and Kelly 1995: 295) has proved pivotal to the best work undertaken in this field.

Forbes worked, alongside her peers, for the broader establishment of the credentials of film studies as a justified and indeed necessary focus for academic study. The parallel movement of this breaking down of disciplinary barriers alongside the insistence on building bridges between film studies, cultural studies and modern language studies has resulted in the concomitant opening up of cinema studies to broader contexts of (national) production and reception (to include art history, socio-political discourse and wider cultural movements) that is so characteristic of Forbes' work on French film.[4] The primary example of this work remains Forbes' monograph, *The Cinema in France: After the New Wave*, which served not only to recontextualize the New Wave but also to address the different modes through which French cinema had been approached, 'overcoming the aestheticoideological rupture of 1968' (Forbes 1992a: 258). The volume offers illuminating interventions in established key debates around the function of the auteur, 'women film-makers', popular cinema and the cross-cultural impact of genre, and also a prescient identification of future focus on mutations in documentary, the (representational) crisis of masculinity and the complexities of representing popular memory. The book remains notable for its detailed engagement with film-makers who were not comfortable choices as part of any canon (Akerman, Doillon, Eustache, Tavernier) and a spectrum of theoretical discourses, some of which were familiar within film studies at the time (Bazin, Deleuze, Foucault), and others that were not yet part of the mainstream of cultural studies (such as Rancière). Forbes' dual aims – to present the dynamic between the sociopolitical contextualization of the films discussed and an assertion of film-makers' primary concerns, 'not to change society but to change the cinema' (Forbes 1992a: 261) – are combined in her central desire to persuade audiences and distributors to look beyond the (internationally) known quantities of French cinema to discover the 'undeservedly unfamiliar' (Forbes 1992a: 261).

Such concerns remain central to Forbes' article '*Pierrot le fou* and Post-New Wave French Cinema'. Its selection here is not triggered by its status as one of Forbes' last published pieces; rather, it was chosen for two other reasons: first, it is one of the most complex and suggestive responses to Godard's charming provocation; and second, it is a clear example of the coexistence in Forbes' work of the rigorous contextualization of film into historical, socio-economic and philosophical frameworks alongside a clear focus on the detailed specificities of the filmic text. Laura Mulvey identified just such qualities. In a response to Forbes' 1997 monograph on *Les Enfants du paradis/Children of Paradise* (Carné 1945), she describes the 'combination of unusual cinematic insight and careful historical research that took me beyond a blind spot, a prejudice against one of the great masterpieces of cinema' (Mulvey 2003: 278). Always fired by an 'increasing dissatisfaction with the way film histories have been written in the past' (Forbes and Street 2000: x), Forbes' work here approaches the film as a nexus for key debates on the dominant debates of French film studies: the question of the nature and function of the figure of the auteur; the complex generic and filial mutual fascinations of Franco-American cultural relations (see also Forbes 2003); and shifting definitions of realism. *Pierrot le fou*, with its ludic generic affiliations, dense intertextual play and overpoweringly reflexive discourses on painting, representation and narrative, provides an exemplary textual arena for these trajectories. Forbes' analysis is informed by her refusal to view the New Wave as a monolithic category, or to approach Godard's *Pierrot le fou* as an isolated, iconic text; rather she views it as a link between his films of the 1960s and his later productions. *Pierrot le fou* is also liberated from an auteurist bubble and presented as containing traces of wider shifts in French socio-economic and cultural history as indeed a pivotal textual moment that 'predicts the ruins of one aesthetic and the birth of another' (Forbes 2000: 108).

Working from the general acceptance that 'the auteur has always been a fiction, a polemical device used to promote a certain kind of *reading* rather than a particular kind of writing' (Forbes 1992a: 4), Forbes reveals the ways in which *Pierrot le fou*'s ironic challenge to the aesthetics of the film-makers directly evoked within it (Fuller, Leacock) can be seen to anticipate Godard's later dismissals of the auteur figure as a fantasy of patriarchal control. In a parallel argument, Forbes contests reductive associations of the New Wave with a positive modernity represented by a young generation unfettered by familial ties or social structures, to identify the (narrative) crisis of the central couple in *Pierrot le fou* as a precursor of Godard's shift to representations of familial structures in his post-1968 films (Forbes 2000: 113), familial structures haunted by the same pernicious fantasies of paternity and patriarchy.

The New Wave's quest for American texts to adapt for the screen and Godard's recurrent reworkings 'in an obviously minor key' (Forbes 2000: 109) of dominant American genres are contextualized as constituent elements in the consequent naturalization of the domestication of American forms. In a framework that follows Bloom's (1973) 'anxiety of influence', Forbes demonstrates how the complex interplay of influence and difference in Franco-American cultural relations, and the working-through of the creative tension between Hollywood and French film production, reflects and generates a perception of the American presence as both threat and regenerative model, thus fuelling French cultural anxiety (Forbes 2000: 109). Forbes presents *Pierrot le fou* as a marker in French attitudes towards the United States as contemporary news reports of US war atrocities reinforced the discourse of imperialism that dominated contemporary debate. In the face of dominant critical response that foregrounds Godard's auteurist deviations from the written intertext, Forbes highlights the residual similarities between *Pierrot le fou* and Lionel White's novel *Obsession*, from which Godard loosely adapted this film, including the central exploration of identity as performance (Forbes 2000: 116).

The question of the singular creativity of the auteur is also challenged through the almost overwhelming proliferation of intertextual references in *Pierrot le fou*. Forbes goes beyond the standard listing of intertexts to home in on their central function in terms of narrative and characterization. While the alignment of Ferdinand and Marianne with the grotesque characters of the comic strip 'La Bande des Pieds nickelés' and their pantomiming of war adds further humour to visual gags in the early sequences of the film, Forbes makes a convincing case that Godard is in fact not arguing for a ludic emulation of such forms, but is already positioning them in unfavourable comparison to the emergent popular, politicized forms of satirical cartoons and café théâtre. *Pierrot le fou*'s concern with performance reveals the central characters' search for compatible models and genres as a desperate attempt to advance or escape their narrative, yet a particular sensitivity of this piece leads Forbes to identify a further element in the couple's constructions of self, which stages their doomed romance as 'an encounter between "high" and "low" culture that divides along gender lines' (Forbes 2000: 117). Thus Forbes reads the final sequence as Ferdinand's betrayal by Marianne, and by the popular culture with which she is associated, as the codes of her chosen genre of thriller demand that she fulfil her role as femme fatale; this undermines Ferdinand's playful staging of a dynamite-fuelled, cartoon finale and provides the final tragedy when the fuse he lights reveals its stubbornly realist provenance (Forbes 2000: 109).

The great merit of Forbes' article is its ability to construct and uncover links between these central debates, and thus questions of familial structures, authority and patriarchy are linked to legacies of realism.[5] Forbes begins from the allegorical instance of Ferdinand's nostalgia for the naming of telephone exchanges after authors and the 'forgetting' of Balzac (Forbes 2000: 116), moving to a reading of lateral pans as a critique of modern society's lack of depth and the 'failure of the modern' (Forbes 2000: 126) to then reveal Godard's evocations of Rimbaudian synaesthesia and Velazquez as signalling an aesthetic shift from surfaces to sensual and painterly depth, 'from unchecked modernization to new pastoralism' (Forbes 2000: 128). *Pierrot le fou*'s lack of historical dimension is thus constructed as a 'series of superimposed presents' (Forbes 2000: 128) that accepts history not as a resurrection of the past but as a continuous present and prefigures the 'musée imaginaire' of Godard's later *Histoire(s) du cinéma* (Forbes 2000: 129).

I am not suggesting an exclusive pairing of the rhyming couple of Godard and Audiard, yet several of the central issues and trajectories marked out in Forbes' piece on *Pierrot le fou* find clear resonance in Audiard's work, and in *De battre mon coeur s'est arrête/The Beat That My Heart Skipped* (Audiard 2004) in particular. First, Forbes' linking of Godard's challenge to the status of the auteur with his renewed representation of familial structures and paternal authority proves central to readings of Audiard's oeuvre. It is notable that, while the life stories of many directors of the New Wave echo Daney's self-definition as a *ciné-fils* (Daney 1992), Jacques Audiard's lineage goes beyond this to include his biological father, the successful scriptwriter Michel Audiard. More detailed analyses of Audiard's multilayered engagements with tropes of oedipal filiation have been proposed elsewhere (Dobson 2007, 2008), yet the striking recurrence of sinister father figures who are agents of stasis, dominance and the violent policing of identity can be read more broadly as a critique of the filiative model of the auteur. Audiard's recurrent response remains the liberation of the *ciné-fils* through the marked intervention through adaptation of existing texts, generic hybridization and challenges to realism from within. While it is arguably the very consistency of such concerns that associate him, paradoxically, with the auteurist tradition, his films can be read as a challenge to paternal authority (although arguably not to patriarchal authority) through their insistence on a mode of adaptation that avoids the direct weight of heritage and legacy and invokes the more subversive Deleuzian 'involution' that remains creative: 'to involve is to form a block that runs *its own line* between the terms in play and beneath assignable relations' (Deleuze and Guattari 1988: 238–39). Thus Audiard's films reflect the generic preferences of his father (the *polar*/thriller) yet hybridize them to thus permit generic elements to serve as liberational, performative frameworks for his protagonists rather than narrative and iconographic constraints. *De battre* remains a response to *Fingers* (Toback 1978), yet while several sequences are replicated in very faithful detail (the final fight, Tom's lunch dates with his father), Audiard undertakes a radical change in the film's ending, saving his central character from a series of crises in sexual, racial and filial identity.

Unlike the youthful icons of the New Wave, many films of the 'new' New Wave of the late 1990s feature central protagonists whose lack of social and familial frameworks leads not to liberation but alienation. Audiard's protagonists, however, struggle to free themselves from familial constructs of identity through performance, creativity and reinvention. The narrative and *mise-en-scène* of *De battre* privilege an intimate reading of its oedipal crisis of filiation, yet questions of paternity and what constitutes a father reflect the wider contemporary social discourses around evolutions in family structures and their recognition in constitutional law through the PACS legislation of the mid-1990s. Although *De battre* shares with *Pierrot le fou* a relative 'lack of historical dimension' (Forbes 2000: 128), we can assert parallels between Tom's search for an identity, and concomitant struggle with filial models, with questions of '*patrie*' and belonging in contemporary France. The French family firm, identified overwhelmingly with a homosocial milieu and fraternal clan, are threatened by the newly ascendant Russian Mafioso, yet I would argue that it is not in these confrontational dynamics that socio-political and cultural anxieties might be revealed. The

De battre mon cœur s'est arrêté – Tom and his father.

father's occupation, and that of Tom and his peers, involves the violent eviction of tenants and the destructive protection of property, which implicate the Parisian urban landscape and marker of national identity in order for it to serve not as an illustration of modernization (as in the New Wave) or of alienation (as in the 'new' New Wave), but as evidence of the corrupt entrepreneurial and state practices that render the national (city) space ever more exclusive and excluding. In contrast to the low-lit spaces of Tom's apartment, the bought, sold and stolen spaces of property development are valued neither as habitat nor shelter, but only hold greatest capital value when they are uninhabited, and indeed temporarily uninhabitable, in an extreme commodification of space. These sites of violent, multiple exclusions constitute the negative of shared place, of France's historical self-representation as 'terre d'accueil' in which the fostering of community or the negotiation of new identities might take place. It is noticeable that the violent episodes in the film all target ethnic 'others': the precarious communities forcibly evicted from their flats, the owners of the couscous restaurant (and even Minskov) are victims of a series of assaults that, in the first case, are sanctioned by discourses of corrupt capitalist development in league with government officials. The lack of place afforded these groups serves as a metaphor for wider exclusions in suggesting their position in relation to the definitions of nationality and citizenry: their treatment provides a marked contrast with the situation of the overseas students at the Conservatoire who, due to the support of linguistic and cultural capital, achieve some stability.

Discourses of national, *cultural* filiations are also articulated in *De battre*. Yet Audiard *fils* escapes the direct '*boulimie citationnelle*' of the national filmic heritage (here again, specifically the New Wave) that Goldberg claims leads contemporary French film-makers to 'allow their parents to be reborn through them, to dance with ghosts' (Goldberg 2008). Forbes notes that 'by 1974 the long love affair with American popular fiction and popular cinema which had sustained the New Wave had definitively ended' (Forbes 2000: 111), yet in a strangely cyclical move, it is precisely this period of American independent cinema that provides the strongest intertexts for Audiard, found in its most explicit form to date in *De battre* and its response to one of the lesser-known films of that period, *Fingers* (Toback 1978). Tom's characterization, the dramatic close ups of his incongruous cowboy boots, the careful mirroring of de Niro's leather-jacketed silhouette and the retro styling of his headphones produce a nostalgic fetishization of independent New York cinema of the 1970s. Indeed unused sequences involving Tom travelling to New York in pursuit of Aline, whilst threatening a heavy-handed indication of the film's heritage, would have provided a fascinatingly self-conscious insertion of Tom into a contemporary version of his generic milieu that recalls Ferdinand's attempts to construct his own identity through visual and textual citation. The establishment of such clear narrative and visual intertexts can be read in the context of Forbes' assertion of the role of particular genres (for her, the *policier*) in articulating broader historical and socio-political relationships between France and the United States (Forbes 1992a).

Yet, in a parallel move to that adopted by the reflexive discourses of *Pierrot le fou*, Tom's identity is not only torn between that of paternal and maternal genealogies but also between their respective identifications with high and low culture. While the criminal adventures of the business practices of father and son are associated with the look of New York independent cinema, the non-realist rites of passage narrative of his aspirations to emulate his mother's career as a concert pianist is associated with the indices of a European heritage of high culture. These range from the recurring motifs of the Bach cantata he must master, through the footage of a pianist's hands that evoke *Nosferatu* (Murnau 1922), icon of a European pedigree of Expressionist cinema, to the clearly identified couture of the Yves St Laurent shirt worn for his audition. The non-standard slang used in Tom's deals contrasts with the established lineage of the Italian musical notation through which Tom must initially communicate with Miao-Lin. The idyllic calm of her apartment and the maternal enclave of high culture that, through the use of music technology, he builds in his apartment are vehemently protected from the generic spaces and characters associated with the crime thriller. Indeed, sequences showing Tom thumping out popular tunes on a bar piano that would have muddied such distinctions between worlds – and introduced intrusive parallels with *Tirez sur le pianiste/Shoot the Pianist* (Truffaut 1960) – were filmed but not included, and the only overlap between such discourses remains his compulsive miming of the piece on the bar top in which the music remains unheard and inaccessible to those around him.

The gendering of popular and high cultures in *De battre* remains the reverse of that to which Forbes draws our attention in *Pierrot le Fou*. The strict, patriarchal hierarchies and strikingly homosocial milieux notable throughout Audiard's films dominate *De battre*, where even the presence of the mother and of female lovers and teachers is contained within a narrative that insists on the association of Tom's final, compromised identity with that of the alternative father figure, Monsieur Fox.[6] It is striking that, while the association of two women, Tom's dead mother and Miao-Lin, with high culture is privileged through recurrent *mise-en-scène* that stresses communication, articulation, the sensual and self-realization – for example, the progressive reframings of Tom and Miao-Lin in her apartment in which the revelation of increasing physical proximity denotes a shared cultural affinity (rather than romance) – their position in the narrative remains contained and modified by the highly gendered transfers between cultural and economic capital, achieved first by Monsieur Fox, as the mother's agent, and then by Tom as he adopts this role in relation to Miao-Lin. In the same way that, through the technological and spatial construction of the sanctuary of his apartment, Tom was able to manage his mother's presence after her death, he is ultimately able to control aspects of Miao-Lin's possession of the cultural capital of the concert pianist through his superior fluency in French and his aptitude for cutting deals. While I have suggested elsewhere (Dobson 2007) that the ambiguities of the ending (has Tom succeeded in resolving maternal and paternal genealogies? Has he escaped the (oedipal) father? Is his new identity a liberating hybrid or a reductive compromise?) posit a predominantly positive model for the formation of an assured, performative identity, it can also be read as a critique of the rampant commodification of both (French) space and culture. Through his new identity, revealed teasingly as Miao-Lin's manager, Tom achieves a achieves a conversion of the cultural capital of his mother's and Miao-Lin's talent into economic capital through his function as agent and broker of deals with recording companies and concert halls. This conversion echoes the commodification of empty space so central to his corrupt business practices, and so closely associated with the paternal through his father or the substitute father figure of Monsieur Fox. Tom fails to exact the *dénouement* anticipated through the generic codes of the thriller (and through the ending of the 'source text' *Fingers*) of avenging his father's murder by killing Minskov, yet his bloodied return to the concert hall, which can be read as a marker of his 'taming' by high culture and romantic love, may indeed signal a different revenge, one exacted upon a feminized high culture that denied him primary access. The emphasis throughout the film on Tom's hands and their foregrounding as markers of creativity, sensuality and humanity is accompanied by the recurrent presence of the more banal prop of his briefcase as symbol of the greed and corruption of the world of real estate. The final sequences reveal Tom's use of his briefcase as avenging weapon against Minskov, but the physical awkwardness of its cradled presence in the final concert hall sequence also suggests that it represents a vengeance of another type. We may, in this light, read the ending not as a straightforward redemption of Tom's identity by high culture and romantic love, but as his reassertion of a gendered authority over the high culture that has been associated with women throughout the film. The close-up of Tom's hand on Miao-Lin's nape indicates not tenderness but possession as it facilitates the brokering of new deals, and his father's throwaway comment that he viewed Monsieur Fox as 'a pimp' may provide an eerie anticipation of Tom's new role.

A final parallel provoked by Forbes' piece on *Pierrot le fou* falls in the realm of the treatment of realism. While Audiard's films cannot be described as engaging in anything approaching the 'new pastoral'[7] that Forbes identifies in the aesthetics of Godard's text, they do include serial disruptions of the norms of realist narrative that share some characteristics of Godardian tactics. Audiard's narrative insistence on the potential for radical change in protagonists through an adoption of self-consciously performative identities continues to disrupt the taut psychological realism that an audience might anticipate from his choice of generic frameworks. In *De battre*, realism is also disrupted through the *mise-en-scène* of set pieces (the maternal shrine of Tom's apartment, the compulsive rehearsals – *répétitions* – of Tom's fledgling identity as pianist, the allegorical castration of the audition scene and the suspense of the final concert hall sequence), which evoke scenarios of both dream and nightmare through their low lighting, explicit staging and use of the Lynchian red theatre drapes that reveal knowing access to other worlds. Audiard's insistence on the 'plan incliné' works to destabilize the conventional realist point of view and gives formal warning of a slippage in the real. As happens throughout Audiard's oeuvre, the narrative drive of *De battre* (towards redemption, revenge, romance) is disrupted and suspended by shots that foreground a *mise-en-abyme* of conventions of visual representation – not here in reference to comic book art or Velazquez as in *Pierrot le fou*, but to the construction of the film's own visual codes. Tom demands that his lover, Aline, remain perfectly framed in a doorway, and spectatorial gratification follows as we share in viewing that same composition. Shots of shifting light on a carpet and a close-up of soft fabric textures serve to evoke Tom's sensual awakening through love and music, and also suspend the diegesis to suggest a potential identity that is perhaps based less on seeking new roles and reformulating narratives than on a focus on the sensual experience of the self in the time and space of the present – a rare luxury in realist narrative. Indeed, one recurrent Audardian motif – the poetic foregrounding of unexplained, hovering light – forms a striking link with the use of lights on the car windscreen in *Pierrot le fou* (Forbes 2000: 124).

This proposition of parallels and connections between Godard and Audiard, between Ferdinand/Pierrot and Tom, pivots on a central point asserted throughout Forbes' work across film studies and cultural studies that the construction of new identities and the intervention in familiar narratives must always be read across a dynamics of aesthetic, cultural and socio-political discourses. The implications of such an approach assure a non-vengeful negotiation of the relationship between the cultural specificities of a French film history dominated by the figure of the auteur and the vast constellation of other intertexts.

Notes

1. These include obituaries in *The Guardian* (Edgar 2001) and *The Independent* (Reader 2001c), *French Cultural Studies* (Marshall 2003a) and *Studies in French Cinema* (Harris 2001a).
2. Editors' note: Although this chapter is included in Part 1 of this volume in an abridged version, references given here are for the full text original version.
3. Contributions cover psychoanalytical readings of Eustache, shifting definitions of (cinematic) realism, Audrey Hepburn's European star identity, representation of maternal identities in Truffaut, comparative study of French and British intellectuals, the problematics of Bourdieu's politics and the representation of America in French film.
4. The boundaries and definitions of national cinemas are also questioned and contextualized in a consideration of French cinema in relation to its other European counterparts in the first volume of its kind, *European Cinema: An Introduction* (Forbes and Street 2000).
5. For further reflection on Forbes' work on realism, see Jeancolas (2003).
6. Audiard's latest film, *Un Prophète/A Prophet* (2009), posits an even more exaggerated model through the dominant setting of the men's prison.
7. Indeed, any such idea is explicitly mocked in the hilarious opening sequence of *Regarde les hommes tomber/See How They Fall* (Audiard 1994).

Chapter 9

Jill Forbes: The Continued Conversation

Sue Harris

The death of Jill Forbes was marked in an obituary published in only the second issue of *Studies in French Cinema* (Harris 2001a) at a time when family, friends and colleagues alike were still reeling from the loss of our much-loved friend. Her premature death from lung cancer silenced one of the most eloquent voices in our field, and it was nigh on impossible to accept that so much intellectual and personal energy had been so suddenly stopped in its tracks. Some nine years on, we miss her no less; in fact, her professional absence remains acute to those who worked alongside her on various projects that have since come to fruition. However, time and distance, and a wealth of new research produced by both established and emerging scholars in the intervening years, have confirmed what we knew then, and what proved to be a comfort of sorts at the time: that Jill's vast body of research in the area of French cultural studies mattered hugely, and that her influence lives on in the thriving research community in French film studies that we celebrate in this volume and in our many academic institutions.

As Jill's first doctoral student, sometime colleague and close friend, I was privileged to write the obituary mentioned above on behalf of the editorial and advisory body of the journal. Jill was an enthusiastic supporter of the *Studies in French Cinema* journal project from its inception, and was an original member of the editorial board. The obituaries and tributes that appeared there and elsewhere – in the national press (Edgar 2001; Reader 2001c) and in leading disciplinary journals (Reader 2002b; Marshall 2003a) – stressed Jill's qualities as a researcher, teacher and ambassador for her subject, and the writers were united in their acknowledgement of Jill's pioneering role in our disciplinary research. It is fitting that, at a moment when we collectively take stock of the significance and achievements of French film studies as a discipline, we remember Jill – who, had she lived, might now be contemplating retirement alongside her peers – and attempt to offer some kind of assessment of the important work she did and the influence she had on a generation of scholars. What I hope to convey in this chapter is both my personal appreciation for Jill's work, and an account of how she influenced my own work and scholarly practice. Perhaps more substantially, I hope to give a sense of how the woman with whom I spent so many wonderful hours in conversation saw dialogue itself as being central to her scholarship and its dissemination. Jill Forbes was not simply a pioneer of French film studies, she was a committed and generous facilitator in the development of careers, curricula and cultural understanding, and in the advancement of the kind of critical thinking we may sometimes take for granted today.

Reviewing her published research and professional service in the years up to and including the year of her death, one is struck by the enabling quality of almost everything Jill did. In addition to her academic and journalistic writing, Jill was a prodigious organizer and participant in events and conferences, and her portfolio of activities included editorial service on international journals, membership and chairmanship of public organizations, as well as management, teaching, examining and guest lecturing in institutions with diverse student populations. Her most significant editorial work was with the journal *French Cultural Studies*, which she co-founded in 1989 with Professors Mike Kelly, Nick Hewitt and Brian Rigby. The focus of the journal on modern French culture as manifested in audiovisual media, the visual and performing arts, and the institutions of culture offered a much-needed academic outlet for new kinds of scholarly research. As Mike Kelly suggested in the first editorial:

> The enormous interest and importance of this fertile cultural field is not matched by the scant attention it receives in existing scholarly publications, and the primary aim of this journal is to remedy that deficiency ... *French Cultural Studies* has been developed and supported by scholars and teachers who felt the lack of a forum and a resource in several important and rapidly developing areas of French Studies. (Kelly 1990: 2–3)

The journal's championing of cinema as an object of cultural study resulted in the publication of a series of special issues focused on wholly or partly on cinema (Reader 1996c; Marshall 2003b; Harris 2004), issues that provide lasting evidence of the impact of Jill's intellectual choices and active mentoring, while documenting the growing acceptance of French film studies within the academy.[1] Jill's talent for identifying genuine gaps in scholarship is evident in the content and range of her many publications, from her earliest (*INA: French for Innovation*, 1984) to the last before her death (*European Cinema: An Introduction* – Forbes and Street 2000). Indeed, as in the case of *European Cinema*, it is typical of Jill that some of her most important books carry the subtitle 'Introduction', a designation that on the surface could easily mislead. Jill's books could never be deemed 'introductory' in the sense of offering simple surveys of a subject. They are, however, determinedly 'introductory' in that they are have frequently been conceived with the university syllabus and the needs of university lecturers in mind.

European Cinema's concerns with the notion of European cinema and how it might be defined and studied was, as Jill and Sarah state in their opening paragraph, 'inspired by the attempts of its authors to design and teach an undergraduate course in European cinema' (Forbes and Street 2000: ix). Writing and teaching in the mid- to late 1990s, the authors responded to what they deemed to be the urgency of questions about European cinema and a dissatisfaction with the way film histories had so far been written, coupled with the paucity of current literature devoted to questions of the European – or, to use a term now in general circulation, transnational cinema. The book contains an extended introduction that probes a range of considerations relating to economics, politics, ideology, aesthetics and style, and concludes with an invaluable list of suggestions for further reading. The second part of the book is a series of detailed case studies, with individual essays by Jill and Sarah Street on French and British cinema respectively, and contributions by a range of colleagues from the University of Bristol (where the book was conceived) specializing in Italian, Spanish, German and Russian national cinemas.

Again, it was typical of Jill to find ways of pooling the expertise of a group of people who may have worked together as teachers for any number of years without necessarily finding an outlet for collaborative research work. The acknowledged support of the (then) Arts and Humanities Research Board testifies to the originality and anticipated impact of the book, and the plethora of later publications in the area of European cinema confirms the validity of the this early investigation.[2] This book, like others authored by Jill, was genuinely introductory inasmuch as there was nothing else in circulation at the time that could claim to cover the same ground for the same readerships. Her characteristically sympathetic approach, combining authoritative scholarship with an accessible written style, and her expectation that the book should provide a platform for further study rather than serve as a vehicle to jump through the hoops of undergraduate assessment tasks, sets Jill's work apart from the mainstream, and accounts for the continued inclusion of her studies on countless university reading lists around the world.

Jill's conviction about the holistic nature of French cultural studies was actively demonstrated in a co-authored book aimed at university language teaching, *Contemporary France: Essays and Texts on Politics, Economics and Society* (Forbes, Hewlett and Nectoux 1994, 2nd edition 2001), and her series editorship with Longman that included similar texts relating to Germany and Spain. In particular, *French Cultural Studies: An Introduction* (co-edited with Michael Kelly) is a work that remains perennially relevant, and whose content belies its modest title. Bringing together some of the United Kingdom's most eminent scholars, the book offers an interdisciplinary evaluation of French cultural forms since 1870, and a consideration of the evolving narrative of French cultural identity through a prism of nation, class and gender. The structuring principle expressed in the introduction (following Levi-Strauss) is that:

> if a society's culture is the language in which it speaks to itself, then French society obviously speaks to itself in many voices. The richness and multiplicity of its cultural discourses are a guarantee that it will continue to find powerful and vivid ways of articulating new identities. (Forbes and Kelly 1995: 7)

This belief that culture is best understood as a complex and ongoing conversation was fundamental to Jill's academic scholarship, and for her French cinema was one voice among many in France's cultural expression. It was, nevertheless, her passion and was arguably at the core of her wide constellation of interests. For her it was simple: responses (if not actual answers) to many of the questions we might ask about France, French culture and French intellectual life are to be found in the cinema; and the cinema, in turn, is a vital component of French intellectual life. As she reminds us in *The Cinema in France: After the New Wave,* the first of two influential monographs she published in the 1990s, 'this is a two-way process' (Forbes 1992a: 1). (The other monograph, *Les Enfants du paradis,* is discussed below).

Unsurprisingly, Jill's landmark study – described by the editors of a special issue of *Esprit Créateur* as a 'breakthrough text' (Higgins et al. 2002: 4) – wears its intentions to engage the reader on its sleeve, inspired as it is by her sense of service to a community of readers and film lovers. In her own words: 'This book has been written for both students and teachers of the cinema and for readers whose main focus of interest is France and French culture' (Forbes 1992a: 1). In her brief introduction, Jill appeals to her readers, most provocatively those students and teachers schooled in the British literary tradition of French studies, to take the cultural significance of French cinema seriously. In an era when French cinema is widely taught in universities and schools, and when a journal like *Studies in French Cinema* exists to serve a vibrant community of committed scholars, it may be hard to imagine a time when the validity of cinema as an object of critical study needed to be argued and defended. But to cast back just two decades to 1991, when Jill was appointed Professor of French at the University of Strathclyde, an ostensibly progressive 'new' university in a city that had as recently as 1990 celebrated its status as a European City of Culture, cinema was still an entirely unknown element on the undergraduate curriculum.

Such was Jill's energy that within the space of only a few years she had introduced a specialist undergraduate option in post-New Wave cinema, gained her first doctoral student and ensured that student was employable and able to introduce her own portfolio of French cinema courses to another Scottish university – and thus began my own journey which took me from being a lecturer in French at the University of Stirling to current chair of a growing young Department of Film Studies at Queen Mary, University of London. One of my own published essays stems from my first experience of being taught by Jill when, as a graduate teaching assistant in French, I had the privilege of sitting in on her final-year undergraduate classes at Strathclyde. She asked me to prepare a seminar presentation on *La Petite Voleuse* (1988), a then recent film by Truffaut's some-time protégé Claude Miller, no mean task for someone who had last presented a seminar paper some six years previously and who had no experience whatsoever of analyzing film. But Jill's immediate enthusiasm for the ideas I tentatively expressed about narratives of motherhood was initially surprising, then infectious, and the film itself became a staple of my own teaching for some years to come. I regret, of course, that she did not live to see the piece turned into a formal article in the journal she co-founded, and on whose editorial board I now serve (Harris 2003).

Miller was one of a number of French directors little known outside France whose films were discussed in *The Cinema in France: After the New Wave*. Christine Scollen-Jimack, reviewing the book for *Screen*, noted the breadth and ambition of the book, acknowledging that: 'Since it is clearly impossible to deal exhaustively with the totality of output in France over the past twenty-five years, Forbes has had to construct her own canon, which some readers may be unwilling to accept' (Scollen-Jimack 1994: 96). Scollen-Jimack's assessment of the book as 'avoiding the trap of mere compilation' and of conveying an immense amount of information 'that can only otherwise be gleaned by minute perusal of French cinema journals' recognizes the scope and complexity of a work 'which must have entailed agonizing choices'. Jill's focus was the work of a new generation of film-makers who, by and large, began their careers after 1968, and the choices she made were not so much agonizing as profoundly challenging. As figures of continuing innovation, Godard and Varda both find their place there (Truffaut too, but perhaps less convincingly); however, the originality of the book lies in the introduction it provides to a host of (then) less familiar names, including Philippe Garrel, Jean Eustache, Jacques Doillon, Maurice Pialat, René Allio and André Téchiné. Doillon, whose film career began with *L'An 01/ The Year 01* in 1973, was a particular personal favourite of Jill's, and on the publication of her book she was delighted to receive a handwritten letter from the director, thanking her for her attention to his work and for advocating it to viewers and scholars outside France.

Of particular influence in my own career trajectory was Jill's chapter on new French comedy, featuring the first assessment in an English-language publication of the films of maverick *provocateur* Bertrand Blier. Jill's confidence in her own work and in the profound needs of the research culture was such that she never shied away from what was difficult or unfashionable – or, in Blier's case, frequently tasteless. While the 1980s saw considerable academic attention paid to the work of the *cinéma du look*, sleek modernist films that found a willing public among French youth and on the international art-house circuit, Jill's work probed the rather more murky depths of the domestic popular cinema, including sometimes unsavoury, but incontrovertibly important, films in French cultural life. Jill's discussion of Blier's *Les Valseuses/Going Places* (1973), *Tenue de Soirée/Ménage* (1986) and *Trop belle pour toi/Too Beautiful for You* (1989) is criticized by Scollen-Jimack for 'minimizing his overwhelming misogyny: an aspect of his films that is not easy, for any woman, let alone a feminist, to ignore or forgive' (Scollen-Jimack 1994: 98). Jill's contention, however – and this is a lesson that I have passed on to my own students at every possible opportunity – was that it didn't matter whether one 'liked' a film or not; rather, it was incumbent upon the cultural studies scholar to identify and examine precisely those cultural and ideological manifestations that were most difficult to grasp, process and interpret.

As she noted in the opening words of her plenary lecture to the Society for French Studies in 1996 (published in the third section of this volume), we are all 'distant observers' of foreign cultures; distanced first by the obvious interpretative difficulties of cultures that – no matter how well we come to know them – nevertheless remain ever fractionally out of reach; and distanced also by the very privilege of the 'capacity for totalisation' that we develop as observers who are looked to for explanation, synthesis, summary. As Jill eloquently and perceptively argued, the dialectic of closeness and distance, internality and externality, is one of the fascinating paradoxes of cultural studies, perhaps above all in the cinema where the immediacy of perception tends to obscure the necessity for reflection. Her consummate ability to reflect on, and defend (unpopular) popular cinema – in this case, arguing that Blier's work is an important example of how domestic mainstream cinema engages with long-established French traditions of satire, derision and subversion – confers upon her writing a rare authority, as well as an important model for future researchers.

Significant, too, is Jill's defence of the figure of the auteur, which she readily admits could be perceived as provocative in the post-Structuralist period. Jill's defiant stance that 'it would be perverse to ignore it' (Forbes 1992a: 4) is another example of her fundamental awareness of her own status as a 'distant observer', reminding us that we cannot operate selectively according to preferred ideological positions. For Jill – as indeed for the Manchester University French Film Directors series which began publication in 1998, and now boasts some 30 monographs on individual film-makers – the auteur continues to matter a great deal in evaluations of a national cinema so profoundly steeped in debate about the concept. Taking a lead from Peter Wollen, Jill asserts that 'in film criticism, unlike literary criticism, the auteur has always been a fiction, a polemical device used to support a certain kind of *reading* rather than a particular kind of writing' (Forbes 1992a: 4) and points out that:

> to talk of the auteur cinema is not to deny the essentially collaborative nature of film making or the social, political or ideological context in which it takes place. But for the post-1968 French film-maker to be or not be an auteur is to adopt a position in relation to the industry, to the *nouvelle vague*, to gender, and to the audience. (Forbes 1992a: 4)

For Jill, the relevance is wholly valid: there is 'a recognizable economy of the auteur cinema in France that is constituted by the marriage of specific production practices with the pursuit of thematic continuities' (1992a: 259) – and which thus merits our fullest consideration.

The aims of the book in question were multiple, but also very simple. In Jill's own words, she hoped:

> to change the conventional view of French cinema which prevails in English-speaking countries, a view which tends to concentrate narrowly on the survivors of the *nouvelle vague* and on the commercially successful work of directors such as Beineix, Besson and Carax, to the exclusion of much else that is worthwhile. (Forbes 1992a: 1)

In itself, this was a valid aim of her scholarship, and the proliferation of the field of study since is evidence of the impact of her pioneering work. As Phil Powrie notes in his assessment of the doctoral theses on French cinema produced since the early 1970s through to 2002, directors such as Eustache, Garrel and Pialat are now as frequently studied as canonical luminaries such as Bresson, Duras, Renoir, Resnais and Truffaut (Powrie 2003: 202). We might take the intended impact on future academic study as a given of any scholarship. But Jill hoped for more, and already had her sights set on what today's academic world would term 'knowledge transfer', or dissemination of scholarly work among generalists and the non-academic professional sector. The final words of the book firmly reiterate the desire to expand the horizons of conservative viewers, but more importantly what Jill hoped was to 'persuade, above all, distributors [outside of France] of the value and interest of the undeservedly unfamiliar' (Forbes 1992a: 261).

Jill's dialogue with her own book continued throughout her career and beyond, in the form of publications by students she mentored and peers she influenced: my own book on Blier was published by Manchester University Press in 2001, a matter of weeks after her death (Harris 2001b); Bill Marshall's (2007) book on Téchiné (French Film Directors) is dedicated to Jill Forbes, 'another Téchiné fan'; and Lynn Higgins' monograph on Tavernier is forthcoming with MUP at the time of writing. A scholarship set up in Jill's memory at Queen Mary, to enable doctoral research in one or more of her primary areas of interest, saw the award in 2007 of a PhD on the subject of 'The French Cinema and Hollywood: A Study of Two Systems from the Arrival of Sound to the Collapse of the Production Code' (Drazin 2007), sections of which will soon be published in *The Faber History of French Cinema* (Drazin, forthcoming). A major thread of Jill's book was precisely a consideration of French cinema's relationship with American cinema, not simply as a dialogue between the *Cahiers du cinéma* critics and the Hollywood greats, but more subtly in terms of the important but largely unacknowledged renewal of French cinema in the 1970s, a decade that has frequently been seen as unmarked by a school or movement. Jill's book was the first to recuperate this unfashionable decade, showing how American cinema functions as a clear intertext in a valuable renewal of film form, most notably in the work of Bertrand Tavernier and Alain Corneau: of the latter, she notes that he is 'typical of his generation in his enthusiasm for certain aspects of American popular culture and in his breadth of knowledge of the cinema, and his films are designed to appeal to an audience with comparable interests' (Forbes 1992a: 67). Jill's chapters on women film-makers, on Jean Eustache, and on René Allio and the 'new history film' offered particularly inspiring assessments of 1970s French cinema, and have proved to be the platform for three important essays that were all published posthumously: 'Gender and Space in *Cléo de 5 à 7*' (Forbes 2002a), 'Matricides' (Forbes 2002b) and 'Psychoanalysis as Narrative in Films by Jean Eustache' (Forbes 2003). The richness and critical subtlety of these essays allow us to trace the evolution of Jill's thinking over a significant period of years, and provide a legacy that we can treasure.

Jill's second major contribution to scholarship in the 1990s was her book on Marcel Carné's *Les Enfants du paradis/Children of Paradise* (1945), published in the prestigious BFI Film Classics series (Forbes 1997). This book, which Keith Reader (2001c) has described as 'model of erudition and lucidity', can trace its origins to an earlier article entitled 'The Liberation of the French Cinema?' (Forbes 1994), in which Jill offers a probing discussion of Carné's Occupation and post-Liberation films. Noting that *Les Visiteurs du Soir/The Devil's Envoys* (1942) and *Les Enfants du Paradis* are both 'explicitly and programmatically national cultural products' (Forbes 1994: 256), Jill goes on to offer a rare assessment of *Les Portes de la Nuit/ Gates of the Night* (1946), a film that was roundly criticized as a megalomaniac folly on the part of Carné, whose artistic extravagance was perceived as considerably at odds with the climate of austerity that prevailed in France in the years following the war. For Jill, whose interest in questions of film architecture in general, and inter-war French set design in particular, were beginning to take shape, the investigation of these films was centred not around their function as allegories of French life under the Occupation, but rather in their signalling of an 'aesthetic revolution' in French cinema practice at the very moment when history suggests the national industry was at its most depleted and constrained. Jill takes these ideas much further in the BFI book, insisting on the film's use of an architectural paradigm as an assertion of the popular revolutionary tradition in a modern France living under oppression. For Jill, it is the very scale of the film, including its detailed reconstruction of the popular *quartiers* of Paris, that constitutes a reflection on the politics of culture and affirms the radical force of culture in French history. The film's literal staging of popular culture in the form of theatre and performance, the notorious Boulevard du Crime and the transgressions of the popular audience are a defiant riposte to the provincialism and regressive 'heritage' politics of the Vichy regime. As Jill demonstrates, the film's codes of gender, genre and class provide a positive message, and 'the essential link which allows the visual to be understood politically and transgression to be seen as a more creative and radical act than opposition or resistance' (Forbes 1997: 72). As theorist Laura Mulvey – confessing herself to be no fan of the film – notes in the tribute volume of *French Cultural Studies,* Jill's writing had the ability to challenge and persuade even those scholars we might assume to be utterly certain of their critical position. As she says:

> Reading an intelligent, well informed and perceptive book about a favourite film may be a fun and rewarding experience but a book that makes visible and tangible a film's previously unperceived qualities is surprising and more profoundly rewarding. The pay-off is double: discovering the book leads to the discovery of the film. (Mulvey 2003: 278)

'To the Distant Observer' (Forbes 1996) builds on the same 1994 article and, although a spoken lecture, gives a real flavour of the new major work in which Jill was engaged at the time of her death. Jill's interest in the design practice of the French studios in the inter-war years, and the ways in which the transition to sound exposed the inadequacies of French film technology, had been germinating for a number of years, and was sure to be another major contribution to scholarship in film and French cultural history. After her death, the project was 'adopted' by myself and Sarah Street, and with the collaboration of German film specialist Professor Tim Bergfelder we succeeded in publishing a book that, while in no way the one Jill would have written, we hope is one that she would have valued and found a useful contribution to the field.

Our book, *Film Architecture and the Transnational Imagination: Set Design in 1930s European Cinema* (Bergfelder et al. 2007), consciously engaged with the core priorities of Jill's research, while redirecting the focus in line with the interests and expertise of a diverse team of researchers. The decision to privilege the period of the late 1920s to the late 1930s stemmed from our like-minded assessment of the period as a pivotal one in European film history: a decade in which studio-based production dominated, and in which production practices across Europe were transformed by new technologies, new artistic currents and the mobility of technical personnel from East (notably Russia and Hungary) to West (Germany, France and Britain). While it was clear from Jill's initial research that the set designer was a significant stylistic force in landmark French productions such as *La Kermesse héroïque/Carnival in Flanders* (Feyder 1935) and *Les Enfants du Paradis*, work on the broader impact of designers on European cinema – and the consequences of this for questions of both national identity and film authorship – remained to be done. Our hypothesis – that identifiable professional practices developed within a framework of cross-national mobility, and that questions of visual style and spatial organization in European cinema of the era are best understood in this historically specific context – was tested through a comparative analysis of films produced by different studios, working with a mobile cohort of designers, in three separate countries.

Our investigation of an array of archival material – memoirs, drawings, personal letters, studio plans, itemized budgets, photograph collections – belonging to key figures (Lazare Meerson, Alfred Junge, Eugène Lourié, Vincent Korda and Alberto Cavalcanti, to name but the most prominent) revealed that the role of the set designer on a given project was far more complex, and far more influential, than had generally been assumed. But in order to demonstrate this, we had to first confront the relative lack of resources available to film studies to conceptualize set design as an element of critical practice, and to account for its performative function in both film narrative and the analysis of *mise-en-scène*. The challenge that Jill had set in her work, and to which we responded, was to undertake the study of a filmic element characterized by its ephemeral and fragmentary qualities – artificial, 'disposable architecture' that bears little relation to real space, but whose success is measured in terms of verisimilitude and authenticity, and that is paradoxically at its most persuasive when it remains imperceptible as decor to the viewer. Tellingly, the aspiration to invisibility that underpins much set design is inseparable from the set designer's status as an invisible figure in film history. Our study, in tandem with Jill's research, seeks to rectify this neglect, while adding a new perspective on the cultural influence of cinema in the period in question.

From the French-centred study that Jill set in motion, *Film Architecture and the Transnational Imagination* evolved in a spirit of collaborative scholarship into a European study, concluding that many themes, preoccupations and practices were not confined to particular national cinemas, and that there was a far greater degree of similarity between German, French and British films of the 1930s than had hitherto been recognized. My own specific section on the meticulous, lyrical imagining of Paris begun by Meerson in *Sous les Toits de Paris/Beneath the Rooftops of Paris* (Clair 1930), and indeed the broader interrogation of familiar visual worlds recreated by distant, and crucially mobile, observers is, I hope, evidence of our continued conversation with Jill. In this case, perhaps more than any other, her work provided the actual foundations for a new way of thinking, and for the type of collaborative work she enthusiastically promoted.

There has always been a sense among Jill's close friends that her best research was still ahead of her. We can only speculate about where her scholarship would have taken her or us, but we know for certain that we could not be celebrating our disciplinary achievements in quite the same way today were it not for the work she did, and the generosity with which she did it in her all too short professional life.[3]

Notes

1. Editorial and advisory board work elsewhere included the journals *French Studies*, *Sites* (USA), *Monash Romance Studies* and *Australian French Studies* (Australia) and *Paragraph*, of which she was a founder-editor, on which she served from 1984–95.
2. See, for example, Aitkin (2001); Fowler (2002); Ezra (2003); Everett (2005); and Wood (2007).
3. The title of this article is inspired by Jean-Pierre Jeancolas's (2003) tribute to Jill entitled 'Jill Forbes, ou la conversation interrompue'.

Chapter 10

Political Threads and Material Memory: Mayo's Wardrobe for *Casque d'or* (1952)

Jennie Cousins

In terms of prior academic study, few have shared Professor Susan Hayward's interest and enthusiasm for the so-called 'Golden Age' of 1950s French costume drama. Despite constituting 15 per cent of all films at the time, featuring exquisitely dressed stars and being popular with the cinema going public, the 1950s costume drama has, like the majority of 1950s French cinema, been remembered with indifference by academics (Powrie 2004a: 5). Unwilling to let a whole decade of costume drama production slide into obscurity, Hayward has drawn back the dust cloth from this veiled genre in her recent research. In so doing, she has initiated fresh seams for discussion in 1950s French cinema and the costume drama as generic type.

Hayward's analysis of Simone Signoret's dress code created by costume designer Antoine Mayo in *Casque d'or/Golden Helmet* (Becker 1952) in the publications 'Signoret's Star Persona and Redressing the Costume Cinema: Jacques Becker's *Casque d'or* (1952)' (2004a), and *Simone Signoret, the Star as Cultural Sign* (2004b), sparked my own interest in the 1950s costume film, encouraging me to delve deeper into the wardrobes responsible for so much of the look of this genre. In particular, it was Hayward's (gender) political reading of Mayo's treatment of corsetry in relation to Signoret's star body and identity that intrigued me. Costume drama has often been viewed as a genre that sidelines history and politics in favour of romance and fashion (Bruzzi 1997: 35). Yet, in Hayward's analysis of *Casque d'or*, it is romance and fashion that become politicized through the use of the film's *Belle Époque* timeframe. This is typical of Hayward's influential approach of looking at, and finding value in, that which others may have under-estimated.

Set in what Leahy terms the genuine '*milieu*' of 1900s working-class Paris (2007: 1), *Casque d'or* recounts the love story of Marie (Simone Signoret) and Manda (Serge Reggiani), against the backdrop of the actions of a gang of *apaches* led by the duplicitous Leca (Claude Dauphin). The couple meet at a *guinguette* where Manda is working as a carpenter and, to the displeasure of her lover/pimp, Roland (William Sabatier), Marie asks Manda to dance. The following day, Leca offers to buy Marie from Roland; she does not give him an answer and instead visits Manda. However, finding that Manda is engaged to his *patron's* daughter, Marie goes to the Ange Gabriel, a café and dancehall, and accepts Leca's offer only to have Manda arrive. Unaware of Marie's deal with Leca, Manda duels with and kills Roland, and narrowly escapes the police. Marie then engineers a meeting with Manda in Joinville, and they spend two snatched days of happiness together, but their union is cut short when Manda learns that his friend, Raymond (Raymond Bussières), has been falsely accused of Roland's murder by Leca. Manda turns himself in to face the guillotine, but not before shooting the treacherous *apache* boss.

By 1950s standards of costume cinema, which tends to focus on bourgeois literary adaptations, *Casque d'or* is atypical in its focus on the working class and its inclusion of a female protagonist with agency via Signoret's Marie, who troubles patriarchal structures of power (Hayward 2004a: 26). Hayward recognizes this unusual treatment of class and gender in *Casque d'or*, referring to the film as 'an elegiac treatise on sexual equality [and] an appeal against the inhumanity of the death penalty, which make it on both counts a very modern film' (2004a: 26). Such modernity deepens Becker's atypical use of the costume drama, for the genre is traditionally nostalgic and conservative rather than progressive in its ideals. Yet *Casque d'or* is not without nostalgia for working-class solidarity (which, as we shall see, is linked to Manda and his actions), and this seems to have clouded the impact of Becker's forward-looking ideas on equal rights and social advancement, and their relevance to the time of the film's release. Contemporary reviews of the film have generally failed to pick up on any relevance *Casque d'or* may have had to the socio-political situation of the 1950s – the one exception being Roger Boussinot's review in *Les Lettres françaises*, which commented on the film's gender relations (Leahy 2007: 79–80) – and in Dudley Andrew's analysis, he finds 'difficulty ... in linking the film to the social issues of the day' (2000: 116). Yet, to the contrary, Hayward has claimed that: 'In speaking from the past, Becker was in fact making a statement about the present' (2000a: 20). I will now explore this reading of the film's contemporary relevance.

The 1950s were a politically turbulent decade in France. As Hayward summarizes, the political climate of 1951 when *Casque d'or* was being made was characterized by a swing to the right. The coalition left known as the Third Force, which had been in power since 1947, came to an end due to American pressure. Marshall Aid would be granted only on the condition that the French Communist Party (PCF) had no authority, and so communist cabinet ministers were relieved of their posts. By 1951, the left coalition was disintegrating without the support of the PCF. By 1952, the right had taken power and former collaborators, such as Antoine Pinay (who was appointed prime minister), were granted office (2000a: 20). This political situation, coupled with a tightening of censorship on visual media, renders Becker's choice of the costume drama 'as a background for radical statements ... clearer' (2000a: 20). As Hayward continues: 'Read in this light, the shooting of Leca, a collaborator with the police and an informer, now takes on stronger political connotations, as does the film as a whole' (2000a: 20). I am intrigued by the way in which these political connotations are expressed in *Casque d'or*, for – as I will explain in conjunction with Hayward's analysis – they are stitched into the costume design of the film as much as the narrative. It is in this vestimentary area that my own research intersects with Hayward's, in particular her analysis of corsetry in relation to Marie/Signoret, to which I shall now turn.

Due to their body-sculpting qualities, foundation garments such as the corset are the costume drama's first level of historical signification in terms of costume design, for a particular historical silhouette can immediately signify a past era – for example, the S-bend silhouette is a visual marker of the *Belle Époque*, and so what one would assume

Marie exhibits (Cousins 2009: 130–32). Furthermore, functioning as what we might term fabric gender armour, foundation garments are the site/sight upon which discourses of sexuality, (gender) identity and politics are layered. However, such discourses, along with the corset that generates them, are usually hidden beneath outer clothing. Yet, as Hayward has noted with regard to Marie, Mayo's treatment of corsetry is very different from that of many other costume designers working in 1950s costume cinema, for Marie has no corset beneath her clothes. Instead, Mayo externalizes her corset, placing it at a visual rather than a hidden level:

> In effect, that desired object [the corset] (as far as the male is concerned) is not just missing. Marie has put it elsewhere. It is worn outside in the reduced form of her belt, and not on the inside … The belt becomes an ironic commentary on masculine desire and power: she first exteriorises it and then diminishes it. (Hayward 2004a: 26)

Hayward reads this externalizing of the corset as a sartorial interruption, explaining how, in putting the corset outside her clothes, Marie troubles the shell that prevents one from seeing sexuality by putting her corseted carapace into the public arena. This notion of perturbing the public arena is particularly pertinent given that when we first see Marie she is on her way to the *guinguette* to dance with her friends (assorted prostitutes and *apaches*), much to the dismay of some of the clientele. In putting the corset over her clothes, negotiations between the forbidden, desiring body and the social body that is insulated from private fantasies are disrupted. For underwear, particularly corsetry, is the site/sight of the body's unwrapping, a gateway to naked flesh (Hayward 2004a: 27). In collapsing the boundaries of dress, which mediate between the individual body and the social body, Marie's corset-belt becomes an uncomfortable confrontation with desire. Her body is not disciplined by the corset and her desire is not mediated by it. In short, she is an undisciplined and thus unruly body. As a result of being an unruly body of undisciplined desire, Marie negates the passivity and conformity that a patriarchally dominated socio-political system demands of her, and this is how her agency manifests itself through Mayo's reworking of corsetry. The political and sartorial message is clear: Marie disrupts (Hayward 2004a: 27).

Hayward's reading of Marie's corset-belt illustrates how Mayo's costume design, like Becker's atypical treatment of the costume drama, goes against expectations of the genre. Women's dress in 1950s costume drama is frequently characterized by constraint, provided courtesy of the corset and the crinoline in their varying fashionable forms. Male clothing is also characterized by restraint in this genre, in the guise of the uniform – be it the aristocratic suit or militaristic dress. In this respect, Mayo's loose-fitting costume design for Reggiani's Manda is also unusual. Furthermore, the designer places importance on the male waist in *Casque d'or*, as I will now illustrate by comparing and contrasting the costumes of Manda and Leca, in particular the fabrics they wear, in conjunction with Hayward's reading of Mayo's corsetry outlined above.

Material memories: Manda's bruised masculinity and Leca's apparel of amnesia

Hayward's analysis of Marie's, Manda's and Leca's dress calls attention to how Marie mirrors different sartorial aspects of the two men throughout the film:

> Her [Marie's] clothes mirror in look, but not entirely in *fabric*, those of Manda – his dark velvet trousers and striped cotton shirt. But of course they also mirror the clothes she wore in the opening sequence and when she went to visit Leca … The stripes on the collar of Marie's blouse fall in the same diagonal direction as the stripes on Leca's shirt … Thus, much as Marie's clothes appear to align her with Manda, they fail to be totally free from connotations with Leca and his own desire for her. (2000a: 25, my emphasis)

It is the reference to different types of fabric that is particularly interesting here in terms of Mayo's masculine wardrobes, for Manda and Leca are dressed in very different types of cloth – Manda favouring heavy cottons and velvets, and Leca opting for light silks and satins.

Compared with Leca's flashy dress, Manda's garb is a simpler affair; however, this is not to say that his dress is less complex a signifier of meaning, for Manda is undoubtedly sartorially complex. Leca's attire consists of three-piece suits marked with patterns (stripes, polka dots, stars), his shirts and waistcoats cut from fabrics with a sheen (silks and satins). They are clothes that conceal the body by deflecting attention away from the corporeal; their patterns and lustred surfaces draw attention to themselves by flagging up their fine tailoring rather than the flesh beneath. Manda, on the other hand, is clothed in soft, open fabrics that reveal his body. His sleeves are frequently rolled up and his shirt is unbuttoned at the neck, unlike Leca who is always buttoned up and tucked in (Leahy 2007: 51).

From this accessibility of the body, one can read Manda as being unbound by the rigid constraints and codes of masculinity to which Leca and his *apaches* adhere. Indeed, as I will illustrate, following Hayward and Leahy, Manda 'embodies a new kind of masculinity' (Leahy 2007: 22). Mayo's dress for Manda authentically replicates the working-class fashions of flat cap, cotton shirt, loose trousers and wide cummerbund-like band at the waist, indicating both Manda's profession as a carpenter and his working-class credentials. His appearance honours the traditions of the older working-class generation and their artisan way of working. Such an association with the working class is strengthened via the presence of the renowned cinematic icon of French working-class masculinity, Gaston Modot as Manda's *patron*. This emphasis on and intertextuality with working-class icons and iconography lends Reggiani's already sartorially authentic depiction of Manda further weight. Indeed, Manda becomes the embodiment of the working class laid bare in *Casque d'or*, both literally and figuratively, for Reggiani's is the only body to be seen unclothed during the film's narrative.

Manda's costume in some ways shares Marie's external corsetry via the wide band of cloth at his waist (see Figure 11.1). Although it appears less like a traditional women's foundation garment than Marie's corset-belt, Manda's cummerbund-style cloth could be read as alluding to the lesser-worn male corset. Male corset-wearing has always been considered controversial (Steele 2001: 38), and has been practised only by small numbers of certain groups. For example, in the nineteenth century, male corset-wearing was associated with a few military men, dandies, corset-enthusiasts and cross-dressers, but certainly not the mainstream (Steele 2001: 38). None of these social groupings seems to be a natural fit for Manda and his cummerbund-corset, but then again he is not putting the corset where it is supposed to be, for it is externalized. However, Manda retains the controversial aspect of male corset wearing through what his cummerbund-corset comes to represent in addition to his working-class roots. In the same way that Hayward reads Marie's corset-belt, Manda's own pseudo-corset becomes a site/sight of information, exchange and economies of desire. For example, it is where he places Marie's letter to him, tucking it into the centre of the cloth. In this respect, Manda's cummerbund-corset is similar in function to whalebone/wooden busks, where love notes would be carved and then slotted into the corset to keep its structure – desire kept next to the body. Yet Manda places this desire at one remove away from the body, for his cummerbund-corset is over his clothing. Akin to Hayward's observation of Marie, Manda exteriorizes discourses of desire that are usually kept within the liminal space between body and undergarment. Consequently, Hayward's interpretation of the external corset as a confrontation with desire is also applicable to Manda. As such, Marie and Manda mirror each other in both costume and desire.

Of Marie and Manda's mutual desire, Hayward has commented that 'what is suggested … is sexuality as flowing both within and between bodies, rather than something rigid and contained and measurable only against the phallus' (2004a: 19). This flow between the bodies of Marie and Manda is enabled via their repositioning of the 'corset' over outer clothing, the desire with which the garment becomes imbued radiates out rather than being tightly laced away. Thus there is a sartorial equality of power between them in terms of their desire, which Hayward speaks of as softening their characters (2000a: 19). Such softening is replicated in the external 'corsets' they share, which become waist-defining but not structuring garments of display rather than hidden body scaffolding. Yet there is a further significance to Manda's dress, which is to be found in Mayo's choice of fabrics.

Because they are worn against the skin, fabrics record bodily actions. By this I mean that, through everyday use, fabrics document our movements through their patterns of wear and tear, record our locations through the particles (such as pollen and dirt) that become trapped in their fibres, and even take on the smells of our bodies and environments. Through simply wearing clothes, the deterioration of the fabrics from which they are constructed becomes a process through which our lives are captured. In short, fabrics become imbued with what I will term material memories, echoes of our lives in action when dressed. Obviously some fabrics are more susceptible to attrition than others; the more three-dimensional a fabric, the more successful it will be in exhibiting patterns of wear and tear and attracting exterior matter into its fibres. For example, velvet has a very three-dimensional surface and so 'bruises' with wear, making its material memories visible. Notably, Manda's trousers are cut from velvet and thus show the material memories of past actions through bruising. This notion of clothing being able to show the impact of past actions takes on further significance in the costume drama, a genre that recreates the past yet can never escape the timeframe of its production period. Therefore, the clothing worn in *Casque d'or* is simultaneously documenting the imagined past of its narrative (*Belle Époque*) as well as the present moment of its production (1950s) through the creation of material memories that belong to both timeframes, which is most apparent in Manda's bruised velvet trousers (see image overleaf).

It is through such visible evidence of material memories in Manda's costume that my analysis of *Casque d'or* further intersects with that of Hayward, who we will remember stated that: 'In speaking from the past, Becker was in fact making a statement about the present' (2000a: 20). In acknowledging the costume drama's dual occupation of two timeframes, Hayward has identified how Becker has attempted to speak to the present via the guise of the past in terms of gender relations and social progress (2000a: 20). Expanding on this, I would suggest that *Casque d'or*'s costume design is also part of this process, because the material memories in the fabrics Mayo uses belong to both the 1950s and the imagined *Belle Époque*. In this respect, Manda's velvet bruises at an individual character level represent his actions and their consequences. For example, his carpentry trade, his dancing with Marie, his duel with Roland are all marked in the velvet he wears via the deterioration the fabric exhibits in this imagined *Belle Époque* timeframe. However, when considered in the early 1950s timeframe of the film's production, these fabric bruises can also be interpreted as representative of material memories caused by contemporary actions.

On an individual level, these material memories are a by-product of Reggiani's actions as both himself and Manda. Yet, given the shared left-wing position of Becker, Reggiani, Mayo and many other cast and crew members (Leahy 2007: 4; Malliarakis 2002: 20), it is not unreasonable to imagine that Manda's performance and costume become imbued with some contemporary political trace, particularly given Becker's labelling as a 'social film-maker' (Hayward 2000a: 20). Indeed, Manda's masculinity differs from expected male behaviour in both the *Belle Époque* and the 1950s, a difference demonstrated in Manda's conduct throughout the film. Although a man of few words, he is willing and able to negotiate with the other sex, making him an authentic rather than stereotyped masculinity, and he is unyielding in his defence of and fight for the truth in *Casque d'or*. For example, he cannot let Raymond take the blame for Roland's murder even though he knows it will lead to his own demise. While this points to a nostalgic view of working-class solidarity in the *Belle Époque* setting of the film, I would suggest that Manda's actions, and the material memories that result from these actions, also comment allegorically on masculinity in the 1950s.

Battered by the loss of one and a half million people (mostly men) and facing changes in society and traditional gender roles, France's post-war masculinity was in crisis – a crisis the government endeavoured to resolve by implementing misogynistic measures to encourage women to stay in the domestic sphere and reproduce, measures which were in full swing by the 1950s (Duchen 1994: 2–3). This drive to the domestic was coupled with kick-starting the nation's rebuilding and modernization on both a social and economic scale. In order to begin this dual process of reconstruction and adopt the new, the legacy of the Occupation and the horrors of war became a scar to be covered over. This scar was in part camouflaged

Casque d'or – Manda's cummerbund-corset and bruised velvet.

by the strict legislation of women (the metaphorical embodiment of the nation), evidenced by measures such as 'the single-wage benefit, generous allowances for large families and the fact that husbands could still prevent their wives from working until 1965' (Leahy 2007: 28), as well as encouraging an acceptably conservative masculinity. Once this process was underway, the procedure of forgetting and fabricating could begin. The myth of the Resistance in particular became heavily embroidered, with De Gaulle championing the myth of France's unified resistance to Nazi occupation (Paxton 2001). In short, in an attempt to revert to a system that privileged and rehabilitated France's bruised masculinity, misogyny and national amnesia were embraced. In remembering one's history wrongly, national cohesion can be maintained. As Hayward has commented: 'We need only think all too briefly of the post-occupation period in France to realize the self-serving purpose and necessity of national amnesia' (2000: 83). Above all, forgetting the past and denying the horrors of war in this period were paramount. The bruises should not show.

Yet the bruises (the material memories of his actions) do show on Manda's velvet trousers. The fabric of his costume does not forget, but records events as they happen – unlike the post-war period in which national amnesia is embraced. As such, the bruises Manda sports can be read as an allegory of bruised masculinity in the post-war period, and a refusal to let the horrors of wartime go unmarked. Manda actively resists misogyny and denial (the tools being used by the government to try to resolve the crisis in French masculinity and shattered national identity) in the narrative through his equality with Marie and loyalty to Raymond. Accordingly, Manda's death in *Casque d'or* reflects the 1950s' unwillingness to listen to an alternative male voice or be reminded of uncomfortable recent history. This is why Manda's progressive politics and working-class solidarity, as demonstrated through his actions, must be cut off (he is guillotined). There is no space for fresh ideology in this restrictive post-war context, as evidenced by the American-led eviction of the PCF (the emblematic party of the working class) from government and the return to power of former collaborators such as Antoine Pinay (Hayward 2000a: 20).

The topic of collaboration is further commented on in *Casque d'or* through Mayo's costume for Leca, as I shall now explain. Leca is symbolic of the old tradition of patriarchy within the film. As the head of the 'family' of *apaches*, he stands for the patriarch, the father who ultimately has power over his boys. Leca monitors his *apaches'* finances (only he has the key to the safe), clothing (he chastises Raymond and Billy for wearing caps rather than hats), time (he frequently checks his watch and organizes the gang's routine), discipline (he punishes Fredo for taking the money) and women (he takes Marie from Roland). Contrary to Manda's soft, open silhouette, which reveals his body, Leca is attired in such a way that the corporeal is concealed. As Leahy has commented: 'Unlike Manda, where what you see is what you get, Leca's appearance hides what lies beneath: the bourgeois wine merchant hides the gangster, the jovial boss hides the violent disciplinarian, the dapper and suave exterior hides the cowardly and treacherous nature within' (2007: 60–61).

When one first encounters Leca at his house, he is dressed in a white shirt shot through with a two-colour pinstripe tucked into dark, extremely high-waisted single-pinstripe

Casque d'or – Leca's multi-layering.

trousers. Over this combination he sports an expensive-looking satin waistcoat, which is dark in colour and patterned with a star motif. He is accessorized with a gold pocket watch and a geometrically patterned silk tie complete with tie-pin. It is clear that Leca takes pride in his appearance. Such a preoccupation with the sartorial links Leca to a long tradition of narcissistic and dandified Franco-American gangsters, for whom clothing is directly equated with status, money and style. Bruzzi has identified such narcissism as being an element that distinguishes the gangster from other masculine archetypes, and that such vanity is demonstrated by the gangster via both 'a preoccupation with the appearance of others and a self-conscious regard for his own' (Bruzzi 1997: 67). Leca is certainly a vain character, shown frequently checking his reflection. He is also fixated on personal grooming: we see him shaving and Marie knowingly flatters him by remarking on his change of hair parting. Such vanity and grooming tie into Bruzzi's reading of the gangster, but in the case of *Casque d'or* it would appear that there is something extra going on behind Leca's façade.

The heavy patterning of Leca's costume is undoubtedly a symbol of wealth and status. His adoption of clothes worn by the bourgeoisie illustrates his class ambitions. Yet this extreme patterning deflects attention away from the corporeal by drawing attention to itself and its surface rather than the body it attires. In addition, the sheen of Leca's silk garments also deflects attention away from the flesh that wears them. Furthermore, they are not easy to read in terms of their material memory, for they never appear to crease and their lustre makes them seem to be almost wipe-clean. Therefore, the actions of Leca and the movements they produce appear to go unrecorded – unlike Manda, whose velvet trousers show his every motion. In short, Leca's clothes display themselves rather than his body, and in so doing function as a cover-up. Nothing sticks. To unpick this further, I need to return to the 1950s timeframe.

Whereas the velvet bruises of Manda's trousers refuse to collude with the process of erasing the past, Leca's costume *does* collaborate in the process of national amnesia. Indeed, collaboration is key for, as Leahy notes, *Casque d'or* explicitly refers to 'France's recent history through Leca's double dealings and denunciations' (2007: 16). In opposition to Manda's materiality of truth, Leca has threads of collaboration and cover-up stitched into his costume. Read in this light, the wipe-clean appearance of Leca's clothing sartorially translates as an allegory of the nation's desire to wipe clean the stain of collaboration from the collective conscience. As unstitched above, Leca's costume deflects attention away from corporeal truth. Expanding on this, one can observe that the layering of patterns in Leca's clothing translates as layer upon layer of fabricated 'truth' covering up reality. Therefore, Leca's costume replicates the way in which the French national psyche wanted not only to conceal but efface the murky truth of collaboration. This is a point that takes on an ironical turn due to Claude Dauphin's resistance efforts during World War II – see Leahy (2007: 57).

Maintaining this state of national amnesia was paramount for 1950s France, and one can read Leca's upholding of personal appearance and reputation as emblematic of this. Leca does not want his shady deals (his collaboration) to be discovered, so he fixes and controls events in order to either erase or rewrite them. For example, Leca takes charge of the impending duel between Manda and Roland, insisting that they use his knife even though Roland has several on his person. He also tells Raymond to keep the dead Roland's watch to remember his friend by, knowing that he will later use this object of transference to set Raymond up. This then resonates with the 1950s timeframe by illustrating how dangerous memory, remembering and being in possession of the truth can be, for it goes directly against the prevailing climate of national amnesia. For example, Leca has Anatole killed for having witnessed the duel and thus being privy to the reality of the situation. Leca is therefore the controller of history, amending events through accessories and adornments, in particular watches and weapons.

However, one must not forget the foundation of inquiry in this chapter – Hayward's reading of the external corset. Unlike his *apaches*, who have various pseudo-corsets in the form of cummerbunds and wide belts, Leca does not appear to be 'corseted'. Yet his waist is still a focal point for his costume, due to the extremely high-waisted trousers he wears. In fact, his waist becomes the point where at least three layers of fabric overlap at any one time: his shirt being tucked into his trousers and his waistcoat covering both of these layers. The excessive height of Leca's trousers and the layering of fabric function to protect this vulnerable area of the body; it is as reinforced as possible without a corset. Again, one may interpret these multiple fabric layers as referring to Leca's manipulated and multi-layered versions of the truth, yet there is something else going on here. In order to divine what this may be, we need to understand why Leca does not wear a pseudo-corset.

We have already discovered that Mayo does not discriminate in terms of gender with regards to 'corset'-wearing, for he makes both the male and the female waist sites/sights of equal importance within *Casque d'or*. Yet none of these garments is a corset in the traditional sense, for they do not function as undergarments. Instead, Mayo takes the interior and externalizes it. As such, liminality is put into the public arena along with other sociological, sexual, political, cultural and economic readings. In summary, the externalized corset becomes a junction for such sartorial/corporeal discourses. Yet Leca deliberately attempts to suppress any discourses in terms of material memory that his clothing may have through wearing lustred fabrics that remain unmarked, without material memory. This, then, is the reason why Leca does not wear an exterior pseudo-corset but rather chooses to triply strap himself into multiple layers of shiny fabric, for he wishes to silence any discourses of truth generated by material memories of actions that might expose his double-dealings and denunciations. Thus, once more, Leca can be linked to the process of covering up traces of collaboration. The denial of material memory implicit in his costume ultimately speaks volumes about the difficulty that France as a nation was having in facing up to the realities of World War II and its consequences – difficulties that were still troubling the nation at the time of *Casque d'or*'s release.

Building on Hayward's assertion that *Casque d'or* does have contemporary political resonance, this analysis of Mayo's masculine wardrobes has extended Hayward's reading of the designer's external corsetry and woven it into the concept of material memory. It is via the process of material memory that *Casque d'or*'s costume design takes on a political edge, supporting Becker's atypical use of the costume drama genre, which Hayward has identified as a space in which to make 'radical statements' on gender, social progress and the socio-political situation of the 1950s (2004a: 20). As in Hayward's own work, Becker's film subverts expectations, finds political resonance in the unexpected and stands the test of time. As Leahy remarks, '*Casque d'or* offers a sort of "collective memory" to a nation busy forgetting its recent past' (2007: 90) – a collective memory which goes against the 'voluntary myopia' that marks much 1950s cinema (Hayward 1993: 188).

Chapter 11

'Une vraie famille Benetton': Maternal Metaphors of Nation in *Il y a longtemps que je t'aime* (2008) – a Response to Susan Hayward

Sarah Leahy

W hether she is addressing stars (Simone Signoret, in Hayward 2004b), directors (Luc Besson in Hayward 1998; Hayward and Powrie 2006), genres (her forthcoming work on 1950s costume drama (Hayward 2010), French national cinema (Hayward 2005), or questions of national cinema more generally (Hayward 1993, 2000a, 2000b), Susan Hayward's approach to whichever facet of French cinema she is exploring is always multiple, deploying sets of questions to interrogate our assumptions in many-layered analyses that frequently raise as many questions as they answer, and that always provoke the reader to think about the subject in new and exciting ways. Thus Hayward's contribution to French film studies to date has done much to demonstrate precisely the cultural, ideological and ethical complexities of cinema as institution, industry and art form. As she herself put it in 'National Cinemas and the Body Politic', cinema itself 'in its hybridity ... cannot help but challenge modernist (binary) thought, however implicitly' (Hayward 2000a: 97). So, for example, in 'National Cinemas and the Body Politic', she interrogates the idea of nation, not in order to challenge its relevance but to reveal it as a cultural construction bound up with other patriarchal constructs – notably those of self and other. Her mapping of the nation on to the psychoanalytic concept of the subject also reveals the links between nationhood and the gendered subject – the sexed body – and even more specifically with the maternal body, as we shall see later in this chapter.

Hayward's discussion of the national and the maternal is framed in the context of a debate around national cinemas, in which she urges the need to look beyond dominant images and discourses mobilized in the construction of the national to bodies that are often excluded from such discourse (and thus from representation and articulation as subjects). In the context of a contemporary French society where universalist Republican values are arguably being tested to their limits, such bodies that articulate their difference – postcolonial bodies, queer bodies, disabled bodies, elderly bodies, child bodies – 'trouble' the illusory construction of nation as a unified entity. However, rather than reinforcing a binary structure in which these bodies are other to the nation's self, Hayward prefers to conceive of the nation in terms of Grewal and Kaplan's notion of 'scattered hegemonies' (Grewal and Kaplan 1994; Hayward 2000a: 106). This term, Hayward argues, is useful because it enables us to think in terms of difference rather than otherness, allowing for relations between groupings ('voices/hegemonies/ideologies') which may potentially overlap, but which are also limited in number. And she goes on to show that cinema is a powerful tool in revealing these scattered hegemonies, 'exposing in just this way, the subject-nation's masquerade as an idealized image or unified subject' (Hayward 2000a: 106).

One of the key ways in which this masquerade of the unified nation-subject is achieved is through the essentializing images of nation as woman, and more particularly as mother. As Hayward has put it in another of her essays on national cinemas: 'We fight and die for the mother nation; when we leave we return to our mother-nation; the colonized refer to the colonizing country as mother-country. When "she" is invaded by the enemy, she is "raped"' (Hayward 2000b: 97). We begin to see, then, how closely the national and the maternal are imbricated, as well as the potential impact that this figurative relationship has on women's bodies and on cultural constructions of motherhood, as Hayward goes on to consider, following Judith Butler:

> If as Judith Butler explains (1993), the only time that a woman's body 'matters' (counts as matter) is when she is the reproducer of life (as mother) then we can perceive why nations valorize the female body in distinct discourses that represent her as reproducer of the nation. (Hayward 2000a: 112)

This is never more true than in times of conflict, or of rebuilding the nation post-conflict, when images of the nurturing female body are used as rallying points. However, as Hayward also argues, such conflation of body and nation also conversely leads to the female body – the reproductive body – becoming the site of conflict itself, as can be seen from the use of rape as a systematic tactic of genocide in the Balkan conflicts, in Rwanda and currently in the Democratic Republic of Congo, Sudan and numerous other conflicts. It is clear, then, that this relationship is more than just discursive: it has very real consequences for women as actions prosecuted in the name of nationalist agendas continue to materially affect their bodies, most particularly as sexual and reproductive bodies.

At the end of 'National Cinemas and the Body Politic', Hayward sets a challenge for the reader to ponder the role of cinema that enables the sexed female body – straitjacketed by national discourses into an uncomfortable and precarious transvestite masquerade – to emerge in multiple and scattered forms, crossing (transgressing) national, sexual and gender boundaries to threaten the unity of the nation-subject (Hayward 2000a: 112). In this chapter, I attempt to take up this challenge by considering how a reframing of cultural constructions of the maternal body in particular might also pose a challenge to the unified nation-subject, especially if this entails a questioning of the ties that link motherhood and nation.

Philippe Claudel's 2008 film *Il y a longtemps que je t'aime/I've Loved You So Long* also explores the links between the maternal and the national, through a foregrounding of both maternal relationships and of national and transnational identities within the family. Following her release from prison, Juliette (Kristin Scott Thomas) comes to stay with her younger sister, Léa (Elsa Zylberstein), and Léa's family. The film follows the relationship between the two sisters as they come to know each other again. We gradually learn more about Juliette – including the fact that she had served her sentence for killing her six-year-old son – as we follow her tentative reintegration into society, through conversations principally with her sister but also with her parole officer, Capitaine Fauré (Frédéric Pierrot), her social worker, prospective employers and with one of Léa's colleagues, Michel (Laurent Grévill). The reasons for her actions are only explained fully at the end of the film. Claudel's film sets this personal trauma within the family context, but also against a background of traumatic experiences resulting from international conflicts, all of which are in some way bound up here with motherhood.

There are three sets of maternal relationships at the heart of the film: the first is that of Juliette and Pierre; the second is that of Léa and her adopted daughters; and the third is that of Juliette and Léa with their own mother. Fathers are also present in the film, but they are far from traditional paternal figures of authority: Léa's husband Luc is pushed to one side by the arrival of Juliette, whom he resents; Luc's father, 'Papy Paul', is a benign, childlike and silent presence, unable to speak after a stroke; Juliette's ex-husband is only ever mentioned in relation to their divorce or her trial; Capitaine Fauré's wife and child live far away after their divorce, and his loneliness eventually drives him to commit suicide. This insistent sidelining, combined with the narrative focus on the two sisters, places a strong emphasis on the maternal relationship.

Another way in which the maternal relationship is privileged is how the film features motherhood, in many varieties and at many stages: from pregnancy and birth through to adult woman caring for her elderly mother; from the consequences of infanticide to international adoption; from loving sacrifice to complete rejection. And these relationships are framed within an understanding of the family that exceeds the context of the national, whether that be through inter-marriage, adoption, or enforced or voluntary relocation. So, for example, Juliette and her sister Léa are the daughters of a French father (now dead) and an English mother (Claire Johnston). Léa's husband Luc (Serge Hazanavicius), born and bred in Lorraine – a region with a long history of border disputes – is the son of a Polish father, Papy Paul/Grandpa Paul (Jean-Claude Arnaud) and a Russian mother who is now dead. Léa and Luc have themselves adopted two young Vietnamese girls: Clélis, or P'tit Lys as she is known (Lise Ségur), and Emélia (Lily-Rose). This 'melting pot' theme also extends to the secondary characters: Léa and Luc's friends Samir and Kaisha are Iraqi refugees now settled in France.

This, then, could perhaps be read as a family of 'scattered hegemonies', a family characterized and ultimately united by their respective differences rather than marginalized by their apparent otherness.[1] The fact that national identity is brought into play within such a firmly domestic context, where the effects of a fifteen-year-old trauma on Juliette and her family are traced demonstrates how closely intertwined family and nation can be. The question then becomes, does this film in fact offer a model of integration and assimiliation along patriarchal and republican lines which presents the family (and the nation) as a unified subject; or does the emphasis placed on the maternal role within this transnational context rather open up to another possible way of reading the family/nation? Over a dinner of quiche Lorraine, Léa explains the various national origins of her family to Juliette soon after her arrival, jokily describing them as '*une vraie famille Benetton*'. Léa's gently self-mocking reference to the Benetton 'United Colours' slogan places an emphasis on the transnational family accommodating difference across three generations, almost from the beginning of the film. However, it also implicitly at least raises the question of commodification and even exploitation: accusations that were levelled against the notorious Benetton advertisements created by Oliviero Toscani, of deploying deliberately controversial images of suffering and conflict in the service of selling luxury clothing to middle-class westerners (Silvana da Rosa 2001: 61). Léa's metaphor appears particularly loaded, then, given the association of international adoption with similar fears of commodification and exploitation of developing countries by western consumers (Brysk 2004).

As the above discussion of Hayward's work in this area shows, the maternal signifier is a shifting one with respect to the concept of nation: one moment, the mother is the nation, for whom her sons and daughters must sacrifice themselves; the next she is the other against whom the nation-subject defines himself. In neither case is she the subject; rather, as Hayward explains, this patriarchal 'valorization' of the maternal body as a metaphor for the nation 'does not release [the woman] from her imprisonment within the Imaginary' (Hayward 2000: 112). Applying a Lacanian understanding of the nation as a subject that needs to forge for itself the illusion of a unified identity, the maternal body exists only in the Imaginary realm as the means by which the nation-subject comes to (mis)recognize itself as unified. She is thus stuck in the position of the 'other', imprisoned in her maternal state (the one which matters) from which she can break free only by assuming a precarious, transvestite identity through which she may (in Lacanian terms) access the Symbolic.

In this scheme of things, then, motherhood – along with femininity – remains tied to certain myths, well-worn clichés that can be seen to emerge in cinema particularly at times when the nation-subject is under threat. One example cited by Hayward is *Le Voile bleu/The Blue Veil* (Stelli 1942), which stars Gaby Morlay as a mother whose child has died, and who then gives her service to the nation as a nanny, reliving her trauma every time she leaves one family to move on to another (Hayward 2000b: 98). Such images continue to propagate a dominant cultural understanding of the maternal relation as one of self-abnegation, where the mother's subjectivity is subordinated to that of her child.[2] However, in post-war France too, natalist and family policies were foregrounded, so that motherhood continued to be seen as a primary role for women (see, for example, Badinter 2001 and 2010; Cova 1997; Duchen 1994: 96–127 for an analysis of the shifting discourses on motherhood). Images of good and evil have dominated cultural representations of motherhood: as Kaplan puts it, the Ideal 'angel' mother is pitted against her evil 'witch' opposite (Kaplan 1992: 9).

These cultural constructions of motherhood are arguably predicated on a psychoanalytic model of the maternal relation, which is one of symbiotic fusion followed by (painful) rupture. In such a model, the mother is an ambivalent figure: our first love object but also our first taste of difference, and thus a source of anxiety. Within such a framework, then, the relation to the other must always be problematic – a potential source of anxiety or threat – since it is based on the initial recognition of difference experienced as a traumatic moment. *Il y a longtemps que je t'aime* offers a different perspective on this relationship by placing the emphasis on mothers and their experience of the maternal relation rather than privileging the viewpoint of the grown-up child-subject – arguably the most common narrative perspective. Indeed, as E. Ann Kaplan points out, most scholarly discourses respond to this 'othering' of the mother: 'Few scholars had been interested in understanding her positioning or her social role from *inside* the mother's discourse' (Kaplan 1992: 3). And, as she goes on to point out 'the discovery of subjectivity … with Freud and his theory of the unconscious … did not lead to discussion of the *mother's* subjectivity; rather it produced the mother as the one through whom "I", the child, *become* a subject' (Kaplan 1992: 8). While representations of maternal subjectivity may now be more common than when Kaplan was writing, they are still far from frequent, and in focusing on mothers as subjects in their own right, *Il y a longtemps* is part of a rather exclusive group.[3] What makes *Il y a longtemps* a particularly interesting case is the range of experiences of motherhood within which Juliette's trauma is contextualized. The fact that the two central mothers are also sisters, coming to terms with their own relationship after fifteen years of separation following the traumatic events that led to Juliette's imprisonment, offers a further dimension of female solidarity within which to contextualize the maternal relations – a dimension that arguably further displaces the paternal as Léa's husband Luc is pushed to one side to make room for the prodigal sister's return. And while *Il y a longtemps* can be seen to offer a nod of acknowledgement to the traditional division of maternal representations into 'good' and 'bad' mothers through the figures of Léa and Juliette (and indeed their own mother), its complex characterization and focus on the maternal perspective ensure that it does not fall into stereotypical binaries.

Maternal trauma: The mother who matters

Juliette is both mother and not mother, since her son is dead. Since we do not know of his existence until approximately one-third of the way into the film, we must also construct her as a mother retrospectively. Our view is complicated by the fact that we learn simultaneously that she was a mother and that she has killed her son, when she is tackled directly about her crime by a prospective employer. Having guessed her crime by the length of her sentence, he demands to know whom she had killed. She eventually admits: 'My son. My six-year-old son.' Thus it emerges that Juliette has violently transgressed the notion of the maternal body as the one that matters. Indeed, her resulting punishment has been like an effacement of her body and her own existence, hidden away from society in her cell (from which, we later learn, she was allowed only limited release in order to pace within a walled courtyard), known by her fellow-prisoners as *'l'absente'*, divorced by her husband whom she has not seen since her trial, and disowned by her parents who also forbade Léa any contact with her sister. However, Juliette's punishment is not only externally imposed from the state and her family. The end of the film (though we have guessed before this point) reveals that Juliette's crime was in fact an act of euthanasia performed by a doctor-mother on her child who was suffering from a degenerative disease which, we glean, she had passed on to him.

Her punishment is thus also self-imposed through her refusal to speak – to explain her act – and through her own self-effacement. The woman who emerges from prison is withdrawn almost to the point of hostility, dressed in brown and grey clothes whose shapelessness disguises and hides the body beneath them, and whose face – bare of make-up – reflects the grey tones of her surroundings in the anonymous airport arrivals lounge. In terms introduced by Butler and applied to French cinema by Hayward, this is a woman who is determined not to 'matter'. Juliette deliberately withdraws herself from the world around her as the recurring images emphasizing her isolation demonstrate. These shots, which linger on her sitting and smoking, often in her room, are characterized by a slow zoom forward, highlighting her entrapment. This is further emphasized by the *mise-en-scène* (windows and doors are reminiscent of prison bars; staircase and landing filmed like a prison gallery). Juliette may be free from jail, but she is far from free of her act.

Throughout almost the entire film, Juliette is unable to speak about her act or the reasons for it – paradoxically, it is as if the act of murder has reversed the act of giving birth to her son, and she now carries Pierre inside her. In psychoanalytic terms, it is the recreation of the symbiotic bond between mother and son that leaves her, as well as him, in the realm of the Real (death).[4] This helps to explain why she is unable to speak of her act. The Real has no language, so to rationalize her act in words would entail a return to the Symbolic realm and a betrayal of her dead son – a final severing of the umbilical bond. When Juliette finally speaks of the act to Léa, she describes how she injected her son and then lay down with him until the morning, emphasizing physical proximity and that: 'After that, nothing else mattered. I wanted to go to prison.' As she speaks these words, she holds the photo of Pierre that she keeps under her pillow along with the poem he wrote her on the back of the medical analysis form. The picture shows a close up of a blond boy with large, dark eyes looking away from the camera with a half-smile on his face. Emma Wilson, discussing another film that features a large-eyed dead child, *Trois couleurs: Bleu/Three Colours: Blue* (Kieslowski 1993), emphasizes that: 'Cinema is a mourning art, as Bazin, Barthes and others remind us' (Wilson 2003: 26). Here, then, we see the image of Pierre – withheld until the final moments of the film – making present the boy whose absence lies at the heart of the film. However, as we know, this presence – also the presence of the cinematic image – is not real, but corresponds rather to a misrecognition. Thus this is a presence always already marked by absence: in keeping the photo, Juliette keeps an object that retains a direct link to her son, but at the same time this object can only remind her of his absence, the lack that now defines her – which, as we have seen, she has come to paradoxically embody. It is striking that Pierre is not even named until close to the end of the film when Juliette utters his name to Léa. Up to that point, he has been referred to directly only twice and both times as her child and in reference to his killing (Luc: 'She killed her kid'; and Juliette, in response to a direct question asking whom she killed: 'My son. My six-year-old son.')

If these signs of Pierre do not appear until almost the end of the film, there are other ways in which the missing child is evoked, most obviously through Léa and Luc's adopted daughters, especially P'tit Lys, who is only a little older than Pierre was when he died. In some ways the exact opposite of this little blond boy, P'tit Lys clearly provokes Juliette's ambivalence, as she awakens memories with her very presence, her incessant yet innocent questioning always threatening to dismantle the flimsy web of lies her parents and aunt have concocted to explain the sudden arrival in their life of 'Tata Juliette' (she has been 'travelling'). If, on one level, she represents Pierre, P'tit Lys also stands in for Léa, asking Juliette to recall her own childhood with questions about her mother when she was young, and through their piano sessions, where Juliette teaches her to play a song she and Léa played as children, the nursery rhyme that gives the film its title and that insists on the bonds of memory: 'I've loved you so long, I'll never forget you.'

Léa's is the other childhood presence that haunts Juliette. For Juliette, caught between the refusal of the present – an inability to 'move on' that for her entails giving up her son – and a fear of the void of a post-prison existence, the memory of her sister as a child is what brought her back, as she tells Michel: 'It's for that little girl that I decided to come back.'

The sisters' past recurs throughout the film in their own conversations, too, which shuttle back and forth between the pre-trauma past and the present. It is in evoking these childhood memories that the sisters begin to re-establish their own bond – a bond that initially seems fragile and stretched beyond repair. This fragility is demonstrated when Léa becomes upset after she is unable to remember their regular visits to a Rouen tearoom. For her, the memories represent not just a nostalgia for a pre-trauma past, but also the possibility of a future relationship with a sister she had thought lost, and thus of understanding why Juliette killed her son.

Juliette's trauma – as well as her maternal bond – is figured as intensely personal and private. Her apparently monstrous act has left her without purpose: as a mother without a child, she no longer matters. This is emphasized still further by the fact that she can no longer practise as a doctor. However, as the film progresses, we witness Juliette's gradual rehabilitation through her tentative connection with others: Léa, P'tit Lys and Michel. So, while the revelation of Pierre at the end of the film through his photographic image, his poem and her telling of his story can in some ways be seen as the breaking of the bond that binds Juliette to her son, it is also the means by which he emerges – even as a memory – into the world, thus allowing Juliette to finally accept the possibility of difference in the form of other people.

Postcolonial motherhood: Scattered hegemonies

While Juliette's trauma and its impact on her family are clearly the focus of the film, this is contextualized against a wider background of traumatic experience: all of the major characters are marked by some trauma in their past, or in their family history. Trauma is portrayed here in terms of its impact on individuals and those surrounding them in terms of everyday experience within the domestic sphere: thus the Iraq war, post-World War II mass migrations and Vietnamese postcolonial history are alluded to in terms of their (often indirect and delayed) impact on individuals and families. So Samir and Kaisha, we come to understand, are refugees who are now cut off from their family as a result of the Iraq war. We are told that Luc's parents came to France (indeed to Lorraine) from Poland just after the war – again, we do not know why, but they were doubtless just two out of countless refugees in a war-torn Europe.

Nor do we learn the circumstances in which Clélis or Emélia's parents gave them up for adoption, though their family context is clearly the decades of conflict that continued in Vietnam after French colonial withdrawal. By considering the effects of such events at an individual level – thus drawing parallels with private traumas such as the death of Michel's wife in a car accident many years earlier – Claudel could be accused of evacuating the political, of 'reducing' these events somehow to the micro-level of the personal. Further, by referring to them only in a rather schematic way (a photo, a dinner table discussion of family origins), he might be seen as reducing the people affected to a range of clichés. However, the fact that all of these characters are seen also to be engaged in other experiences and in a network of relationships, thus ensuring that none of them is defined by trauma or as victims, makes another reading possible. This would suggest that in humanizing the effects of trauma by showing – however briefly or suggestively – their cost at the domestic level of the family, the film offers points of possible identification between the secondary characters and Juliette, and also more importantly with the audience. The result is to break a rather introspective and potentially self-pitying focus on Juliette by forcing a recognition of the wider world. This is a wider world still perhaps defined in domestic terms, but a domestic sphere that reaches beyond borders and embraces difference. This brings us back to the concept of scattered hegemonies, which – as we have seen – offer a non-hierarchical conception of differences that may overlap and touch upon each other. In *Il y a longtemps*, different groups can be defined on the one hand through national origins, but also (and perhaps more pertinently) through shared experience (as far as this is possible) of traumatic events. And it is these experiences that ultimately provide the characters with the potential for common understanding. Here, then, we see maternal relations that are framed on the one hand at the domestic level of the family, and on the other within a global context, arguably bypassing the national.

This is especially true of Léa's family which, as we have seen, she characterizes as '*une vraie famille Benetton*', highlighting the multinational origins of its members: both she and Luc are of mixed parentage, while their children have been adopted from Vietnam. While transnational migration is sometimes characterized as yet another example of the way western capitalism exploits the resources of developing countries, seen in the wider context of child migration, the picture appears more complex. As Alison Brysk (2004: 172) points out, adoption is the only form of migration where the rights of children are taken into consideration, and which entails a transfer of nationality, thus ensuring that the child then 'belongs' to the country of the adoptive parents. This is not, as she goes on to explain, necessarily the case for children born of migrant parents, or for children left behind by migrant parents.

Transnational adoption has had an impact on the cultural institution of the family, leading to the globalization of the 'most private and local social unit' (Brysk 2004: 167). The fact that the majority of adopted children are not orphans, but have at least one living parent who is often forced to give them up due to economic hardship and 'social pressure' (Brysk 2004: 164), further complicates this notion of the global family. In *Il y a longtemps*, this is the case for one of the two children: Léa declares to Juliette that she and Luc have carefully documented P'tit Lys's origins, including the contact details for her mother, in case she should want to meet her at some point in the future, though they were not able to do the same for Emélia, for whom no information could be found. It is also perhaps worth mentioning the gender bias that exists in inter-country adoption: as in Claudel's film, the majority of adopted children are girls, responding to a 'patrimonial logic whereby females' identity is mutable and their citizenship correspondingly disposable' (Brysk 2004: 165).

In the context of this discussion, there is one final point to be made regarding the power relations that structure transnational adoption. According to Altstein and Simon, cited by Brysk: 'Reproductive patterns in receiving countries have led to a shift in focus "from parentless children to childless couples"' (Brysk 2004: 165). However, rather than a simple match of a surplus on the one hand responding to a lack on the other, this shift has arguably led to an increased commodification of 'parentless' children – many of whom, as we have seen, are not in fact parentless but are given up for adoption by parents in dire need.

Just as 'orphans' put up for adoption are often not in fact parentless, in *Il y a longtemps* neither are Léa and Luc an infertile, childless couple. It is Léa's refusal of pregnancy and childbirth that pushes them to adopt: she declares to Juliette that she 'did not want to carry a child in her belly'. When Juliette – taken aback – responds that this is a reaction to her own actions, Léa's only response is to say that she has never thought about why. Since Léa is apparently ignorant of Pierre's genetic illness until the end of the film, it is intriguing that her rejection is specifically of biological motherhood, and emphatically not of the cultural maternal role. And yet it is against this role that Juliette has most dramatically transgressed. The question then becomes not only why Léa has refused pregnancy, but also why she has decided to adopt from abroad, and specifically from Vietnam. The answer may lie – at least partially – in one aspect of transnational adoption and power relations between the countries involved that Brysk does not explicitly discuss: the history of colonialism which, as with other forms of migration, clearly influences the flows of inter-country adoption.

In France, Vietnam is now the fifth most popular country for international adoptions (2008 saw 284 Vietnamese children adopted in France out of a total of 3271 international adoptions) and, with the exception of Haiti which gained independence in the early 19th century, has the highest adoption rate of all France's former colonies.[5] If the issue of international adoption can be seen as a rather vexed one in terms of the potential reification of children, then this is even more true within this postcolonial context. Indeed, the adoptive relation is one that was made explicit in French colonial discourse on Indochina, as Nicola Cooper's discussion of Régis Wargnier's *Indochine/Indochina* (1993) makes clear. While 'the adoptive and protective mother', played by Deneuve, embodies colonial France, 'Camille

[Linh Dan Pham], the adopted daughter, represents Indochina, *la fille adoptée de la France* [original emphasis]: an indigenous orphan, she is the subject of narration and the object of metropolitan desire' (Cooper 2001: 208).

While Claudel's film has no scenes set in Vietnam, and does not refer directly to the decolonization, the presence of the two children recalls the former link between the two countries, and a continued 'metropolitan desire' for the exotic East, here again embodied as orphan girls and expressed through Léa's longing descriptions of their visits to Vietnam. Yet this desire is not represented in a fetishistic way. The house contains no obvious mementos of their trips to Vietnam, and the camera does not specifically dwell on the children. It is Léa herself who – with the jokey reference to Benetton – shows her awareness of the dangers of commodification. P'tit Lys functions as a catalyst for Juliette's reintegration, and especially with regard to the relationship between the two sisters, yet she is also a subject in her own right, referring to her own history by asking Juliette whether she knew her when she was little, when her parents got her from Vietnam, and showing her own desires and determination by firmly stating her opinions and by sticking with her piano lessons until she can eventually play the song with both hands – which, significantly, she does alone, turning back to the piano with a determined shrug when her 'audience' is called away.

In revealing a range of maternal relations which go beyond the national context, then, Claudel's film not only depicts what Hayward has termed the 'differently desiring' scattered hegemonies (2000a: 106) within the nation-family; it could also be said to 'drop the mask' of the nation's simulacrum as unified subject. This is how, even with its focus on such an intensely personal trauma of one mother, this film also demands our engagement with a world beyond the self.

Notes

1. I am indebted to Will Higbee for his insightful comments on this point, and on drafts of this chapter.
2. In Vichy France this was taken to an extreme under its severe anti-abortion laws, which deemed that the foetus should be saved in preference to the mother, as we see for example in Clouzot's 1943 film, *Le Corbeau/The Raven*.
3. Examples of other contemporary French films which focus on mothers include *Indochine* (Wargnier 1993), *Trois couleurs: Bleu/Three Colours: Blue* (Kieslowski 1993), *Y aura-t-il de la neige à Noël/Will It Snow for Christmas?* (Veysset 1996) and *Martha ... Martha ...* (Veysset 2001).
4. A similar bond exists in Claudel's novel *La Petite fille de Monsieur Linh* (2005). Claudel explores the trauma of Vietnamese refugees arriving in France via the character of Monsieur Linh, who refuses to be separated even for an instant from his 'granddaughter', whom he rescued from the rice paddy where her parents were killed in a bombing raid. The end of the novel reveals what we have come to suspect from the descriptions of the 'child's' extreme docility: that it was his granddaughter and not her doll who lay decapitated in the field, and it is her doll that he has so carefully looked after throughout his journey to France. And just as Juliette is unable to speak about the events

surrounding Pierre's death, Monsieur Linh is trapped in a kind of silence: he is unable to speak French, but neither can he communicate with the fellow refugees who share his dormitory and who mock him for his senility and weakness.

5. Interestingly, according to Brysk, many Islamic countries do not allow adoption 'because Islam states that children's identity and inheritance belong to their biological families and cannot be transferred to another family' (Brysk 2004: 163). This suggests that, even where it is permitted, attitudes may mean that it is more restricted than in non-Islamic countries, and could explain why France's North African former colonies do not feature on the list. The most popular countries in descending order in 2008 were Haiti, Russia, Ethiopia and Colombia, while the only other former French colonies to feature in the top ten countries were Mali and Côte d'Ivoire. For further information on international adoption in France, see the Ambafrance website: <www.diplomatie.gouv.fr/fr/IMG/pdf/conditions_pays_2009.pdf> (accessed 7 August 2009); <www.diplomatie.gouv.fr/fr/actions-france_830/adoption-internationale_2605/statistiques_5424/statistiques-2008_70404.html> (accessed 7 August 2009).

Chapter 12

Phil Powrie: French Film Studies as a Heterotopic Field

Ann Davies

In writing this chapter, I am perhaps committing a transgression on one level, since I come from a background of research into not French but rather Spanish cinema. We like to assume that our academic field, whatever it be, will welcome all comers – but not necessarily to critique, and not necessarily to assume the same authority as those who work in the field on a daily basis. French cinema has by now become an established field of academic study that has survived in part, like any academic field, in being able to adopt and adapt new approaches and insights; however, the definition of French cinema as a distinct field of study necessarily carries with it the implication of limiting parameters – that is, after all, part of the point of such a definition. I mention this not so much to draw attention to my own status, or indeed to apologize for it, as to claim that the goal of this chapter is to embrace an approach that French film scholar Phil Powrie has himself adopted in his work on French film. He has not only been a pioneer in the field but a pioneer in the approach that French film, far from being a hermetically sealed entity, is a thing of contradiction, ragged at the edges and with holes at its heart, but a substantial structure for all that. Powrie has assisted materially in mapping out the terrain of French cinema through various monographs and edited collections (Powrie 1997, 1999, 2006c; Powrie and Reader 2002) as well as being a founder of the journal *Studies in French Cinema*. To that extent, his scholarship has had a consolidating impulse within the field. But Powrie's work on French cinema also demonstrates a fascination not only with concepts of outside and inside within French films but the passage between the two, which in turn undermines the binary of inside and outside as a whole. This fascination encompasses his work on Besson and Beineix and, more recently, the actor Pierre Batcheff; the work on film adaptations of Carmen. To some extent, it also includes his interest in the relationship between music and film, given music's interstitial status in film – there but often not there, a noise of which the screen characters can only be aware if it is diegetic. Thus his work explores not only the centre but the peripheries of French film; furthermore, it establishes through the exploration of the passage between supposed binaries a trace that applies to the in and out of French cinema and its academic study. I will argue that this body of work, notwithstanding Powrie's unwillingness to be hemmed in by strict parameters, is of a piece, demonstrating that French cinema is something to be seen from both within *and* without, and that the passage between this in and out of French cinema is itself of some significance. I would like to claim here that the notion of the passage enables the outside to come *into* the inside and see the inside from both within and without, much as I aim to do here from my standpoint as a Hispanic film scholar. Thus, in writing this chapter, I hope I am carrying out such an act of passage.

This act, I would argue, is a heterotopic one. The Foucauldian notion of the heterotopia has been familiar to scholars for some time now, deriving both from Michel Foucault's essay 'Of Other Spaces' (Foucault 1986) and also his introduction to *The Order of Things* (Foucault 1994). Foucault suggests a version of the heterotopia that creates 'a space of illusion that exposes every real space, all the sites inside of which human life is partitioned, as still more illusory', or alternatively, 'a space that is other, another real space, as perfect, as meticulous, as well arranged as ours is messy, ill constructed, and jumbled' (Foucault 1986). French cinema studies encompasses all these ideas – it is an illusion of order that nonetheless recognizes the very real chaos from which derives an idealistic impulse to classification and order. Much of what Foucault says in both 'Des espaces autres' and *The Order of Things* can apply to the vexed question of a national cinema, a field that can contain contradictory definitions to the extent that it might even, taken to an extreme, resemble Borges' strange classification scheme that Foucault cites in *The Order of Things* (1994: xv) – as Foucault says: 'Each of these strange categories can be assigned a precise meaning and a demonstrable content.' And he goes on to say: 'We are all familiar with the disconcerting effect of the proximity of extremes, or, quite simply, with the sudden vicinity of things that have no relation to each other; the mere act of enumeration that heaps them all together has a power of enchantment all its own' (1994: xvi).

The field of French cinema (as with other national cinemas) does not immediately resemble the apparently illogical jumble of categories in Borges' list, but we should not forget that part of what is being celebrated in this collection of essays is an act of naming and also of enumeration, the conceptualization of French cinema and the decision about what belongs under this umbrella. Perhaps we can perceive a category such as French cinema to have the potential to be classified in ways that seem strange beyond the 'normal' classification processes; and to recognize this is to appreciate the potential of an academic field to shift its parameters to include concepts that hitherto fell outside it. Conceivably, anything might be named and added. Powrie's work plays with this concept of the inclusion of the illogical celebrated by Borges and Foucault, the borderline moment of decision wherein we decide whether a filmic element makes that film clearly French or whether it does not fit.

French cinema as an ideal field might be compared with Foucault's notion of the utopia (which itself stands in contrast to the heterotopia), the utopia offering 'consolation: although they have no real locality there is nevertheless a fantastic, untroubled region in which they are able to unfold'. If the utopia and the heterotopia stand in contrast, nonetheless the two coexist in the desired ideal of an academic field that is clearly defined and bounded. But they also existence in apparent opposition in that it becomes impossible 'to name this *and* that, because they [heterotopias] shatter or tangle common names, because they destroy … that less apparent syntax which causes words and things (next to and opposite one another) to "hold together"' (Foucault 1994: xviii). Here we come to the perennial difficulty experienced by scholars of national cinemas as to precisely what it is they are studying, what falls within the parameters of the field and what does not. There is no neat, systematic way of defining what a French film is: does it include only those films that deal with French matters, can it include co-productions, and so on? I doubt that any scholar by now wishes to realize the ideal by laying down in fixity, once and for all, what French cinema is: French cinema is heterotopic because it includes within it things that contradict each other but utopian in that the impulse to name it 'French cinema' goes against the clashes and contradictions that the heterotopia propounds. It is thus both utopian and heterotopic, both being 'spaces, as it were, which are linked with all the others, which however contradict all the other sites' (Foucault 2000: 178). As Benjamin Gennochio says:

> Acting as points of a kind of mediatory enablement rather than fencing off any discontinuous ground, Foucault's descriptions suggest that we scrutinize and question the implications and possibilities of the slips, exceptions, oddities lurking at the very limits of the system that defines for us what is thinkable, sayable, knowable. The heterotopia is thus more of an idea about space than any actual place. It is an idea that insists that the ordering of spatial systems is subjective and arbitrary in that we know nothing of the initial totality that it must presuppose. It is an idea which consequently produces/theorizes space as transient, contestory, plagued by lapses and ruptured sites. (Gennochio 1995: 43)

Gennochio observes that many theorists of social space have drawn on and developed Foucault's heterotopia 'to reveal the possibility of socially constructed counter-sites embodying a form of "resistance" to our increasingly surveyed, segregated and simulated socio-spatial order' (1995: 36). But Gennochio argues that 'in any attempt to mobilize the category of an outside or absolutely differentiated space, it follows logically that the simple naming or theoretical recognition of that difference always to some degree flattens or precludes, by definition, the very possibility of its arrival as such' (1995: 39). So, he states rhetorically, 'what cannot be designated a heterotopia?' (1995: 39). But I believe that the notion of the passage between spaces that are not only differentiated but opposed may help overcome this problem. French cinema as a field is not stable: there is always the potential for new films and new theorizations to disrupt what has been established so far. French film scholars work with this ever-present possibility, so that the simple awareness of it precludes Gennochio's flattening process. But of course, the possibility can be ignored or denied. Powrie's work, however, draws explicit attention to the oscillation between utopia and heterotopia, between inside and outside – indeed, his work celebrates it.

Powrie has done much to establish a core around French cinema with his books on French cinema of the 1980s and 1990s (Powrie 1997, 1999), his edited collection for Wallflower's 24 Frames series (Powrie 2006c) and the co-authored student's guide to the field (Powrie and Reader 2002). He has also done the requisite auteur study, though few might have chosen such a maverick subject as Jean-Jacques Beineix (Powrie 2001a, 2001b). Yet here too there are references to a spaces that resemble heterotopias, such as the anamorphs Powrie identifies as the root of Beineix's central characters, 'the empty hub around which revolve the vortices of images and words in play, something like a fifth of November sparkler describing runic figures in the dark night of the interpretative gesture' (Powrie 2001a: 204). In the end,

'Beineix's protagonists are merely locations' (2001a: 205). The sense of emptiness and lack is picked up once more in Powrie and Susan Hayward's introduction to their edited collection on Besson, in which they describe excess as one element of Besson's style, and say that this excess 'is one of violence and points to a lack, to an emptiness of meaning ... the characters ... are empty and ahistorical' (Hayward and Powrie 2006: 1).

Powrie furthermore argues that, of all the world cinemas, the French one matters most in contesting the domination of Hollywood because France produces the most European films, because of the pivotal role of France in cinema history, and because of the importance of cinema in the specificity of French culture (Powrie 2006c: 1). Here he insists on French cinema studies as a field, and a core one, distinct from other cinemas and specific to France. Yet on the very next page he raises the issue of stars as a problematic way of defining what French cinema is (2006c: 2–3), and from his point of view there is a clear sense that a national cinema can look different from the inside and from the outside, as illustrated by the example of Jean-Paul Belmondo, known primarily for his Godard films internationally, but for police comedies within France itself (2006c: 3). These points suggest the simultaneous impulse in Powrie's work to lay the foundations of the field of French cinema studies and to chip away at the foundations he himself has helped to lay.

This chapter takes three specific examples in which Powrie demonstrates the heterotopian nature of French film. In each example, we find this heterotopia embodied and thus made manifest on screen: the body, like the French film in which it participates, brings to the fore the porosity of bodily borders as well as cinematic ones. Consider, for example, Powrie's most recent work on the French film actor Pierre Batcheff, notable in particular for his involvement in Surrealist cinema. In his co-written article with Eric Rebillard, Powrie posits Batcheff as a Surrealist star, and the authors pursue the elusive nature of the actor as both a pin-up and as an active participant in avant-garde cinema. Batcheff was an early example of a French film star: the article offers film stills and illustrations from magazines that depict him as the sensual leading man, an early object of desire. But the star himself took pains to create some distance from the commercial roles he undertook and sought actively for a more 'authentic' essence in his work. Powrie and Rebillard suggest that Batcheff's detachment from his commercial roles can also be seen in his vacant look – looking elsewhere, not here (Powrie and Rebillard 2008: 167). Batcheff, they argue, acts almost as an empty space: 'He is there without being there; or, rather he is *there*, somewhere else, rather than being *here*; Batcheff is an absent presence' (Powrie and Rebillard 2008: 163). They make particular play with Batcheff's Russian origins, often mentioned in the press of the time, and argue that 'Oriental' associations may have been highlighted too, given the link in the popular imagination of the time between Russia and China: they state that French attitudes to Russia incorporated a notion of Russians as 'the savage other' (2008: 164). They further comment that 'it is also likely that Batcheff would have been a vehicle for the working out of fantasies and fears relating to the frontiers of "North Europeanness"' (2008: 166). Thus Batcheff combined elements of Russia, China and also Arabia, given the links to Rudolph Valentino and his Arabic roles.

While Powrie and Rebillard define Batcheff as a Surrealist star and emphasize the possibility that such a notion is a contradiction in terms, we could arguably also call him a heterotopic star in that Batcheff embodies many contradictory characteristics, including being both French and yet not French, situated squarely within the French cinema industry and yet indicating a space both inside and outside of it. It could also be argued that Batcheff demonstrates how French cinema plays with the border between commercial and art cinema, and enables a passage between the two. The authors argue that 'doublings and splittings inform Batcheff's star persona: fatalist and enterprising; sensitive and savage; French and Russian; masculine and feminine. These criss-cross and form the texture of Batcheff's performance' (Powrie and Rebillard 2008: 175). But they also stress that we should not simply consider this in terms of binaries; rather, these concepts form a 'fluid network' that can be described as 'hysterical convulsions' (2008: 175). The concepts of the network and the hysterical convulsion suggest both the movement and the confusion between the inside and outside of French cinema. It is apt, then, that the authors describe this in terms of dislocation, as a star out of place:

> his mysterious otherness, the sign of a being-other, of a being-elsewhere, cryptic and dislocated. Batcheff has always already vacated the location in which he acts; he is, as we suggested earlier, an absent presence, liminally there, but fundamentally elsewhere, figured by his deathly immobility and his deflected gaze, the looking away or off. In that sense he can never be graspable or recoverable. (2008: 170–71)

While this impossibility of recovery lying within Batcheff's persona might coincide with the 'failure to arrive' that Gennochio observed within the heterotopia, as cited above, Batcheff offers the embodiment of an oscillation between inside and out, here and there, commercial and art house, French and not French, thus a passageway on multiple levels. This sense of passage is further enhanced by Batcheff's association with director Luis Buñuel. Of all directors, Buñuel is one of the hardest to place in terms of a national cinema: though Spanish, he nonetheless made many films outside of Spain, and arguably his greatest classics – including those starring Batcheff – were made in France. Many of his Spanish-language films were made in exile in Mexico, while his first Spanish film for many years, *Viridiana* (1961), made for an uncomfortable homecoming, since the film – sponsored by the Spanish government – was feted at Cannes but subsequently banned by the Vatican, to the discomfort of the Catholically minded Franco regime in power in Spain at the time. Buñuel, like Batcheff, is an infiltrator into French cinema who deliberately questioned the boundaries of the cinema he was making. But it is Batcheff who renders the porosity of national boundaries visible: he embodies it.

If Batcheff acts as a nexus of inside and outside for Powrie, the latter's interest in such a nexus is even more apparent with the project he initiated that addressed film adaptations of *Carmen*. The *Carmen* story quintessentially demonstrates the difficulty of assigning nationality, since although the story purports to be about Spain and the fiery passions between its cold north and a south that is ethnically 'other', it in fact derives from France and the nineteenth century taste for bourgeois slumming in a land that was ethnically 'other' in its entirety. Thus the story speaks to French as much as Spanish concerns (and Spanish culture and film has manifested its own fascination, but also irritation at a figure foisted on it by its northern neighbours). Since cinema came into being, there have been some 90 film versions of the story at the last count: some thirteen of these (including co-productions) are French, but we also find versions made in Spain, the United States, Germany, South Africa, Venezuela, the Netherlands, Italy, and so on, as the tale of *Carmen* fits neatly with a penchant for indulging in sexual desire with low-life women that crosses national boundaries, even though it can also invoke them. Powrie pushes his exploration further in his own interest in those *Carmen* films that occupy marginal and maybe disreputable niches within film – even marginality possesses its own margin – including the films that push the sexual desire so far that they dissolve into pornography and leave artistic pretensions behind.

Powrie observes: 'Carmen ... functions ... as a model for excessive and uncontainable desire ... dystopia and utopia are mobilized together, and in doing so are constantly displaced' (Powrie et al. 2007: 17). *Carmen* acts as another form of passage between binaries, here between not only desire and fear but between self and ethnic other, more specifically a civilized France and a primitive Spain which nonetheless carries its own levels of self and other through the binary of Spaniard and Gypsy. *Carmen* is a centrifugal force, pulling self and nation to the margins and borders: 'There is no center because the center is always already at the margins, pulled there by desire for difference' (Powrie et al. 2007: 19). The fascination of the passage between France and not-France embedded in Mérimée's original *Carmen* novella and the better-known opera by Bizet has in turn given rise to a significant corpus of French and French-language films within the larger category of *Carmen* adaptations. When writing more specifically about the French *Carmen* films, Powrie observes that they suggest:

> the urge to return to an origin, superficially the Spain before Romantic tourism had made of it a slummer's paradise; not even Spain, of course, but the not-France, the anywhere other than France, what comes 'before'. Before what? If only there were a simple answer. (Powrie et al. 2007: 107–8)

Powrie concludes of the French *Carmens*:

> They ... reveal a systematic fear. It is a fear not so much of 'woman-as-enigma' ... as of what 'woman-as enigma' hides: the fear of not knowing who 'we' (the 'French') are ... Carmen is reaffirmed as the perfect postmodern icon: on the margins, on the move, erring constantly, an 'error' without origin herself, and signaling in herself the impossibility of origin, the lure of 'identity'. (Powrie et al. 2007: 153)

We have here again the passage between utopia and heterotopia, intricately imbricated with questions of national identity and the simultaneous impulse to define it and inability to place it. Like Batcheff, *Carmen* is an embodiment of the passage that links and confuses heterotopia, reflected in Powrie's fascination with entry and exit in the *mise-en-scène* and camera work of Calmettes' Carmen of 1910 (Powrie et al. 2007: 110–20), and later with the film's play between inside and outside (Powrie et al. 2007: 114).

If the investigations into *Carmen* suggest a movement across bodily borders, a similar process of in and out can be discerned in terms of the male body in French film and Powrie's interest in the abject and the cloacal. He explores the question in his discussion of French films of the 1990s (Powrie 2004), relating the abject firmly to masculinity, and tracing links between Gaspar Noé's *Seul contre tous/I Stand Alone* (1998) and Martin Scorsese's *Taxi Driver* (1976) in these terms. He notes that the ghost of scenes from *Taxi Driver* trace themselves across *Seul contre tous* in 'a kind of slippage ... fluid play, which matches the obsession with abject fluids evident in both films' (Powrie 2004: 209). It is also, of course, a fluid play between French and American cinema. Powrie sees within the film an obsession with holes, representing both the vaginal and anal, and thus the collapse of sexual difference (Powrie 2004: 211) and a collapse of boundaries into the faecal and abject (Powrie 2004: 213). In his discussion of Luc Besson's *Léon* (1994), he looks again at the masculine in terms of cloacal imagery, a reference to what is within and yet must be denied, and which facilitates in and out, rejection and expulsion. One of Powrie's purposes is to move away from the common motif of father–daughter relationships found in this film and in many places in French cinema, and towards suggestions of the homoerotic and the problematization of masculine identity (Powrie 2006a: 147). Yet there is also interest in space, particularly the contradictory meaning of the lavatory: '*Léon* establishes a shifting, hybrid space which is more intestinal than labyrinthine.' The lavatory is an abject space 'associated with violence and detritus', but also a place of purification – literally 'the place where one washes oneself' (Powrie 2006a: 152), and furthermore the place wherein homoeroticism is both disavowed and an ever-present possibility.

Given that the cloacal takes the heterotopic passage to extremes, it is perhaps no surprise that Powrie finds plenty of shiftiness about place in *Léon*. Examples are the foreign accents of Léon and Stansfield – particularly the latter, which is 'unstable, difficult to position in relation to place' (Powrie 2006a: 154); the in-betweenness of Besson (including that of national identity) noted by other critics (Powrie 2006b: 77); and Léon's open coat that signifies 'European innocence ranged against American corruption' (Powrie 2006b: 80). The film in particular offers an in and out centred on French cinema, with a French actor playing an Italian, versus a British actor playing an American, in an American film genre. The film 'is interesting ... partly for the way in which it plays with the conventions of the American gangster, pitching American identity against a vague Europeanness ... but also because it foregrounds the issue of national identity through its deconstruction and destruction of costume: the stereotypical American gangster is blown up by the dishevelled anarchic European' (Powrie 2006b: 80). Nonetheless, Besson's work is for Powrie crucial to an understanding of contemporary French society. Despite its literal eccentricity (Powrie 2006b: 75), it is 'anchored in a French cinematic tradition'. As Powrie goes on to explain, 'Besson's work is pulled between national traditions: it is French, but it is also American, so that it is not always easy to decide whether his films ...

are Americanized French cinema, or Gallicized American cinema' (Powrie 2006b: 76). Again, then, Powrie has picked out the contradictory notion of the passage on multiple levels – clean and abject, French and not French.

Thus the heterotopia of French cinema, as we have seen, can be embodied, and Powrie's work on Batcheff, Carmen and masculinity demonstrates his fascination with that embodiment. In each case, the heterotopic nature of French film manifests itself through the body – Batcheff's dual nature written across his features, Carmen as female proclaiming otherness as both desirable and fearful, the male body as porous and thus fragile, very prone to the abject. Each embodiment depends on the sense of passage to and fro; indeed, without this embodiment there would be no passage. The body is thus both solid and tangible, yet hints at its own dissolution: through Batcheff's absence even while he is present; through Carmen's constant death and resurrection through the various remakes in within French film and elsewhere; through the wastes of the masculine body. But the heterotopian body in these cases becomes even more contradictory by the fact of being rendered virtual rather than tangible through the film medium. They are, like Batcheff, there and not there. It comes as no surprise, then, that there is little fixity in terms of Frenchness: Powrie renders Frenchness heterotopic through the body. If Batcheff as national pin-up nonetheless has a suggestion of other nations traced across his facial features, then the *Carmen* story derives from a French desire to go slumming and enjoy the passage away from bourgeois culture – and back again – across and through the foreign woman's body. And in Besson's work we find that the anxiety and fascination around the cloacal is mirrored in the confusion over national identity, where actors adopt different nationalities from their own, where accent and costume raise awareness of identities other than the home one, and where genre allows French and American cinemas to both confront and to merge into each other. Powrie's service to French cinema studies is thus dual: he has helped, as I said earlier, to foster French cinema as a distinct field of study, but simultaneously he has called our attention to the holes in that field, to the sites/sights of passage. And this is an approach that we can adopt elsewhere when looking at other national cinemas, not so much to define them but to look precisely at a field's holes and contradictions as an integral part of that cinema.

In his co-written introduction to the volume *The Trouble with Men* (Powrie et al. 2004a: 14), Powrie argues: 'What we hope to have to done … is to locate *moments of becoming*, the interstitial moments which undermine fixed ontologies, as cinema attempts to come to terms with change.' To my mind, this is exactly what he tries to do in and with the field of French cinema. Not only has Powrie helped to lay the foundations of French film studies, but his work has been crucial in opening up the field to dialogue and negotiation with scholarship from outside. Powrie's work not only posits the French film scholar as able to go beyond borders, but as occupying an academic field that turns out to be heterotopic, in which French film exists alongside other texts and arguments deriving from them that not only straddle the borders but challenge them, so that French film studies carries the potential to contradict its own existence. Powrie's scholarship suggests this not so much to undermine the field of French film studies but to posit national cinema scholarship as a constant – and fruitful – site of tension, a constant act of passage.

Chapter 13

Men in Unfamiliar Places: A Response to Phil Powrie

Alison Smith

Phil Powrie's 1997 book *French Cinema in the 1980s: Nostalgia and the Crisis of Masculinity* established the idea of a 'crisis of masculinity' almost as a commonplace of French filmic identity in that period. Since its publication, work on problematic masculinities in general, and in film and visual culture in particular, has multiplied, and thanks in part to Professor Powrie the specific issues of French representation have remained at the forefront.

Representing masculinity visually has never been a simple enterprise. As Solomon-Godeau (1997: 33) suggests, for the last two centuries masculinity has *always* been in crisis – or at least in a state of dynamic tension requiring constant reassurance and reassessment. Unsurprisingly, then, while the terms of negotiation are in constant flux, the crisis of the 1980s was not resolved or exorcized in the ensuing twenty years. In this context, in *The Trouble with Men*, Powrie, Davies and Babington point to the greater recognition accorded to representations of the vulnerable and damaged male body, to which they tentatively attribute a 'redemptive' or reconstructive role, whereby 'the damaged male … forces male and female viewers to reconstruct a theoretical space which precedes patriarchal law' (2004a: 14).

While much of the work on vulnerable or damaged masculinity in contemporary French cinema has centred on relatively experimental or extreme production – see Powrie's (2004b) own essay on Gaspar Noé's films in *The Trouble With Men* – mainstream cinema has also continued to worry at the subject, with perhaps more unease at the prospect of resigning itself to a pre-patriarchal, renewable space or of consigning its protagonists to the indignities of abjection analyzed by Powrie (2004) or Keith Reader (2006). The two films that will be addressed in this article, Michel Blanc's *Mauvaise passe/The Escort* (1999) and Yvan Attal's *Ma femme est une actrice/My Wife is an Actress* (2001), are mainstream works, thoroughly imbricated in the thriving celebrity culture of the French screen. Both centre on a male protagonist struggling to come to terms with a fraying social and sexual identity; they were released within two years of each other, and both stage their protagonists' dramas across the English Channel, setting the scene of their self-questioning in large part in London.[1]

There seems at first glance no particularly pressing reason why French film-makers should look to London for their projects at the turn of the millennium. Pathé Pictures' London division had certainly been the recipient of a coveted lottery franchise, but its involvement in these three films seems to have been merely as distributor. Although the Blair government had made some changes to film financing rules on its accession in 1997 (BFI 2008), these had largely been for the benefit of British producers, and while the Film Policy Review Group had produced a paper in 1998 recommending extension of tax relief to foreign productions, there seem to have been no actual steps taken before 2001 (Block et al. 2001: 69–70). Yvan Attal recalls that shooting in London was costly and restricted, and that 'for production reasons, everything that could be done in Paris we did there' (Attal 2002). Certainly European co-productions were officially being encouraged at several levels, including in the United Kingdom, but neither of these two films is a co-production. Perhaps more importantly, an inclination towards English-language production was fashionable in the French film industry at the turn of the millennium; producers had been impressed by the international successes of Luc Besson and were eager to access the Anglophone market, and Claude Berri – personally involved with both films – was an outspoken supporter of English-language projects. But whatever pressure directors may have been under to work in English, there were also personal and artistic reasons for these displacements, and the protagonists' various encounters with London undoubtedly affect the form in which their male trouble is manifested: in different ways according to the different responses of the film-makers to the associations of the capital. In both films, London and Paris are constructed as two poles, with Paris – rarely seen in *Mauvaise passe*, but quite prominent in *Ma femme est une actrice* – being the place of the protagonist's 'normal' life, which he deconstructs and reconstructs in the course of confusing and chaotic experiences across the Channel. It seems credible, therefore, to propose that for these Frenchmen, London functions as a place of 'heterospection', to borrow a term from Powrie's work on the Foucauldian concept of heterotopia (e.g. Powrie 2005) – certainly for the protagonists, but perhaps also for the kind of audience that both directors probably envisaged.

Throughout the 1980s and early 1990s, Thatcherism was 'the most important influence shaping cinematic London', with directors concerned primarily to illustrate the city's polarization into the London of the 'rich and selfish' and the London of the 'poor and helpless' (Mazierska and Rascaroli 2003: 167). The social British cinema of the Thatcher era had a considerable impact in France, and its survival as a national image can be seen in the three projects we are discussing. All mobilize personnel closely associated with it, most obviously Hanif Kureishi as scriptwriter for *Mauvaise passe* and *Intimacy*, but also a galaxy of actors recognizable from the London of Stephen Frears and Mike Leigh, including Frances Barber (Frears' Rosie in *Sammy and Rosie Get Laid*, [Frears, 1987]) in a small part in *Mauvaise passe*. The associations of Thatcherism are probably most evident in *Mauvaise passe*, but visual memories of this cinema persist in both films. For these French directors, the London of the turn of the millennium is also a London of cinematic memory and association, its significance partly determined by its recent past. Possibly for 'production reasons', as Attal said, contact with the city is largely restricted to actors and one or two carefully selected iconic shots: it becomes a site of displacement, a network of associations, a catalyst for the protagonists' reworking of both their manhood and their Frenchness.

Mauvaise passe (Michel Blanc, 1999)

Mauvaise passe was certainly an unexpected project for its director, Michel Blanc, the small bald fall-guy of the Splendid stable. It was only his third feature film as director, and the first in which he did not appear; it was a drama when audiences associated Blanc with comedy, and it was overwhelmingly in English when his previous project, *Grosse fatigue/Dead Tired* (1994), was perhaps most remembered for the impassioned defence of the Frenchness of French cinema with which it had ended. In discussing *Mauvaise passe*, Blanc claimed to identify with his protagonist Pierre precisely in his desire for a drastic break with his previous work and his perception of himself as director and actor (Blanc, in Brunet 1999).

Pierre (Daniel Auteuil) is a middle-aged Parisian literature professor who has just left his wife, son, job and home. At the beginning of the film, he is shacked up in a seedy hotel in Bayswater, dilatorily attempting to write a novel. His crumbling fortunes turn when he encounters Tom (Stuart Townsend), a young Englishman who introduces him to a new career as an expensive male escort. Pierre's improbable success at thus commercializing his manhood creates a new framework within which to read his life.

The first image of *Mauvaise passe*, an unidentifiable expanse of dirty greyish-white water accompanied by dripping sounds, places us from the start in the realm of male crisis at its most dramatic. Apparently unbounded and certainly unpleasant, it recalls all the associations of leakiness and fluidity associated with the Kristevan abject (Kristeva 1980). The fact that it might be the water of the Thames just as easily as the contents of a grubby hotel basin – which, in fact, it proves to be – leaves us initially uncertain as to whether it is a résumé of the state of the protagonist or the state of the world: when the camera tracks upwards to reveal mucky taps and a tube of toothpaste, the nasty liquid acquires a corporeal dimension at the same time as its scale is reduced and bounded by the bowl. Pierre himself only appears gradually – as it were, as an extension of his basin: first a hand reaching out to the glass of whisky also balanced beside the taps, then a brief glimpse of his bespectacled head, then another hand that soon abandons its pen for a cigarette. The camera frames him in extreme, dingy close-up, drastically restricting his space: he is a man in a very tight corner.

In the course of the following sequences, the multiple failures and lacks that characterize his position will be revealed one after the other. His lack of experience of the city he is in – indeed, it would seem, of any city at all – as well as his hesitant command of the ambient language is revealed when he is inveigled into a Soho nightclub, cheated and beaten up. Although this incident results in his encounter with Tom, its most immediate effect is to damage him physically, leaving him with a bandaged hand. The following morning his credit card refuses to function, and in order to earn money he practically begs a job as temporary washer-up in Tom's café and sandwich bar, work that requires him to don an apron and, once again, to find himself in forced proximity to a bowl full of dirty water. Although he has presented himself to Tom, and to the audience, as a novelist in the course of preparing a new work, his evasiveness before any further questioning on the subject, as well as the readiness with which his hands find other occupations than writing, quickly arouse our suspicions; the confession that he has never actually written a line, and hasn't yet found the inspiration to begin, is surprising only in terms of the time it takes to arrive. When, finally, he confides that he has ceased to function physically as well, the information is already practically superfluous, not least because the film has taken pains to associate Pierre's subsidiary failings with his virility or lack of it. This is most obvious in an associative editing chain leading from Tom's declaration that, since Pierre doesn't have a condom to lend him, he'll 'find a machine' to a close-up of Pierre's bandaged – therefore recognizable – hand feeding his cash card, unsuccessfully, into a cash machine before ceremonially burning it before the astonished eyes of a young homeless woman.

Pierre has thus come to London in all senses down and out, and he enacts for the audience a sequence of symbolic castrations, which only confirms what is already fact: if he burns his cash card, it is because he *already* has no money. He has also come as the result of a violent rejection of his past life in France, although he keeps a residual umbilical link in place with occasional telephone calls. The French past is a space associated with family, although the precise nature of Pierre's family ties, like much else, is revealed only gradually. It is a place of stability, and as such the focus of his sudden revolt (the revelation of the rut he was caught in, he tells Tom, came to him while 'on the toilet'; there could hardly be a more direct statement of the status of the world he is pushing away). It is also a place of culture, given his career as a literature professor – a culture to be possessed rather than created, certainly, but since Pierre is unable to reinvent himself in a new place as a producer of literature, his intellectual and artistic existence seems bound to his past. Home, family, stability and the voice of his wife berating him in French across the phone wires: the reassuring, but smothering values of a stereotypically maternal space are thus associated with all that Pierre has left behind. The story of his reinvention of himself as a successful gigolo in a new country is in large part the story of the recuperation of his Frenchness and his culture in the service of an affirmation of his manhood – or, perhaps more accurately, in the service of the *marketing* of his manhood. For if France is identified with a number of 'heritage' values on which Pierre has contemptuously turned his back (and we shall see later that this is an ambivalent rejection), then London is above all a space of transaction – of money, of branding, of (false) advertisement and glittering surface.

Blanc's London is in fact conspicuous by its invisibility. With the exception of three short and variously nondescript thoroughfares that serve to *brand* their respective inhabitants – a bustling pedestrian alley outside Tom's coffee-shop, the walkway of a rundown council block in front of the Cockney prostitute Kim's childhood home and a charming, but slightly unsettling, cobbled jetty in front of Pierre's new dockland residence – the city appears only as a medley of coloured lights or chaotic fly-posters on restrictive walls. If, as the neon sign reflected on Tom's café door announces, it may seem 'EXOTIC' to the bewildered Pierre of the early sequences, its defining feature is its two-dimensionality. What 'exoticism' there may be comes from the range of human types incarnated by the assorted actors, many of which are self-consciously superficial – Pierre's glamorous first client greets the news of his inexperience with a 'This is about to get interesting' lifted straight from the opening scenes of

Mauvaise passe – Blanc's anonymous London.

Dr No (Young 1962), while Kim's impish androgyny, offhand amorality and brutal 'partner' make her a twenty-first century combination of Nancy and the Artful Dodger. Eroticism itself becomes a commodity, naturally given the narrative *milieu*, but its commodification is repeatedly emphasized by different characters as something which in changing the meaning of sex simultaneously reduces its danger and *increases* its value. 'It all seemed so natural. It's just sex … But then I realized it actually was business' is how Tom describes his discovery of his vocation, and a few minutes later he fends off a still-shocked Pierre with 'There's no lies between us … It's just business.'

Such is the stereotype of London, still redolent of the associations of Thatcherism, with which Blanc confronts his emasculated French innocent. Eventually the claim that 'business' is somehow an assurance against 'lies' will prove to be more than hollow, but to begin with it proves most adaptable to Pierre's needs. In the repackaging that he undergoes for the agency, it is those characteristics most associated with his past that prove his most potent selling point: his French accent, his culture ('There's more body-builders than university lecturers on [the agency's] books'), his ability to whisper fluent Baudelaire into clients' receptive ears. Even Auteuil's less than imposing figure and Pierre's unpromising combination of middle age and emotional immaturity are marshalled in the service of advertisement; his promotional leaflet, captioned 'Le Mâle', photographs him in huddled pose, biting his thumb as he looks out at the punter: somewhere between babyhood, provocation and Rodin's Thinker. 'It's perfect for the clientele,' Tom tells him. 'Your niche market.' And within this fluid economy, which transmutes and transposes culture and language, sex and money in a series of endlessly renewed present moments, Pierre becomes a new man: sexually, financially and linguistically, his life begins to flow again.

The rehabilitation that London affords Pierre provoked one critic, writing for *Cahiers du cinéma*, to see in *Mauvaise passe* a straightforward apology for the neo-liberal dream: 'a Frenchman gripped by the liberal fever (for the *liberty* dear to neo-liberal economists). *Easy money* and an easy life against the demands of a relationship and the weight of culture' (Chauvin 1999). This may skate over both the eventual destruction wrought by Pierre's over-eager adoption of the values of transaction and branding, and the absence of any creative re-empowerment from the system of present exchange he sets in train in London, but it is nonetheless troubling, for Pierre ends the film back in London, restored to potency through a combination of a filtered past with the most cynical of his newly acquired attitudes. However, the end of his first adventure leaves him once again financially and sexually insolvent, reliant on credit and cocaine, rejected by his new associates (a sign, perhaps, of the 'foreignness' of these values), staring once more into a boundless expanse of dirty water, which this time really is the river.

The reconquering of his French manhood requires a *return* to the space of the past – but it is a space that, while undoubtedly nostalgic, has been de-feminized, transferred from the realm of mother and family to that of an absent father. If, as Powrie claims in his study of the function of the nostalgia film (Powrie 1997: 26), 'the nostalgia film … returns spectators, both male and female, to Mother while reminding them of the loss incurred', Pierre's rediscovery of the space of his origins is dependent on complete repression of that loss. The feminine is not merely silenced, it is eliminated. Thus Pierre returns to France in response to news of his father's illness. After meeting his wife in an impersonal glass airport hall and learning that she wants to divorce him, a brief meeting with his sick father ends, in contrast to that with his wife, with reconciliation and the offer of the use of his house, 'since I'm not there'.

The paternal house figures a perfect nostalgic space – a rural France shown briefly but in luscious, clear deep-focus. A taxi carries Pierre through vineyards to the magnificent mansion. Birds twitter as he opens the door. The subsequent fade to black elides the time that Pierre presumably spends in this beautiful space, maternal in implication but explicitly attributed to the father's control. In fact, if we are to accept Powrie's attribution of the nostalgic rural space to the mother, it could be argued that this unrepresented (unrepresentable?) period of calm and creativity figures an oedipal surrender: Pierre's father, in offering him the use of his house, has raised the most fundamental of all taboos. Such a reading might be implicit, but it is also unimaginable, itself repressed by the film into an ellipse, a hasty fade-out. From this unspeakable interlude, Blanc will return him once again to London, this time bearing final proof of his reaffirmed virility in the form of the completed best-seller he has drawn from his London experiences, sublimated and controlled. The very last sequence, which shows Pierre consummating his triumph with his publisher's wife, is extremely ambivalent – the camera lingers on a small handful of money on the bedside table before drifting to the window to frame a street bedecked with Christmas lights in an orgasmic consumerist fountain; while the two songs – the first in the film – which introduce the credit sequence contrast the nostalgic French romanticism of 'Hymne à l'amour' with a rather less heartening English lyric, Barry Adamson's 'My Aimless Love'. But *Mauvaise passe* does end with some resolution, however temporary, to Pierre's crisis of national and sexual identity: a resolution that simultaneously eliminates from his life anything French and feminine – his wife divorced, his utopian home passed to him by his father and absorbed by the film into silence – and that subordinates this particular English woman, and by extension all others, to his cross-Channel fascination. It is something of a desperate ending, and one that perhaps elides the true nature of the crisis of masculinity by displacing it on to a crisis of cultural identity, where Blanc feels himself to be on surer ground.

Ma femme est une actrice (Yvan Attal, 2001)

Yvan Attal is himself an actor, and his wife is Charlotte Gainsbourg. His first feature film, in which he plays Yvan, sportswriter husband to bilingual film star Charlotte, was thus a deliberate choreography of the couple's celebrity status, a calculated mix of autobiographical accuracy and outrageous fiction. It is, in generic terms, a romantic comedy about jealousy. The fictional Yvan starts the film discontented at being forced to live in his wife's shadow, a discontent he is unable to express to her. When a film project takes her to London to play opposite an adulated English actor, Yvan's discontent translates into fury against the institution of cinema in general, and Charlotte's co-star John (Terence Stamp) in particular, and his irrational nagging leads to a brief separation before the generically inevitable reconciliation. A parallel sub-plot, entirely Paris-based, recounts the constant quarrels between Yvan's sister Nathalie (Noémie Lvovsky) and her husband over whether or not their unborn son should be circumcised. The sub-plot thus links concerns over masculinity with concerns over Nathalie's – and by extension Yvan's – Jewishness, a question that can thereby largely be evacuated from the main plot while remaining tacitly present, especially in Yvan's ambivalent responses to his sister's arguments.

While *Mauvaise passe* begins with the protagonist's most intimate situation, imaging his desperate psychological straits in an unrecognizable, anonymous space, the first post-credit sequence of *Ma femme est une actrice*, by contrast, concentrates on place and society, gender and the city of Paris. Over a montage that starts with the Eiffel Tower and then presents a variety of women of all ages, shapes and sizes engaged in typical Parisian activities, a man's voice-over, not yet recognizable as Attal's or indeed as belonging to the narrative at all, regales us with a series of statistics regarding the gender balance of the Parisian population, from which it transpires that the city (apparently) contains *'une proportion de 1.4 femmes pour un homme. Pas mal*/A proportion of 1.4 women to one man. Not bad'. The end of this opening sequence reveals Yvan/Attal as a small man. Like Pierre/Auteuil in *Mauvaise passe*, Yvan/Attal is relatively short, slight and dark, with a tendency to five o'clock shadow. Though he will constantly be contrasted with taller, broader, less light-absorbent fellow-actors, Yvan's masculinity is mischievously over-determined. Employed in the very male activity of football journalism, he appears first coming down the stadium stairs from the privileged lair of the 'Tribune de Presse', then in front of computer screens where he alternates match results and pictures of curvaceous women, with the occasional screen-wide caption GOAL! If Yvan's occupation constitutes a declaration of triumphant maleness, however, it is a feeble fiction. In the company of Charlotte, the magnetism of *her* occupation, which constantly draws complete strangers into the frame she shares with Yvan and others, renders him literally transparent. In the course of the first few sequences, in which Yvan's life with Charlotte in Paris is presented, Attal several times employs the same intriguing shot structure, in which Yvan, in the foreground and in clear focus, appears in both sides of a shot/counter-shot series constructed on the exchanged gazes of Charlotte and an admirer. While they are framed behind him, and slightly hazily, the dynamics of the editing and the eyeline matching give them full control of the narration; Yvan thus being at once central to this experience – *his* experience – and rendered invisible. What's more, her prestige translates into an almost magical social power: whether it be placating the traffic police or booking a table in the trendiest restaurant, Charlotte can, Yvan cannot. Even his personal sexual attraction, he suggests, is enhanced or perhaps even brought into being by the fact that he is M. Charlotte. If the symbolic phallic economy is in any way to be measured as the capacity for social action, then there is no doubt that Yvan's sense of possession is, from the start of the film, shaky in the extreme, and dependent for any meaningful affirmation on a process of fetishization, then of dogged attachment to his wife. Charlotte has absolute social power (Charlotte *is* the phallus) but Yvan, at least in Paris, 'has' (and is subordinate to) Charlotte.

Charlotte's work in London, then, threatens Yvan's unstable equilibrium first by virtue of mere separation. Although, as the couple tell each other, the physical distance is not great, and the film will indeed constantly bridge it – Attal gives considerable time and prominence to the Eurostar journeys that connect the two poles of the film – cultural and linguistic distance make it further, and the personal cultural distance that separates Yvan from 'the world of the cinema' will eventually give him the sense of being definitively cut off from her. When interviewed, Attal said his first priority was that the film should involve displacement: 'I wanted this story to take place somewhere other than France because of the distance, which accentuates anxiety and jealousy' (Attal, in Brunet 2001). London thus becomes for Yvan – as indeed it did for Pierre – a kind of modern crisis heterotopia (Foucault 1986), self-selected for Pierre, but imposed on Yvan by the contingencies of Charlotte's career. The choice of city may seem to have been arbitrary (Blanc's Pierre declares that he came to London because 'the flights to Rome and Barcelona were full'), selected for convenience or to correspond to the cultural affinities of the real Charlotte Gainsbourg. In the same interview, Attal offers a decidedly inconclusive, even perverse, reason for the choice: 'I chose England because I wanted that glamour, that magic, that belongs to the actresses who we see parading in the credits sequence. It was also a way of paying homage to certain American comedies that possess that glamour.' As this quotation suggests, the glamorous actresses who appear in the film's credit sequence, while certainly Anglophone, are not English, and contemporary London is likely to be unreadable as a signifier of golden-age Hollywood. Fortunately, Attal's London is not in fact so disembodied as these quotations might suggest, and the associations that he marshalls around it do indeed contribute to defining Yvan's insecurities and the ways in which national – and cultural – and gender identities may interact.

Compared with *Mauvaise passe*, *Ma femme est une actrice* has few London scenes, but Attal does take the trouble to make the city recognizable to us. Although, as mentioned above, production difficulties induced him to reduce London locations to a minimum, those he selects are unique and generally extremely familiar, including to a French audience of discerning tourists: the Houses of Parliament as instant visual shorthand, but also the then-new Tate Modern, the Tower Record Store at Piccadilly Circus (sadly deceased) or the Royal Court Theatre. The fabric of the city is thus to some extent intercalated into the film. In the context that concerns us here, it is perhaps the combination of meanings that Attal accumulates in the Tate Modern that can best illustrate the attractive menace which London represents for Yvan. The giant chimney of the old power-station, appearing on the screen in immediate counterpoint to a furious argument in Paris over the unborn nephew's embryonic penis, offers a jokey diagram of the city as supermale, an overwhelming rival that offers Yvan no chance. It is not, however, accidental that the particular site of this challenge is also a temple of culture (and as such foreign territory to the self-consciously laddish Yvan), nor that if he is filling his time by a trip there it is, unbeknownst to him, on the recommendation of the English arch-rival's human incarnation, John – or Terence Stamp.

Ma femme est une actrice – Yvan and Charlotte in Tower Records.

It is eventually in the character of John, and around Stamp's persona, that Attal will crystallize most thoroughly an alternative masculinity placed in, and lived through, London. Long before his appearance, the character is charged with symbolic weight and a surplus of adjectives: 'génial', 'sublime', 'extraordinaire' 'très séduisant' ('very seductive'). Although the level-headed Charlotte seems immune to the ambient hero-worship of her co-star, and even amused by it, the fascination that we observe exerted by *her* star power is, in fact, seemingly infinitely multiplied when evoking *his*: as a group of star-struck theatre students sum him up for a dismayed Yvan, he is nothing less than 'le mec' ('the man'). And indeed, the narrative will confirm that, despite the many contradictions between the character and the image proposed for him, he is indeed seductive, and a serious challenge to Yvan.

The casting of Terence Stamp itself set in motion contradictory connotations, of which Attal was very much aware. He could figure the quintessential Englishman – the 'Limey' with well-tended roots in East London – but also a cosmopolitan European art cinema and the transatlantic 1960s counter-culture; his film career had certainly seen him cast several times as a seducer or *homme fatal*, but his very seductiveness had been built in large part on skilful manipulation of gender marginality; and he was 62 in 2001, and looked it. His John accentuates all the traits most problematic for a prospective male icon. His age and thinning hair are brought to the fore by frequent close-ups; his body, inasmuch as we get a sense of it, seems frail rather than physically impressive; when not in costume for the film within the film, his favoured wear is a dressing-gown. Again and again throughout the film, he presents a display of weakness, uncertainty or vulnerability at moments when it would seem most urgent to impress: offering childish scribbles alongside elegantly skilful sketches, discussing his failed marriage, losing at chess, mispronouncing French phrases, and getting elegantly but slurringly drunk when alone with Charlotte and a handful of adoring young women from the crew. The paradox, not unpredictably, is that while Yvan pounces on all such 'failings' to reassure himself of John's inadequacy as a man, they are precisely the qualities that make him attractive to Charlotte while the film's brash director, David (Keith Allen), only irritates her. She finds John 'touching'; she is visibly embarrassed by Yvan's efforts to seize the linguistic high ground unexpectedly offered to him; and it is through a combination of his ill-judged jealous assertiveness and John's drunken rendition of Shakespeare's sonnets that she does, temporarily, succumb to the charm of the 'other'.

In *Ma femme est une actrice*, then, England, in the person of Stamp, confronts the unsophisticated Yvan with a calculated performance both of high culture and of 'the redemptive function of damage' (Powrie et al. 2004a: 13). It is this that endangers Yvan's status as husband and lover, rather than the punkish hypermasculinity represented by David, or the incomprehensible – but quite innocuous – naked member with which he is confronted on an unfortunate visit to the film set. This vision of masculinity in the raw may perhaps startle an audience by dint of its incongruity in a romantic comedy, and it disturbs poor Yvan to such a point that he faints; however, the joke – for us, and on him – is in the entirely workaday, asexual and therefore unthreatening reasons why this particular male body happens to be exposing its maleness. In *Ma femme est une actrice*, the more the signs of masculinity are apparently flaunted, the less power and prestige they command. Although the eventual resolution, which not only restores Charlotte to Yvan but offers prospective parenthood as a way to recast their initially awkward couple, is rather hastily conceived, there are a number of signs throughout the film that suggest Yvan *will* eventually 'deserve' his restoration by retaining the lesson learned through London, and learning to cultivate those traits – vulnerability, sensitivity, creativity – that he has always read, conventionally, as weaknesses.[2]

Conclusion

The two films considered in this essay both stage a dramatic reassessment of their protagonists' masculinity through the experiences that these French men encounter across the Channel, in London. Although they read the nexus between the city, Frenchness/foreignness and male crisis in different ways, it seems beyond coincidence that such different films should have chosen to combine these factors in such a short space of time. This brief examination under the auspices of Phil Powrie's combined work on space and masculinity has, I hope, taken a first step to exploring the significance which an unfamiliar place – in particular, the unfamiliar space of England, of the city, of London in its multiple uniqueness – can acquire to a reassessment of the troubles of being a Frenchman at the turn of the millennium.

Notes

1. The same pattern is detectable, with perhaps an even stronger sense of displacement, in another high-profile project of 2001, Patrick Chéreau's *Intimacy*. Chéreau's main protagonist is himself a Londoner and the narrative is almost wholly British; it was the project as a whole that enacted the cross-Channel encounter in this case. Chéreau's exploration of masculinity in crisis is much more radical than either of the films discussed in detail here, and his engagement with the life and fabric of contemporary London is also fuller. I regret that considerations of space prevented this article from extending its scope to the case of *Intimacy*.
2. Although the film's two stories coexist rather awkwardly, Yvan's ambivalent feelings about his Jewishness should probably be included here. As Michele Aaron reminds us, a persistent strand of anti-Semitic rhetoric in the early part of the century, culminating in the work of Otto Weininger in 1906, had equated Jewishness, dismissively, with an undesirable femininity, thus 'mak[ing] th[e] crisis of masculinity a Jewish condition' (Aaron 2004: 92). In 2001, a perceived resurgence in French anti-Semitism was making headlines in France and abroad: for a French Jewish film-maker, the subject was both inescapable and invasive, and Attal's unwillingness either to ignore it or to be engulfed by it is understandable.

Chapter 14

To Elicit and Elude: The Film Writing of Keith Reader

Douglas Morrey

In a career that has ranged widely across the various appurtenances of French Studies, including literature, cultural studies and critical theory, it is his work on French cinema that will most memorably have defined the scholarship of Keith Reader. Having begun his film writing with two general-interest volumes addressed to a wide audience – *The Cinema: A History* (1979) and *Cultures on Celluloid* (1981) – Reader has gone on to produce a formidable range of articles, chapters and monographs on French cinema, which display an admirably comprehensive knowledge of the field while frequently returning to and reassessing a handful of his favourite films and directors: *Les Enfants du paradis/Children of Paradise* (Carné 1945), *La Maman et la putain/The Mother and the Whore* (Eustache 1973), films by Alain Resnais – in particular *L'Année dernière à Marienbad/Last Year in Marienbad* (1961) and *Mon oncle d'Amérique/My American Uncle* (1980) – and, of course, the work of Robert Bresson and Jean Renoir. In all of this writing, Reader has gradually carved out a singular body of work that testifies to the key role of cinema in creating, reflecting, developing and disseminating those images, myths and stories that bolster French national identity.

In many ways, the flavour of Reader's writing about French cinema has been typical of British academics working in the humanities over the past three decades. His early work demonstrates commitment to a socialist politics that becomes increasingly informed by theory (especially Lacan and Deleuze) before moving to a more historically inflected textual analysis that nonetheless continues to draw on theory and to observe a political agenda. But Reader is no mere follower of fashion. If his work on Popular Front cinema (1986) considers the inheritance of that coalition in the context of a critical assessment of François Mitterrand's first Socialist government, Reader's writing has also attentively charted the eclipse of the political in French social and cinematic life, lamenting in particular the bastardized legacy of May 1968 – what he has called 'the reduction of social conflict to an ill-defined generational consensus' (1992: 99). Hence perhaps his attraction to the work of Michel Houellebecq, and the sensitivity with which he has described, in the work of that author and its film adaptation, the separation of spheres of cultural, political, commercial and sexual activity into so many mutually exclusive domains with no subtending logic between them (2001b: 120–21). If Reader's politics are never tokenistic, nor is he one to hide behind the modish jargon of theory. His writing demonstrates a thorough assimilation of the most important lessons of post-structuralism, yet Reader always wears his theory lightly, allowing it to illuminate the interpretation of those familiar with theory without distracting from the discussion of the films at hand. It is, for instance, enough simply to mention that *La*

Règle du jeu/The Rules of the Game (Renoir 1939) is a film populated by 'desiring machines', or that its prescient relation to historical events makes it a 'hauntological text *avant la lettre*' (Reader forthcoming) – the point is clear enough for readers without theory while, for those who know Deleuze and Derrida, the film is suddenly bathed in a new and intriguing light. Robert de la Chesnaye's absurd, malfunctioning music machines thus begin to seem like a literal extension of the cogs of desire that pull the characters of the film together, while the *danse macabre* unfolding against the eerie automatism of the player piano bespeaks not just the blind on-rush of history, but also a *text* that escapes its creator's control, saying more than its author could ever have intended. Similarly, Reader suggests that the elliptical style of *Le Journal d'un curé de campagne/Diary of a Country Priest* (Bresson 1951) has important things to say about 'speech, writing and silence' (Reader 2000a: 41) without needing to betray the film's discreet aesthetic with a didactic marshalling of Derrida and Blanchot. The nature of language, heavy with the weight of the already-said and the unsayable, means that speech and writing are always inhabited by a silence that they can never fully articulate, while even the deepest silence is pregnant, to our ears, with words. For post-structuralist theory, this unreachable emptiness at the heart of language takes on something of the ineffability of the sacred, a connection that swells for us out of the stillness of Bresson's film.

The accessible way in which Reader incorporates theory into his writing is but one instance of his eminent readability, a consequence perhaps of his early training in writing works designed to facilitate the populist dissemination of film history. The encyclopaedic, and frequently comparative, nature of his early books is perhaps also responsible for a certain preference for intertextuality when interpreting films. Reader will frequently illuminate a film by reference to other works by its director or stars, or simply by evoking other movies that share its themes or imagery. Reader knows full well that everything we write, like everything we watch, already bears the imprint of pre-existing texts, though he is self-deprecating enough to acknowledge that 'done by students, that is plagiarism; done by authors and academics, intertextuality!' (Reader 2000b: 41). Above all, though, this intertextuality testifies to Reader's genuine love of, and voracious appetite for, cinema. It is perhaps this undisguised enthusiasm that makes his writing most engaging – for instance, when he relates the epiphanic personal experiences that have determined his research projects: the unexpected tears he cried when screening Bresson films to a class full of students (Reader 2000a: ix); the 'one-off screening of a rare Renoir' that inspired an article on *Le Testament du docteur Cordelier/Experiment in Evil* (Renoir 1959), the reading of whose own intertext, *Dr Jekyll and Mr Hyde*, caused the resurgence of memories from a troubled childhood (Reader 1990: 187); or the admission that his book *The Abject Object* can ultimately be traced back to Reader's fascination with a scene in *La Dernière femme/The Last Woman* (Ferreri 1976), in which Gérard Depardieu castrates himself with an electric carving knife (Reader 2006: 165).

If this autobiographical inflection makes Reader's work particularly accessible to students, then so too does his constant concern for the physical availability of films. Time and again in his books and articles, Reader will raise this issue, pointing out how and where films can be viewed, and, perhaps more importantly, when they cannot. Reader is never afraid to admit in print when he has been unable to see a film that might otherwise have enriched his analysis. As such, he appears perhaps more human than those academics who have spent their lives in libraries, archives and museums. Reader, at least, has spent his in the cinema. As a result, Reader's work on French cinema has covered mainly fairly well-known or canonical films. There is perhaps a slight danger thereby of accepting a consensual view of the subject – as when Reader readily accepts the wider availability of Renoir's pre-war work as sufficient evidence for its greater significance (Reader forthcoming). By the same token, though, Reader evinces a healthy disregard for the academic snobbery that sometimes prizes films for their very obscurity. He is suspicious of the way in which Godard's recent films have been 'extremely difficult to see, often extremely difficult to watch, but it sometimes seems all but impossible to avoid reading about', as though their very inaccessibility were 'proof of their revolutionary seriousness' (Reader 2004: 75–76). In summary, we might note that Reader, with admirably democratizing intentions, has never taken his eye from the political and economic realities of *distribution*, whether of popular French cinema (the UK release of *Le Bonheur est dans le pré/Happiness is in the Field* [Chatiliez 1995], he suggests, has a lot to do with Eric Cantona [Reader 1999: 108]) or of academic publishing (he once regretted, in conversation with me, that a proposed monograph on *La Maman et la putain* had been refused on the grounds that no subtitled DVD was currently available).

Reader's work is frequently permeated by a dry but irrepressible sense of humour. For example, discussing British cinema of World War II in his first book, he sardonically observes that 'it is difficult to see how James Mason chastising Margaret Lockwood's treacherous actress with a riding-whip in Leslie Arliss's *The Man in Grey* (1943) could have helped in the struggle against Nazism' (Reader 1979: 75). He pokes fun at the critically naïve view of Renoir as a 'supremely tolerant humanist' by noting that such beings 'cannot by definition sully themselves with commitment to anything (including presumably supremely tolerant humanism)' (Reader 1986: 41). Even his beloved Bresson feels the bite of Reader's wit when he mischievously remarks that *Les Anges du péché/Angels of the Streets* (1943) may be difficult to take seriously for 'an Anglo-American audience whose repertoire of cinematic nuns is likely to be headed by Julie Andrews in *The Sound of Music*' (Reader 2000a: 14). But he is funniest, perhaps, in his occasional self-righteous eviscerations of bad movies. Of *Le Grand bleu/The Big Blue* (Besson 1988) he writes: 'What, after all, are the film's dolphins but benignly anthropomorphic variations on the theme of *Jaws* – "good castrators" for those late 1980s that asked for no better than to have their ideological testicles chewed off with painless (and preferably presidential) teeth?' (Reader 1992: 102).

This earthy iconoclasm also means that Reader is more than happy, on occasion, to break the unwritten rules of academic discourse. In a contribution to a book about intertextuality, Reader proposes 'to deal with the vexed question of what a "text" is by ignoring it' (Reader 1990: 176). The very title of a 1992 article – 'How to Avoid Becoming a Middle-aged Fogey, with Reference to Three Recent Popular French Films' – should be sufficient evidence of its irreverence. On a number of occasions, Reader indulges in that ultimate critical no-no that consists of treating the characters of a film as though they were real people and imagining what their lives might become after the end of the narrative. What could be seen as a rather guileless trope becomes, in Reader's writing, a thought experiment with pedagogic uses. Thus the political significance of *La Maman et la putain* is made plain if we imagine that Alexandre and Gilberte's relationship was born in the ferment of May 1968 – and Reader reasons that 'in a film whose characters do little else but tell speculative stories ... I see no reason for curbing my own *libido narrandi*' (Reader 1993b: 95). Similarly, imagining the future destiny of characters from *Mon oncle d'Amérique* allows Reader to trace the descent of the 1968 generation into Mitterrandian socialism and 'the school of tender managerialism' (Reader 1996a: 183). Casting back in the other direction from 1968, he wonders whether the unruly class of schoolboys in *Les 400 coups/The 400 Blows* (Truffaut 1959) represents the first cinematic foreshadowing of the turbulence of May, and might even have gone on to form the Seine-et-Oise Liberation Front from Godard's *Week End* (1967) (Reader 2004: 89). If film characters take on a life of their own in Reader's writing, it is partly because he also enjoys playing the game – dear to David Thomson – of imagining alternative film histories. Sometimes this may be pure fantasy – as when he seeks to cast Maria Casarès as Madame de Merteuil in an adaptation of *Les Liaisons dangereuses* (Reader 2000a: 24) – but elsewhere it proves revealing about the text at hand: the futility of the exercise of trying to imagine Jean Gabin playing any of the male roles in *La Règle du jeu* speaks volumes about the kind of masculinity on display in that film (Reader forthcoming).

It is this mixture of an encyclopaedic knowledge of cinema with an eye for a telling detail that allows Reader often to sum up the essence of a film with a single line or a single idea. Thus *A bout de souffle/Breathless* (Godard 1960) is 'a marathon of indecisiveness' (Reader 1979: 134) and *Pierrot le fou* (Godard 1965), 'the greatest of all films about being in love' (1979: 155). The observation that all the characters of *La Règle du jeu* are childless tells us much about the sterility of the world on display (Reader forthcoming). The trouble with Jacques Tati's post-*Hulot* films is neatly summed up in half a sentence of Reader's film history: 'the intricacy of their crafting tends to work against the humour rather than with it' (Reader 1979: 160). Sometimes a remark that is memorable enough to change the way we look at cinema will take us by surprise in a seemingly unrelated context. It is in the Bresson book that Reader divides mid-century cinema into those directors, like Godard, 'whose work cries out for colour from the very beginning' and those films, like *Marienbad*, 'that would be inconceivable other than in black and white' (Reader 2000a: 98). It is a remark that suggests our division of cinema into classical and modern may be overly simplistic and that Resnais's work, for all its discontinuous editing, retains a sober classicism that is perhaps incompatible with the brash impudence of Godard's forward-looking aesthetic. At other times, a new spark of understanding is produced by an unexpected juxtaposition. Who would think of comparing *L'Atalante/L'Atalante* (Vigo 1934) with *King Kong* (Cooper 1933)? Yet Reader sees a certain 'urban paranoia' that is common to both (Reader 1981: 123), suggesting that the Depression of the 1930s gave rise to new strains of magic realism on both sides of the Atlantic as the cinema both documented, and sought to escape from, urban realities of crime and poverty. Sometimes, again, this is deliberately provocative, as when Reader compares *Mon oncle d'Amérique* by the ultra-formalist and alarmingly serious Alain Resnais to both *Eugénie Grandet* and Monty Python (Reader 1996a: 177, 179), or in the suggestion that *Le Grand bleu* is just *The Rocky Horror Picture Show* (Sharman 1975) without the ironic self-awareness (Reader 1992: 101). Elsewhere, the sense of the comparison runs deeper. It is commonplace to align Jean Renoir with Orson Welles in terms of their camera work, but Reader sees more sinister parallels between *La Règle du jeu* and *Citizen Kane* (Welles 1941): 'Both films know something that the characters within them do not (Kane's secret, the impending collapse of the old France), and both endings have been given intensified force by events subsequent to the making of the films (Welles' blighted career, the onset of war).' It is the difference in the treatment of these secrets – the 'American populism' of Welles' omniscient camera versus the 'uneasy harmony' of a rotten aristocracy unbalanced by the death of André Jurieux and the departure of Octave – that reveals the nature of the gulf between Hollywood and European cinema (Reader 1981: 137).

In this way, and like all the most thoughtful scholars, Reader is able to see past the obvious and move beyond received wisdom. Some of his most thought-provoking reflections on French cinema have concerned the New Wave, whose official history for academics, students and the general public alike is frequently encapsulated in a handful of clichés, one of the most common of these being that the New Wave was a film movement dedicated to youth. However, Reader remarks that actual adolescents (as opposed to children and young adults) are all but absent from the cinema of the period (Reader 1996b). The New Wave films were shot on location in Paris and *A bout de souffle* stands as the ultimate iconic love letter to the city. No doubt; however, as Reader points out, if 'the film is certainly Parisian … its characters are not' (Reader 1981: 140): Michel is desperately trying to escape the city and Patricia remains a foreigner within it. The affection with which the film regards Paris is overtly tinged with nostalgia and regret – for a belonging that has been lost or will never be known. The received wisdom on Godard (himself an outsider in Paris) is that the early, funny films (to borrow from Woody Allen) gave way in the late 1960s to a difficult didacticism from which the director would never entirely return. But for Reader, a film like *Bande à part/Band of Outsiders* (Godard 1964) is 'darker and less good-natured … than its overall tone may seem to suggest'. In particular, the way in which the cartoon violence of the characters co-exists with their expressionless reading of newspaper reports about genocide in Rwanda evokes a world 'in which violences of different kinds sit side by side without connecting tissue' (Reader 2004: 83). Un-recuperated by the rhetoric of dialectical materialism, these contradictions are allowed to stand with all their disturbing force and, as Reader points out, they constitute a damning commentary on 'the levelling, banalising effects of the spectacle' (Reader 2004: 83).

What, then, will be Reader's ultimate legacy for French film studies? It is difficult, perhaps, to align Reader's work with a single innovative area in the field, in the same way that Ginette Vincendeau invited us to reconceptualize French cinema of the 1930s and introduced the study of French film stars; or in Carrie Tarr's focus on women and Beurs in French films and French film-making; or in Phil Powrie's commitment to contemporary French cinema. Reader's work has ranged widely, and as such has been well placed to give us a sense of French cinema as a whole. In particular, Reader's writing has often been attentive to the role of cinema in French national myth-making. In *Cultures on Celluloid*, he writes that 'the dialectic between the time about which a film is (ostensibly) made and the time of its making often comes into sharper focus in French cinema because of the greater weight frequently accorded to specific historical events, and – just as importantly – because of the tendency to transmute history into myth whose importance in France is clear' (Reader 1981: 113). By returning throughout his career to certain key films, and through them to particular historical moments in twentieth century France, Reader has been able to reassess the shifting cultural signification of those moments. His work on Popular Front cinema thus aligns three key dates – 1936, 1968 and 1981 – noting how the carnival spirit of May 1968 picked up on the historical memory of the Popular Front, itself later alluded to by some of the first reforms introduced by Mitterrand's Socialist government. Writing in 1986, as the initial sense of hope that greeted this government had begun to wane, Reader's critical dissection of an analytic tradition that sought to pull the political teeth from a film like *Le Crime de Monsieur Lange/The Crime of Monsieur Lange* (Renoir 1936) acts also as a warning about the way in which the militant intentions of wider political movements can become defused by a vague and nostalgic rhetoric of community. In a similar way, Reader traces across a number of films and a number of articles the sadly ironic inheritance of 1968, from the disillusionment of *La Maman et la putain*, through the managerialism of *Mon oncle d'Amérique*, to the anomie of *Extension du domaine de la lutte/Whatever* (Harel 1999). Reader is aware that myths are nonetheless necessary to a sense of who we are, and that what ultimately makes *La Maman et la putain* so moving is its 'awareness that the loss of meta-narrative, even one so inconclusive – in one sense so un-narrative-like – as May 1968, is tragic' (Reader 1993b: 97). But nor can national myths be produced on the spot by the apparatus of consumer capitalism, as demonstrated by the derisory example of *Le Grand bleu*, with its 'commercially-packaged hunger for transcendence' (Reader 1992: 101). To some extent, though, the mythologizing tendency of cinema is inevitable by simple virtue of its iconicity and, in a kind of self-fulfilling prophecy, certain types of image take on an inescapably fabulous quality if only through their repeated reflection in cinema. Thus Reader concludes an article on cinematic representations of Paris with the suggestion that: 'It appears well-nigh impossible to film Paris without in some way celebrating it, perhaps because it has so uniquely close a connection with cinema' (Reader 1993a: 415).

This example of Paris should not distract us from the fact that Reader's writing on French cinema has often had an unusual, but welcome, focus on *la France profonde*, one of the most pervasive and enduring of myths about French national identity. This is reflected in his interest in the representation of provincial France, often – in a tradition that Reader dates from *Le Corbeau/The Raven* (Clouzot 1943) – as 'the site *par excellence* of hypocrisy and rancorous intrigue' (Reader 1981: 128); but also in his occasional attempts to take the temperature of *la France profonde*, so to speak, through an analysis of those films that are being screened, and watched, by the average provincial filmgoer: *La Vie est un long fleuve tranquille/Life is a Long, Quiet River* (Chatiliez 1988), *Le Grand bleu, Camille Claudel* (Nuytten 1988) or *Le Bonheur est dans le pré* (1995). At the same time, although the examples may be more metropolitan, Reader has also shown an interest in a significant, if sometimes overlooked strand of French film-making that depicts the lives of ordinary people largely consumed by the pleasures and pressures of work – again, *Mon oncle d'Amérique* and *Extension du domaine de la lutte* – 'lives that are extraordinary only in their unremitting ordinariness' (Reader 2001b: 119). *La France profonde*, of course, is no less mythical than the capital to which it is opposed. In *Mon oncle d'Amérique*, it is evoked in an elegiac tone 'as an Alice-in-Wonderland retreat, a *résidence secondaire* in time as well as space' (Reader 1996a: 180). In the films of Étienne Chatiliez, *la France profonde* is an idealized location, 'unpolluted by technical and cultural change', a 'toytown surrogate' for the real provincial France, 'as idealized and constructed as Alexander Mackendrick's Hebrides in *Whisky Galore* (1949) or indeed Capra's small-town America'. The presence of actors like Michel Serrault, Sabine Azéma and Eddy Mitchell ultimately gives the game away: this is 'a Parisian weekend cottage-owner's vision of rural France' (Reader 1999: 113).

If *la France profonde* effectively remains invisible in French cinema, at least outside the work of documentary film-makers like Raymond Depardon and Nicolas Philibert, its trace can perhaps be found wherever we see characters *eating*. Another of Reader's overlooked contributions to French film studies – in keeping with his healthy appetite and his recent publications on French gastronomy (Reader 2002a; Dauncey and Reader 2003) – has been his frequent attention to the cultural role of food in French cinema. Part of the controversial impact of Vigo's *Zéro de conduite/Zéro de conduite* (1933), suggests Reader, lies in its disrespect for food: 'Nothing was better calculated to elicit howls of chauvinistic rage than a combined assault on the educational system and the institutional catering of the supposed intellectual and gastronomic centre of the civilized world' (Reader 1981: 122). The psycho-sexual (and perhaps, by extension, socio-political) pathology of the characters in *La Maman et la putain* is most effectively demonstrated by their lack of appetite, the fact that their heroic consumption of cigarettes and alcohol is never seen to be balanced out by the ingestion of solid food (Reader 1993b: 97). *Mon oncle d'Amérique*'s survey of the effects of spreading globalization on France is partly demonstrated through food, by the way in which local specialties of *rillettes* and pike *au beurre blanc* are co-opted by the multinational Novotel chain. Meanwhile, the effect of these socio-economic changes on the characters' physical and mental health is shown by their troubled relationship to food or, as Reader puts it, their transformation into 'walking digestive disaster zones'. For Gérard Depardieu, 'of all actors to be associated with failed or joyless meals reinforces the film's pervasive sense of *jouissance*-free lives' (Reader 1996a: 182). *Le Bonheur est dans le pré* signals its *France profonde* credentials through the characters' 'cavalier consumption of foie gras and Armagnac' in a rather stylized, and dated, opposition to the 'kiwi-fruit style of cooking' assumed to be *de rigueur* in the metropolis (Reader 1999: 107). It is with relish that Reader relates set designer Alexandre Trauner's opinion that the hurried mealtimes necessitated by the frenzied production schedule of the 1930s brought about the premature demise of his mentor, Lazare Meerson, a victim of the industry's 'permanent dyspepsia' (Reader 2000b: 35). Could Jean Renoir's standing within the classic French cinema have had something to do with his appetite? Reader can't resist commenting on the breakfast order of Octave, played by Renoir, in *La Règle du jeu*: his request for eggs, bacon and white wine constitutes 'more serious, even perhaps more virile, fare than the "Continental breakfast" he was unable to face a moment ago' (Reader forthcoming).

All joking apart, perhaps Reader's most lasting gift to scholarship on French cinema will have been his contribution to Renoir studies. As already mentioned, he has played a significant role in the critical evaluation of *Le Crime de Monsieur Lange*, condemning the way in which the film has been depoliticized 'in the unspoken name of an ideology of humanist consensus' (Reader 1986: 42). With his customary irreverence, Reader takes to task the sacred cow of André Bazin and his well-known formalist analysis of *Lange*'s courtyard, reminding us that 'communities and topography alike are rooted in the system of class-relations which shortly after the making of *Lange* the PCF would attempt to change' (Reader 1986: 45). Reader's impatience with the view of Renoir as a 'jovially unthreatening humanist' (Reader 1990: 179) also feeds into his interpretation of *Le Testament du docteur Cordelier*. Reader suggests that this view of the director may have something to do with 'the increasingly rotund benignity of his silhouette' (Reader 1990: 179), turning him into a sort of '"Father Christmas" figure' (1990: 180), but that, with *Le Testament du docteur Cordelier*, framed by Renoir's own rather patrician presentation of the narrative to a television audience, he is deliberately seeking to undermine this persona. Thus Monsieur Opale – the Mr Hyde to Cordelier's Dr Jekyll – gives free rein to the anti-social drives that had been more carefully repressed in earlier characters like Boudu or Octave: as Reader puts it, 'Opale's leering viciousness is surely an agonistic attack on his less malign predecessors' (1990: 183). In a reassessment of *Le Crime de Monsieur Lange*, first published in 2000 and reproduced in Chapter 5 of this volume, Reader further teased out the more sinister, less jolly aspects of Renoir's work. He points out, for instance, the rather ominous way in which 'dissident or recalcitrant elements in *Le Crime de Monsieur Lange*'s view of community can safely be marginalized as buffoons' (Reader 2000c: 291; see also chapter 5, p. 74). Picking up Bazin's spatial analysis of the film, he further notes the way in which the 'bleakly horizontal' disposition of the final shot, in which Lange and Valentine escape over the border, seems to contradict or negate the communal circularity that has gone before (2000c: 293). As such, the couple's farewell to France perhaps marks the beginning of the end of Renoir's own cinematic relationship with that country, a deep understanding of French social life that he would never entirely regain after the exile of the war years (2000c: 295). Of course, the pivotal role in bringing about Renoir's exile is usually attributed to his misunderstood masterpiece *La Règle du jeu*, and it is fitting that we should end this chapter by evoking Reader's most recent, and perhaps most accomplished, work within film studies: his extraordinarily detailed yet admirably concise analysis of 'this Everest of the French cinema' (Reader forthcoming). Reader had already suggested, in passing, that Renoir's film is in many ways the hinge around which French cinema of the twentieth century turns:

Neither truly 'classic' – though the summit of the French cinema that generally goes by that name – nor yet 'modern(ist)', *La Règle du jeu* marks the transition *par excellence* from one kind of cinema to another. (Powrie and Reader 2002: 12)

In his monograph on the film, Reader succeeds in making the case that *La Règle du jeu* is 'central not only to French cinema, but to the whole history of French and indeed European culture' (Reader forthcoming). In one of his typically intriguing juxtapositions, he offers – and with a nod to his own, distant PhD thesis – Stendhal as a significant literary antecedent for Renoir: 'a romantic cynic writing in a classical style at a time of immense social upheaval' (Reader forthcoming).

It is a comment of Reader's upon *La Règle du jeu* that may perhaps afford us the opportunity to conclude. Evaluating various suggestions of the theatrical structure underlying Renoir's film (a five-act comedy? a tripartite structure? etc.), Reader notes the way in which '*La Règle du jeu* at once elicits and eludes such analysis, hinting at a kind of order whose reassurance remains perpetually out of reach' (Reader forthcoming). Reader captures well, it seems to me, the mysterious quality of *La Règle du jeu* that makes it eminently re-viewable and that also makes it at once exciting and somehow infuriatingly difficult to teach. Like all great works of art, Renoir's film readily draws comment but, even after thousands of words have been expended upon it, its mystery and its appeal remain intact, untouched. Reader's work, I suggest, has always been sensitive to this quality of the best French cinema. If he has returned so frequently to the same films, it is because they continue to call for our interpretation while forever evading our grasp. We could analyze every line in *La Maman et la putain* yet never quite understand the well-spring from which its compulsive logorrhea spills. In mapping the precise movements of the characters through La Colinière, we risk losing sight of the truly *unhinged* nature of the social breakdown depicted in *La Règle du jeu*. Reader's writing on French cinema seems to have found a way to preserve the enigmatic and urgent allure of the films. Not for him the kind of systematic, exhaustive textual analysis that leaves no room for alternative interpretations, nor the will to ascribe all films and film-makers to a single, over-riding theory, ideology or agenda. Instead, as we have seen, Reader's work is able to suggest interpretations that are allowed to grow and test themselves in the mind of the reader; it reveals a cinema always in dynamic interaction with itself (through other films) and with its society; and it seeks above all to remain faithful to the charms and curiosities that draw us to the cinema in the first place.

Chapter 15

Sexuality (and Resnais): A Response to Keith Reader

Emma Wilson

Following Douglas Morrey's important acclamation of Keith Reader's work on the history and politics of French film, my focus is narrower and in a sense more personal. Keith's work, I argue, has been exemplary and agenda-setting in its moves to consider French cinema in a broader cultural, social, and (as I emphasize) affective context. Keith, as his readers are well aware, is a passionate cinephile with an utterly enviable knowledge of French cinema from its origins to the contemporary moment. Colleagues working in film will have had the experience of uncannily encountering Keith Reader, who seems almost ubiquitous, in the cinemas and film libraries of London and Paris. They will have engaged with him in long extended conversations about film, embellished by an encyclopedic range of references and borrowed from him treasured copies of films that have long fallen out of distribution. Keith has been an extraordinarily generous and committed mentor to colleagues, to early career researchers and to graduate students in the field. Cinema is a singular passion in his work and he has proved an eloquent devotee of film, through his many reviews in *Sight and Sound* and in his wide, eclectic and imaginative range of critical articles. Yet film has always also been seen in the richest set of contexts, brought into comparison with literature and with other media, and examined within a range of questions about desire, belief and appetite, about politics, power and knowledge, which encourage the most engaged apprehension of cinema as means of mediation and expression. This attention to context is found, for example, in his case study (with Rachel Edwards) of the affair of the Papin sisters (Edwards and Reader 2001), as well as in his most recent work, a cultural history of the Bastille/Faubourg Saint-Antoine area of Paris.

From the wonderfully thick and textured fabric of Keith's research, I draw out here the threads of thinking about sexuality and gender to consider the influence and innovation of this particular area in his work. Ginette Vincendeau, Susan Hayward and Carrie Tarr, amongst others, have offered politically and culturally engaged understandings of the place of women in French cinema, and have written brilliantly on the imagery and iconicity of French women, both directors and stars. Phil Powrie has pursued such feminist lines as well, considering masculinity afresh and drawing in sensitive and powerful arguments about representations of women and of children. In a different range of writing, buoyed by the work of these contemporaries, Keith has been singularly attentive to the complexities of the intersection between sexuality and gender. His work has brought into sharp focus the attention French film has afforded to the sexual relation, and to heterosexuality in particular, as fraught, intoxicating, phantasmatic and conflicted. It is perhaps perverse to pick out these threads in Keith's writing. They should more properly be seen as interwoven into the set of arguments about film and politics that Douglas Morrey has identified so richly in Keith's work in his chapter in this volume (see Chapter 14). I am offering a partial reading here, but one that intends to respond affectively to one of the keenest, most original areas in Keith's tremendous body of work to date.

In 2008, Keith published a ground-breaking article, 'Another Deleuzian Resnais: *L'Année dernière à Marienbad/Last Year in Marienbad* (1961) as Conflict Between Sadism and Masochism'. Where Deleuze's work on the time-image has been a returning point of reference in work on *Marienbad*, Keith characteristically adds a new facet to studies of Resnais, considering this glacial and hypnotic film in dialogue with Deleuze on masochism. The fit is so true, and so revelatory, that it seems surprising that the two have not been thought together before. Keith, steeped in theory, makes the link others have missed and looks outwards, beyond the time-image, to consider how Resnais instantiates thinking about some of the psycho-sexual concerns that Deleuze has illuminated as well.

I want to pause here to look at the stages of Keith's argument. The alignment of *Marienbad* with Deleuze on masochism comes first in a sensory and affective apprehension of Resnais's film. Keith observes: 'The images and tropes of masochism as detailed by Deleuze are so vividly and insistently present in Resnais's film that it can almost be seen as a *mise en images* of the Deleuze text' (Reader 2008: 150). Keith responds to the 'distinctive iconography of masochism' in the film that is 'dominated by statues, stone women and a "suprasensual emotionality, surrounded with ice and protected by fur" ([Deleuze] 1967: 46–47)' (Reader 2008: 150). The comparison is embedded immediately in this sensory apprehension of how Deleuze on masochism and Resnais connect, and connections too between Deleuze's recognition of Masoch's origins at the boundary of Central and Eastern Europe, his Slavic fascination and 'the glacial imagery that pervades his work' (Reader 2008: 150). But this coinciding, or coincidence, between *Marienbad* and the material world of Masoch, as represented by Deleuze, is only the prelude to a shimmering intellectual argument that then is allowed to unfurl.

Keith speaks of the significance to his study of the 'psychic determination of masochism' (Reader 2008: 150). He shows very feelingly how, to patriarchy, Deleuze opposes 'the maternal and matriarchal world of the masochist, which seeks to punish and indeed to exclude the father by way of a contract between the chastising mother-figure and the chastised male' (Reader 2008: 151). Keith shows how Deleuze draws on the work of Theodor Reik, for whom '"[m]asochistic practices are but an acting out of preceding phantasies, daydreams that are transferred into reality" (Reik 1941: 49)' (2008: 151). Reik places emphasis in particular on the lability of the masochistic fantasy, and such recognition is used to powerful effect in Keith's writing. There is no sense that the relation between masochism and *Marienbad* is illustrative or fixed. Keith's account is sensitive throughout to the extraordinary unfixability of the film, to what he describes as 'the film's evident recalcitrance to a narrativization it at the same time inescapably invites' (Reader 2008: 151). Such recalcitrance is reflected, or more properly respected, in the moves of Keith's argument to elucidate not masochism alone, but 'a rivalry between the sadistic and the masochistic realm – a rivalry whose issue, inevitably for so hyper-ambiguous a film, is indeterminate, though tending perhaps towards the ascendancy of masochism' (Reader 2008: 150). And if masochism is ascendant, it claims this position in particular as a consequence of its lability.

As the article continues, it effectively flips back to Deleuze on the time-image, finding congruence, in 'Marienbad's Möbius-like textual space' (Reader 2008: 154), between the lability and mirroring of Reik's masochism and the refracting and immobilizing mirrors of Marienbad's decor. Decor and iconography are seen as key to the film. Keith argues indeed that in the highly designed space of 'the imaginary room' in Marienbad, that room of mirrors hesitantly inhabited by A (Delphine Seyrig), '[the] Sadean and the masochistic universe ... at once vie and coexist, through X's direction of A's memories and movements ("narrative" and control) on the one hand, and the deployment of mirrors and doublings ("decor" and stasis) on the other' (Reader 2008: 155). Recognition of this coexistence leads towards the most coruscating passages of the piece and Keith's revision of readings of the troubled scene of A's possession by X (Giorgio Albertazzi).

This scene marks a point of interference and difference between screenplay and film, where Robbe-Grillet narrates a rape sequence, while Resnais replaces this with enigmatic shots of resistance or blocking, their opacity drawing attention in effect to the excision that has taken place. Keith ingeniously plots the rivalry between sadism and masochism across the axes of Robbe-Grillet and Resnais's creative collaboration. If Robbe-Grillet's sadistic scenario is removed, it is replaced by an alternative masochistic scene that has significant consequences for readings of representations of gender and sexuality in Resnais.

Looking at the blanched shots where A is seen, over-exposed, like Masoch's Wanda in her white feathery negligee, Keith comments on the absence of X from these shots, and on the way his absence eliminates any possibility of sensory contact between the couple. He goes on, in a deft move reminiscent of the startling comparison of L'Atalante (Vigo 1934) and King Kong (Cooper 1933) remarked by Morrey, to marshall Titanic (Cameron 1997), or at least Žižek's reading thereof, to bring Marienbad into focus. When Rose exclaims, 'Nothing can take us apart! I'll never let you go!', as Žižek writes: 'The act that accompanies these pathetic words is the opposite gesture of letting him go, of gently pushing him away, so that he gets sucked into the dark water – a perfect exemplification of Lacan's thesis that the elevation to the status of symbolic authority has to be paid for by the death, murder even, of its empirical bearer' (Žižek 1999: vii). Keith sees, for this scenario, a mirror image in Marienbad. Teasingly leaving his own question open, he asks: 'Could A's outstretched arms not likewise be seen as pushing X away at the same time as they welcome him, thereby ambiguously granting and denying him "the status of symbolic authority" that acceding to his version of events would confer?' (Reader 2008: 156). Such a reading instantly suspends conclusions on the film. While Keith acknowledges that A's welcome is sensuous, he sees it leaving X 'within the close-yet/because-distant world of the Deleuzian masochist rather than transcending it towards some fusional realm' (Reader 2008: 156). What this reading implies for readings of gender and sexuality in Resnais (and indeed in film of the period more broadly) is, I suggest, highly significant. I focus here particularly on how Keith's work has changed my own reading of the film.

A number of readings of *Marienbad*, my own included, have tended to place A as a victim of the plot's sexual and autocratic machinations. Keith's analysis, at a stroke, opens the possibility that X, as much as A – or perhaps more so – is a victim, however willing, of their encounter. Where in my recent reading of *Marienbad*, I laid emphasis on questions the film raises about 'what it means to construct a fantasy for two' (Wilson 2006b: 73, cited in Reader 2008: 153), my argument tended to privilege the possibility of moving towards what Keith describes as some fusional realm. I argued: 'Where at the start of the film the man and the woman appear as two separate, autonomous individuals, the effect of *L'Année dernière à Marienbad* as it continues is to make us increasingly uncertain about the limits of the subjectivity and desire of these lovers' (Wilson 2006b: 75). I located this uncertainty and fusion directly in the fantasy and game-playing of the individuals, and in the film's strategies of rendering uncertain the ownership of the subjective images, imaginary or mnemonic it insistently displays. For me, the film's approach to intersubjectivity, the shared bond that tends towards fusion and the indeterminacy of boundaries, risked a lapse too into psychosis in the darkness and madness of the end of the film. For Keith, that fusional realm – which he argues specifically is not accessed by X and A – would seem to be tied rather to erotic congress and to the affective and visceral coupling of lovers.

Keith's reading strikes me afresh with uncertainty and opens the play of meanings of the film. My point of contact with the article – its *punctum*, moment of piercing truth and affective curiosity – comes in its vision of A as '"icy-emotional-cruel" (Deleuze 1967: 45) mother' and, at the same time, as 'jubilantly greeting hetaera' (2008: 156). I too, unconsciously identifying the masochist tendency of the film, considered the statuary of the film. But rather than conjure Deleuze, I turned to the work of Barbara Johnson to attempt some notion of a Parnassian aesthetics in *Marienbad* (Wilson 2006b: 82–83). Grappling with the ambiguities of the film, I argued:

> In a film whose aesthetic depends on the statue, on frozen motion and marmoreal timelessness, Resnais's heroine remains contrarily febrile, moving, sentient, though vulnerable. She is never the statue whose pose reveals her pleasure. Resnais refuses to allow her to be tied up (as in Robbe-Grillet's fantasy) but instead allows her to move freely. (Wilson 2006b: 83)

I responded here to the moves between the icy and the erotic that the film undoubtedly explores, as does Keith. My feminist agenda led me to construe A as vulnerable, moving imperceptibly from an apprehension of her as sentient (not numb or frozen) to a sense of her fragility. My reading also constructed a liberatory agenda for her; implicit in my pleasure in the film was a sense that Resnais constructed his female figure as free-moving, and as a desiring and volitional subject. Her volition may entangle her in her intersubjective play with X, but this, my argument suggested, is only an unfortunate corollary of her free movement as subject, of Resnais's free thinking and of his unfixing of patriarchal fantasy.

Reading Keith has made evident to me a limit in my thinking and a failure in my imagination. Going back to the film, from his perspective, has made it open up differently to me. Indeed, this mercurial quality, this lability, is precisely what *Marienbad* seems ultimately to be about (as Keith and I both acknowledge in our different ways). I failed to imagine the scene from the viewpoint of the male desiring subject. I failed to see its gestures outside the sadistic scenario fleshed out more fully in Robbe-Grillet's screenplay. Here is what I now see in the film, following my reading of Keith's essay.

In the scene in *Marienbad* at 1:18, the pace of the tracking camera through the film's corridors, the strident music accumulating sensation, the urgency of the scene's passage towards its point of culmination, appear to conjure a subject position whose emotions and sensations are transported through the shot. Any distance between the point of view of the camera and the subjectivity of a desiring viewer seems elided and the camera work and soundtrack seem at one with a desiring consciousness. As the film races towards A, her figure in white is seen illuminated, framed by the doorway to her over-exposed bedroom. She is not vulnerable here, nor is she free-moving. A stands still and tranquil. She seems to me now a totemic figure, a mother goddess swathed in the fabric and feathers of her lovely peignoir. The actress does not flee before the camera, nor does the character before the figure (or apparatus) that seems to move towards her with such velocity and intent. She confronts what approaches her with apparent equanimity. Her bodily presence here seems strikingly different from that of the fragile and contorting figure seen, held and caressed in the various walks through the gardens of *Marienbad*. As the camera reaches her, she still does not recoil or protect herself. Again, vulnerability and fear are not evidenced here. Instead, she is seen three times raising her arms in this deliriously unreadable gesture, which each time I view seems to me more exultant and erotic, yet divisive. Keith's ambivalent reading, his hypothesis that A's outstretched arms are pushing X away *at the same time as* they welcome him, seems brilliant indeed, and utterly acute in its response to the film's politics and tempo.

Keith takes forward his reading, pursuing ambivalence (and impossibility) by aligning A's gesture, and its ambivalence, with the writing of Jean-Luc Nancy on touch. Looking at Nancy's essay, *Noli me tangere*, Keith cites the philosopher on Christ's words to Mary Magdalene: 'For him Christ's words imply "do not seek to touch or to hold on to what is essentially moving away, and in so doing touches you with its very distance" (Nancy 2003: 30)' (Reader 2008: 156). Nancy's image of this interrupted touch, its impossible relation, takes Keith back to the masochistic contract. He finds in Nancy breathtakingly congruent words for Wanda's final abandonment of Séverin (in Masoch's novella): '"You hold nothing, you cannot hold or hold onto anything, and that is what you must love and know. That is what a loving knowledge is all about. Love what escapes you, love the one who is going away. Love their going away." (2003: 61)' (Reader 2008: 156)

In forthcoming work, also in response to Keith's article on *Marienbad*, I will explore the implications of this interpretation of a loving knowledge, and love of what escapes you, for *Marienbad*, thinking, through Levinas, about the film's recall of images from *Nuit et brouillard/Night and Fog* (Resnais 1955), and about the necrophilic imbrication of death,

L'Année dernière à Marienbad – A simultaneously pushing away and welcoming X.

desire and vulnerability. But this again will be a different reading. What I hope to hold on to for the moment is the sense of the implications of Keith's reading of the scenario in *Marienbad* as staging of masochism. On one level, his reading is revelatory in its ability to work closely from the evidence of the images, from the affect and texture of what is to hand (yet always intriguingly elusive), and this I hope to have gone some way towards illustrating. Yet the interpretation of *Marienbad* is also indicative of a further tendency in Keith's writing in general, revealed in his interest in masochism as a scenario of desire that rethinks (gendered) power relations. Keith's work has been extraordinary in its ability to respond to feminism and to the work of feminists, to pursue a gender equality agenda, and to offer coruscating new perspectives in this field. In particular, Keith has renewed thinking about heterosexuality on film and in twentieth century culture, drawing new attention to its difficulties, vulnerabilities and perversions. So, in the remainder of this chapter, I ask what the work on *Marienbad* reveals about the further trends in his work and about his perspective on sexuality and gender.

Keith's work on *Marienbad* reveals a heightened sensitivity to the range of representations of women and investments in their visual and psychic construction. In his contribution to Alex Hughes' and James Williams' volume *Gender and French Cinema* (Reader 2001a), Keith offers a startling analysis of Arletty and the range of roles she has played. Referencing the work of Ginette Vincendeau and Susan Hayward, Keith acknowledges 'the greater scope that star-studies affords to investigations of gender' (Reader 2001a: 63). Looking at Arletty intricately through Judith Butler, Keith analyzes the ways in which Arletty, through her roles, her performance style, her body morphology and the very timbre of her voice, builds a corpus of work that effectively plays with gender (Reader 2001a: 64). Keith shows how such work references a range of fantasies of femininity, writing: 'Arletty partakes of some of the most tenacious archetypes of modern femininity – the whore-with-a-heart-of-gold in *Hôtel du Nord* (Carné 1938); the *femme fatale* in *Les Enfants du paradis/Children of Paradise* (Carné, 1945); the incestuous mother-figure in Roger Richebé's *Gibier de potence/Gigolo* (1951)' (Reader 2001a: 65). In *Les Enfants du paradis*, Arletty represents 'femininity in all its enigmatic inconstancy' (Reader 2001a: 72), as well as introducing elements of gender ambiguity in particular through her relation to Baptiste. Keith is sensitive to 'the range of gendered possibilities she embodies' (Reader 2001a: 72), and argues that extremely important among these is that of the mother. With due levity, he continues:

> This may at first appear bizarre, given Arletty's own strident rejection of motherhood and the fact that in none of her major screen roles does she play a mother. But the 'mother' to be referred to here is to be understood less in a biological than in a figurative sense, deriving from Gilles Deleuze's construction of a certain kind of mother-figure in *Masochism* (1967). (Reader 2001a: 72)

The work on Arletty prefigures his study of masochism in *Marienbad*, and shows the development of feminist or post-feminist thinking, also referencing the work of Gaylyn

Studlar, about power relations within representations of gender and viewing scenarios. Critical here is the sense, in the first place, that femininity (and masculinity, for that matter, but more on that later) are multi-faceted and mercurial; and second that within this panoply of gender performances, power, autonomous desire and even phallic subjectivity are – and, more generously, should be – also the preserve of women. (He acknowledges humorously in this piece that 'reality, for some of us at least, may of course be significantly improved and enriched by the availability of an erotic, non-castratory mother figure' [Reader 2001a: 73]).

In his co-authored work with Rachel Edwards on the Papin sisters, again drawing together film and critical and cultural context, Keith takes forward thinking about cultural and psychic fascination with 'wayward' women (Edwards and Reader 2001: 51). At the opposite extreme, in his work on Robert Bresson (Reader 2000a), he considers the representation of the *femme douce* in Bresson's work in some depth, bringing debates about gender to the analysis of Bresson's corpus for the first time. Keith's analysis of *Au hasard Balthazar* is suitably brisk in this respect as he comments: 'Marie is later to tell her mother that she does whatever Gérard tells her to and would kill herself if he asked her – a depth of self-abnegation that marks her out as the most extreme, even pathological example of the *femme douce* in Bresson's work' (Reader 2000a: 83). It is certainly a fascination with the range of representations of women, and their sexual and political positioning, that spreads across these works, but I would say that it is questions of female power and autonomy (and their correlative effects on the construction of masculinity) that come to dominate in Keith's work.

This position on feminism and femininity is witnessed in Keith's telling analysis of the Gabrielle Russier affair (Reader 2005). Gabrielle Russier was a schoolteacher prosecuted by the French State for her affair with a much younger male pupil. The affair culminated in her suicide in 1969. Keith explains the interest of the affair, in particular in understanding of the period immediately following May 1968 and its aftermath:

> The affair, indeed, forms a kind of prism through which changes in attitudes within and between French and Anglophone cultures across the past thirty-five years are refracted – attitudes towards gender, class, the pedagogic relationship and the boundaries between private and public life. (Reader 2005: 9)

The article is of telling interest, in terms of gender, in its defence of and fascination with 'the autonomously desiring woman' (Reader 2005: 11) and the challenge she posed in France, and particularly a Mediterranean context, in the late 1960s. By considering the Gabrielle Russier affair within a broader set of questions about gender, sexuality, pedagogy and inter-generational relationships, Keith offers consideration of changed attitudes and mores in a French and also in a US or UK context, noting an inverted gender imbalance post-feminism. He observes that suspicion 'in a feminist – some would say "post-feminist" – era, now bears far more heavily, particularly in the United States, on male desire, fraught as it at least potentially is with greater scope for the abuse of power' (Reader 2005: 11).

As well as femininity, Keith is also concerned with masculinity – the roles and desires open to men. This dual perspective, and his refusal to privilege one over the other, makes him such an astute reader of *L'Année dernière à Marienbad*, amongst so many other films. The questioning of how feminism has reconfigured gender roles comes to the fore in his recent major book *The Abject Object: Avatars of the Phallus in Contemporary French Theory, Literature and Film* (Reader 2006). This volume pursues in part his critical interest in female autonomy and power, and in the lability of feminine roles. He offers a virtuoso reading of Christine Angot's 'phallic narrative transvestism' (Reader 2006: 151–63), fuelled by close attention to the shifting subject positions and the uneasy ventriloquism of Angot's prose. He returns, too, to dualities (or pluralities) of femininity in discussion of *La Maman et la putain/The Mother and the Whore* (Eustache 1973), one of the films to which he has returned at different times in his writing. Of particular brilliance in his discussion of the film is his recognition that 'the film's narrative as it unfolds works to reverse the two women's roles' (Reader 2006: 176). The mother and the whore, figures also conjured in Delphine Seyrig's sumptuous, illuminated gestures in *Marienbad*, merge into one another, their roles reversed.

The Abject Object pursues this consideration of femininity and constructed in the (French) filmic and literary imagination; in line with Keith's attention to heterosexuality, and to its more melancholic guises, the volume also studies with specific intensity the fate of masculinity under feminism. That such an account should be so robust, so humorous, yet also laced with pathos and a reckoning with the costs of crisis, testifies to the strength and originality of Keith's critical positioning.

Early in the volume, he proposes 'masculinity, the ostensible domain of the phallus, inexorably dwells under the sign of its own abjection' (Reader 2006: 11). He effectively shows the ways in which Phil Powrie's work has paved the way for his own, noting:

> What Phil Powrie terms 'the crisis of masculinity which has begun in the 1970s with the advent of feminism' (Powrie 1997: 8) is a well-attested phenomenon in contemporary Western cultures, often seen as a response to the return of the repressed Other that is woman. Masculinity challenged, masculinity distressed, masculinity tormented is a central feature of the modern-day gender landscape. (Reader 2006: 11)

The texts Keith addresses in the volume, including novels by Bataille and Houellebecq, and such contemporary films as *Le Pornographe/The Pornographer* (Bonello 2001) and *Seul contre tous/I stand alone* (Noé 1998), in his words 'locate that challenge, that distress, that torment at the heart of masculinity, perhaps indissociable from its very constitution' (Reader 2006: 11). Gender trouble is configured in the volume as source of distress *and* opportunity. There is a radical move to think these two at once and to record the more outlandish bodily experiences and sensations to which they give rise. Keith here references Kristeva on abjection, and a further series of ambiguous games with the mother, as well as writing with elegance on Lacan and the phallus. In his eloquent conclusion he notes with due effect:

The calling into question of what once seemed self-evident gender boundaries may be liberating, as with much queer theory, but with any other kind of liberation it comes at a price, increasing the scope for felt impoverishment as well as enrichment of what it means to be a man. (Reader 2006: 205)

What I find trenchant in Keith's work is his unflinching analysis of the full complexities of identification and desire, of power and projection, in thinking gender and sexuality. His work offers a thoroughly engaged response to those ethically and culturally adventurous areas addressed by French film (and writing) of the modern era. His work newly responds to the psychological complexity brought to representations of the heterosexual love relation and finds this complexity integrally bound up with questions about representation and interpretation. Politically engaged in broader questions of context, personally involved in his work, marvellously frank and clear-sighted, Keith as critic offers rare and intense companionship for Anglophone analysts of modern French culture.

Chapter 16

Of Spaces and Difference in *La Graine et le mulet* (2007): A Dialogue with Carrie Tarr

Will Higbee

There is a moment early in Abdellatif Kechiche's award-winning third feature *La Graine et le mulet/Couscous* (2007) where Slimane, the film's central protagonist, reveals to his eldest daughter (Karima) and her husband (José) that he is to be laid off from the shipyard in Sète, a port on France's southern Mediterranean coast, where he has worked for over 30 years. José summarizes both the broader economic climate and his father-in-law's particular predicament in the following way: 'It's simple. They no longer want French workers.' The logic of José's argument is as direct as it is familiar: in search of ever greater profits, French companies would prefer to source cheap migrant labour than paying a French workforce what it is worth. Such a comment even has the potential to lead to the kind of xenophobic protectionism that sees immigrant workers presented as a scapegoats in times of economic decline,[1] though this is emphatically *not* the case in *La Graine et le mulet*.

What is so intriguing about José's remark, located in a secondary scene early in the film, is precisely to whom the comment refers. For the 'French' worker in question is Slimane, a Tunisian immigrant, the very person who would previously have been identified as the foreigner accused of 'stealing' French jobs. We might argue that the fact Slimane is identified as French and not 'immigrant' by a member of his own extended family (his son-in-law) is evidence that such a pronouncement is not representative of a significant shift in the broader public view of the presence (and permanence) of the North African diasporas in France. In fact, Slimane's identification as part of the working-class community of Sète in *La Graine et le mulet* is far more complex than José's initial remark might suggest. We learn, for example, that Slimane worked as an undeclared immigrant for many years following his arrival in Sète and so will not receive the full amount of redundancy pay to which he should be entitled – an indication of his legal and economic marginalization and a suggestion that for Slimane there has been a gradual process of integration into the 'French' working-class community. Indeed, this very sense of inclusion is challenged later in the film, when familiar prejudices about the North African immigrant 'other' seem to re-emerge through veiled remarks from health inspectors and fellow restaurateurs as Slimane attempts to launch his floating couscous restaurant.

And yet, despite the presence of these (depressingly) familiar barriers and prejudices in the narrative, when watching *La Graine et le mulet* one is struck by the way in which, without eliding or denying their difference, Kechiche's film already seems to have moved beyond the position of affirming the rightful place of North African immigrants and their descendants in France – a theme that so preoccupied earlier beur cinema of the 1980s and

1990s and continues to dominate the narratives of many Maghrebi-French authored films of the 2000s.[2] In keeping with Kechiche's stated aim in *La Graine et le mulet* to explore this familial narrative with the context of a socio-economic milieu (the working-class community of Sète) rather than through the exoticized difference of an ethnic minority community,[3] Slimane is first introduced to us in the context of class (at work in the shipyard and then in conversation with local fisherman on the quay), before being located in the domestic context of the family home where ethnic differences (such as the couscous of the film's title) are arguably more pronounced.

Therefore, although the central protagonists of *La Graine et le mulet* are of immigrant origin, the film is not specifically concerned with an 'immigrant' narrative. Rather, I would suggest that it is a narrative about a working-class family living in Sète whose members happen to be of North African origin. Writing in *Cahiers du cinéma*, Jean Michel Frodon described the film as: 'not a beur film, nor a film about immigrants but a film about France today' (2007: 10). This view was shared by many French critics who made a point of identifying the Frenchness of Kechiche's particular brand of social cinema, placing him as the natural heir to Renoir, Sautet and Pialat (Kaganski 2007; Delorme 2007: 11). In addition to the overwhelmingly positive critical response, the film amassed a string of awards at various festivals and at the Césars (the French equivalent of the Oscars), where it won four awards including best director and best film, not to mention an audience of 800,000 spectators in France – a considerable achievement for what was essentially a medium-budget, auteur-led production with a cast of relative unknowns and first-time actors.

In terms of both its narrative focus and its reception by French audiences and critics, *La Graine et le mulet* arguably marks an undeniable shift in the identification with Maghrebi-French film-making from immigrant to national cinema.[4] This transformation is, moreover, paralleled in Kechiche's own career trajectory: from an actor who first appeared in *Le Thé à la menthe/Mint Tea* (Bahloul 1984) as a streetwise Algerian immigrant, to the director of a film that identifies Kechiche as the latest in a long line of French social realist auteurs.[5] It is this shift, I suggest, that marks *La Graine et le mulet* as arguably the most significant film by a French director of Maghrebi-immigrant origin to have emerged in France since Mehdi Charef's *Le Thé au harem d'Archimède/Tea in the Harem* signalled the 'arrival' of beur cinema in 1985.

A consideration of when and why immigrant cinema becomes national cinema, and what *La Graine et le mulet* might have to tell us about how far Maghrebi-French film-making has come (or not) since the early 1980s inevitably draws me to the work of Carrie Tarr. Since the publication of her article 'Questions of Identity in Beur Cinema' in the early 1990s (Tarr 1993b; see also Chapter 6 of this volume), Tarr has been charting how Maghrebi-French and North African émigré film-makers reframe the way that difference is conceptualized in the context of French national cinema and in relation to ongoing debates about national identity in a multicultural, postcolonial France. For Tarr, the work of film-makers of Maghrebi descent in France is more than just a question of representation; it also becomes a way of 'negotiating their own position within French society' (Tarr 2005: 210). Despite the increasingly popular successes of certain Maghrebi French and North African film-makers since the late 1990s,[6] Tarr's work has not lost sight of the film-making from within the North African diaspora that continues to take place on the margins (financially and politically) of French cinema – see, for example, her work on directors such Ameur-Zaïmeche and Ghorab-Volta (Tarr 2005: 167–86). In a similar way, when writing about Maghrebi-French film-making in the context of French national cinema, Tarr has always looked within and beyond the boundaries of the national, conscious of the specific local and global contexts within which these films are produced and the ways in which such contexts intersect with debates surrounding French national cinema and French identity. In a recent publication (Tarr 2009), she thus identifies an urgent need for Maghrebi-French film-making to be placed in 'in dialogue with constructions of Franco-Arab cultures, relations and identities in the cinemas of the Maghreb' in order to offer 'a polycentric vision which not only acknowledges the voices and gazes of those previously confined to the periphery but also enables cultures (or ethnicities) to be seen "in relation"' (Tarr 2009: 291–92). Moreover, as her contribution in Chapter 23 of this volume (on Jewish-Arab relations in French and Maghrebi cinemas) shows, Tarr's work continues to emphasize the need to avoid the careless homogenizing of the Maghreb through an exploration the range of differences and identities (individual and collective) that emerge in films on both sides of the Mediterranean.

Carrie Tarr's pioneering work on Maghrebi-French and North African émigré film-making in France thus combines an encyclopedic knowledge of films and film-makers from the North African diaspora in France with an awareness of, and sensitivity to, the nuanced connections between colonial history, contemporary debates concerning immigration, national identity and the Republican model, and the politics of representing difference in a multicultural, postcolonial France. Her sophisticated analysis of Maghrebi-French and North African émigré cinemas in France is further enriched by the application of Anglo-American theoretical discourses (cultural studies, postcolonial theory) that until recently have largely been ignored by French academics in the field. Her approach brings to mind Bakhtin's insistence on the value of interrogating culture from *without*:

> In order to understand, it is immensely important for the person who understands to be located outside the object of his or her creative understanding – in time, in space, in culture ... Such a dialogic encounter of two cultures does not result in merging or mixing. Each retains its own unity and open totality, but they are mutually enriched. (Bakhtin, in Willemen 1994: 199)

In this way, Tarr's research and publications have introduced a whole generation of scholars to films and film-makers that for too long have remained barely visible to both Anglophone and Francophone audiences.[7]

While consistently championing Maghrebi-French film-making, Tarr has never shied away from questioning the limitations of certain films and film-makers in their failure to offer progressive representations of difference, particularly in relation to gender and sexuality (see, for example, her critique of the representation of women in Charef's landmark film *Le Thé au harem d'Archimède* (Tarr 2005: 33–34). Her work has also been keenly aware of the dangers of effacing the politics of representation through an engagement with the mainstream – asking, for instance, what is at stake when Maghrebi-French directors such as Djamel Bensalah and stars such as Jamel Debbouze employ genre cinema to engage with a mainstream French audience, and whether such a crossing over simply means 'selling out' (Tarr 2005: 168–71). In the conclusion to her landmark publication *Reframing Difference: Beur and Banlieue Filmmaking in France* (Tarr 2005: 210–13), she notes that, in spite of the progress made since the emergence of beur cinema in the mid-1980s, a number of critical absences or representational blindspots remain: the continued paucity of female-centred narratives in Maghrebi-French authored films; the lack of a balanced exploration of the place of Islam in France; an uneasiness on the part of Maghrebi-French film-makers at foregrounding narratives involving inter-ethnic romance; and, finally, the continuing representation of the (male) Maghrebi-French protagonist as unable or unwilling to find a place within French society that is not based on an interstitial or marginalized identity – leading to the inability to construct what Tarr refers to as 'narratives of empowerment' (2005: 213). Crucially, Tarr identifies the critical absences listed above as intrinsically allied to the construction of space in Maghrebi-French film-making. Too many narratives, she argues, find it difficult or virtually impossible to construct a space and thus a place for their (mostly masculine) protagonists outside the *cité* – the run-down, working-class housing estates of the deprived urban periphery. Almost inevitably, the *cité* becomes the focal point for these protagonists, coded as a masculine site of violence, delinquency and alterity, regardless of whether or not this is the film-maker's intention.

For the remainder of this chapter, I intend to enter into a dialogue with Tarr's work in order to analyze a recent and key intervention in Maghrebi-French film-making: *La Graine et le mulet*. I argue for the importance of this film in that it directly addresses some of Tarr's earlier criticisms (outlined above) concerning the shortcomings of Maghrebi-French film-making to date, in particular a dearth of strong roles for female protagonists. The film is also significant, I suggest, for the way in which it refuses to identify its working-class protagonists as prisoners of their social environment, confined to the emblematically marginal spaces of the *cité* – another aspect of Maghrebi-French film-making directly analyzed by Tarr's work.

Undoubtedly, Tarr's inquiry into how difference (of ethnicity, gender, sexuality, class, age) is represented spatially in Maghrebi-French film-making reflects the fact that Maghrebi-French film-making, by attempting to argue for the rightful place of citizens of Maghrebi descent in the French Republic, is itself in part preoccupied with representing space as a means of constructing identity. The locale of the *cité*, the contested spaces of the nation state, the hidden histories of North African immigration to France and the intensely personal return narratives of the 2000s that transport us across the Mediterranean are all examples of the extent to which the politics of (diasporic) identity are spatially coded in Maghrebi-French film-making. These films explore the spaces of difference as well as the differences such spaces make, along with the boundaries (real and imagined) that such spaces can bring

La Graine et le mulet.

between margin/centre, inclusion/exclusion, France/Maghreb, national/transnational and *cité*/city.

Nevertheless, as Carrie Tarr reminds us repeatedly in her writing on Maghrebi-French and North African émigré film-making, while such spaces may be inscribed with a difference that has the potential to mark its inhabitants as 'other' to a mainstream audience, they are never as fixed or absolute as more Eurocentric readings of these films and film-makers would have us believe. Indeed, it is from these supposed spaces of difference and alterity that discourse and representations can emerge with the potential to transform our understanding of French national and cultural identity in the postcolonial present. With these ideas firmly in mind, let us now turn our attention to an analysis of space and difference in *La Graine et le mulet*.

Many French reviewers have rightly commented on the importance of language in determining the structure, identity and 'authenticity' of *La Graine et le mulet*.[8] While not wishing to downplay the obvious importance of language in all of Kechiche's films to date, I would argue that the spaces in which these words are uttered are of equal significance.[9] *La Graine et le mulet* is, first, defined by its setting in the port of Sète.[10] The film's geographical location, on the Mediterranean coast, facing out towards North Africa, offers the possibility of the port functioning as a cross-cultural contact zone between France and the Maghreb. However, unlike the larger, more industrial southern port of Marseille that features in films such as *Bye-bye* (Dridi 1995), *Comme un aimant/The Magnet* (Saleh and Akhenaton 2000) and *Samia* (Faucon 2001), Sète is not considered a symbolic point of arrival and departure, nor is it an historical point of cultural intersection between France and the Maghreb. Rather, Sète is characterized primarily as an historic fishing port.[11] Of equal significance for a film that seeks to locate its Maghrebi protagonists in relation to class as much as ethnic difference is the fact that, while the port remains a major commercial fishing centre, the town's economy is increasingly dependent on tourism. In the opening scene of *La Graine et le mulet*, we are immediately introduced to this tension between the old and new economies of Sète, as the camera is placed alongside a group of tourists taking a boat tour of the port led by Madjid, who is later identified as Slimane's eldest son. As the boat navigates the port's interior canals leading to the harbour, Madjid draws the tourists' attention on one side to the piles of scrap metal destined for Turkey (lamenting the fact that 'France used to make ovens, now it seems we've run out of matches') and on the other to '*la criée du poisson*', the spot where a port employee used to announce the arrival of the day's catch at market until, as Madjid notes, 'everything became computerized'. Madjid then abandons his post – much to his colleague's annoyance – in order to meet below deck with his lover, and from this apparently random *histoire de cul*[12] we are abruptly transported to the adjacent shipyard in which Slimane works, and from which he will soon be made redundant.

Through the opening sequence, Sète is thus introduced as a port that is rapidly losing links to its industrial past; the working-class community of fishermen and shipyards are being reduced to little more than a sideshow for the pleasure cruises that pass by. The extent to which the difference is inscribed in the spaces of the port has as much to do with class as it does with ethnicity. As Kechiche has himself acknowledged, it is this theme of the loss of a traditional place for the working-class families of Sète within the local economy that preoccupies Kechiche more in *La Graine et le mulet* than the question of the place of the North African community (and their French-born descendents) within French society (Kechiche 2008).

Locating *La Graine et le mulet* in Sète, Kechiche continues the trend established earlier in the 2000s by certain Maghrebi-French film-makers of moving away from the Parisian urban periphery, and more specifically the run-down housing estates on the fringes of Paris as the exclusive setting for beur protagonists (see Tarr 2005; Higbee 2007). However, unlike other films released since 2000, such as *Jeunesse dorée/Golden Youth* (Ghorab Volta 2002) and *Drôle de Félix/The Adventures of Felix* (Ducastel and Martineau 2000), in which the Maghrebi-immigrant protagonists actively journey 'beyond' the *banlieue* into new and unfamiliar spaces of *la France profonde*, or else attempt to reconnect with their Maghrebi roots through a return to the *bled* (family home in the Maghreb) (cf. *Tenja/Testament* [Legzouli 2005]; *Exils/Exiles* [Gatlif 2004]; *Bled Number One/Back Home* [Ameur-Zaïmeche 2006]), the spaces occupied by the protagonists of *La Graine et le mulet* are settled and familiar. Kechiche thus emphasizes the sedentary nature of the North African diaspora in France rather than the sense of rupture, displacement or a continuing search for place that dominates the narratives of so much Maghrebi-French and North African émigré film-making. The protagonists of *La Graine et le mulet* may well undergo change, most obviously due to the effects of Slimane's redundancy, but Sète is their home, and even the first-generation immigrants have no intention of leaving. Following news of his redundancy, Slimane politely entertains his sons' suggestions that he return to the *bled*. Yet his response, which comes through his subsequent actions and *not* words, is to set up his own business (the couscous restaurant-boat moored in Sète), building a legacy for his children in France, not the Maghreb. Moreover, unlike other films by Maghrebi-French film-makers, or focusing on protagonists of Maghrebi-descent situated on the south Mediterranean coast (most obviously *Bye-bye*), the port location does not function metonymically to express a desire for return to the Maghreb and the ambivalent pull between host and homeland for the diasporic subject. Whereas in *Bye-bye* Ismael is repeatedly framed staring out across the Mediterranean at the boats carrying passengers between France and the Maghreb, the view from the window of Slimane's lodgings is of the internal waterways of Sète; it does not look out to sea. Similarly, the boat that Slimane buys and restores with his redundancy money (named 'La Source', thus evoking a sense of roots or origins) is not intended as a vessel to transport him back to the Maghreb. Rather, the floating restaurant remains on the waterways of Sète – destined for, of all places, Quai de la République. In fact, the boat never arrives at this prime tourist location due to problems with red tape, and is instead (symbolically) moored near the Hôtel de l'Orient.

This is not to say that markers of ethnic difference are absent from *La Graine et le mulet*. Consider, for example, the extended family meal sequence sixteen minutes into the film in which questions of ethnic and linguistic difference, and the tensions that such difference can produce (as well as the sense of enrichment that such differences bring), are openly discussed by Mario and Lilia over the fish couscous 'prepared with love' by Souad for the assembled guests. The meal itself brings together members of the multi-ethnic working-class community of Sète – friends and extended family – who are of Tunisian, Italian and Russian origin. In cinematic terms, the sequence is a *tour de force* that identifies Kechiche as a worthy successor to auteurs such as Renoir and Pialat for its honest and respectful depiction of social relations and human interaction. What distinguishes Kechiche from earlier/other Maghrebi-French directors, though – and what marks out *La Graine et le mulet* as a landmark film in the history of Maghrebi-French film-making – is that Kechiche fully acknowledges the difference of his Maghrebi-French and North African immigrant protagonists without ever making this the determining or deciding factor surrounding their place within French society, or indeed their identification as 'other'. Compare, for example, the treatment of Maghrebi-French cultural difference in *La Graine et le mulet* with earlier beur films of the 1980s, in which the characters reject or elide their parents' North African cultural heritage in favour of an identification with multi-ethnic *banlieue* youth culture, or more recent films such as *Hexagone* (Chibane 1994), which offer a beur-centred narrative that places the Maghrebi-French experience quite clearly in a space (the disadvantaged urban periphery) that is characterized as marginal in relation to wider French society.[13]

In this sense, it could be argued that *La Graine et le mulet* is profoundly Republican in character. It is no accident that the most explicit discussion of difference takes place over the family meal in the private/domestic sphere, while the difference on display at the opening night of the restaurant (to which I shall return later) is quite clearly contained within a space that intends to transfer the intimacy of the family couscous meal to the public space of the restaurant. Similarly, the title of the film itself – *La Graine et le mulet*, 'the grain and the mullet' – provides a reference to the key ingredients of the North African dish at the centre of the film's narrative, without (in line with the French Republican model) drawing attention to its difference, in a way that the more exotic-sounding title *Couscous*, chosen for the film's US and UK release, necessarily does.

However, this is not to say that Kechiche offers a naïve or unproblematic representation of the realities of living with difference in *La Graine et le mulet*. While Slimane finds acceptance and tolerance within the working-class community in Sète, he confronts a hostility bordering on casual racism when he meets with the health and safety inspector from the council, who continually reminds him of how things are done 'here' (in France), the implication being that Slimane is not 'from here'. Furthermore, *La Graine et le mulet* explores what Avtar Brah (1996: 172) describes as the contingent nature of diasporic identities: how, in a variety of social and cultural locations/situations, and depending on the location of the utterance, act or social relations, the difference of diaspora for the North African immigrant population manifests itself in local, regional, national and transnational terms. This occurs most obviously in the symbolically named Hôtel de l'Orient, the bar and hotel owned by Latifa (Slim's partner), which provides lodgings and a communal meeting point for many of Sète's North African émigré workers. The sights and sounds of the North African diaspora (the traditional food, song and dance of the Maghreb) are foregrounded in the bar. Similarly, when Slimane ascends the staircase to his lodgings, his footsteps mingle with the sound of traditional North African music emanating from his neighbour's room. And yet, rather than suggesting a state of enforced exile or longing for the North African 'homeland', the bar instead stands as a marker that the presence of the immigrants who lodge there is anything but temporary. The terrace of the Hôtel de l'Orient functions as focal space for the North African émigrés who lodge there to pass the time and gossip. The (highly amusing) sequence in which they sit outside the bar discussing the complications of both Slimane's personal life and business venture identifies them as a chorus within the film, a dramatic technique that has led a number of critics to draw comparisons with Pagnol's films of the 1930s,[14] a further suggestion that the difference being displayed in *La Graine et le mulet* here is as much meridional as it is Maghrebi.

Various social spaces, public and domestic, are represented in *La Graine et le mulet*: the port as both a site of work and leisure; the bank where Rym and Slimane apply for their loan and offices at the town hall where they request the relevant permissions to open their business; the shipyard and quayside where Slim renovates La Source; the modest, working-class apartments of Slim's estranged wife (Souad), his daughter (Karima) and his son (Madjid). Of these various locations, the port, family home and Hôtel de l'Orient are the principal geographical locations of the film. It is, however, in the space of the boat that Slimane renovates and transforms into a floating couscous restaurant that all of the protagonists who occupy the various spaces of the film converge in the final third of *La Graine et le mulet* – indeed, the boat is the central location for the final hour of the film. The boat therefore functions as a space of encounter, performance and intercultural exchange that is both real and metonymic. The final part of my analysis will thus move on to consider how space is inscribed with the politics of difference in *La Graine et le mulet*.

The boat itself is representative of the transformation of Sète from an industrial port to a city whose economy is increasingly dependent on the service industries of the restaurant trade and tourism. Significantly, Slimane begins his renovation of the boat in an area of the port that now appears to be devoid of any industrial activity. As he arrives with Rym on the back of his moped to inspect the boat for the first time, idle cranes surround scrap metal on an empty quayside, seeming to reinforce Madjid's earlier comments about the decline of manufacturing and industry in France. When his renovation of the boat is complete, Slimane then transports the vessel from the vestiges of the industrial port to the site of Sète's new economy: the quayside dominated by leisure boats and restaurants.

Like the Hôtel de l'Orient, the boat itself offers a further indication of the sedentary nature of the North African immigrant population (and thus diasporic identity) within Sète. Just as Slim's view from the Hôtel de l'Orient doesn't look out across the Mediterranean, the floating restaurant is, as we have already noted, moored on the waterways of Sète. But whereas the Hôtel de l'Orient is overwhelmingly identified as a relatively closed diasporic space associated with the local North African immigrant community, the boat offers the possibility of intercultural exchange between French and North African protagonists –

though, as I will suggest in a moment, Kechiche refuses any simplistic or naïve notion of this space as a site of an unproblematic or convivial multiculture.[15] In this respect, the boat also functions as a point of convergence for the public and private in the film. It is, after all, the space where Slim hopes to transform the '*couscous d'amour*' prepared lovingly by Souad for family and friends from a simple family meal into an object of capital exchange to be consumed by a paying (French) clientèle.

The boat is therefore simultaneously presented in the film as a real social space (the floating restaurant) and a performative space. Most obviously, it is the space in which the band of first-generation North African émigrés provides musical entertainment to accompany for the meal, as well as the location where Rym performs her belly dance – a calculated and increasingly desperate risk to buy time as Slimane searches in vain for Souad, Madjid and the missing couscous. Kechiche has spoken of the theatricality associated with the extended meal scenes in *La Graine et le mulet*, and how the boat continues this sense of spectacle and performance (Domenach and Rouyer 2007: 20). The interior is decorated with drapes, palm-trees and clichéd paintings of camels resting by an oasis, while the invited friends and prominent local businesspeople and members of the town council must wait on the quayside in darkness before Slim illuminates the boat, opens the doors and quite literally lets the drama of the evening unfold.

The boat is also transformed into a performative space in which the possibilities of encounter between Maghrebi and French culture can be tested, a metonymic site in which the dynamic politics of multiculturalism in contemporary French society are played out in the micro-environment of the floating restaurant. Olfa (Slim's youngest daughter) welcomes French guests by placing her hand on her heart – a typical Arabic greeting indicating a potentially convivial space that can promote tolerance and respect through intercultural exchange. However, Kechiche quickly dismisses any possibility that the boat should turn into some utopian site of unproblematic multicultural harmony. The assembled local dignitaries congratulate Slimane on his 'success' in patronizing terms that verge on neo-colonial paternalism, describing his business venture as 'a human adventure', and joining together in a nervous chorus of 'Inch Allah' to toast the restaurant's opening night. Local French restaurateurs who have been invited to the opening use language that is couched in racist undertones: one makes the comment about granting the permit for the restaurant that 'We're not savages'. However, Kechiche refuses any simplistic division between 'us and them' that divides the bad French (racists) from the innocent Maghrebi protagonists by suggesting, through the context of these remarks, that such hostility could be motivated as much by a fear of further competition in an already overcrowded market as by any deep-seated and aggressive racist beliefs. Moreover, the director shows that the Maghrebi protagonists of his film are equally susceptible to applying stereotypical judgements – such as when Lilia suggests that the best way to placate the French guests who are becoming increasingly impatient for their meal to be served is to ply them with alcohol, commenting 'Give them a drink and they forget about everything, including their wives – and I should know'.

Finally, despite being a space conceived, constructed and presided over by Slimane, the boat is ultimately a space that is dominated and directed by the women of the film. Though it is Slimane's vision (as well as his physical labour) that transforms the wrecked boat into a floating restaurant, it is Rym who convinces the bank to lend the money and the council to grant a permit for the business. Similarly, while a taciturn Slimane presides over the front of house, the women are the driving force behind this new entrepreneurial venture, as well as the public face of the restaurant. It is Souad who prepares all the food upon which the restaurant's success or failure will depend, and Karima, Olfa and Lilia who effectively take charge of service on the restaurant's opening night. In contrast, Madjid flees his responsibilities at the restaurant when his mistress arrives with her husband as one of the invited guests from the council, while Rhiad bows his head and mumbles to his sisters when attempting to cover for the absence of his elder brother. Even Slimane eventually abandons the restaurant to embark on a futile and ultimately tragic search for the missing couscous, leaving the Maghrebi women to hold the fort and deal with the increasingly restless guests. In the end, it is Rym who takes a calculated risk – reducing herself to eroticized object (much to the delight of the men on the boat) by performing a belly dance in a desperate attempt to buy time, while her mother returns to the Hôtel de l'Orient to prepare more couscous for the invited guests.

Thinking of the way space is inscribed to suggest feminine control of the narrative leads us to conclude that *La Graine et le mulet* offers precisely the kind of female-centred narrative that Carrie Tarr has, on a number of occasions, noted as conspicuous by its absence from the majority of Maghrebi-French film-making to date (Tarr 2005: 94–95). And yet, just as Kechiche rejects the boat as site of unproblematic convivial multiculture, so he also refuses to identify it as a utopian sight of female solidarity. An uneasy truce exists between Slimane's daughters and the women of his new 'family'. Karima and Olfa are barely able to contain their disgust when Latifa and Rym arrive unannounced on the opening night. Elsewhere, the women of the family (led by Souad) are shown as complicit in hiding Madjid's serial adultery from his Russian immigrant wife Julia by receiving calls and passing on messages from his mistresses. Perhaps most troubling, though, is the fact that Rym's presence as a forceful, uncompromising and fiercely independent, young female voice in the film (a sight that is all too rare in Maghrebi-French film-making) is entirely undercut by her belly-dancing performance at the end of the film. Even if we read her performance as a calculated risk, which could be interpreted along the lines of Rivière's notion of the female masquerade (Rivière 1929) – provocatively objectifying her femininity and exposing her body at the end of the film to save the restaurant from disaster on the opening night – her highly sexualized performance and the camera's fetishizing fragmentation of her body through extreme close-ups, combined with the lascivious gaze of both the assembled French guests and the North African musicians, presents an unsettling final image for any feminist reading of the film.

Yet Kechiche refuses to present a schematic discourse that demonizes the French while presenting the North African and Maghrebi-French protagonists as entirely virtuous 'victims', or one that embraces a naïve and excessively optimistic view of either gender equality or convivial multiculture in postcolonial France – which could, for example, have come in the form of an upbeat ending closing on resolution and success for Slimane and his extended family – such as that found in *Baton Rouge* (Bouchareb 1985) where, having been deported from the United States, the two beur protagonists set up a successful burger bar in their local neighbourhood upon their return to France. Instead, he offers a more honest portrayal of multicuturalism and intercultural exchange as a work in progress in contemporary France, with its 'vitality, conflicts, hopes and contradictions' (Kaganski 2007).

The very fact that Kechiche feels able to end *La Graine et le mulet* with the failure of the restaurant and the death of Slimane suggests a new-found confidence on the part of the Maghrebi-French film-maker – and one that Carrie Tarr's work has long wished for, in which Maghrebi-French film-making does not simply become a 'sop to the liberal critical conscience', but rather a cinema that 'calls French identity as well as beur identity', and by extension the place of the North African diaspora in France, into question (Tarr 2005: 46). In short, Kechiche offers –perhaps for the first time in Maghrebi-French film-making – the possibility for difference, and the spaces that such difference makes, to be celebrated, critiqued and explored as part of a French national and not solely 'immigrant' cinema.[16]

Notes

1. Think, for example, of the unfounded claims made by the far right during periods of high unemployment in France in the 1980s and 1990s of 'three million unemployed: three million immigrants'.
2. In this sense, it is consistent with other developments in Maghrebi-French film-making of the 2000s, such as the proliferation of return narratives, in which the diasporic or hybrid identity is considered in the context of a return to the North African *bled* or village as opposed to its rightful place within French society (see Higbee forthcoming).
3. See, for example, the interview with Kechiche that appears on the UK DVD release of *La Graine et le mulet* (Artificial Eye 2008).
4. See also sections on *La Graine et le mulet* in Ginette Vincendeau's Chapter 24 of this book for further discussion of *La Graine et le mulet* as French 'national' cinema.
5. Born in Tunisia in 1960, Kechiche moved to Nice with his parents at the age of six, where he was raised on a working-class council estate. Emerging from a background in French theatre in the 1970s, Kechiche took various roles as a screen actor in the early 1980s. Most notably, he performed the lead role of a young, attractive, streetwise Algerian immigrant living in Paris in *Le Thé à la menthe*, a film released a year before *Le Thé au harem d'Archimède* brought the attention of beur cinema to a wider French public. With the release of his debut feature, *La Faute à Voltaire* (Kechiche 2001), he established himself as a new Maghrebi-French writer/director to watch. His second feature, *L'Esquive*, followed in 2004, enjoying both critical and relative commercial success (over 400,000 spectators in France and two Césars). Kechiche built further on the success of *L'Esquive* with *La Graine et le mulet* and is currently working on *Venus noir/Black Venus*, due for release in 2010.
6. In addition to *La Graine et le mulet*, we might also include here films such as *Le Ciel, les oiseaux... et ta mere!/Homeboys on the Beach* (Bensalah 1999), *Chouchou* (Allouache 2003) and *Indigènes/ Days of Glory* (Bouchareb 2006).

7. Her expertise in this field was recognized in 2007 when she was asked to select a series of films by Maghrebi-French directors for the ArteEast festival in New York. The festival was accompanied by a special dossier published by *Cineaste* and edited by Tarr, entitled 'Beur is Beautiful' (Tarr 2007).

8. See, for example, Masson (2007: 14–15); Frodon (2007: 9–10).

9. In *La Faute à Voltaire*, the immigrant hostel, psychiatric hospital and metro function as the hidden or liminal spaces in contemporary French society navigated by Tunisian immigrant Jallel following his arrival in France. Similarly, the decision to stage *L'Esquive*'s narrative in the *cité* is crucial in that it gives a voice to dispossessed and alienated *banlieue* youth while simultaneously subverting stereotypes of the deprived urban periphery as a cultural wasteland: the sights and sounds of Marivaux's *Le Jeu de l'Amour et du Hasard* (1730) are entwined with the relentless verbal sparring or *tchatche* of the young people on the estate and the personal dramas that inhabit this forgotten social space of contemporary France.

10. Originally, Kechiche had intended to shoot the film in Nice (his home town), further emphasizing the film's semi-autobiographical nature by casting his father in the lead role. In the in end, however, his father's untimely death prior to production led the director to seek an alternative port location on the Mediterranean coast. Filming in Nice, Kechiche suggested, would simply have been too painful following the loss of his father (Domenach and Rouyer 2007).

11. Until *La Graine et le mulet*, Sète was most famously associated in cinematic terms with Agnès Varda's *La Pointe courte* (1954), a film that juxtaposed the breakdown of a relationship between a young French couple returning from Paris with documentary footage of the local fishing community whose livelihood was being transformed by the arrival of modern industrial fishing practices.

12. Only later do we fully understand the significance of this opening sequence and the identity of Madjid's French lover. Madjid flees the opening night of his father's restaurant in order to avoid meeting his lover, who is attending the event with her husband (and guest of honour) the deputy mayor. In his haste to leave, Madjid drives off with the couscous in the boot of his car, setting in motion the chain of events that will end with the death of his father.

13. Kechiche's film also departs from earlier beur and Maghrebi-French film-making in the sense that he refuses to play on a sense of generational conflict between first-generation North African immigrants and their French-born descendants. Instead, the Maghrebi-French protagonists display a profound respect and genuine affection for their parents.

14. Numerous reviewers have picked up on this point when writing about the film. See, for example, Kaganski (2007) and Vincendeau (2008).

15. I am using the term 'convivial multiculture' here as it has been developed by Paul Gilroy in *After Empire: Multiculture or Postcolonial Melancholia* as 'an ordinary, demotic multiculturalism that is not the outcome of government drift and institutional indifference but … which is distinguished by some notable demands for hospitality, conviviality, justice and mutual care … a mature response to diversity, plurality and differentiation … oriented by routine, everyday exposure to difference' (Gilroy 2004: 108–9).

16. I am grateful to Sarah Leahy for her careful reading and insightful feedback on drafts of this chapter.

Chapter 17

Cinema, the Second Sex and Studies of French Women's Films in the 2000s

Kate Ince

Carrie Tarr's publications on French women's film-making have been fundamental to establishing it as an area of research for Anglophone studies of French cinema. Starting with her article on Jacqueline Audry's *Olivia* (Tarr 1993a), Tarr has approached the domain from different directions, most fully and directly in the major study *Cinema and the Second Sex: Women's Filmmaking in France in the 1980s and 1990s*, which she co-wrote with Brigitte Rollet (2001), but also in her monograph on Diane Kurys (Tarr 1999), a 2003 article on the 1970s films of Yannick Bellon, in essays reprinted as chapters in her book *Reframing Difference: Beur and Banlieue Film-making in France* (Tarr 2005) and in a co-edited special journal issue on the representation of the body in French women's writing and film-making to which she contributed a discussion of Marina de Van's *Dans ma peau/In My Skin* (2002) (Tarr 2006). Retracing the trajectory she has followed through the area that has formed one of the two major foci of her research into French cinema (the other being beur, *banlieue* and transnational French film) can serve as a useful *piste de reflexion* on the achievements and progress of research into French women's cinematic production, as well as on the state of the field itself.

That field – the achievements and fortunes of French *réalisatrices* – was looking particularly healthy at the turn of the millennium, the point at which *Cinema and the Second Sex* concludes, since no fewer than 37 films directed by women were released in 2000 against an average of just over seventeen per year in the 1990s (a total of 174 between 1990 and 1999). It was also in 2000 that a female director – Tonie Marshall for *Vénus Beauté (Institut)/Venus Beauty Salon* – was awarded the César for best director for the first time since 1985, one of four awards her film brought her (Tarr with Rollet 2001: 1). If success at the annual Césars ceremony is taken as a measure, women directors' fortunes have improved significantly over the 2000s: Agnès Jaoui's *Le Goût des autres/The Taste of Others* won Best Film in 2001, an achievement repeated by Pascale Ferran's *Lady Chatterley* in 2007, which also garnered the Best Actress award for its star Marina Hands. Unfortunately, however, it does not seem that studies of female-authored films have kept pace with the increase in production and growing recognition by the industry achieved by women directors: from a critical point of view, it is auteurs Claire Denis and Catherine Breillat who have attracted the lion's share of interest, with several major studies each.[1] The sad early death of Françoise Audé deprived French feminist film criticism of one of its major figures, and perhaps of further studies to supplement the two major ones she had completed by 2002 (Audé 1981, 2002), so although books on women auteurs have appeared in English and in French throughout the first decade of the 2000s, there has been no substantial new study of French women's cinema to supplement those that documented the field up to the turn of the century.[2] In 2001, Tarr and Rollet seemed understandably confident 'that other researchers will take up where [our study] ends and produce other analyses of how films made in France are inflected by questions of gender' (2001: 9), but at the end of the first decade of the twenty-first century, we at least have to ask whether that confidence might have been misplaced.

Because *Cinema and the Second Sex* treats almost exactly the same historical period as Audé's *Cinéma d'elles, 1981–2001*, a comparison of the two books may reveal whether the differences of critical style that have often been observed between Anglophone and Francophone approaches to academic film study are as apparent in books on female directors as they are generally.[3] In this regard, it is of immediate interest that Tarr and Rollet entitle Part I of *Cinema and the Second Sex* 'Personal Films', but do not employ the critical category of the auteur, even though the double-bind of auteur status for French women directors – it functions as a sign of acceptance into the industry but is widely understood, because of the universalism of French discourses, 'to transcend the particularities of gender, sexual orientation and ethnicity' (Tarr with Rollet 2001: 10) – is an issue illuminatingly discussed in their introduction. For Audé, on the other hand, the concept of the 'auteure' is central, as we shall see. Would organizing Part I of *Cinema and the Second Sex* by director have been a better way to present the critical accounts of the 50 or more films it covers than in its chapters 'Growing Up', 'The Age of Possibilities', 'Couples', 'Families' and 'Work, Art and Citizenship'? An answer to this question depends at least partly, of course, on the aims of the study. Tarr and Rollet stated these as being 'to redress gaps and absences in the critical recognition of women's film-making in France by providing information about the range of feature films and feature-length documentary and essay films directed by women in the 1980s and 1990s', and 'to trace through and explore the evolution of the kinds of films women have been making during a period dominated by 'postfeminist' assumptions' (Tarr with Rollet 2001: 2–3). They do not mention 'contributing to a systematic history of French women's film-making' among their aims, and Tarr is obviously aware of the difficulties and pitfalls of over-ambitious history-writing, since she specifies that *Cinema and the Second Sex* is not an exhaustive study, in part because it proved practically impossible to view more than 75 per cent of the basic corpus. (The book's other anticipated limits are that it does not include more than incidental comment on 'French language films directed by women from other countries' or on 'women's short and medium-length films or televisions films' [Tarr with Rollet 2001: 16].) The themes that are used to organize the five chapters of Part I – 'Growing Up', 'The Age of Possibilities', etc. – require contextualization of a different kind than the scrutiny of selected directors' trajectory into (and within) the male-dominated film industry supplied by Audé in *Cinéma d'elles*. What these chapters do reveal are some major thematic concerns: that childhood and adolescence are a key theme in women's film-making ('Growing Up'); that 'feel-good' films about heterosexual relationships are the exception in the films women made during this period ('Couples'); and that 'the interrogation of motherhood and mother–daughter relationships, a facet of films by directors influenced by the 1970s women's movement, has also surfaced in films by younger women in the 1990s' (Tarr with

Rollet 2001: 131, in 'Families'). By addressing issues of class, ethnicity and citizenship, and by including consideration of documentary and essay films in addition to narrative features, 'Work, Art and Citizenship', the final chapter of Part I, is perhaps the most satisfying of all for the feminist reader seeking an appraisal of cinema's part in contributing to and reflecting on the social progress made by women in France by the end of the twentieth century.

Comparing the organization of *Cinema and the Second Sex* to Audé's *Cinéma d'elles, 1981–2001* is also instructive. Whereas the whole of Part II of Tarr and Rollet's book is devoted to genre films (comedies, crime dramas, road movies and historical films), Audé finds a substantial contribution to genre cinema by women directors only in the areas of the *polar* (Yannick Bellon's *La triche/The Cheat* and Christine Pascal's *La garce*, both from 1984, stand out) and comedy, where the box-office successes of Coline Serreau and Josiane Balasko enjoyed such pre-eminence during the two decades under scrutiny. The British critic finds far more genre films among women's cinematic output of a twenty-year period than the French one does, in other words. As if to reinforce this difference between the broader and more subtle approach to genre(s) in Anglophone criticism, compared with the French preference for aesthetics and the auteur, Audé, in contrast to Tarr and Rollet, does devote a distinct section of her book (the last) to auteures[4] – Breillat, Denis, Dominique Cabrera, Jeanne Labrune, Laetitia Masson, Sandrine Veysset and Agnès Varda – even although all these seven except Veysset have already been discussed in other chapters (Labrune in 'Cinéma de genre', Breillat in 'Moeurs', Denis, Masson, Cabrera and Labrune in different sub-categories of 'Fictions sociétales', Varda in 'Documentaires', and Masson in the chapter entitled 'La forme, la pensée'). By indicating the contrast between Audé's organization of her discussion of films around the individual, named director – a choice clearly determined in part by her working context (a national film industry that still has a larger output of auteur cinema than most others) – and Tarr and Rollet's decision to let the content of film narratives guide the structure of their investigation – effectively adopted in Part I of *Cinema and the Second Sex* as well as in Part II on genres – I do not mean to reinforce an evaluating binary opposition between French and Anglophone styles of film criticism. What I do mean to ask is whether the additional focus on individual careers within the industry afforded by the 'French' (Audé's) approach might be of particular value in a young and developing field such as female-authored film, which could not meaningfully be addressed *as* a field until the 1970s.

An alternative to the non-individualized mode of grouping women's films that Tarr and Rollet adopt in *Cinema and the Second Sex*[5] is in any case offered by the Tarr's detailed study of a single director – Diane Kurys – which she completed before moving on to her investigation of the broader field of French women's film-making. Kurys' career was, evidently, far from over at this point: in 1999 she had made eight films, a number now augmented by the divorce comedy drama *Je reste!/I'm staying!* (2003), the comedy *L'anniversaire* (2005) and the biopic *Sagan* (2008), initially made as a TV mini-series of two 90-minute parts then released in a two-hour theatrical version. It was, however, already characterized by the particular success of the autobiographically inspired *Diabolo menthe* (1977) and *Coup de foudre/Entre nous*

(1983). The conclusion to *Diane Kurys* is entitled 'Kurys' Authorial Signature', and Tarr begins it by claiming that Kurys' series of 'semi-autobiographical' films – even *Un homme amoureux/A Man in Love* (1987), a 'contemporary love story inspired by fantasy rather than fact' (Tarr 1999: 72) that self-reflexively takes the position of women within the film industry as a main theme – 'provide a unique source for the analysis of female authorship' (Tarr 1999: 140). How 'unique' this source can be is questionable, when Tarr herself counts at least twenty female directors as active in France in 1999 (Tarr with Rollet 2001: 293), even if probably fewer than ten of these had as substantial a body of work to their credit as Kurys. But the analysis of female authorship Tarr achieves in *Diane Kurys* fully bears out my sense – and Tarr's 1999 intimation – that (feminist) criticism of women's cinema has much to gain from studies of individual directors. It is the ambivalence of Kurys' authorial signature that proves so suggestive in relation to her gender, an ambivalence that Tarr argues is due 'on the one hand to the need for successful woman directors to find survival strategies within a misogynist French film industry, and on the other to the particularities of Kurys' own formative experiences' (Tarr 1999: 140): Kurys' Russian Jewish parents married in a Vichy detention camp for Jewish refugees during World War II then separated, in part because of Kurys' mother's close friendship with another woman (the story of *Coup de foudre*). Kurys had a 'rebellious and troubled' (Tarr 1999: 12) childhood and adolescence as the younger daughter of a single mother in Paris, running away aged fifteen to spend a year in an Israeli kibbutz before becoming involved in the Paris-based *événements* of 1968. The way Kurys' life and her films are interwoven furnishes her cinema with '[t]he most significant component of Kurys' authorial signature … the series of female characters who act as the author's stand-ins' (Tarr 1999: 141). These characters often bear a striking physical resemblance to Kurys, and continuities among them are very apparent; however, although this 'Kurys figure' can be found in all the director's films up to 1999, 'the refusal of a fully autobiographical voice means that [the films] often do not fully acknowledge the Kurys figure as their subject' (Tarr 1999: 142). Authorship is simultaneously affirmed and denied (or at least qualified) in a manner that recalls the difficulty faced by all French directors attempting to give expression to an identity that is in any way 'different' from the neutral, unmarked individuality implied in the post-1789 Republican tradition. Over the last twenty years (since the first *affaire du foulard* in the late 1980s), French public life has seen countless cultural and legal dramas of this kind. The careers of film directors who are female, queer or of French-North African origin, to name but the three most common 'different' identities, depend not only upon proving artistic and technical skill equal to the white male majority, but on negotiating this additional hurdle in personal expression. In the case of Diane Kurys, Tarr detects an 'underlying personal psychodrama' (Tarr 1999: 148) across her films, indicating that psychological as well as socio-political conflicts of identity are at work. Kurys' films are all 'personal', and depict a range of interpersonal relationships among which those between sisters, mother and daughter, and adult women and men predominate – the kind of material that makes a study of her work valuable to the consideration of the field of women's cinema as well as in its own right, as part of a 'French Film Directors' series. It seems to me that similarly intricate negotiations around the adoption of a woman's voice might be found in the work of a number of other French women directors (Catherine Corsini? Anne Fontaine?) if their films were only accorded the extended analysis granted to Tarr by the monograph format of Manchester University Press's series, which (it is worth noting) has not yet been attempted by any French publishing house.[6] *Diabolo menthe* and *Coup de foudre* not only gained audiences of approximately 2.3 and 1.3 million in France (Tarr 1999: 150), but are easily identified as having the most 'overtly woman-centred focus' among Kurys' films (Tarr 1999: 4), and have remained her best-known productions into the 2000s, a testament to the vitality and historical importance of films made by women in the 1970s and early 1980s, before anyone thought to ask whether Western societies had entered a 'post-feminist' era.

Between *Cinema and the Second Sex* and the most recent of Tarr's publications on French women's film-making I shall discuss here, the co-edited journal issue 'Focalizing the Body in Contemporary Women's Writing and Filmmaking in France' (Rye and Tarr 2006), she contributed an article about the 1970s films of Yannick Bellon to an early issue of *Studies in French Cinema* (Tarr 2003). (The same issue, incidentally, contains an article by Geneviève Sellier, the other major French commentator apart from Audé on the representation of women and gender in French cinema, whose writings in this area cannot be ignored, even if she has not tended to focus on female directors in the way Audé and Tarr have.)[7] In 'Feminist Influences on the Work of Yannick Bellon in the 1970s', initially given as a paper at the second annual Studies in French Cinema conference in 2002, Tarr supplies a necessarily far more condensed analysis of the most productive period of Bellon's career than she did of Kurys' in *Diane Kurys*, but one that admirably accomplishes the task at hand – that is, to remedy the unavailability of anything but the briefest critical consideration of 'one of France's most commercially successful women directors' (Tarr 2003: 55). The lack of criticism on Bellon is indicated by Tarr's bibliography, which lists only reviews of Bellon's films *Quelque part quelqu'un/Somewhere, Someone* (1972), *La Femme de Jean/John's Wife* (1974) and *L'Amour violé/Rape of Love* (1978), three short interviews with Bellon, and books by Audé, Denise Brahimi, Jean-Pierre Jeancolas and René Prédal that devote limited space to Bellon's output (Audé 1981; Brahimi 1999; Jeancolas 1979; Prédal 1991). By treating *Quelque part quelqu'un* and *Jamais plus toujours/Never Again Always* (1976) as 'art films' and *La Femme de Jean* and *L'Amour violé* as 'women's films', and setting out the commonalities between them, Tarr reaches sound and thought-provoking conclusions about the way Bellon's films construct women *and* men. If she (like the films themselves) still seems troubled by the way that both the 'women's films' *and* the 'art films' remain 'obsessed with women's relationships with men' (Tarr 2003: 64), this surely points forward to one key development in feminist film criticism since 2003: the centrality taken up by questions of embodiment, desire and subjectivity.

'Focalizing the Body in Contemporary Women's Writing and Filmmaking in France' (Rye and Tarr 2006) emerged from an identically entitled conference organized by Rye and Tarr and held at the Institute of Germanic and Romance Studies in October 2004. Although the volume's essays (like the conference papers) consider women writers as well as film-makers, the four essays on French *réalisatrices* treat many of the most talked-about and/or critically acclaimed French films of recent years, whether directed by men or women – Sandrine Veysset's *Y aura-t-il de la neige à Noël?/Will it snow for Christmas?* (1996), Catherine Breillat's *Romance* (1999), Virginie Despentes and Coralie Trinh-Thi's *Baise-moi* (2000), Claire Denis's *Trouble Every Day* (2001) and *Vendredi soir/Friday night* (2002), and Agnès Varda's *Les Glaneurs et la glaneuse/The Gleaners and I* (2000). (The less widely seen films discussed are Laetitia Masson's *En avoir ou pas/To Have [or not]* [1995], Laurence Ferreira-Barbosa's *Motus* [2003], Martine Dugowson's *Mina Tannenbaum* [1994] and Veysset's *Martha... Martha...* [2001].) By focusing on the issue of the body in representation, the volume allows what might now be called 'the phenomenological turn' in film theory and criticism of the 2000s, in particular the notion of 'haptic optics' described by Laura Marks in *The Skin of the Film*, to come into view. (Marks [2000: xi] defines 'haptic visuality' as 'the way vision itself can be tactile, as though one were touching a film with one's eyes'.) One of the best observers of the way haptic visuality works in Claire Denis's and other contemporary French films is Martine Beugnet (2004, 2006, 2007), and Beugnet's essay for Rye and Tarr's volume examines how the history of the cinematic close-up is bound up with that of the 'formation du corps cinématographique' (Beugnet 2006: 24) – the phrase is Pascal Bonitzer's – and then explores the re-mappings of the cinematographic body undertaken by the close-up camerawork of Denis, Varda, Breillat and Masson respectively. Emma Wilson, in an essay entitled simply 'Women Filming Children', investigates how the foregrounding of the subjectivity and bodily experience of child protagonists in Martine Dugowson's *Mina Tannenbaum* and Sandrine Veysset's *Martha ... Martha* displaces 'the fetishistic gaze of dominant cinema' (Wilson 2006a: 105) – a displacement initially noted by Tarr and Rollet in *Cinema and the Second Sex*, as Wilson acknowledges. Tarr's own contribution to 'Focalizing the Body' is a thorough and carefully crafted exploration of Marina de Van's first feature film, *Dans ma peau* (2002) which, as she starts by noting, 'was awarded the 2003 Prix Très Spécial by French journalists as the most disturbing, iconoclastic film of the year' (Tarr 2006: 78). In order to bring out the extremely unsettling nature of de Van's fictional but undoubtedly personal investigation of a woman (Esther)'s descent into self-harming (de Van, who is known in France for the perturbing and transgressive representations of the body featured in her own shorts and collaborations with François Ozon, plays Esther herself), Tarr adopts a kind of twin-track approach, paying attention both to the visual 'body horror' that results from Esther's self-mutilations and to how the subject of self-harming comments on women's lives and situations in contemporary society. Unsurprisingly, the tension between these two perspectives – one of which necessarily spectacularizes the suffering female body while the other attempts to understand Esther and examine the social pressures that have contributed to her extreme behaviour – keeps resurfacing in Tarr's discussion. So although it seems quite legitimate to describe *Dans ma peau* as a 'taboo-defying study of a monstrous female body ... [which] invites analysis in terms of Kristeva's concept of the abject' and what Barbara Creed, in her study of film, feminism and psychoanalysis, has named 'the monstrous feminine' (Tarr 2006: 78), it is fascinating to learn that 'De Van had apparently wanted to show the wounds on Esther's body from Esther's point of view, not as monstrous, but as a landscape of forms and colours (as in certain scientific photographs) and therefore as abstract rather than repulsive; unfortunately such effects were beyond her budget' (Tarr 2006: 86). De Van's film, like Esther's self-harming, not only 'makes deviance a poetic, aesthetic experience' (Tarr 2006: 86): its *mise-en-scène* of alienation and suffering seems largely driven by ethical concerns. As well as asserting subjectivity, the title *Dans ma peau* seems to resonate with a kind of appeal from Esther/De Van to inhabit her skin, at least imaginatively. In its sober, careful emplotment of the advancing stages of a woman's sensual self-destructiveness (the long final sequence 'is the most testing for the spectator and takes the mutilation of the body to its most extreme point' (Tarr 2006: 84), although the final shot can be read as offering 'a more productive perspective' (Tarr 2006: 85), *Dans ma peau* – which is for obvious reasons often compared to Denis's *Trouble Every Day* – seems like the more intelligent film. By fearlessly exploring the difficult subject of self-harming, it undoubtedly comes closer to the reality of contemporary women's lives than Denis's film. Tarr's beautifully written and finely judged assessment of de Van's début feature is the first substantial essay to give the film the critical attention it undoubtedly deserves.

As I asserted at the start of this essay, Carrie Tarr's publications on French women's film-making have been fundamental to establishing it as an area of research for Anglophone studies of French cinema. Her monograph on Kurys, the co-authored *Cinema and the Second Sex*, her work on Yannick Bellon and Marina de Van, and her collaboration with Gill Rye on the 'Focalizing the Body' volume not only add up to a more substantial body of work on French women's cinematic production than that of any other British researcher; they address films, directors and issues often not considered by anyone else. Retracing the trajectory she has followed through the field to date has uncovered a great deal about the progress and current state of research into films made by French women since the 1970s – progress that has been considerable but is currently less buoyant than might be hoped, especially given the steadily increasing proportion of national annual production women's films represent in France.[8] However, the cluster of studies of female auteurs' films that have appeared in the 2000s is one indication of the vital role Carrie's work has played in opening up the field of French women's cinematic production for serious consideration; another is the conference on 'French women's cinema 2000–2010' she and I are co-organizing in December 2010, just as the first decade of the twenty-first century – and the first new decade of French women's cinema to elapse since the publication of *Cinema and the Second Sex* – comes to a close. It says much about Carrie's abilities and achievements as a scholar and her qualities as a person that she is committing to such a project at this point in her career (just as she retires from her post as Professor of Film at Kingston University). We hope that our conference will bring together most, if not all, of the scholars and critics in Britain, France and the United States (and hopefully other countries too) who have worked or are now working on contemporary French women's cinematic production. It is a tribute to Carrie's pioneering work that a conference devoted to this topic promises to be such an exciting occasion.

Notes

1. In particular, Beugnet (2004); Mayne (2005); Clouzot (2004); Keesey (2009); Vasse (2004).
2. A recent special journal issue goes some way, but not very far, towards remedying this critical gap (Tourret 2009).
3. For discussion of these differences of critical style, see (for example), Powrie and Reader (2002: 51), where the authors attribute the favouring of 'the popular, whether the popular genres of comedy and police thriller, or stars' to the permeation of film studies by cultural studies in the 1980s and 1990s. According to Powrie and Reader, a privileging of the director as 'auteur' is the approach 'favoured by many university courses, whether in France, the UK or the USA' (2002: 51), but since cultural studies has made far less impact on academic courses in France than it has in the United Kingdom or United States, I would argue that this permeation of film studies by cultural studies cannot have occurred to the same extent in France as it has in the United Kingdom or United States.
4. Audé feminizes the term auteur, whereas I prefer not to.
5. It is noteworthy that Noël Burch and Geneviève Sellier's *La Drôle de guerre des sexes du cinéma français 1930–1956* (Burch and Sellier 1996) also adopts this approach.
6. It is apparently with slight surprise that Françoise Audé notes the existence of an entire volume devoted to Kurys, whom she considers 'a film-maker too careful to have real appeal', with a career already in decline by the late 1980s (Audé 2002: 66). The University of Illinois Press's 'Contemporary Film Directors' series now fulfils a similar role to MUP's director-based ones, and as far as women's film-making is concerned, contains volumes on Claire Denis (Mayne 2005), Jane Campion (McHugh 2007) and Sally Potter (Fowler 2008). French directors featured in the series in addition to Denis are Chris Marker (Alter 2006), and Jean-Pierre Jeunet (Ezra 2008).
7. Sellier's most important publications are Burch and Sellier 1996 and Sellier 2005.
8. Over the eight years from 2000 to 2007, I have calculated (Ince 2008a: 281), women in France have directed an average of thirty films each year, or approximately 14.4 per cent of average annual national production, as compared to Tarr's figure of 13.7 per cent for the 1990s (Tarr with Rollet 2001: 3).

Chapter 18

The Bafflement of Gabin and Raimu and the Breathlessness of Belmondo: A Dialogue with the Work of Ginette Vincendeau

Martin O'Shaughnessy

W hat is written here has its initial roots in a puzzlement at a bafflement. Watching Pagnol's famously misogynistic *La Femme du Boulanger/The Baker's Wife* (1938), I was intrigued by a sense that the baker of the film's title, played by the great Raimu, had never and could never really understand what had happened to him when his young wife (Ginette Leclerc) ran off with a decidedly hunky Italian shepherd (Charles Moulin). Clearly, he was fully – if belatedly – aware of his *cocufiage*, not least because, this being a Pagnol film, the word *cocu* more than once made itself heard. However, there seemed to be something more to Raimu's character's bafflement than this, something that the character could never understand. I had a similar feeling when watching Grémillon's remarkable reflexive engagement with stardom in *Gueule d'amour/Lady Killer* (1937) where the hero – played by the great Jean Gabin – having been the darling of a garrison town, is thrown into an eventually murderous disarray when he falls for an elegant kept woman, played by Mireille Balin. While the disarray of his character could partly be explained, like that of Raimu, at the level of plot there also seemed to be something more to it, something of which the film was aware but that the hero could not be allowed to recognize or understand, something intrinsically connected to the nature of masculine stardom. When it came to Belmondo, the issue was less bafflement than breathlessness. I was intrigued by how, in Godard's *A bout de souffle/Breathless* (1959), the Belmondo character was simultaneously all surface and an existential hero who lived life with heroic intensity. It seemed to me that this ultimately untenable combination of features was in some way tied to the character's own breathlessness and his impossible need to run ever faster to escape his own contradictions. At the same time, it again also pointed towards a more general tension within male stardom itself.[1]

As I tried to ponder the stars' bafflement and breathlessness and the underlying issues about male stardom that they raised, I was inevitably and repeatedly drawn to the writings of Ginette Vincendeau, whose work on French stardom occupies such a central place in a field that it almost single-handedly opened up and still undoubtedly dominates. First came the compelling examination of Gabin's mythical status as star, Frenchman and male in *Jean Gabin: anatomie d'un mythe* (Gauteur and Vincendeau 1993), a work that not only effectively inaugurated French star studies in the English-speaking academy but also took star studies to a French audience. Second, and most importantly, there was *Stars and Stardom in French Cinema* (Vincendeau 2000), a remarkably wide-ranging, assured and persuasive work. If its scope, its ability to range from Max Linder to Juliette Binoche, was intimidatingly impressive, its real strength lay in its capacity to combine a thorough insider's knowledge of socio-cultural contexts with a highly sophisticated and nuanced use of the essential tools of cinematic analysis. Much work on stars tends to be narrowly textual. In contrast, that of Vincendeau shows how profitably close analysis of film and performance can be combined with an awareness of genre, technological change and political economy. Third and more recently came the important *Journeys of Desire: European Actors in Hollywood, a Critical Companion* (Phillips and Vincendeau 2006). While star studies had very fruitfully looked at stars within a national socio-cultural frame, they risked under-estimating the transnational dynamics always at play in cinematic production. *Journeys of Desire* provides a precious corrective. Its exploration of the cultural translations that occurred when stars moved to Hollywood and its capacity to explain their very different impacts there make for compelling reading. Problematizing dominant understandings of the national in a different way, Ginette Vincendeau has also recently turned her attention to the place of southern French stars such as Raimu and Fernandel in classic French cinema (Vincendeau 2007b). Again combining a tremendous knowledge of cultural contexts and forms with rigorous and nuanced attention to details of film style and performance, she convincingly articulates how southern stars offer an alternative version of the nation and of national masculinities. Adding to her work on Pagnol in the classic *French Film: Texts and Contexts* (Hayward and Vincendeau 1990), this more recent work is hopefully part of a larger project that will give Pagnol and the French south some well-deserved attention.

Pagnol takes us back towards Raimu and *La Femme du Boulanger*. Vincendeau has pointed to the overwhelmingly patriarchal nature of the *cinéma méridional* of the classic era: a cinema dominated by male stars and logocentric films where 'verbal mastery is the preserve of male characters and actors' (Vincendeau 2007b: 226). She has noted, too, how the films 'on the whole enact conservative gender relationships, building a world governed by the figure of the father and the subjection of women' (Vincendeau 2007b: 225). Yet, as she commented in her earlier work on Pagnol's Marseille trilogy, the director's films also tend to engage in a disarmingly explicit way with the mechanics of desire and repression that propel their narratives (Vincendeau 1990: 68–69). Because of this, they lay bare the tensions and frustrations that lie within the patriarchal family and the patriarchal order more generally (Vincendeau 1990: 76). *La Femme du Boulanger* responds well to a reading along these lines. The film is (rightly) seen as misogynistic because of the way the men of the town form a local *union sacrée* in order to bring the unfaithful wife back to her husband while silencing the other women who might comment on the drama. However, before this occurs the film has shown a remarkable awareness of female desire and its frustration within the patriarchal order, not least in the scene when the wife comes out from behind the bakery counter to breathe in the shepherd's smell even as, in a highly suggestive gesture, she puts bread into his sack. Another particularly telling scene shows the Italian shepherd and some companions as they sing her a romantic song under the bakery window, their foreign tones

Opposite: *La Femme du boulanger* – different pleasures in response to the shepherds' serenade.

disrupting the cosily Franco-French soundscape of the village. Not quite sure whether he is hearing Corsican, Piedmontese or Arabic, the naïve baker assumes that the spectacle is in his honour. Filled with desire for the handsome shepherd, his wife sees it rather differently. As spectators, we cannot help now viewing her portly, mature husband and the bedroom she must share with him rather differently too!

Part of the daring of this scene is the way it foregrounds the woman's sexual frustration but another part of it is its reflexivity. Does not the woman's desiring look out of the window upon an eroticized transnational spectacle say something about the kind of transgressive publicness produced by cinema itself along lines described by Miriam Hansen and James and Stephanie Donald?[2] While the film seems, on the surface, to confirm a male monopoly of the word and of the public sphere – women being brought 'home' or driven indoors – at a deeper level, it suggests cinema's own capacity to challenge that domination – a capacity that, at the level of the diegesis, can never be acknowledged. Part of a traditional male-centred publicness, the baker's identity seems to be defined by his work – he is 'le boulanger' – and by what he makes – the bread that nourishes the community. But defined also by the woman's (non)-desiring look upon him as an unerotic body, his identity is effectively fissured in ways with which he cannot fully engage. Hence, perhaps, his deeper bafflement. His surface confusion, rooted in his slow realization of his wife's infidelity, will diminish as the narrative unfolds. This deeper bafflement, grounded in an objectification and decentring of the male of which he cannot be self-reflexively aware and with which the story cannot explicitly engage, is condemned to last. It is the surface confusion, of course, that generates explicit signals: the benign smile even as his wife's seduction has begun; the bemused refusal to recognize an unacceptable truth; the verbose impotence of a character unable to deal with the situation. These surface disturbances are, I would argue, the diegetic echoes of cinema's more profound destabilization of the masculine.

The roots of Gabin's equally unthinkable bafflement in *Gueule d'amour* are somewhat similar. Building on Geneviève Sellier's work on the film, Vincendeau has shown how his character is the focus of admiring looks from both men and women in a way that effectively feminizes and objectifies him (Sellier 1989; Gauteur and Vincendeau 1993: 188). Like *La Femme du Boulanger*, but in a much more sustained way, the film develops an implicit reflexive engagement with cinema and the subversive forms of publicness it develops. In the early part of the film, the Gabin character, a Spahi or colonial soldier, is effectively a 'star', an object of mass consumption, as all the women in the barracks town are drawn to him and pass photographs of him between themselves. His dashing handsomeness makes him a very different screen presence to Pagnol's 'homely' baker, yet his character's identity is nonetheless fissured in a similar way: on the one hand, as a soldier he belongs to a traditional masculine public sphere defined by virile action and inner strength; on the other, he is part of an emergent, frivolous, feminized consumer economy that reconfigures his identity as erotic, objectified surface. This eroticization of Gabin's image is discussed by Vincendeau in her co-authored book with Gauteur (Gauteur and Vincendeau 1993: 184–90) as well as in her *Pépé le Moko*, where she notes the capacity of the gangster genre to which *Pépé le Moko*

Gueule d'amour – a baffled Jean Gabin comforted by René Lefèvre.

(Duvivier 1937) belongs to allow a narcissistic display of masculine elegance yet maintain an image of 'rugged masculinity' (Vincendeau 1998: 41). Her preference in those works, and in *Stars and Stardom*, is to connect the 'feminization' of the Gabin persona to its capacity to incorporate the feminine and thus to achieve a mythic universality that helps explain the star's appeal to a mixed public despite its masculine core (Gauteur and Vincendeau 1993: 190–203; Vincendeau 2000: 76–77). While recognizing the power of this explanation, I prefer to underscore the instability of the Gabin persona. If the star image can help reconcile tensions, it can also force them to the surface. The kind of focus on how star images serve to dramatize yet stabilize social contradictions inaugurated by Richard Dyer has the virtue of allowing readings of stars to be tied to social evolution in often compelling ways (Dyer 1979). Yet it runs the risk of underestimating cinema's own role in the production of contradiction. Part of an emergent consumer economy, classical cinema was far from neutrally situated with respect to social change. Configuring male stars as unstable objects to be consumed frivolously by a mixed public, it sat uneasily with a heavily patriarchal public sphere with its serious, durable masculinities.

Another clue as to why the Gabin of *Gueule d'amour* may look so thoroughly baffled, with explicit signals (bemusement, hurt, frustration, passivity) again pointing to more profound underlying disturbances, is the way in which the film seems to lurch from one genre to another as its story unfolds. If it starts out as something akin to the *comédie troupière*, it ends as tragic melodrama. Within the former genre, the Gabin character's conquests can be joked about with the *copains* who, as Vincendeau has shown, so typically surrounded him and in contrast to whose defects or excesses his idealized masculinity '*degré zéro*' was habitually defined (Gauteur and Vincendeau 1993: 180-84). Yet, as his character is detached from the group and falls under the destructive spell of Balin's *femme fatale* in a way that leads to her death and his exile, the film shifts to melodramatic mode. While it would surely be too neat and too easy to tie this generic shift to the need to provide different pleasures to male and female spectators, something along those lines surely plays a major part in generating such generic instability, the fragility and vulnerability of the Gabin persona that comes to the fore in the melodramatic part (Gauteur and Vincendeau 1993: 119-23) making him much more available to a protective, feminine gaze. It is surely a commonplace by now to suggest that stars may be configured differently as they move from one medium such as cinema to another such as popular cinema magazines, or from film to film? But it is perhaps less obvious that they be may also be configured differently through the course of a single film as it seeks to offer a variety of pleasures to a diverse audience.

Some confirmation of the argument so far can perhaps be found in an earlier Gabin film, the 'Diva' movie *Paris-Béguin/The Darling of Paris* (Genina 1931), perhaps the first to locate him in what Vincendeau labels 'his typical 1930s habitat: pessimistic melodramas in working-class or underworld settings' (Vincendeau 2000: 61). The film is particularly interesting because, like *La Femme du Boulanger* and *Gueule d'amour*, it reflexively engages with the transgressiveness of cinema, albeit implicitly. Its heroine is a star singer (played by Jane Marnac). Gabin plays a criminal who breaks into her room, and for whose charms she falls. The affair ends tragically as Gabin's character, wrongly suspected of informing, is murdered by another gangster played by Jean Max. The grief-stricken Diva brings his story into her own stage show, where it is reworked as an Orientalist drama for the mixed audience of the theatre, moving in the process from a hard, masculine genre of the gangster to the softer, feminized world of the exotic fantasy. Picking up the core Gabin persona at a decidedly embryonic stage, the film underscores its availability for a narrative driven by female desire. Its capacity to detach itself from the star and to shift as it moves across genres suggests how the world of spectacle (of theatre or cinema) can produce an unstable, superficial, eroticized masculinity for a mixed public.

Only embryonic in *Paris-Béguin*, the Gabin persona firms up around the time of Duvivier's *La Bandera/Escape from Yesterday* (1935), as Vincendeau has shown (Vincendeau 2000: 64–69). She sees the film as a felicitous coming together of 'Duvivier's penchant for men's stories' with 'Gabin's physique and performance style'. Contrasting the film to the couple-centred *Le Grand Jeu* (Feyder 1934) and *Morocco* (Von Sternberg 1930) – both also set in colonial space – she notes how: 'In *La Bandera* … the central conflict takes place between soldiers and addresses, through the military institution, a construction of masculinity defined by the relationships between men and not by the relationships between men and women.' She adds: 'The woman [Annabella] is, as it were, part of the decor. The film clearly addresses spectators constructed as masculine (whether they are men or women)' (Vincendeau 2000: 67). With typical attention to detail, she notes how Gabin occupies 145 of the film's 417 shots while Annabella only has 39 (Gauteur and Vincendeau 1993: 124), an astonishing imbalance given the latter's prominent profile at the time and her high-ranking in star popularity polls (Crisp 2002: 268–69). She notes, too, how *La Bandera* seems to respond to wishes expressed in an article by Jean-Fayard in popular cinema journal *Pour vous*, in which he deplores the excessive sensibility of the French cultural climate in general and film melodrama in particular while calling for 'a virile cinema' (Vincendeau 2000: 67).

When doing some work on colonial cinema as a (supposedly) coherent genre, my own eyes were caught by another piece in the popular cinematic press, this time clearly directed at women (O'Shaughnessy 2005). Written by critic Nino Frank and entitled 'Puis voici mon coeur' ('So here is my heart'), the piece framed a series of films, covering a very diverse generic range, as different romantic fantasies. Each fantasy ('*L'amour bel canto*', '*l'amour espionnage*', etc.) was accompanied by a still showing the lead couple from a film. *La Bandera* figured as 'Moroccan love', a variant of the broader category of 'military love' (Frank 1937: 8–9). Always aware of the importance of popular cinema magazines in the construction of star images, Vincendeau reminds us how their main appeal during the classic era was to women, something 'confirmed by editorial and advertising references to fashion, shopping and grooming … and sections entitled "Pour vous Mesdames"' (Vincendeau 2000: 16). The article I had come across referencing *La Bandera* as female fantasy was thus not something exceptional. It suggested how the cinematic press might serve as a key base for the construction of a female spectatorship in a way perhaps still insufficiently taken into account when we analyze the 'gendering' of classic French cinema.[3] Intriguingly, it perhaps implied how a film that Vincendeau undoubtedly rightly sees as an essentially male-centred text might nonetheless house something very different, which again points to the necessary instability of films' generic identity as they sought to build in different audience appeals. Very much in the minority, the scenes with Annabella seem to shift the film away from a virile colonial narrative into a soft, escapist exoticism in a way that not only *interrupts* the masculinist central story but also *contaminates* it, making Gabin's character's virile suffering available for an erotically charged look.

One of the many important contributions that Vincendeau has made to the field of French cinema studies is to try to move us away from an over-concentration on canonical and auteur films that risks fundamentally distorting our area of research. Her own work on Gabin, on other stars and on popular film – *La Bandera* being a case in point – avoids this pitfall. *Stars and Stardom* is typical in this respect, giving as much attention to a figure like Louis de Funès, whose stardom was almost entirely constructed in 'low' popular comedies, as to Jeanne Moreau or Catherine Deneuve, whose stardom lies at the quality or art-house end of the spectrum. In the same work, Vincendeau also reminds us that our retrospective understanding of 1930s French film tends to privilege mythical figures like Gabin, Charles Boyer, Michelle Morgan or Arletty at the expense of names like Annabella or Victor Francen, huge figures at the time (Vincendeau 2000: 26). Taking my cue from this, I would now like to bring a relatively neglected star, Harry Baur, into the picture to broaden and develop my argument.

Another of the heavy, mature males who dominated the French cinema of the latter 1930s (Burch and Sellier 1996), the physically imposing Baur was typically seen in heavyweight dramas such as Raymond Bernard's *Les Misérables* (1934) (see Figure 22.1 in Chapter 22 of this book), Robert Siodmak's *Mollenard/Hatred* (1938) or Marcel L'Herbier's *Les Hommes nouveaux* (1936).[4] In the last-mentioned film, he plays the part of a settler in colonial Morocco. Initially shown building roads and then captured by rebels, he is later picked up when he has risen to the status of an entrepreneur and is engaged in the public works that are 'developing' the country. The film seems an entirely masculine drama: military action, manual labour and entrepreneurship are tied together as part of a shared national project, taking the film close to colonial propaganda. However, the tone shifts sharply when the hero meets Christiane (Nathalie Paley), a beautiful young widow, on board a boat on a trip back to the colony from France. The hero falls for the woman and marries her. All seems set fair until she bumps by chance into Henri de Chassagnes (Max Michel), the dashing military officer she once loved. The ins and outs of the plot are not worth explaining here, but what is of note is how the woman's introduction changes everything. The initial focus on masculine activities, male groups and virile bodies in action partly gives way to the consumerist pleasure of watching the range of gowns worn by the very elegant heroine. At the same time, the masculinity defined by virile action in the world is now reconfigured within the romance, even as the heroine's viewpoint serves to anchor a feminine look on actions and people. The unstable males mutate before our eyes. No longer simply an action hero, the young officer is reconfigured as a dashing object of feminine desire. No longer simply defined by his deeds and his place within different male groups, the hero is reframed as a suffering, jealous figure, unable – like Raimu in *La Femme du Boulanger* – to excite a woman's desiring gaze even as he develops the emotional complexity that might make him worthy of her interest. Having begun by seeming to promote the kind of 'serious' masculinities consonant with the colonial project and with a conventionally defined male-centred public sphere, *Les Hommes nouveaux* mutates into something more 'frivolous' as it responds to the need to offer a range of generic pleasures to a mixed audience. One way to read the Baur persona here would be to underscore its capacity to resolve social tensions through its ability to be both proletarian and bourgeois (the early road digging and the later entrepreneurialism), masculine and feminine (competitively strong yet sensitively vulnerable), a versatility also in evidence in Bernard's *Les Misérables*, as Reader shows in this volume (see Chapter 22). But another way to view it would emphasize an instability tied to cinema's need to mount different audience appeals and its capacity to generate forms of publicness that necessarily sat uneasily alongside dominant patriarchal norms.

If we accept that the baffled and unstable nature of the male stars in the films considered is intrinsically tied to the fact that cinema, as a forerunner of the consumer economy, was to some extent 'out of phase' with its time, then we should also accept that this out-of-phaseness was something that would inevitably diminish as consumerism became more prominent in the course of the *Trente Glorieuses*. As production became less central, as the cult of the image became prevalent and as the public sphere became less rigidly gendered, the gap between normative masculinities and cinematic ones would become more easily bridgeable and star personae would more easily be able to engage reflexively with their own consumability and instability. Something along these lines would be suggested by Vincendeau's compelling analysis of Delon and Belmondo, the unsmiling and smiling icons of their period.

With typical attention to evolutions in film style, Vincendeau notes how two young stars were able to respond to fundamental changes in screen technology and in the screen image. With specific reference to Belmondo, she notes: 'Belmondo's energy … made him perfect for the new adventure movies, which demanded stars who could move and fill the newly wide screen' (Vincendeau 2000: 168). Broadening the focus to take in Delon, she notes: 'The move to wide-screen, colour and location shooting demanded new types of performance for which … both stars' youthful bodies were perfectly suited' (Vincendeau 2000: 183). Belmondo and Delon were not the first stars to place the athletic male body on display. Jean Marais, Gérard Philippe and Henri Vidal had already done so; however, as Vincendeau comments, 'they did so in distinctly non-realist genres: the swashbuckler for Marais and Philippe, the Italian *peplum* for Vidal. Delon and Belmondo's originality was to offer male erotic display in recognizable, contemporary settings, clothes and situations' (Vincendeau 2000: 183). The self-conscious display of the eroticized male had become possible, as Vincendeau notes, because of changing lifestyles: 'The move to a consumer and leisure society and the rise of tourism which accompanied the French 'economic miracle' of the post-war period … provided motivations for the films to display 'modern' locations, objects and behaviours' (Vincendeau 2000: 183). This shift to *explicit* display meant that Belmondo and Delon could embody a *knowing* objectification of the male star – something particularly marked in the case of Delon, whose early films 'are structured around the narcissistic display of his face and body' (Vincendeau 2000: 174). It is this capacity for self-conscious, narcissistic self-display that particularly interests me here. Gabin, Raimu and Baur, male stars of an earlier generation, were already consumable, objectified males, men of fleeting surface as well as of durable depth, but they could not be allowed to be aware of this without running ahead of their time. With Delon and Belmondo, the times had caught up and male stars could be narcissistically aware of their objectification and no longer needed to be baffled.

However, as the need for bafflement diminished, the need for breathlessness increased. Cinema might no longer seem out of phase with its time, but hegemonic constructions of masculinity still were. A masculinity still predominantly defined by action in the world and by naturalized domination of self, others and public space sat ill with the increasingly androgynous world brought by the social transformations of the post-war period. It would have to run increasingly hard to stay ahead. Nowhere is this better expressed than in *A bout de souffle*, another brilliantly self-reflexive commentary on the intersection of masculinity and the image economy. As the film begins, the hero Poiccard (Belmondo) seems part of a securely male world. He steals a large American car from a US serviceman and finds in its glove compartment the revolver that he uses to kill one of the policemen who pursues him on the road. At the same time, he borrows his image from Bogart, as in the famous scene where he self-consciously imitates Bogart's gesture of running his thumb over his upper lip while looking at the poster for Mark Robson's 1956 Bogart vehicle *The Harder They Fall* (Vincendeau 2000: 164). This is a masculinity that might seem to have successfully updated itself for the world of the (borrowed) image and the (stolen) consumerist icon, able to exist narcissistically on the surface and still be resolutely virile. However, when we look a little further, the world of the film is increasingly androgynous. Poiccard might speed away from Marseille at the wheel of an American car, but he arrives sedately in Paris as a passenger in a 2CV driven by a woman. If the increasingly central media economy can be plundered for icons of masculinity (Bogart), it is also a place where gendered differences are undermined. Poiccard is bent on reaching CineCittá, but his girlfriend Patricia already works as a journalist, while an ex-girlfriend works in television. Moreover, as we will all remember from the film's conclusion, Patricia is able to steal the same gesture from him that he had stolen from Bogart. A heroic masculinity that lives on the edge sits ill with the detachable superficiality of consumer goods and fleeting images so the hero must drive himself to the limits to maintain traditional gender demarcations. This no doubt explains his breathlessness.

The Gabin of the classic period was associated with traditionally masculine professions (Vincendeau 2000: 71), defined in contrast to other members of male groups (Gauteur and Vincendeau 1993: 180–84) and associated with male places (the locomotive platform of *La Bête humaine/The Human Beast* [Renoir 1938], the prisoner-of-war camp of *La Grande*

Illusion/Grand Illusion [Renoir 1937], the factory of *Le Jour se lève/Daybreak* [Carné 1939]) (Gauteur and Vincendeau 1993: 177–80). The personae of Delon and Belmondo cannot be grounded in such a solidly masculine universe. Much more typically, they are defined as isolated individuals who have to set themselves against their world – setting them, as Vincendeau tellingly puts it, against 'the "soft" ethos of the 1970s' (Vincendeau 2000: 185) in order to assert a masculinity no longer reflected in what surrounds it (Austin 2003: 58–59). Their early image was rooted in a criminality that, unlike that of Gabin, isolated them from the group (Vincendeau 2000: 159, 181). Their later personae became markedly conservative. Cinema could still be out of phase with its time and its society, after all. A masculine stardom that had once been able to move ahead of its period by developing consumable, unstable males could also run behind its times by refusing to acknowledge social evolution.

Of course, in the same way as the bafflement that I attribute to Raimu, Gabin and Baur should not be read in too narrowly literal a way, the breathlessness I associate with Belmondo and Delon should not simply be seen as something associated with the strains of kinetic on-screen activity, not least because of Delon's generally cooler, more languorous screen presence (Vincendeau 2000: 179). Rather, like that earlier bafflement, it should be seen as the result of underlying tensions (between the 'hard' male and a 'soft' society, between a 'deep' existentially defined masculine and the shifting superficiality of the image economy) that at times break through the textual surface and express themselves through the isolation, vulnerability or exhaustion of the hard male body (Vincendeau 2000: 185).

Vincendeau's different works set a challenge to all those researching on French stars to somehow go beyond what she has written. As she herself would be the first to point out, there is still much to be done. Her work has concentrated in tremendously productive ways on the major, 'mythical' stars. There are a host of lesser but still important figures that need attention. *Stars and Stardom* devotes some important pages to the political economy of stardom but much more clearly needs to be done in that area if we are to develop a clearer understanding of the role of stars in the production, distribution and exhibition of French cinema.[5] *Stars and Stardom* underlines the role of the popular cinema press in generating star personae, but more work is still needed on it – and especially on its capacity, during the 'classic' period, to sustain a distinctly feminine look upon films and stars. Vincendeau's writing on how southern French film stars develop a different version of Frenchness (Vincendeau 2007b) surely invites us to look more at how, for example, the rising generation of beur stars might be helping to reinvent a sense of nation and national belonging. Her co-edited work on European actors in Hollywood could also be seen as an invitation to ponder the role of foreign stars in the French industry (Phillips and Vincendeau 2006). It is not easy to know how French star studies may be redefined in the years ahead. We can be sure, however, that the person who defined the field initially will play a lead role in moving it forward through her own work and in dialogue with others. Hopefully this piece will have contributed to that dialogue and suggested some possible areas that may also repay further thought.

Notes

1. For a more developed version of some of the arguments developed here about the complexities of male stardom, see O'Shaughnessy (2007).
2. Referring specifically to early cinema, Hansen suggests that, due to the diversity of what was shown and an as yet undomesticated audience, cinema was able to function as an alternative public sphere within which a public of women or of immigrants were able to self-reflexively engage with the American experience of the modern. She argues that this capacity was curtailed as classic narrative cinema, synchronized sound and accommodation of the audience to bourgeois norms came to produce a more passive, standardized and massified experience (Hansen 1991: 90–125). Broadening the historical application of her argument, Donald and Donald suggest that, contrary to those who defend a highly normative sense of 'serious' publicness, cinema in general 'makes available structures of visibility, modes of conduct and practices of judgement, which together constitute a culture of public participation' (2000: 114).
3. Leila Wimmer (2008) explores how the popular cinematic press served as a key site for women's negotiation of modernity. She sees the same press as a key locus of a popular, feminine cinephilia neglected in existing accounts of French cinephilia.
4. Reader's Chapter 22 in this volume underscores the undeserved critical neglect that has befallen Bernard's adaptation of Hugo's *Les Misérables*. In the same piece, he reminds us of the place of Harry Baur as one of the leading performers in 1930s French cinema, alongside actors such as Raimu.
5. Although it is a relatively short piece, Creton (2007) shows how productive an attention to political economy can be when dealing with stardom. On a larger scale, McDonald (2000) gives political economy and star labour a central role in his analysis of Hollywood stardom, thus providing a vital corrective to the predominant text-centred approaches.

Chapter 19

Placing French Film History

Alastair Phillips

S ometime during my mid-teens, late one night on BBC2, I watched my very first French film, Julien Duvivier's classic gangster tale *Pépé le Moko/Pépé le Moko* (1937). I have remembered the longing in the tragic face of Jean Gabin at the gates of the port in Algiers ever since. Little did I realise then that I would still be thinking about this experience a quarter of a century later when called upon to consider the immeasurable contribution that Ginette Vincendeau has made to the development of French film studies. I was initially reminded of Gabin's face some time later when, in the year before starting my BA in Film and Media Studies with Art History at the University of Stirling, I found myself working at the British Film Institute and gorging on a lengthy season of French film classics at the National Film Theatre that included Marcel Carné's moving and atmospheric *Le Quai des brumes/Port of Shadows* (1938) and *Le Jour se lève/Daybreak* (1939).

I ended up being inspired by my first degree partly because it allowed me to combine a sense of learning spanning the centuries with exposure to a field that was only just finding its way. Where else was I going to study Piero della Francesca in the morning and Douglas Sirk in the afternoon? Film studies was still a nascent discipline, and much of what I read by Richard Dyer, Laura Mulvey and Christian Metz, amongst others, had only recently been published or translated. There was very little to read on French cinema then that matched the vigour and theoretical sophistication of the important work being done on American cinema.[1] There was also little emphasis on the kind of work that I was beginning to enjoy in art history that married close textual analysis with theoretical explanation and rigorous historical contextualization. For me, reading Vincendeau's first published work on Jean Gabin in *Screen* in 1985 began to change all this. 'Community, Nostalgia and the Spectacle of Masculinity' (Vincendeau 1985a, reproduced in slightly abridged form as Chapter 7 of this volume) was the first article in English to make me think seriously about the possibility of a different form of film studies – and I have continued to return to it ever since, first as one of Professor Vincendeau's students at the University of Warwick in the 1990s, and second when coming to terms with its legacy in the light of this anniversary publication.

In this chapter, I therefore want to begin by presenting an assessment of Vincendeau's formative work in *Screen* through an examination of its core critical perspectives on the stardom of Jean Gabin. As Vincendeau herself would proudly say, there has been little she has said since that has not, in some way, referred to the enduring importance of France's leading screen figure of the twentieth century. Although I will concentrate on this particular journal article – taken, by the way, from a key chapter in her PhD (the United Kingdom's first in film studies and still probably the most widely referenced unpublished doctoral thesis in the field) – I will also refer to the influential nexus of Gabin-related publications that have appeared subsequently. Second, I want to highlight the crucial fact that this work was not placed in a French studies journal at all, but in what was then, and is arguably still today, the leading film studies journal in the English language. This is important because it also allows us to consider the ways in which Vincendeau's writing also contributed to a realignment of priorities in the light of 'the historical turn' then confronting film studies after the sedimentation of *Screen*'s earlier influential work on psychoanalysis, post-1968 Marxism and the politics of narrative realism. Here, I thus wish to position Ginette's work more in relation to her practice as a theoretically informed film historian, and I want to do this by considering two overlapping vantage points: first, that of the intersection between gender, class and performance; and second, that of the intersection between questions of popular cinema, national identity and genre.

As has been the case with much of her subsequent intellectual work, Vincendeau's initial conception of Gabin's significance drew on key currents in the French and English language academy in terms of its pairing of Roland Barthes' notion of the significance of myth's ability 'to make the historical appear natural' (Vincendeau 2000: 64) with Richard Dyer's groundbreaking work on the intertextual nature of film stardom (Dyer 1979). Dyer's writing, in particular, allowed Vincendeau to posit that in order to unpick the mythological construction of such a figure as 'Jean Gabin', one must see this process in terms of 'an intricate … construction which radiates through not only the films themselves, but also an array of other texts such as memoirs and testimonies (his and others), fan magazines, newspaper reports, plays, music-hall shows and songs' (Vincendeau 1985a: 19). This was crucial, for by seeing Gabin in the 1930s as both a figure defined in relation to a (largely male) community within the text, and a figure mediated within a broader network of mass cultural intertexts, Vincendeau was able to conceive a set of revealing propositions that demonstrated Gabin's historical significance, not simply as an existential tragic hero whose fate merely echoed a broader sense of cultural and political defeat, but as an emblematic figure capable of articulating profound and enduring divisions within French society concerning gender, class and national identity.

How was this achieved? First, I think it was necessary to articulate a network of fluid spectatorial relations within the two films discussed in the article: the previously mentioned *Pépé le Moko* and *La Belle équipe/They Were Five* (Duvivier 1936). The influential way in which these relations were defined was in terms of spectacle – a notion initially drawn from Steve Neale's pioneering work on masculinity published a few years earlier in *Screen* (Neale 1983). Here, the term was synthesized to encompass a sense of the diegetic male community's gaze upon the figure in its midst that, importantly, also constituted its exception. Thus, like the non-diegetic audience within the cinema, the communities within the films' actual narratives were also simultaneously transformed into spectators. It was:

> through their common look at a spectacle that the communities [were] constructed
> as important structures within the film[s]: passive in the sense that they [were] not

themselves performing, and active through their gaze at, and therefore construction of, the performer, Jean Gabin. (Vincendeau 1985a: 24)

This realization that French cinema of the 1930s could be defined as an intricately organised field of shared social practice, as well as mass entertainment, forced the question of what these audiences were actually looking at when they gazed at the spectacular figure of Gabin. Furthermore, what conclusions could one draw from the fact that, in each case within these films, the hero played by Gabin ends in failure rather than success?

The key to answering these points can be found, I think, in the second plank of Vincendeau's overall formulation of the nature of Gabin's significance, resting – much like the very phenomenon of stardom itself – on a series of paradoxes mediated principally through the act of performance. The fundamental duality that Vincendeau notes – and I think this is also crucial to understanding her analysis of other male French stars within popular narrative cinema such as Gérard Depardieu (Vincendeau 1993) – is that there is a particular correlation between Gabin's act of performance *within* the text and how the specific characters he played in turn simultaneously embodied the performance of an ideal masculinity. In both films, she notes:

> masculinity is tested against its own excesses ... Against the excessive values embodied by his friends and accomplices, the Gabin hero stands as the norm ... Whereas they are one-dimensional and therefore incomplete, he is complex and complete, but the ideal masculinity he represents, being the result of a comparison to extremes rather than the positive affirmation of particular attributes, is strangely lacking in substance. (Vincendeau 1985a: 32)

It is, in other words, 'a definition of masculinity which is more passive than active, more negative than positive' (Vincendeau 1985a: 32). This paradox, unique to the case of Gabin, is thus 'underlined and echoed in the contradiction between the place of the Gabin hero *within* the group (where he reigns supreme) and his place *outside* it, where he is variously an outcast, a deviant or a solitary "anti-hero"' (Vincendeau 1985a: 33). It is also, crucially from a film studies perspective, underscored by the very performance style of Gabin himself in that his mode of self-presentation typically embodied an unusual, but highly attractive, kind of 'degree zero' masculinity characterized by the '*show*' of 'laconic', 'restrained' (Vincendeau 1985a: 36) body movements (with the exception of his famed moments of explosive anger). We are thus given the perfect means to understand the true reality of Gabin's fate. As Vincendeau goes on to argue: 'If women in these two films are the first victims of [this system of working class masculinity in a patriarchal capitalist society] ... in being punished, rejected or marginalised, the heroes are themselves trapped' (Vincendeau 1985a: 36). Gabin's destiny, in particular, is indeed intertwined with his refusal of the realities of the class structure he is also forced to inhabit. Thus, finally, 'the self-generated need for the affirmation of virile values means that the comforting world of the feminine has to be rejected, while physical closeness with other males must be heavily disavowed' (Vincendeau

1985a: 36). In other words: 'Denied (denying himself) both the comforts of the feminine and the rewards of patriarchy, there is no solution left for the Gabin hero but destruction' (Vincendeau 1985a: 37).

In her later work on Gabin's role in *Pépé le Moko*, Vincendeau would extend her analysis of Gabin's paradoxical performativity through an analysis of the film's treatment of costume and space. It also evidently mattered how Gabin's character looked and where he was situated. In the beginnings of a rich vein of work on masculinity and popular French crime cinema, resulting in such publications as her book-length assessment of the career of Jean-Pierre Melville (Vincendeau 2003) and, to a lesser extent, an important survey of classical French *film noir* in Andrew Spicer's groundbreaking *European Film Noir* anthology (Vincendeau 2007a), Vincendeau's BFI Classic on *Pépé le Moko* (1998) argued that the male gangster figure in 1930s French film melded influences from American cinema with a range of specifically French socio-cultural contexts. The point of being a *French* criminal, she points out, is that it is an 'existential' rather than 'functional' matter (Vincendeau 1998: 35). In the reverse of Hollywood's more conventional goal-orientated perspective on the American gangster, the French film gangster – exemplified by Gabin – was represented in terms of a predilection for atmosphere over action. Central to this 'atmosphere' was dress and, in particular, the contradictory means by which the apparent sartorial synergy between Pépé and Gabin himself permitted the 'highly narcissistic display of the male body, while preserving a virile image of "rugged masculinity"' (Vincendeau 1998: 41). The even greater irony of this proposition that especially marked Gabin's configuration of the famous Parisian *apache* was, of course, that 'the star persona of Gabin as "ideal Frenchman"' was actually being 'forged [outside of France] in colonial space' (Vincendeau 1998: 62).[2] This assessment thus allowed Vincendeau to perceive the double bind of the Gabin character in a new light. In a bold move that not uncharacteristically overturned what would be a far more conventional political reading, merely viewing Pépé as an apparently racially superior agent, Vincendeau suggested that we needed to read against the grain to see the ways in which 'Pépé's relation to the Casbah' in the film was 'in itself ambivalent. It protects and imprisons him,' she observes. 'He is both *of* the Casbah and alien to it' (Vincendeau 1998: 63). In other words, rather than simply seeing the relation between Gabin and the narrative space his character inhabits in terms of a form of subjugation in which the colonial location could be said to be 'feminized' by French tutelage, we need to understand that 'the strong eroticisation of the Casbah, its feminine identity, [actually] imprison[s] and feminize[s] him too' (Vincendeau 1998: 63). Gabin's character was thus trapped not only in terms of class and masculinity, but also in terms of the politics of location.[3] Whether it be in relation to Paris, and the particular coordinates of the city evoked in Fréhel's famous song, 'Où est-il donc?' or the treacherous world of the Algerian Casbah, Gabin's working-class persona may have been 'culturally dominant' but crucially it also always, for Vincendeau, remained 'politically subaltern' (Vincendeau 1998: 66).

So far, then, I have begun to identify some of the major critical concerns governing my reading of Vincendeau's work on Gabin as it sought to re-evaluate a number of the actor's key films from the 1930s. I have reiterated that, instead of seeing him simply as an emblematic Poetic Realist anti-hero, somehow presaging a wider sense of subsequent defeat on the part of France in the fraught political climate of the years leading up to the Occupation, we need to relocate Gabin in terms of a more plausible reading based around the politics of gender, class and spectatorial identification. In Vincendeau's own words from the *Screen* article, her work at this point was concerned with how the films in question told 'the story of masculinity or, rather, of one of its possible paths under a patriarchal regime' (Vincendeau 1985a: 31). I have also implied that the significance of Vincendeau's analysis also lay in her ability to marry close textual analysis with a conviction that good theoretically informed writing necessitated the explication of a clear political investment. In a broad sense, I would argue that this was largely defined by the impact of second-wave feminism and the consolidation of cultural studies approaches within British film studies as the discipline itself matured during the first half of the 1980s. In the second part of this chapter, however, I want to address the second part of the quote above that states that 'in this respect, the films carry their own historical and social inscription' (Vincendeau 1985a: 31). This formulation suggests a nod to a kind of critical film history that deserves further explication, and to do this I shall initially turn to another piece of writing published in the same issue of *Screen* as 'Community, Nostalgia and the Spectacle of Masculinity', a report on a major international conference that took place at Cérisy-la-Salle in France in August 1985.

The year of the Cérisy conference also saw a broader return to film history that was marked by two highly influential publications: Robert Allen and Douglas Gomery's informative *Film History: Theory and Practice* (1985) and David Bordwell, Kristin Thompson and Janet Staiger's monumental *The Classical Hollywood Cinema: Film Style and Mode of Production to 1960* (1985). The former, in line with recent work beginning a fundamental re-evaluation of the study of early cinema,[4] proposed a stronger engagement with empirical material at the expense of abstract speculation. It suggested valuable ways of understanding how Hollywood cinema, in particular, functioned as an industry with sources of historical documentation including such items as legal records, fan magazines, production memos or trade papers. Like Barry Salt's contemporaneous investigations into film style and technology (1983), much of this writing eschewed earlier forms of film history that, as Vincendeau pointed out in relation to the French example, had either led to totalizing accounts of the like provided by Georges Sadoul and Jean Mitry or, perhaps more problematically, auteurist narratives proposing a teleological line of (usually male) geniuses taken to be exemplars of the art of cinema. But in this attempt to escape from what Vincendeau in her review called the 'double pitfall of teleology and normativity' (Vincendeau 1985b: 71), a new problem emerged in that aspects of this 'new film history' not only lost sight of the film text itself (in favour of the range of concrete practices that led to its production and consumption), but also the means by which we should interpret the moving image in terms of the fundamental ideas, beliefs and feelings that it helped shape and transmit.[5] As Alison Butler astutely commented in a later *Screen* article, a revisionist screen history was in danger of throwing the baby out with the bathwater. In its valid attempt to localize discrete phenomena, long displaced through such sweeping generalizations as 'the spectator' and 'the classical realist text', this form of film history writing had three problematic, though perhaps unintended, consequences: a separation of cinema from any 'broader socio-cultural context' in favour of seeing it as 'an autonomous artistic-industrial practice'; a displacement of 'questions of thematics and representation' in favour of 'detailed analysis of form'; and finally, the rare subjection of any individual film to substantial 'interpretative critique' (Butler 1992: 414).

I point this out because I think it allows us to get to the crux of what I take Vincendeau's more general contribution to the writing of film history to actually be. I'll begin by going back to the point I made at the beginning of this chapter: that her work on French cinema, especially in its varied local, national and transnational contexts, had in fact already responded quite precisely to Butler's call for an historicized understanding of the ways in which some films may 'neither imitate nor oppose some or all of the codes of Hollywood cinema: they simply give priority instead to more localized approaches to cultural codification' (Butler 1992: 419). I am thinking here, for instance, of another early article published in an anthology of writings for a season of films curated to mark the fiftieth anniversary of the Popular Front. Refuting the prevalent tendency to read Poetic Realist cinema as a direct response to the class politics of the time, Vincendeau proposed that the iconography of populist melodrama (as she prefers to call it) related more to a longer *durée* in which, as a result of the appeal within such films to an essentially nostalgic view of a class-based form of community: 'The historical specificity of these films [was] … much less likely to be found in situations directly contemporary with them than in events or movements situated in a more distant past' (Vincendeau 1986: 100). This cultural formation – constituted, as we have already seen, both within the text in terms of performance[6] and in relation to the text by the spectators in the actual cinema – could thus be linked more to the impact of larger scale changes within the class structure of society that had been generated by the shift from a rural to an industrial economy. Hence the stress in so many of these films, according to Vincendeau, 'on predominately male groups … or excessively patriarchal families' (Vincendeau 1986: 100). In other words, this particular 'localised approach to cultural codification', when teased out in full, would see that '[p]erformance and older entertainment traditions are thus not only the *raison d'être* of many films [of the period], but also the mediating agent between spectators and their own history' (Vincendeau 1986: 100). To put it another way, we can thus see Vincendeau beginning to answer the very question posed at the end of her review of the Cérisy conference. Noting that 'the notions of the object (history of what?), and purpose (history, what for?) of history were often debated by the conference's participants, one crucial question remained to be asked,' she claimed: '*whose* history?' (Vincendeau 1985b: 71)

In order to answer this point of whose history we are discussing, it was evidently necessary for the film historian to review the historiographical reversals noted by Butler and to re-engage more fundamentally with the text, *in relation to* the other documentary materials and empirical evidence now within the grasp of any historically minded film scholar. In other words, as Roger Chartier has put it, by 'avoiding both social reductionism (assuming that everything cultural and political can be explained in terms of social origins) and the mirror-image view that political and intellectual life are entirely autonomous and separate from the social', we may still 'see in social representations and, more broadly, in cultural configurations, not the transcription of pre-existing social relations but rather, on the contrary, one of the sites where social differentiation is constructed' (Chartier 1995: 544). Crucial to this sense of contestation, for Vincendeau, has been the field of an explicitly gendered history, as has been demonstrated in her work, for example, on father–daughter relations in 1930s French films (Vincendeau 1988); melodrama and the woman's film of the 1930s (Vincendeau 1989); and especially the films of Brigitte Bardot during the heyday of her phenomenal stardom during the 1950s into the early 1960s (Vincendeau 2000).[7] In her article on the politics of feminist film history, the American film scholar Patrice Petro noted the significance of Frederic Jameson's notion of two fundamental strands within the writing of history: 'the path of the object, and the path of the subject, the historical origins of the things themselves and that more intangible historicity of the concepts and categories by which we attempt to understand those things' (Petro 1990: 10). Mindful of the ways in which this opposition may fail to take into account 'the paradoxical status of woman in film history as both subject and object of representation', Petro argues forcefully that:

> What is finally at stake for feminism is not so much the problem of claiming too much for textual analysis, but that of claiming too little, thereby leaving the writing of film history to those who would exclude sexual difference from the study of cinema entirely. (Petro 1990: 22

Vincendeau's work on Bardot was a perfect model of the very kind of film history for which Petro is calling. It married a close attention to archival material and textual analysis with a vivid eye for understanding the various means by which Bardot had been interpreted and understood within France as a cultural phenomenon. Her notion that 'Bardot's myth as a star both negotiated and concealed the tensions engendered by her "old and new" femininity' has had a lasting impact on the understanding of female stardom in French cinema, especially in terms of explaining Bardot's fascination for the French – male *and* female – public of the time.

This brings me to the second strand of discussion mentioned earlier concerning questions of the popular, national identity and genre. One of the crucial strands of Vincendeau's work on French cinema has always been an insistence that, in order to fully comprehend the historical significance of a given period, it is important to go beyond the usual vectors of auteurism and assess the films that French audiences actually *saw*. To briefly go back to Bardot, for example, we can only fully understand her significance to a classic *nouvelle vague* film such as *Le Mépris* (Godard 1963) if we locate this within the context of her other roles in more popular films such as *En cas de malheur* (Autant-Lara 1958). Or, to give another example, we can only fully understand the French cinema of the Popular Front era if we make sense of the fact that Marcel Pagnol's *César*, rather than Jean Renoir's *Le Crime de M. Lange*, was the most popular film of 1936. As Vincendeau has put it:

> [R]ather than dismiss most of the 1930s mainstream production for what it was not (aesthetically or politically progressive), it is perhaps time to consider it for what it was: a popular entertainment form which, despite what we may think now, was relevant to its audience in many ways, not least in giving pleasure … Run-of-the-mill features are not just the preserve of the sociologist … they also provide important clues to the functioning of cinema itself. (Vincendeau 1986: 74)

What are the implications of this observation for the writing of a more fully rounded account of French film history? First, this means a challenge to canonicity and the culture of cinephilia. The critical discussion of French cinema outside (and within) France up to the mid-1980s was largely dominated by accounts of the major films by a selected canon of (male) film-makers that included the luminaries of the New Wave, as well as a number of earlier names such as Robert Bresson, Jean Renoir, Abel Gance, and so on. However, Vincendeau's work on, for instance, the 1930s argued for the inclusion of other, less familiar names, such as Pierre Colombier and Yves Mirande, whose now forgotten work was known at the time to legions of French spectators for being part of the popular 'Saturday night cinema'.[8]

Linked to this insight was a claim for the significance of other creative personnel, especially those involved in the writing of the dialogue, such as Henri Jeanson and Charles Spaak. This points to the second fact that a consideration of the cultural specificity of many popular successes requires a closer attention to language, as indeed Vincendeau argues in Chapter 24 of this volume. These films were addressing a national audience destined to find pleasure, at a time of growing competition from American cinema, through an engagement with nationally specific norms of exchange and behaviour. Hence also the need, on Vincendeau's part, to examine the bodily performance styles of star and character actors, especially in relation to their delivery of revealing aspects of dialogue. Third, this emphasis on the word, as well as the image, allows us to see the ways in which Vincendeau's work has quite systematically refused to follow the well-trodden route, typified by such film historians as Maurice Bardèche and Robert Brasillach, of disparaging the theatrical and favouring the supposed purity of the recorded moving image in its own right. As Vincendeau has pointed out, the French film industry of the 1930s, for example, couldn't afford a self-sufficient pool of studio writers à la Hollywood, and instead drew on the proximity to the major film studios of the boulevards. Figures such as Louis Jouvet had two careers cementing a strong relationship between film and theatre audiences. Thus cinema and theatre could be said to have 'worked in a symbiosis – not only in terms of the films themselves, but also of their mode of production' (Vincendeau 1986: 91). This interest in wider traditions of performance and areas of film production conventionally scorned for not being sufficiently 'cinematic' has led to a fourth tenet of Vincendeau's contribution to the study of popular French cinema: an interest in mainstream genres not traditionally considered worthy of serious concern. This has produced valuable critical work, for instance, on Louis de Funès as 'the abject of French cinema' (Vincendeau 2000: 137); the French heritage film, whose representational politics differ significantly from its English counterpart (Vincendeau 2001); and a detailed elaboration of the lineage of French popular crime cinema that has thrown up complex patterns of influence and interference between French and American popular culture (Vincendeau 2003, 2007a).

I want to conclude this chapter by making three brief comments that summarize my assessment of Vincendeau's contribution to French film studies in terms of what I see as a dialectic between the inside and the outside. First, as has been apparent in my discussion, fundamental to any assessment of Vincendeau's work must be an informed understanding of the relations between text and context. As Michèle Lagny (1994) has argued in an account of the politics of writing contemporary film history that deserves to be more widely known:

> Too often, in order to draw the 'historical context', historians use film without knowing much about the rules of film language at the time when a chosen film was made. In doing so, they … overlook the 'filtering' function performed by the microcosm of film language. As for film specialists, they like to use 'context' in order to explain films and their production, without thinking of the double transposition with which the practice of historiography affects the 'contextual facts' they are referring to. (Lagny 1994: 30)

I don't think Vincendeau's work has ever been guilty of these faults. Indeed, through her assiduous use of textual analysis, as well as undisclosed archival material, she has always proposed a Bourdieu-like reading of film that largely matches Lagny's notion of an open 'cinema field' in which 'different forces (economic, social, political, technical, cultural or aesthetic) come into being and confront each other' (Lagny 1994: 41). At the heart of this 'field', however, lies the film text, 'because only the film is the sign that cinema does exist. [In other words] Working from the cinema or on the cinema [always] means starting from the film, and going back to it' (Lagny 1994: 41).

Second, I have also argued that Vincendeau's preoccupation with popular French cinema on its own terms has allowed her to traverse the fault line between high and low culture – between the world of the mass audience and the milieu of the cinephile – with admirable acumen. In doing so, she has broadened our understanding of French cinema in its entirety. And third, going back again to the question of language, I think that it is vital to remark upon the fact that Vincendeau has accomplished all this, for the most part, in her second tongue. This is not only remarkable in its own right, for Vincendeau is undoubtedly one of the finest writers in English-language film studies today, but I think essential to the ways in which we can fully comprehend the force of her argumentation. Writing from within but from without – or, to put it more precisely, from in between – she has consistently placed her own thinking on French film history in such a way that allows a fundamentally unique level of clarification and insight.[9]

Notes

1. Roy Armes' informative but limited survey text (1985), an updating of his earlier publications of the 1970s, serves as an indication of this tendency.
2. The same was also true in *Gueule d'amour* (Grémillon 1937).
3. This means of reading Gabin in terms of deterritorialization resurfaced in a different context in Vincendeau's work on the actor's brief career as an émigré in Hollywood (Vincendeau 2006: 115–24).
4. Initiated by the famous symposium 'Cinema 1900–1906', held at the 1978 FIAF congress in Brighton.
5. I owe this particular formulation to Thomas Elsaesser's critical, but friendly, *Sight & Sound* review of Gomery and Allen, and Bordwell, Thompson and Staiger (Elsaesser 1986: 246–51).
6. The same was also true, Vincendeau argued, in the case of the *chanteuse réaliste*. See also Conway (2004).
7. The contribution of the work of Geneviève Sellier, another participant at the Cérisy conference, is also crucial here. See especially Burch and Sellier (1996).
8. In this work, Vincendeau was undoubtedly influenced by the pioneering contribution of Raymond Chirat.
9. Thanks to Tom Brown for his supportive reading of an earlier draft of this chapter.

References to Part II

Aaron, M. (2004), 'Cinema's Queer Jews: Jewishness and Masculinity in Yiddish Cinema', in P. Powrie, A. Davies and B. Babington (eds), *The Trouble with Men: Masculinities in European and Hollywood Cinema*, London: Wallflower Press, pp. 90–99.

Aitkin, I. (2001), *European Film Theory and Cinema: An Introduction*, Edinburgh: Edinburgh University Press.

Allen, R. and Gomery, D. (1985), *Film History: Theory and Practice*, New York: McGraw-Hill.

Alter, N. (2006), *Chris Marker*, Urbana, IL: University of Illinois Press.

Andrew, D. (2000), '*Casque d'or, casquettes*, A Cask of Aging Wine: Jacques Becker's *Casque d'or* (1952)', in S. Hayward and G. Vincendeau (eds), *French Film: Texts and Contexts*, London: Routledge, pp. 112–26.

Armes, R. (1985), *French Cinema*, Oxford: Oxford University Press.

Attal, Y. (2002), DVD commentary to *Ma Femme est une actrice*, France: Pathé.

Audé, F. (1981), *Ciné-modèles, cinéma d'elles: situations de femmes dans le cinéma français 1956–1979*, Lausanne: Editions l'Age d'Homme.

Audé, F. (2002), *Cinéma d'elles, 1981–2001, situation des femmes cinéastes dans le cinéma français*, Lausanne : Editions l'Age d'Homme.

Austin, G. (2003), *Stars in Modern French Film*, London: Arnold.

Badinter, E. (2001), *L'Amour en plus: Histoire de l'amour maternel (XVIIe–XXe siècle)*, Paris: Flammarion.

Badinter, E. (2010), *Le Conflit: La femme et la mère*, Paris: Flammarion.

Bergfelder, T., Harris, S. and Street, S. (2007), *Film Architecture and the Transnational Imagination: Set Design in 1930s European Cinema*, Amsterdam: Amsterdam University Press.

Beugnet, M. (2004), *Claire Denis*, Manchester: Manchester University Press.

Beugnet, M. (2006), 'Close-up vision: Remapping the body in the Work of Contemporary Women Filmmakers', *Nottingham French Studies*, 45(3), pp. 24–38.

Beugnet, M. (2007), *Cinema and Sensation: French Film and the Art of Transgression*, Edinburgh: Edinburgh University Press.

Block, P., Houseley, W., Nichols, T. and Southwell, R. (2001), *Managing in the Media*, Burlington, MA: Focal Press.

Bloom, H. (1973), *The Anxiety of Influence: A Theory of Poetry*, New York: Oxford University Press.

Bordwell, D., Thompson, K. and Staiger, J. (1985), *The Classical Hollywood Cinema: Film Style and Mode of Production to 1960*, London: Routledge and Kegan Paul.

Brah, A. (1996), *Cartographies of Diaspora: Contesting Identities*, London: Routledge.

Brahimi, D. (1999), *Cinéastes Françaises*, Paris: Collection Textes/Femmes, Fus-Art.

British Film Institute (BFI) (2008), 'Screenonline: The 1997 Finance (No. 2) Act', http://www. screenonline.org.uk/film/id/1011998/index.html. Accessed 16 April 2009.

Brunet, J.-L. (1999), Interview with Michel Blanc, *Alice Cinéma*, 17 November, http://cinema.aliceadsl. fr/article/default.aspx?articleid=AR011778. Accessed 16 April 2009.

Brunet, J.-L. (2001), Interview with Yvan Attal, *Alice Cinéma*, 14 November, http://cinema.aliceadsl. fr/article/default.aspx?articleid=AR013876. Accessed 17 April 2009.

Bruzzi, S. (1997), *Undressing Cinema: Clothing and Identity in the Movies*, London: Routledge.

Brysk, A. (2004), 'Children Across Borders: Patrimony, Property or Persons', in A. Brysk and G. Shafir (eds), *People out of Place: Globalization, Human Rights and the Citizenship Gap*, London: Routledge, pp. 153–73.

Brysk, A. and G. Shafir (eds) (2004), *People out of Place: Globalization, Human Rights and the Citizenship Gap*, London: Routledge.

Burch, N. and Sellier, G. (1996), *La Drôle de guerre des sexes du cinéma français: 1930–1956*, Paris: Nathan.

Butler, A. (1992), 'New Film Histories and the Politics of Location', *Screen*, 33(4), pp. 413–26.

Chartier, R. (1995), 'The World as Representation', in J. Revel and L. Hunt (eds), *Histories. French Constructions of the Past*, New York: The New Press, pp. 544–58.

Chauvin, J.-S. (1999), '*Mauvaise passe*', *Cahiers du cinéma*, 540, p. 126.

Clouzot, C. (2004), *Catherine Breillat: indécence et pureté*, Paris: Cahiers du cinéma.

Conway, K. (2004), *Chanteuse in the City: The Realist Singer in French Film*, Berkeley, CA: University of California Press.

Cooper, N. (2001), *France in Indochina: Colonial Encounters*, Oxford: Berg.

Cousins, J. (2009), 'Mechanised Corsetry: Annenkov, Ophüls and *La Ronde* (1950)', *Studies in French Cinema* 9(2), pp. 127–46.

Cova, A. (1997), *Maternité et droits des femmes en France, XIXe–XXe siècles*, Paris: Anthropos.

Creton, L. (2007), 'L'acteur et le box office: valeur, prix et spéculation dans le champ cinématographique', in V. Amiel, J. Nacache, G. Sellier and C. Viviani (eds), *L'Acteur de Cinéma: approches plurielles*, Rennes: Presses Universitaires de Rennes, pp. 159–73.

Crisp, C. (2002), *Genre, Myth and Convention in the French Cinema, 1929–1939*, Bloomington, IN: Indiana University Press.

Daney, S. (1992), *Itinéraire d'un ciné-fils*, Paris: Jean-Michel Place.

Dauncey, H. and Reader, K. (2003), 'Consumer Culture: Food, Drink and Fashion', in N. Hewitt (ed.), *The Cambridge Companion to Modern French Culture*, Cambridge: Cambridge University Press, pp. 104–24.

Deleuze, G. (1967), *Présentation de Sacher-Masoch*, Paris: Editions de Minuit.

Deleuze, G. and Guattari, F. (1998), *A Thousand Plateaus: Capitalism and Schizophrenia*, London: Athlone.

Delorme, S. (2007), 'Bateau ivre', *Cahiers du cinéma*, 629, pp. 11–13.

Dobson J. (2007), 'Jacques Audiard and the Filial Challenge', *Studies in French Cinema*, 7(3), pp. 179–89.

Dobson J. (2008), 'Jacques Audiard: Contesting Filiations', in K. Ince (ed.), *Five Directors: Auteurism from Assayas to Ozon*, Manchester: Manchester University Press, pp. 38–58.

Domenach, E. and Rouyer, P. (2007), 'Entretien avec Abdellatif Kechiche: Échapper aux règles pour voir la vie se créer', *Positif*, 562, pp. 16–20.

Donald, J. and Donald, S.H. (2000), 'The Publicness of Cinema', in C. Gledhill and L. Williams (eds), *Reinventing Film Studies*, London: Arnold, pp. 114–29.

Drazin, C. (2007), 'The French Cinema and Hollywood: A Study of Two Systems from the Arrival of Sound to the Collapse of the Production Code', PhD thesis, Queen Mary University of London.

Drazin, C. (ed.) (forthcoming), *The Faber History of French Cinema*, London: Faber & Faber.

Duchen, C. (1994), *Women's Rights and Women's Lives in France 1944–1968*, London: Routledge.

Dyer, R. (1979) *Stars*, London: BFI.

Edgar, D. (2001), 'Obituary: Jill Forbes', *The Guardian*, 19 July.

Edwards, R. and Reader, K. (2001), *The Papin Sisters*, Oxford: Oxford University Press.

Elsaesser, T. (1986), 'The New Film History', *Sight and Sound*, 55(4), pp. 246–51.

Everett, W. (2005), *European Identity in Cinema*, Chicago: Chicago University Press.

Ezra, E. (2003), *European Cinema*, Oxford: Oxford University Press.

Ezra, E. (2008), *Jean-Pierre Jeunet*, Urbana, IL: University of Illinois Press.

Faubion, J. (ed.) (2000), *Aesthetics, Method and Epistemology: Essential Works of Foucault 1954–1984*, Vol. 2, London: Penguin.

Forbes, J. (1984), *INA: French for Innovation*, London: BFI.

Forbes, J. (ed.) (1985), *In Memory of Michel Foucault*, special issue of *Paragraph*, 5(1).

Forbes, J. (1992a), *The Cinema in France: After the New Wave*, London and Bloomington, IN: Macmillan and Indiana University Press.

Forbes, J. (ed.) (1992b), *Film and Theory*, special issue of *Paragraph*, 15(3).

Forbes, J. (1993), 'L'Atout de ne pas être un cinéma américain', in R. Prédal (ed.), 'Atouts et faiblesses du cinéma français', *CinémAction*, 66, pp. 178–82.

Forbes, J. (1994), 'The Liberation of the French Cinema?', *French Cultural Studies*, 5(15), pp. 253–63.

Forbes, J. (1996), 'To the Distant Observer', paper presented to Society for French Studies Annual Conference, University of Birmingham.

Forbes, J. (1997), *Les Enfants du paradis*, London and Bloomington, IN: BFI Film Classics and Indiana University Press.

Forbes, J. (1999), 'Politicians and Performers: *Un Héros très discret*', *Australian Journal of French Studies*, 36(1), pp. 125–35.

Forbes, J. (2000), '*Pierrot le fou* and Post-New Wave French Cinema', in D. Wills (ed.), *Jean-Luc Godard's Pierrot le fou*, Cambridge: Cambridge University Press, pp. 108–32.

Forbes, J. (2002a), 'Gender and Space in *Cléo de 5 à 7*', *Studies in French Cinema*, 2(2), pp. 83–89.

Forbes J. (2002b), 'Matricides', in *Gender and French Film Since the New Wave*, special issue of *Esprit Créateur*, 42(1), pp. 62–70.

Forbes, J. (2003), 'Psychoanalysis as Narrative in Films by Jean Eustache', *In memory of Jill Forbes: Cinema and Cultural Studies*, special issue of *French Cultural Studies*, 14(3), pp. 249–56.

Forbes, J. and Hewlett, N. (1994), *Contemporary France: Essays and Texts on Politics, Economics and Society*, London: Addison, Wesley, Longman (2nd ed. 2000).

Forbes J., Hewlett, N. and Nectoux, F. (1994), *Contemporary France: Essays and Texts on Politics, Economics and Society*, London: Addison, Wesley, Longman(2nd ed. 2001).

Forbes, J. and Kelly, M. (eds) (1995), *French Cultural Studies: An Introduction*, Oxford: Oxford University Press.

Forbes, J. and Street, S. (2000), *European Cinema: An Introduction*, London: Palgrave Macmillan.

Foucault, M. (1986), 'Of Other Spaces', *Diacritics*, 16(1), pp. 22–27. Trans. by J. Miskowiec. http://foucault.info/documents/heteroTopia/foucault.heteroTopia.en.html. Accessed 7 May 2005. ['Des Espaces Autres. Hétérotopies', lecture to the Cercle d'études architecturales, 14 mars 1967; originally published in *Architecture, Mouvement, Continuité*, 5 (1984), pp. 46–49.]

Foucault, M. (1994), *The Order of Things: An Archaeology of the Human Sciences*, New York: Vintage.

Fowler, C. (2002), *The European Cinema Reader*, London: Routledge.

Fowler, C. (2008), *Sally Potter*, Urbana, IL: University of Illinois Press.

Frank, N. (1937), 'Puis voici mon coeur', *Pour Vous*, Easter issue, pp. 8–9.

Frodon, J.-M. (2007), 'La Langue d'Abdel et le pays réel', *Cahiers du cinéma*, 629, pp. 9–10.

Gauteur, C. and Vincendeau, G. (1993), *Jean Gabin: anatomie d'un mythe*, Paris: Nathan.

Genocchio, B. (1995), 'Discourse, Discontinuity, Difference: The Question of "Other" Spaces', in S. Watson and K. Gibson (eds), *Postmodern Cities and Spaces*, Oxford: Blackwell, pp. 35–46.

Gilroy, P. (2004), *After Empire: Melancholia or Convivial Culture?*, London: Routledge.

Goldberg, J. (2008) "Faire renaître les parents …' http://www.ouvalecinam.centrepompidou.fr. Accessed 10 October 2009.

Grewal, I. and Kaplan, C. (eds) (1994), *Scattered Hegemonies: Postmodernity and Transnational Feminist Practice*, Minneapolis: University of Minnesota Press.

Hansen, M. (1991), *Babel and Babylon: Spectatorship in American Silent Film*, Cambridge, MA. Harvard University Press.

Harris, S. (2001a), 'Obituary: Professor Jill Forbes', *Studies in French Cinema*, 1(2), p. 68.

Harris, S. (2001b), *Bertrand Blier*, Manchester: Manchester University Press.

Harris, S. (2003), 'Lives out of sequence: Maternal Identity in François Truffaut's *Les 400 coups* (1959) and Claude Miller's *La Petite voleuse* (1988)', *In memory of Jill Forbes: Cinema and Cultural Studies*, special issue of *French Cultural Studies*, 14(3), pp. 299–309.

Harris, S. (ed.) (2004), *New Directions in French Cinema*, special issue of *French Cultural Studies*, 15(3).

Hayward, S. (1993), *French National Cinema*, London: Routledge.

Hayward, S. (1998), *Luc Besson*, Manchester: Manchester University Press.

Hayward, S. (2000a), 'National Cinemas and the Body Politic', in E. Ezra and S. Harris (eds), *France in Focus: Film and National Identity*, Oxford: Berg, pp. 97–113.

Hayward, S. (2000b), 'Framing National Cinemas', in M. Hjort and S. MacKenzie (eds), *Cinema and Nation*, London: Routledge, pp. 88–102.

Hayward, S. (2004a), 'Signoret's Star Persona and Redressing the Costume Cinema: Jacques Becker's *Casque d'or* (1952)', *Studies in French Cinema* 4(1), pp. 15–28.

Hayward, S. (2004b), *Simone Signoret: The Star as Cultural Sign*, New York: Routledge.

Hayward, S. (2005), *French National Cinema*, 2nd ed., London: Routledge.

Hayward, S. (2010), *French Costume Drama of the 1950s: Fashioning Politics in Film*, Bristol: Intellect.

Hayward, S. and Powrie, P. (eds) (2006), *The Films of Luc Besson: Master of Spectacle*, Manchester: Manchester University Press.

Hayward, S. and Powrie, P. (eds) (2007), *Luc Besson: Master of Spectacle*, Manchester: Manchester University Press.

Hayward, S. and Vincendeau, G. (eds) (1990), *French Film: Texts and Contexts*, London: Routledge (2nd ed. 2000).

Higbee, W. (2007), 'Re-presenting the Urban Periphery: Maghrebi-French Filmmaking and the *Banlieue*', *Cineaste* (special supplement, 'Beur is Beautiful'), pp. 8–13.

Higbee W. (forthcoming), "'Et si on allait en Algérie?": Home, Displacement and the Myth of Return in Recent Journey Films by Maghrebi-French and North African Émigré Directors', in V. Swamy and S. Durmelat (eds), *Screening Immigration and Integration in Contemporary France*, Nebraska: University of Nebraska Press.

Higgins, L. (forthcoming), *Bertrand Tavernier*, Manchester: Manchester University Press. Higgins, L., Krauss, D. and Ungar, S. (2002), *Gender and French Film Since the New Wave*, Special issue of *Esprit Créateur*, 42(1).

Ince, K. (2008a), 'From Minor to "Major" Cinema? Women's and Feminist Cinema in France in the 2000s', in '(Retro)projections: French Cinema in the Twenty-first Century', special issue of *Australian Journal of French Studies*, 45(3), pp. 277–88.

Ince, K. (ed.) (2008b), *Five Directors: Auteurism from Assayas to Ozon*, Manchester: Manchester University Press.

Jeancolas, J.-P. (1979), *Le Cinéma des Français: La Ve République 1958–1978*, Paris: Stock.

Jeancolas, J.-P. (2003), 'Jill Forbes ou la conversation interrompue (notes sur le réalisme dans le cinéma français 1895-1939)', *In memory of Jill Forbes: Cinema and Cultural Studies, special issue of French Cultural Studies*, 14(3), pp. 257–63.

Johnson, B. (1998), *The Feminist Difference: Literature, Psychoanalysis, Race and Gender*, Cambridge, MA: Harvard University Press.

Kaganski, S. (2007), '*Couscous*' (review), *Les Inrockuptibles*, 12 December. http://www.lesinrocks.com/cine/cinema-article/article/la-graine-et-le-mulet. Accessed 20 July 2009.

Kaplan, E.A. (1992), 'The Psychoanalytic Sphere and Motherhood Discourse', in *Motherhood and Representation: The Mother in Popular Culture and Melodrama*, London: Routledge, pp. 27–56.

Keesey, D. (2009), *Catherine Breillat*, Manchester: Manchester University Press.

Kelly, M. (1990), 'Editorial', *French Cultural Studies*, 1(1), pp. 1–3.

Kristeva, J. (1980), *Pouvoirs de l'horreur: essai sur l'abjection*, Paris: Seuil.

Lagny, M. (1994), 'Film History: Or History Expropriated', *Film History*, 6, pp. 26–44.

Leahy, S. (2007), *Casque d'or*, London: I.B. Tauris.

Malliarakis, N. (2002), *Mayo, un peintre et le cinéma*, Paris: L'Harmattan.

Marks, L. (2000), *The Skin of the Film: Intercultural Cinema, Embodiment and the Senses*, Durham, NC: Duke University Press.

Marshall, B. (2003a), 'Jill Forbes 1947–2001', *French Cultural Studies*, 14(3), pp. 247–48.

Marshall, B. (ed.) (2003b), *In Memory of Jill Forbes: Cinema and Cultural Studies*, special issue of *French Cultural Studies*, 14(3).

Marshall, B. (2007), *André Téchiné*, Manchester: Manchester University Press.

Masson, A. (2007), '*La Graine et le Mulet*: La parole et le corps', *Positif*, 562, pp. 14–15.

Mayne, J. (2005), *Claire Denis*, Urbana, IL: University of Illinois Press.

Mazierska, E. and Rascaroli, L. (2003), *From Moscow to Madrid: European Cities, Postmodern Cinema*, London: I.B. Tauris.

McDonald, P. (2000), *The Star System: Hollywood's Production of Popular Identities*, London: Wallflower.

McHugh, K. (2007), *Jane Campion*, Urbana, IL: University of Illinois Press.

Mulvey, L. (2003), 'Jill Forbes's Les Enfants du paradis', *In memory of Jill Forbes: Cinema and Cultural Studies, special issue of French Cultural Studies*, 14(3), pp. 278–87.

Nancy, J.-L. (2003), *Noli me tangere*, Paris: Bayard.

Neale, S. (1983), 'Masculinity as Spectacle: Reflections on Men and Mainstream Cinema', *Screen*, 24(6), pp. 2–16.

O'Shaughnessy, M. (2005), 'Incohérence du cinéma colonial, intermittence des plaisirs génériques', in R. Moine (ed.), *Le Cinéma français face aux genres*, Paris: Association Française de Recherche sur l'Histoire du Cinéma, pp. 253–63.

O'Shaughnessy, M. (2007), 'Cinematic Stardom, Shifting Masculinities', in C. Forth and B. Taithe (eds), *French Masculinities: History, Culture and Politics*, Basingstoke: Palgrave, pp. 190–205.

Paxton, R. (2001), *Vichy France, Old Guard and New Order, 1940–1944*, New York: Columbia University Press.

Petro, P. (1990), 'Feminism and Film History', *Camera Obscura*, 22, pp. 8–27.

Phillips, A. and Vincendeau, G. (eds) (2006), *Journeys of Desire: European Actors in Hollywood – a Critical Companion*, London: BFI.

Powrie, P. (1997), *French Cinema in the 1980s: Nostalgia and the Crisis of Masculinity*, Oxford: Clarendon Press.

Powrie, P. (ed.) (1999), *French Cinema in the 1990s: Continuity and Difference*, Oxford: Oxford University Press.

Powrie, P. (2001a), 'The God, the King, the Fool and ØØ: Anamorphosing the Films of Beineix', in A. Hughes and J.S. Williams (eds), *Gender and French Cinema*, Oxford: Berg, pp. 195–207.

Powrie, P. (2001b), *Jean-Jacques Beineix*, Manchester: Manchester University Press.

Powrie, P. (2003), 'Thirty Years of Doctoral Theses on French Cinema', *Studies in French Cinema*, 3(3), pp. 199–203.

Powrie, P. (2004a), 'Fifteen Years of 1950s Cinema', *Studies in French Cinema*, 4(1), pp. 5–13.

Powrie, P. (2004b), 'The W/hole and the Abject', in P. Powrie, A. Davies and B. Babington (eds), *The Trouble with Men: Masculinities in European and Hollywood Cinema*, London: Wallflower Press, pp. 207–17.

Powrie, P. (2005), 'Unfamiliar Places, "Heterospection" and Recent French Films on Children', *Screen*, 46(3), pp. 341–52.

Powrie, P. (2006a), '*Léon* and the Cloacal Labyrinth', in S. Hayward and P. Powrie (eds), *The Films of Luc Besson: Master of Spectacle*, Manchester: Manchester University Press, pp. 147–59.

Powrie, P. (2006b), 'Of Suits and Men in the Films of Luc Besson' in S. Hayward and P. Powrie (eds), *The Films of Luc Besson: Master of Spectacle*, Manchester: Manchester University Press, pp. 75–89.

Powrie, P. (ed.) (2006c), *The Cinema of France*, London: Wallflower Press

Powrie, P., Babington, B., Davies, A. and Perriam, C. (2007), *Carmen on Film: A Cultural History*, Bloomington, IN: Indiana University Press.

Powrie, P., Davies, A. and Babington, B. (2004a), 'Introduction: Turning the Male Inside Out', in P. Powrie, A. Davies and B. Babington (eds), *The Trouble with Men: Masculinities in European and Hollywood Cinema*, London: Wallflower Press, pp. 1–15.

Powrie, P., A. Davies and B. Babington (eds) (2004b), *The Trouble with Men: Masculinities in European and Hollywood Cinema*, London: Wallflower Press.

Powrie, P. and Reader, K. (2002), *French Cinema: A Student's Guide*, London: Arnold.

Powrie, P. and Rebillard, E. (2008), 'Pierre Batcheff, the Surrealist Star', *Studies in French Cinema*, 8(2), pp. 159–77.

Prédal, R. (1991), *Le Cinéma français depuis 1945*, Paris: Nathan.

Reader, K. (1979), *The Cinema: A History*, London: Hodder & Stoughton.

Reader, K. (1981), *Cultures on Celluloid*, London: Quartet Books.

Reader, K. (1986), 'Renoir's Popular Front Films: Texts in Context', in G. Vincendeau and K. Reader (eds), *La Vie est à nous: French Cinema of the Popular Front, 1935–1938*, London: BFI, pp. 37–59.

Reader, K. (1990), 'Literature/cinema/television: Intertextuality in Jean Renoir's *Le Testament du docteur Cordelier*', in M. Worton and J. Still (eds), *Intertextuality: Theories and Practices*, Manchester: Manchester University Press, pp. 176–89.

Reader, K. (1992), 'How to Avoid Becoming a Middle-aged Fogey, with Reference to Three Recent Popular French Films', *Paragraph*, 15(1), pp. 97–104.

Reader, K. (1993a), 'Cinematic Representations of Paris: Vigo/Truffaut/Carax', *Modern & Contemporary France*, 1(4), pp. 409–15.

Reader, K. (1993b), '"Pratiquement plus rien d'intéressant ne se passe": Jean Eustache's *La Maman et la putain*', *Nottingham French Studies*, 32(1), pp. 91–98.

Reader, K. (1996a), 'Giscardian Desiring Machines: Alain Resnais's *Mon oncle d'Amérique*', *Journal of European Studies*, 26, pp. 175–84.

Reader, K. (1996b), '"Tous les garçons et les filles de leur âge": Representations of Youth and Adolescence in Pre-New Wave French Cinema', *French Cultural Studies*, 7, pp. 259–70.

Reader, K. (ed.) (1996c), *One Hundred Years of French Cinema*, special issue of *French Cultural Studies*, 7(3).

Reader, K. (1999), 'Right-Wing Anarchism and *Le Bonheur est dans le pré* (Chatiliez, 1995)', in P. Powrie (ed.), *French Cinema in the 1990s: Continuity and Difference*, Oxford: Oxford University Press, pp. 104–13.

Reader, K. (2000a), *Robert Bresson*, Manchester: Manchester University Press.

Reader, K. (2000b), 'Subtext: Paris of Alexandre Trauner', in M. Konstantarakos (ed.), *Spaces in European Cinema*, Exeter: Intellect, pp. 35–41.

Reader, K. (2000c), 'The Circular Ruins? Frontier, Exile and the Nation in Renoir's *Le Crime de Monsieur Lange*', *French Studies*, 54(3), pp. 287–97.

Reader, K. (2001a), '"Mon cul est intersexuel?": Arletty's Performance of Gender', in A. Hughes and J. Williams (eds), *Gender and French Cinema*, Oxford: Berg, pp. 63–76.

Reader, K. (2001b), 'Jouissance at the Margins: Philippe Harel's *Extension du domaine de la lutte/Whatever*', *Studies in French Cinema*, 1(2), pp. 118–25.

Reader, K. (2001c), 'Jill Forbes. Obituary', *The Independent*, 10 August.

Reader, K. (2002a), 'Leaner and Meaner: From *L'Homme maigre* to *La nouvelle cuisine*', *Contemporary French Civilization*, 26(11), pp. 1–11.

Reader, K. (2002b), 'Obituary: Jill Forbes (1947–2001)', in *French Studies*, 56(1), pp. 143–44.

Reader, K. (2004), 'Godard and Asynchrony', in M. Temple, J.S. Williams and M. Witt (eds), *For Ever Godard*, London: Black Dog Publishing, pp. 72–93.

Reader, K. (2005), 'The Policing of Desire in the Gabrielle Russier Affair', *French Cultural Studies*, 16(1), pp. 5–20.

Reader, K. (2006), *The Abject Object: Avatars of the Phallus in Contemporary French Theory, Literature and Film*, Amsterdam: Rodopi.

Reader, K. (2008), 'Another Deleuzian Resnais: *L'Année dernière à Marienbad* (1961) as a Conflict Between Sadism and Masochism', *Studies in French Cinema*, 8(2), pp. 149–58.

Reader, K. (forthcoming), *La Règle du jeu*, London: I.B. Tauris.

Reik, T. (1941), *Masochism in Modern Man*, trans. M.H. Beigel and G.M. Kurth, New York: Grove Press.

Riviere, J. (1966 [1929]), 'Womanliness as a Masquerade', in H. Ruitenbeek (ed.), *Psychoanalysis and Female Sexuality*, New Haven, NH: College and University Press, pp. 163–75.

Rye, G. and Tarr, C. (2006), 'Focalizing the Body in Contemporary Women's Writing and Filmmaking in France', *Nottingham French Studies*, 45(3), pp. 116–24.

Salt, B. (1983), *Film Style and Technology: History and Analysis*, London: Starword.

Scollen-Jimack, C. (1994), 'Review: Jill Forbes, *The Cinema in France: After the New Wave*', *Screen*, 35(1), pp. 96–99.

Sellier, G. (1989), *Jean Grémillon, le cinéma est à nous*, Paris: Méridiens Klincksieck.

Sellier, G. (2005), *La Nouvelle Vague: un cinéma au masculin singulier*, Paris: CNRS.

Silvana da Rosa, A. (2001), 'The King is Naked: Critical Advertisement and Fashion – the Benetton Phenomenon', in K. Deaux and G. Philogène (eds), *Representations of the Social*, Oxford: Blackwell, pp. 48–82.

Solomon-Godeau, A. (1997), *Male Trouble: A Crisis in Representation*, London: Thames and Hudson.

Steele, V. (2001), *The Corset: A Cultural History*, New Haven, CN: Yale University Press.

Tarr, C. (1993a), 'Ambivalent desires in Jacqueline Audry's *Olivia*', in R. King (ed.), *French Cinema*, special issue of *Nottingham French Studies*, 32(1), pp. 32–42.

Tarr, C. (1993b), 'Questions of Identity in Beur Cinema: From *Tea in the Harem* to *Cheb*', *Screen*, 34(4), pp. 321–42.

Tarr, C. (1999), *Diane Kurys*, Manchester: Manchester University Press.

Tarr, C. (2003), 'Feminist influences on the Work of Yannick Bellon in the 1970s', *Studies in French Cinema*, 3(1), pp. 55–65.

Tarr, C. (2005), *Reframing Difference: Beur and Banlieue Film-making in France*, Manchester: Manchester University Press.

Tarr, C. (2006), 'Director's Cuts: The Aesthetics of Self-Harming in Marina de Van's *Dans ma peau*', *Nottingham French Studies*, 45, pp. 78–91.

Tarr, C. (2007), 'Beur is Beautiful', special supplement, *Cineaste*, November.

Tarr, C. (2009) 'Franco-Arab Dialogues In/between French, Maghrebi-French, and Maghrebi Cinema(s)', *Contemporary French and Francophone Studies*, 13(3), pp. 291–302.

Tarr, C. with Rollet, B. (2001), *Cinema and the Second Sex: Women's Filmmaking in France in the 1980s and 1990s*, London: Continuum.

Tourret, F. (ed.) (2009), 'Le cinéma féminin français contemporain', *Contre Bande*, 18, Paris: Université de Paris I, Panthéon Sorbonne.

Vasse, D. (2004), *Catherine Breillat: un cinéma du rite et de la transgression*, Brussels: Editions Complexe.

Vincendeau, G. (1985a), 'Community, Nostalgia and the Spectacle of Masculinity', *Screen*, 26(6), pp. 18–39.

Vincendeau, G. (1985b), 'New Approaches to Film History', Screen 26(6), pp. 70–73.

Vincendeau, G. (1986), 'The Popular Cinema of the Popular Front', in G. Vincendeau and K. Reader (eds), *La Vie Est A Nous! French Cinema of the Popular Front 1935–1938*, London: BFI, pp. 73–102.

Vincendeau, G. (1988), 'Daddy's Girls: Oedipal Narratives in 1930s French Films', *Iris*, 8, pp. 70–81.

Vincendeau, G. (1989), 'Melodramatic Realism: On Some French Women's Films in the 1930s', *Screen*, 30(3), pp. 51–65.

Vincendeau, G. (1990), 'In the Name of the Father: Marcel Pagnol's "Trilogy" *Marius* (1931), *Fanny* (1932), *César* (1936)', in S. Hayward and G. Vincendeau (eds), *French Film: Texts and Contexts*, London: Routledge, pp. 67–82.

Vincendeau, G. (1993), 'Gérard Depardieu: The Axiom of Contemporary French Cinema', *Screen* 34(4), pp. 343-61.

Vincendeau, G. (1998), *Pépé le Moko*, London: BFI.

Vincendeau, G. (2000), *Stars and Stardom in French Cinema*, London: Continuum.

Vincendeau, G. (ed.) (2001), *Film/Literature/Heritage: A Sight and Sound Reader*, London: BFI.

Vincendeau, G. (2003), *Jean-Pierre Melville, 'An American in Paris'*, London: BFI.

Vincendeau, G. (2006), '"Not for Export": Jean Gabin in Hollywood', in A. Phillips, and G. Vincendeau (eds), *Journeys of Desire: European Actors in Hollywood – A Critical Companion*, London: BFI, pp. 115–24.

Vincendeau, G. (2007a), 'French Film Noir', in A. Spicer (ed.), *European Film Noir*, Manchester: Manchester University Press, pp. 21–54.

Vincendeau, G. (2007b), 'Les acteurs méridionaux dans le cinéma français des années 1930', in V. Amiel, J. Nacache, G. Sellier and C. Viviani (eds), *L'Acteur de Cinéma: approches plurielles*, Rennes: Presses Universitaires de Rennes, pp. 217–32.

Vincendeau, G. (2008), 'Southern Discomfort: Couscous', *Sight and Sound*, 18(7), pp. 46–47.

Willemen, P. (1994), *Looks and Frictions: Essays in Cultural Studies and Film Theory*, London: BFI.

Wilson, E. (2003), *Cinema's Missing Children*, London: Wallflower Press.

Wilson, E. (2006a), 'Women Filming Children', *Nottingham French Studies*, 45, pp. 105–18.

Wilson, E. (2006b), *Alain Resnais*, Manchester: Manchester University Press.

Wimmer, L. (2008) 'Another Cinephilia? Popular Film Journals and Female Publics in the 1930s', unpublished conference paper.

Wood, M. (2007), *Contemporary European Cinema*, Oxford: Oxford University Press.

Žižek, S. (1999), *The Žižek Reader*, eds E. Wright and E. Wright, Oxford: Blackwell.

Part III

Chapter 20

To the Distant Observer

Jill Forbes

It will come as no surprise that, in this centenary year of the cinema, my title is inspired by Noël Burch's marvellous study of Japanese film (Burch 1979). A 'distant observer' usefully describes the position of all those who study foreign cultures, both because of the interpretative difficulties that distance throws up, and because of the privileges that distance confers and the capacity for totalization that it appears, perhaps dangerously, to offer to our gaze. The dialectic of closeness and distance, internality and externality, is one of the fascinating paradoxes of cultural studies – above all, perhaps, in the cinema, where the immediacy of perception tends to obscure the necessity for reflexion. Burch's contention that the Japanese cinema cannot be truly seen by viewers educated in Hollywood conventions, although it is obviously influenced by the *Tel Quel* orientalism of the 1970s, is an important reminder that features such as the organization of space, iconography, lighting, camera positions, as well as gesture and movement, are all conventions which our viewing experiences make us take for granted. Here I propose to 'take seriously the debris of mass culture', as one critic put it, by looking at a corpus in which totality is inscribed and interrogated, imagined and questioned, both by the visual resources of the cinema and cultural distance of those involved in film-making.

The corpus of material I have looked at is the cinematic representation of the city. This is primarily because the city offered the material for the flamboyant exhibition of the visual resources of the medium in films such as René Clair's *Paris qui dort/Paris asleep* (1924) or Dziga Vertov's constructivist *The Man with a Movie Camera* (1929). Here, the film-maker was a maker of collages, a childlike character amusing himself twiddling the buttons of a new machine, his documentary record enlivened and complicated by techniques such as split screen, dissolve, superimposition, slow motion, freeze frame, and so on. In the silent period, the city developed into what might be called a cinematic *topos*. The monumental constructions of Hollywood epics like D.W. Griffith's *Intolerance* (1916), and Cecil B. de Mille's biblical dramas *The Ten Commandments* (1923) or *The King of Kings* (1927), extravagant Italian epics like *Quo Vadis* (1912) all deployed dramatic compositional effects that have been compared to John Martin's Romantic landscapes, while the urban environment acquired a nightmare inflection in the fantastic Expressionist architecture of *Das Cabinet des Dr Caligari/The Cabinet of Dr Caligari* (1920) or the totalitarian geometry of Fritz Lang's *Metropolis* (1927), brilliantly described by David Robinson as a sort of 'concrete martial law'. The spectacularly oppressive set of *Metropolis* was created by a model whose size was magnified by mirrors, combining in this way the fantastic *trucages* of Méliès with contemporary town planning. By contrast, the French and Russian films of the period are not claustral but exuberant: the city is the artist's material and his playground; nature is still close and it determines its rhythm of life; and its representational tradition is still heavily influenced by Impressionism. The Prévert brothers' *Paris la belle/Paris the Beautiful* (1928), Carné's *Nogent, Eldorado du dimanche/Nogent* (1929) and even Vigo's *L'Atalante* (1934) all exploit this pastoral tradition, which is continued ironically by Renoir into the 1930s in *Une Partie de campagne/A Day in the Country* (1936, released 1946) and by Becker into the 1950s with *Casque d'or/Golden Helmet* (1952).

The advent of sound changed all this, destroying at a stroke the *plein air* movement in French film-making and rendering the use of the studio virtually obligatory. While sound was generally welcomed as a miraculous technology capable of further refining the cinema, in France – with its highly developed art film movement, and its commitment to location shooting – the invention was deplored because it would inevitably turn film away from visual composition towards the horror of 'filmed theatre'. The fact that many dreary *boulevard* hits were indeed filmed – or more accurately, transposed to film – in the early 1930s did not help to promote confidence in the resources of sound, and traces of this resistance to the scenario can still be found as late as the 1950s in Truffaut's celebrated polemic in favour of an auteur cinema in which the director, rather than the scriptwriter, calls the shots. The advent of sound exposed the inadequacies of French technology: there was no homegrown system to compete with the American Western Electric or the German Tobis. Many French film-makers found themselves working either in the studios built by the Americans and the Germans in the Paris region or working on German and English language versions of French films, while foreigners invaded French studios in large numbers. Since it was for the time being either impossible, or extremely expensive and difficult, to make films on location, set design became the new imperative. At the Tobis studios at Epinay in the northern suburbs of Paris, the legendary Russian designer Lazare Meerson gathered round him a group of talented individuals, including Alexandre Trauner, his best known disciple, and their designs are to be seen in many of the best known films of the period.

Meerson was born in Russia (now Poland), trained as a painter and left for Germany after the Russian Revolution, reaching Paris in 1924 where he found employment – as did many Russian expatriates – at Alexandre Kamenka's Albatros Films in Montreuil. There he worked with both Feyder on *Gribiche/Mother of Mine* (1925) and Clair on *Un Chapeau de paille d'Italie/An Italian Straw Hat* (1927). But his real influence was felt between 1930 and 1936, when he was head of design at the Tobis studios in Epinay, where he created the sets for Clair's four sound masterpieces, *Sous les toits de Paris/Under the Roofs of Paris* (1930), *Le Million* (1931), *À nous la liberté/Freedom for Us* (1931) and *Quatorze juillet/Bastille Day* (1933), and for Feyder's most celebrated film, *La Kermesse héroique/Carnival in Flanders* (1935). After that he was lured by Alexander Korda to London where he designed, *inter alia, Fires were Started* and where he died in 1938. Alexandre Trauner was a Hungarian who trained as a painter in Budapest and who likewise emigrated because of pre-war anti-Semitism. After having worked as Meerson's assistant, Trauner had a glorious career as the designer for most of Carné's films, including *Quai des brumes/Port of Shadows* (1938),

Hôtel du nord (1939), *Le Jour se lève/Daybreak* (1939), *Les Visiteurs du soir/The Devil's Envoys* (1942) and, of course, *Les Enfants du paradis/Children of Paradise* (1945) and *Les Portes de la nuit* (1946). Having stayed in hiding in France throughout the war, Trauner went to Hollywood in the 1950s, his most memorable creations being Billy Wilder's *The Apartment* (1960) and *Irma la Douce* (1963) and he returned to France in the 1980s where he did, *entre autres*, *Subway* (1985) and Claude Berri's *Tchao Pantin* (1983).

The international celebrity of Trauner's creations, especially *Les Enfants du paradis*, has somewhat eclipsed Meerson, not least because of the latter's untimely death. In fact, so little has been written about Meerson that we rely on Trauner for information about his technique. Trauner explained that set design was not just a matter of a greater or lesser degree of authenticity but, especially in the early years when the technology was very cumbersome, included anticipating what and where the director would want to film, where he would place the camera and actors, how he would wish the set to be lit and what movement he required in both foreground and background. The designer was thus closely involved in the conception of the film from the storyboard stage, and his role was not just to paint a backdrop that looked three-dimensional but to create a convincing world of planes and volumes.

The technical requirements of sound film had immense political and artistic impact, not least because its adepts were mainly foreign. I do not know if French directors' resistance to sound was shared by French-trained technicians, but I do think it likely that the French auteur and art film tradition stretching back to Méliès, who was a veritable *homme-orchestre* of the cinema, meant that there simply were not enough specialized technicians for the job of designing sets for sound stages. In any case, the designers who made their mark were people like Meerson and Trauner in France, or Korda in Britain, who looked at the locations they were required to reproduce with a considerable degree of unfamiliarity because they had not grown up in that environment. So, just as Griffith's designers were able to imagine an ancient Babylon to suit their whim in Hollywood and to create a fantastic architecture which was generically 'Babylonian' so, it seems to me, Meerson and Trauner took the same approach to France, setting out to create generic locations, more often than not of Paris, which represented what Barthes would have called 'parisianité' more than they represented actual city locations (see, for example, Barthes 1957).

Clearly their sets were not created *ex nihilo*, but neither were they precisely intended as faithful reproductions. According to Trauner, design proceeded in three stages: documentation, the maquette (or colour sketch) and construction. In the documentation stage, the designer familiarized himself with the existing visual and literary tradition, even when the set was contemporary: going to the relevant photo or picture library and reading the associated literature – choosing to reproduce locations, in other words, whose salience and exemplarity had already been established. So both for Carné's pre-war film *Drôle de drame/Bizarre, Bizarre* (1937) and for Billy Wilder's *The Private Life of Sherlock Holmes*, made in Hollywood in 1970, he relied on period nineteenth century illustrations of London to recreate the turn-of-the-century Baker Street or for the composite of Edwardian and Victorian London depicted in *Drôle de drame*. For *Hôtel du nord* and *Quai des brumes*, he obviously went to the novels of Dabit and Mac Orlan, with the latter incorporating an interesting transposition of the action from Paris to Le Havre, the better to exploit the metaphor of the port and its visual representation. For *Les Enfants du paradis*, much of the detail of the *boulevard du crime* is lifted from Baudelaire's prose poem 'Le Vieux saltimbanque', while the atmosphere of the *barrière de Ménilmontant* is strongly reminiscent of descriptions in Hugo's *Les Misérables*, though its appearance is inspired by nineteenth century architectural drawings.[1] In interviews and autobiographical writings, Carné and Trauner emphasized this preliminary spadework as absolutely necessary and vital, so that one might be forgiven for thinking that the aim of the sets was to reproduce an original as closely as possible. Yet a glance at Trauner's maquettes illustrates that this was far from being so. *Les Enfants du paradis* was designed when Trauner was hiding *chez* Prévert in the South of France, and reliant on material that Carné could get hold of him from Paris. His boulevard du Temple contains all the 'markers' that show it is the boulevard du Temple, including the theatres and the cabaret 'L'Epie scié', and some – like the Turkish baths which he invented. But it bears little resemblance to his visual sources, which were the architectural drawings held in the Musée Carnavalet. Nor, to my mind, does it resemble the boulevard du Temple as its façades are today –which I take it are not very far removed from their appearance in the 1940s. In fact, the set functions very much like the nineteenth century drawings which allegedly inspired it, as an idealization – no doubt it never was as harmoniously laid out as it appears to be here any more than it was long, brightly lit and crowded as it appears to be in the film. Trauner, like Meerson, detested what he called 'primary realism' ('au premier degré'). This got him into trouble with *Les Portes de la nuit* for, although a set was clearly necessary for a historical reconstruction, critics questioned the cost when it came to contemporary settings. Carné was accused of megalomania, Cocteau remarking 'that he would be capable of reducing Paris to a wasteland if it were necessary', and while he staunchly maintained that filming in situ would have been impossible, he equally admits, in his autobiography, that the set had actually become the principal actor in the film.

Trauner's sets, then, were intended to carry a powerful emotional charge deriving from the activation of artistic memories of places which often no longer existed. Their charm is the charm of recognition, and our pleasure as viewers derives from the fact that the physical environment is exactly as we somehow always expected it to be, that it conforms to an image or an original we carry in our mind's eye, like a recollection of childhood, enhanced or embellished by time. The alleged search for verisimilitude was, so to speak, a blind. The boulevard du Temple is not necessarily as it was, but as we wish to remember it having been – a reconstruction of a memory: longer, more lively, more brightly lit than reality.

Reviewing French sound cinema in an article he wrote in 1933 before he became a well-known director, Carné lamented the passing of the silent period and of films made by 'young people bearing a single portable camera and a few metres of film [who] could allow themselves to be guided purely according to their imagination or their inspiration'. But although 'the Paris of René Clair, so true, so right, moving and feeling, is in reality a Paris of wood and stucco reconstructed in Epinay', he found in it a superior truth:

Les Enfants du paradis – carnival on Trauner's boulevard du crime.

If it's true that we would swear to have met in the street, in the course of our daily lives, the different characters of *Sous les toits de Paris* or *Quatorze juillet*, it is also the case that we would equally swear to have suddenly found ourselves, one day while wandering through the faubourgs, face to face with the streets imagined by Meerson; the dead end with the street singers, the dark lane that runs next to the Petite Ceinture railway in *Sous les toits de Paris*, even though we know them to be built from scratch, move us with their striking authenticity, perhaps even more than if Clair and his gang had really taken themselves off to the actual places of the action. (Carné 1933, reprinted in Chazal 1965: 95)

One of the principal methods by which set design achieved this 'striking authenticity' was through the quest for metonymic exemplarity. This was, in any case, a technique developed in the iconography of the early cinema in which material objects are invested with peculiar resonance. In many of Méliès' films the bourgeois interiors come alive in a quite startling manner: objects move across rooms, appear, disappear, and take on extraordinary dimensions. In Clair's films, with their clear links to Surrealism, objects function both as plot devices – the hat in *Un Chapeau de paille*, the lottery ticket in *Le Million* – and as metonymies. In *A nous la liberté*, the gramophones in the factory multiply by a kind of parthenogenesis, unassisted by human agency. What began as either the celebration of technology, or a critique of capitalism and the industrialization of labour, turned into a design technique.

An entire business grew up to supply Hollywood with images of French, and particularly Parisian, authenticity. Seeberger *frères*, proprietors of a photography business, were commissioned by a Hollywood agent to supply the documentation for items ranging from road signs and policemen's uniforms to café interiors to enable American designers to recreate France in California. This had its comic side: Clair parodied the practice in *The Ghost Goes West* (1935), featuring an American millionaire who buys a Scottish castle and rebuilds it in the American desert; and when Trauner was commissioned by Billy Wilder to design the sets for *Irma la douce* (1963), featuring a prostitute who works in and around Les Halles, he quickly realized that unless the entire crew were to be poisoned by rotting food, the shooting schedule would not permit the use of real meat, fruit and vegetables but would have to rely on polystyrene moulds covered with a thin layer of fresh produce brought in on a daily basis and he had to get from France pictures of animal carcasses which, needless to say, are butchered in quite a different way in the US.

Perhaps because their ultimate destination was known to the photographers, or because of an existing visual tradition, many of the views of objects and people – at least in exterior shots – are placed in perspectives which were subsequently reproduced in film sets. Similarly, Meerson's technique, and he was followed in this by Trauner, was based on the use of

Opposite: The set of *Sous les toits de Paris*, 'built from scratch'.

exaggerated perspective, and on the creation of an illusion of space in which, thanks to the camera, the viewer could see more than would otherwise have been the case. The camera's eye intensified the visual experience, allowing the spectator to penetrate into spaces which would previously have remained unknown or unseen. In both *La Kermesse héroïque* and *Les Enfants du paradis*, part of the set is an elaborately painted perspective, while for the crowd scenes in *Les Enfants du paradis*, children were used as extras in the distant parts of the set to emphasize the changes of scale. In the same way as the selection of objects gives them disproportionate significance, so it seems to me the exaggeration of perspective heightens the utopianism of these sets, reinforcing the viewer's belief that not only is this a complete and self-sufficient world, but a constructed one as well.

It is astonishing how many of these films signal, to an alert viewer, the sources of their illusionism and the conditions of their production. In *La Kermesse héroïque* you will recall that Meerson's sources are placed in a *mise en abyme* in the scene where the Burghers have their portrait painted, a richly intertextual moment referring, as it does, to the habit of reflecting the painter in Flemish portraits. René Clair – who was, as we have seen, the author of one of the most poetic silent films about Paris – only made sound films with great reluctance, which may be why all the films he shot on Meerson's sets offer us, in some way or another, knowledge of their own containment by showing us their enactment in a diegetic space. The opening shot of *Sous les toits* sweeps over the Paris rooftops before descending into a small cobbled square entirely surrounded by tall houses. *Le Million* sets up a contrast between the carefree behaviour of the lottery ticket, forgotten in someone's pocket, casually discarded, blown hither and thither across the city by the wind, and the lumbering attempts of the protagonists to retrieve it. *A nous la liberté* starts in a prison and ends on the open road; starts in a heavily designed art deco set, incorporating all the advances in the rational organization of labour, and ends with its two heroes throwing away wealth and fame in return for a life as tramps. The final moments when the heroes hit the road singing recall those Impressionist landscapes, like Seurat's *Une Baignade à Asnières/Bathers at Asnières*, where popular leisure haunts are depicted against a backdrop of belching chimneys – exactly the sort of place, in fact, that Epinay, the home of the film studios, was itself becoming.

Clair's films are not so much sound films with dialogue as musicals: the characters rarely engage in conversation, but they frequently burst into song – often quite unexpectedly in the middle of the prison in *A nous la liberté*. This may have been what enabled Clair to poeticize the sound revolution, but it is equally a form of auto-referentiality: since the film was being made on a sound stage, its 'sound' will be non-naturalistic, over-determined in some way, while the factory in *A nous la liberté* naturally manufactures records and gramophones.

We find in a great number of these films the camera taking us, the viewers, into an artificial or enclosed world – a castle in *Les Visiteurs du soir*, a walled city in *La Kermesse héroïque*, a prison and a factory in *A nous la liberté* or, when the set is a Paris street, making entirely clear to the viewer the distinction between its inside and outside, between Paris seen from outside and from within. Like the shopping arcades, these films transform exteriors into interiors. In *Le Million* and *Sous les toits de Paris*, the camera descends into an exterior and so transforms it into an interior. In *Les Enfants du paradis*, the camera takes us through the proscenium arch of the theatre into the bustling world of the boulevard du crime and reminds us later, in the scene between Baptiste and Garance at the *barrière de Ménilmontant*, that the action is taking place *intra muros*. Perhaps the most interesting of all because of its contemporary setting, *Les Portes de la nuit* contrasts the realism of the overhead metro with the theatrical illusionism of the street scene below. In this way, Paris is constructed as a film set. Virtually all these films depict the diegetic space thus created as the locus of entertainment, which in turn becomes its *raison d'être* and the justification of its efficacy. All four of Clair's first sound films are built round musical interludes, unmotivated in plot terms, while the entire action of *Quatorze juillet*, as its title indicates, is a festival; in *La Kermesse héroique*, the plot revolves round a fair which takes place within a walled city visited by the Spanish ambassadors; *Hôtel du nord* and *Les Visiteurs du soir* both have seminal dance sequences, the former a 14 July celebration, the latter a gavotte in a medieval castle, while *Les Portes de la nuit* opens with the hero, Diego, descending as it were into the set where he encounters an accordion player singing popular songs under the shelter of the overhead metro, and it later has Diego waltzing with his lover Manou on a building site surrounded by the ruins of classical civilization. In Renoir's *La Chienne/The Bitch* (1931), this convention creates a form of ironic, almost Hitchcockian, suspense when a group of strolling gypsies with a barrel organ performs outside the building in which we know the heroine lies murdered, and traces of this irony can be found as late as the *nouvelle vague* – I am thinking, for example, of the scene in *A bout de souffle/Breathless* (Godard 1960) where Michel is looking for Patricia on the Champs Elysées, which is lined with crowds cheering President Eisenhower on his state visit to Paris. Nevertheless, what began as a critical *mise en abyme* rapidly became a cliché of Paris on film, especially in Hollywood, the first example perhaps being Rouben Mamoulian's *Love Me Tonight* (1932) in which Maurice Chevalier regularly breaks into song and dance routines as he goes about his business as a gentleman's outfitter in Paris.

On the other hand, towards the end of the period in which elaborate sets were either a necessity or vogue, the entertainment which they enclose takes on a critical edge, especially in Carné's films. *Les Enfants du paradis* sets up a comparison between the Rouge-gorge cabaret beyond the *barrière*, to which the actors repair to dance and drink in the first half of the film, and where Baptiste succeeds in taking Garance away from Lacenaire, and the carnival scene on the boulevard at the end of the second part of the film, when he loses her in the crowd; a comparison which is underlined by the use of the same musical theme. In this way, the freedom outside the city which thanks to Hugo was a commonplace of the literature of the period, and the constraint within it, is only heightened by the apparent jollity of the carnival, and renders the boulevard in some way dystopian. In the same way, the 'sound stage Paris' entered into in *Les Portes de la nuit* is a Paris of the black market and corruption, a Paris which has recovered from the euphoria of liberation and woken up to the black realities of hardship and political fighting. Thanks to an insistent orphic theme in *Les Portes de la nuit*, the set becomes the means to transform the entire city into an underworld from

Les Enfants du paradis – the Rouge Gorge cabaret and the Ménilmontant *barrière*.

which, of course, no one escapes. While it might be felt that *Les Enfants du paradis*, with its celebration of the popular and its resolute refusal of the provincial ruralism of Vichy, was an assertion of the vivacity of French urban culture, this message was rapidly tempered by the pessimism of *Les Portes de la nuit*. Meanwhile, the Italian neo-realists, whose work was screened in Paris at the end of the war and made Carné's studio bound film-making seem old-fashioned, showed how the combat had reduced all cities to fragments of décor and convincingly demonstrated the ruins of this aesthetic by depicting, as it were, the aesthetics of ruins. In their construction and their ideology, the film sets and perhaps the cities of the 1930s and 1940s resemble the panoramas of the nineteenth century, destined like Daguerre's Diorama to destruction by fire.

Alongside scenes of history and famous land and sea battles, the panoramas specialized in topographical views, with a preference for the two great metropolises of the period, London and Paris, although Rome, Berlin, Edinburgh, not to speak of Constantinople and Jerusalem, were also popular. They offered the possibility or the fantasy that the entire city could be laid out before the viewer, once again rendering the city comprehensible and restoring the transparency or legibility which, so the argument runs, had been destroyed by political and industrial revolution. The panoramas were the counterpart of and the antidote to the labyrinthine cities imagined by Balzac and Hugo, cities whose denizens created uncertainty and confusion by flouting the so called transparency semiotics of the *ancien régime* – with their characters' disquieting preference for disguise and the need of their naïve heroes to view the city from above or beyond in order to get a grip on reality. Where the panorama differed from landscape painting was in its abolition of the visual and narrative hierarchies traditionally associated with the genre; thus, in Bernard Comment's words, 'confiscating the visual practices of the elite and giving them to the people'. The panorama depended for its effects partly on the authenticity which their creators, like set designers, emphasized was based on extensive documentation *sur place*, and partly on their presentation of the city as a totality – as though it were, in fact, a landscape – so that they often showed London or Paris surrounded by a ring of countryside which was no longer visible to the ordinary city dweller. Reminiscences of this totalization were, as we have seen, part of the standard *mise-en-scène* of Meerson's sets for Clair and Feyder.

The other point of comparison is the sensation induced by a visit to a panorama. It is hard for us now to comprehend the contemporary attraction of panoramas – the only one I have seen personally, at Waterloo, was extremely disappointing. However, our visual expectation and capacities evolve over time and we have to accept they sometimes deceived nineteenth century audiences allegedly to the point of nausea or hysteria. This was because the panorama deliberately disorientated visitors. It was a spectacle 'in the round', which abolished the frame by requiring them to enter through a darkened tunnel in order to induce them to lose their bearings.

As the century progressed, the technology became more sophisticated and the spectacular nature of the experience was enhanced by techniques such as the use of light in Daguerre's Diorama to simulate night and day, and urban representation continued to seek visual mastery: one thinks of Nadar sailing over Paris in a balloon in order to photograph the city, or the Impressionists' preference for the *'vue plongeante'*, the high shot which is often deliberately reiterated in the filming of Meerson's and Trauner's sets. But the cinema was also able to marry the view of the city as a totality with a focus on the individual within it. While few films went to the lengths of *The Cabinet of Dr Caligari*, in which the distortions of the urban environment are the product of a diseased mind, subjectivity is often associated with an interiority that the sets make visible. The cinema does not just offer the possibility of totalization but also of a change of focus, the simultaneous telescopic and microscopic view, reminiscent of Emma Bovary's perception of Rouen which from a distance *'ressemblait à un paysage'* but which close to seemed *'comme un Babylone'*. Thus, if you looked closely at the city, making use of the cinematic zoom to switch, as Proust put it in *Sodome et Gomorrhe*, from 'the contemplation of the geologist' to 'that of the botanist', you might – like Marcel – see corruption on a Babylonian or a biblical scale. This also accounts, I think, for the consistent filmic representation of crowds in the city and the ambiguity with which they are treated. The cinema permitted a scenography in which totalization rapidly evolved into totalitarianism on a spectacular scale. This could lead to Leni Riefenstahl's choreography of the Nuremberg rallies, which we know were designed to be filmed. But it could equally end up as the disposition of choreographed bodies in wildly erotic formations as found in *42nd Street*, *Gold Diggers of 1933* (both 1933) and other Busby Berkeley musicals.

Behind the detail of Meerson's Flanders in *La Kermesse héroïque*, the rejection of industrialization in *A Nous la liberté*, the jumbled gables of Trauner's boulevard du crime and the frenetic activity of the crowds within them lurks the shadow of Le Corbusier's Plan Voisin for Paris, the mad rationalization which would have razed the Marais to the ground and replaced with a grid of clean, high rise buildings in which the messiness of the street was given over to cars and lorries. On the other hand, if not controlled, crowds can easily turn nasty, as they do in *Le Jour se lève* when the hero, confined in his high rise subjectivity, walled up in the room in which he commits the murder in flashback, is contained in a parody of a Le Corbusier tower while the crowd bays for his blood at the base of the building. And in *Les Portes de la nuit*, the overhead metro which provides the kind of rapid transportation system fantasized by Lang in *Metropolis* or Le Corbusier in his plan, overlays the labyrinthine city with a minimum of organization, a grid or network, its supporting pillars incidentally providing a rationalization of space which handily served to divide out the terrain for the prostitutes on the boulevard de Clichy.

Behind all the interwar plans for urban improvement lay the fear not just of crime, dirt and disease, since all those had been present in the nineteenth century – but corruption and contamination of a different kind. Whether Haussmannian rationalization was inspired by public health, military tactics or neo-classical aesthetics, its effect was to cut a swathe through the popular districts of the kind depicted in *Les Enfants du paradis*, juxtaposing in this way a regulated, ordered and above all constructed environment, and the emotional excesses of the individuals within it. However, the contemporary equivalent of the boulevard du crime, the place where humanity in all its excessive variety intermingles in a dangerously uncontrolled fashion, was not to be found in France at all, but in the Casbah of Algiers, a hotbed of criminality and difference, a no-go area controlled by gangs of foreign *mafiosi*. This is the interwar equivalent of the zone beyond the *barrière*, placed alongside the colonial city but separated by a gulf or a wall of cultural difference, turned in on itself like the carnival crowds on the boulevard du crime.

The image of the Casbah in Duvivier's *Pépé le Moko* (1937) – the film which, so to speak, put French North Africa on the criminal map and turned Algiers into the Chicago of the old world – is interesting from a variety of points of view. First, because the Casbah is not rationally organized – it looks, in fact, rather like a brain with CJD – and it is therefore difficult for the European mind (police mind especially) to grasp. Second, it cannot be looked at as a totality, so that the camera can only offer a montage of partial views. But third, despite this, it is filmed like a set. Just as the opening of *Les Portes de la nuit*, which is emphatically not a set, flattens the cityscape and makes Paris look like a constructed backdrop, distance creating a landscape effect, so here the exoticism and danger of the Casbah are mastered by the camera in the establishing or landscape shots, making the viewer feel comfortably in control.

Today, when the technology of film-making no longer requires elaborate sound stages, the architecture of the film set has entered urban design tourism and leisure: the Quai des Jemmapes has been restored to 'look like' the set in *Hôtel du nord*. If you take a trip to the top of the Centre Pompidou, you will see the facades of the plateau Beaubourg restored as though in a film set against the backdrop of the city, which looks like a landscape. The panorama survives in the so-called 'experiences' – Blitz Experience, Great Fire of London Experience, Earthquake Experience – which are the bane of every parent's life and, much more elaborately, in a film show in the round at EuroDisney. In fact, the whole of EuroDisney is authentically fake simulating not just the setting of a colonial settlement in America but using the simulated materials of a film set to do so. This is not the work of Hollywood but of designers working in French studios in the 1930s and 1940s. Millions of people round the world saw *Sous les toits de Paris*, and millions more have seen *Les Enfants du paradis*, but their descendants are alive and well and living in the Service d'urbanisme (Town Planning Service) of the Hôtel de Ville de Paris.[2]

Notes

1. Editors' note: The *barrière de Ménilmontant* refers to the area beyond the city wall and thus situated beyond the reach of Paris tolls and taxes. The area became famous in the late eighteenth and nineteenth centuries for drinking and gambling dens. Ménilmontant was annexed to Paris in 1860.
2. This chapter was delivered by Jill Forbes as a plenary address to the Society of French Studies at their 1996 conference. We are delighted to publish it here for the first time with the kind permission of Jill Forbes' family and the French Department of Queen Mary University of London. As the piece was written to be delivered orally, many references are not available. Translations of quotations in French are by the editors.

Chapter 21

Censoring French 'Cinéma de qualité' – *Bel-Ami* (1954/1957)

Susan Hayward

This chapter seeks to set out three things.[1] The first is to explain the censorship story surrounding Louis Daquin's film *Bel-Ami* (1954, released in France 1957). The second is to bring this significant film back into the orbit of French film history by offering a close textual analysis of it. The third is to suggest that Truffaut's concept of the 'tradition de qualité', which did so much to influence film historians' 'negative' view of France's 1950s cinema, was more of a red herring (or Aunt Sally) than has yet been proposed. On this last point, it is worth re-reading Truffaut's vituperative attack (first published in 1954) on France's cinema of adaptation, which largely dominated the 1950s (up to approximately 60 per cent of all output) and his singling out of two of its greatest exponents, Jean Aurenche and Pierre Bost, for a bitter tirade. As I hope this chapter will demonstrate, Truffaut's claim that this created a formulaic cinema fails to stand up to close scrutiny. Rather, the label 'qualité française' should be taken to mean a specificity in terms of film aesthetics that sought to stand against the American model of film practice.

Perhaps the most protracted censorship story, where the film industry is concerned, was the case of Louis Daquin's *Bel-Ami*. As we can already note, there was a three-year delay in its release in France for reasons that will be made clear below. First, however, it is helpful to remind ourselves of the following political contexts as a way of understanding why this film became such a target for the Commission de Contrôle des Visas. The year 1954 was the real beginning of France's protracted decolonization process. Morocco and Tunisia were in discussion and would gain independence in 1956. The situation in Indochina, which had been at war since 1946, had deteriorated to the extent that France's armed forces suffered an ignominious defeat at the hands of the Viet-minh at Diên Biên Phu. By July of that year, the Geneva agreements were signed and Vietnam was split in two. By November 1954, the Algerian crisis had hit new heights and, to all intents and purposes, France was at war with its colony. Censorship in mainland France was therefore at its peak during the mid-1950s, particularly in relation to Algeria, for reasons of national security. This, then, is the context within which we need to first examine Daquin's ill-fated film.

A brief synopsis begins to reveal why the film posed a problem for the censors. Recently returned from Algeria, where he served for two years as a hussar in the French army, Georges Duroy – known as Bel-Ami because of his good looks – has great ambitions to enter into Parisian society of the mid-1880s. He is, however, penniless. Armed only with his charm and persuasive ways of seduction, this *parvenu* sets out on a campaign to climb the social ladder. His first piece of luck occurs when he bumps into an old army friend, Forestier, who gets him a job as a runner for the right-wing newspaper *La Vie française*, which is owned by the Jewish banker-magnate Monsieur Walter, who uses the paper to make and break governments (and thereby increase his personal fortune and sphere of influence). Georges quickly gets rid of his first mistress, Rachel, a working-class woman of easy virtue but a generous spirit, who hangs out at the Folies-Bergère on the make for a louis or two. She is replaced by a demi-mondaine, Clothilde de Marelle, who helps Georges on his way. She is not the only woman to foster his ambitions, however. Madeleine Forestier, a wealthy bourgeoise of independent means, also takes a shine to him, even though she warns him that she will never be his mistress. She helps Georges write his first article – a piece on Algeria that launches his career as a journalist. He very soon becomes the expert on North African affairs for the newspaper, which his boss Monsieur Walter uses to his advantage to speculate first with and then against the government. After some persuading, he ropes Duroy into a financial scam by playing the card, in his newspaper, of speculation in the stock exchange as to whether France will invade and thereby annex Morocco in retaliation for its purported acts of hostility on French Algerian soil.

Meanwhile, fortunately for Duroy, Forestier dies of tuberculosis and he is able to marry Madeleine, who suggests that he enoble himself to Du Roy Du Cantel. He needs no persuading. She also continues to foster his career by dictating articles to him (much as she did with her former husband). Very soon, though, Georges – a trifle tired of his wife's modern views about marriage (she describes marriage as an equal partnership)[2] and irrationally jealous of her deceased husband – begins to set his ambitions higher still. His next target is his boss's wife, the virtuous and very catholic Madame Walter, whom he easily manages to seduce. She is prone to revealing secrets to her lover, including the fact that his wife, Madeleine, is having an affair with the rather odious and arrogant journalist-turned politician, the minister for foreign affairs, Laroche-Mathieu, whose job Duroy is determined to obtain. Georges catches them *en flagrant délit* and immediately sues for divorce. On the back of the scandal, Laroche-Mathieu resigns his ministerial post. Duroy attempts to persuade Walter to give him the backing of the newspaper to get into politics. However, Walter is getting tired of the upstart Georges Duroy (as indeed are his fellow colleagues at the newspaper), and so fires him. Furious, Georges vows his revenge. He unceremoniously dumps Madame Walter and actively pursues the Walters' virginal daughter, Suzanne. He manages to get her to elope with him, thus forcing the Walters' hand into consenting to the marriage. All is well for Georges Du Roy Du Cantel. He is at the top – or almost, for he still harbours an ambition to enter the Assemblée nationale (his father-in-law can hardly refuse now to help him). As he stares over to the Assemblée from the church steps of la Madeleine, where he has just been married, it is obvious – as the onlooker Rachel remarks – that 'he will soon be minister'.

Censorship stories

Daquin had been trying to get the project of *Bel-Ami* off the ground since 1950 (Daquin 1960: 268). As André Bazin, in a courageous article published in the *Observateur* in 1955, points out, given the political climate of the time in France (war with Algeria), which led to strict censorship, and given the nature of the film's subject-matter (with its references to Algeria and Morocco and corrupt speculation), it was highly unlikely that he would have got the scenario through the pre-censorship board (Bazin, cited in Daquin 1960: 268). In any event, he could not find a French producer to back him. Eventually, Austria – or, more precisely, the then Eastern (communist) bloc of Vienna and Projektograph Film – came to his rescue. They supplied the money and the film stock, Agfacolor, which came from Eastern Germany. However, in exchange Projektograph contracted Daquin to make a German version of the same film, but with Austrian actors and technicians. He agreed, and duly shot both versions in a short turn-around time of ten to twelve weeks. The French version, for its part, was made almost exclusively with French personnel and was edited in Paris. Two small French production and distribution companies (Malherbes and Marceau) were also involved, though at what juncture remains unclear except that it would seem to be at the distribution end of things. However, this was only the start of a series of difficulties to be encountered by the French version of the film, beginning with its 'nationality'. In November 1954 (at its first submission to the Commission of Visa Control), it suited the minister responsible for signing off the exhibition visa – the minister of industry and commerce, André Morice[3] – to deem the film foreign (foreign money, foreign film stock) so he refused to ratify the visa. This was despite the fact that the film had already been awarded French nationality by the Centre national de la cinématographie (CNC) in September – a position the (cowardly) CNC reversed in December 1954 (Daquin 1960: 270). The Commission ordered that all references to Algeria and Morocco be cut. Daquin complied. However, in 1955 (during its second submission for a visa), Morice this time deemed it to be French and banned it in the interests of the nation because 'it gave evidence of a systematic denigration of the nation and placed the accent at a particularly sensitive time on the colonial issue', and it represented a threat to public order (Morice, cited in Daquin 1960: 272–73).

In April 1955, several major film directors and scriptwriters signed a petition demanding that the film be released. Morice again refused (Daquin 1960: 286).[4] The film was the subject of debate at the Assemblée nationale (17 May 1955), with deputies arguing on the one hand that Maupassant's novel, set in 1880–81, was indeed inspired by the Third Republic's first great period of financial speculation, and that it was a true reflection of the moral climate of the late nineteenth century, marked as it was by the collusion of three great powers: money, politics and the press. On the other hand, others – in particular Morice, possibly seeing too many uncomfortable parallels with the contemporary Fourth Republic and the burgeoning crisis in Algeria – argued that Maupassant's *oeuvre* had been misrepresented by the film and used to 'undermine the French nation' (Morice, cited in Daquin 1960: 272). Apparently the film had been screened no less than eighteen times at the Ministry of Information. Yet, for all of that, Morice was no further enlightened and he clearly had not read the novel (as deputies at the Assemblée were quick to point out!) (Daquin 1960: 272–73). Morice insisted on a further cut of two longish sequences. Finally, in 1957, a much-mutilated *Bel-Ami* – reduced from 106 to 86 minutes – was granted general release in France.

As we indicated above, two versions of this film were made, one in French and one in German, with completely distinct exhibition trajectories. The German version came out in Austria and Germany and had a normal shelf-life. As for the French version, although banned in France thanks to the prevarication about its 'nationality', it was possible to distribute the original in its integrity outside of France as an Austrian-produced film. The French version was first released in London in 1954 to considerable acclaim, albeit with an 'X' certificate (Daquin 1960: 270). It was then later redistributed on general release in the United Kingdom in 1956 with the first set of cuts imposed by the Commission (running at 100 minutes). This time, curiously, it obtained less-favourable reviews, doubtless because by now it was tarnished with the story of censorship. As the *Monthly Film Bulletin* put it: 'Louis Daquin and his collaborators have here transformed Guy de Maupassant's story into a fairly thorough Left-wing tract, and it is presumably the numerous references to colonialism and wicked politicians and financiers (modern parallels hinted at) which caused the film to be banned in France' (J.G. 1956). Clearly the reviewer had not read the original novel, either. Maupassant had been to Algeria in 1881, as a special correspondent for the newspaper *Le Gaulois* when much of the North African troubles were brewing. So he had first-hand experience of the effects of colonialism; in his articles, as much as in his novel, he therefore felt compelled to expose the lack of justice towards the Arabs. He sought to challenge prejudice and awaken people's consciousness (Wrona 1999: 386–400). His articles clearly show that he had adopted an anti-colonialist stance and his novel makes no bones about exposing the shenanigans between high finance, the press and politicians, all poised to make money out of the colonies.

The importance of *Bel-Ami*, both as a film and as marking a political moment in France's 1950s history, should therefore not be under-estimated. Let us consider the contexts of this film further. Its director, Louis Daquin, was a member of the Resistance during the war; he was also a member of the French Communist Party – as, indeed, were his two co-dialoguists, Roger Vailland and Vladimir Pozner. Daquin was the General Secretary to the film industry's technicians' trade union (the very institution the 1950s studio bosses railed against). During the 1930s, he had worked with some of the great directors of the time (most directly with Jean Grémillon, whom he greatly admired and from whom he learnt his craft, but also Renoir and Clément). Yet, talented though he was, reaction to his political pedigree from producers and politicians alike was to thwart his ambitions as a film-maker, and he made only nine films in France.[5] As Daquin puts it himself, the system of censorship in place during the 1950s was unrelenting towards him, and the 'Affaire *Bel-Ami*' was the last nail in the coffin as far as his film career was concerned (Daquin 1970: 19). The film was banned for three years and he was never able to work on a film in France again. He went to Romania and East Germany, but to all intents and purposes, his career was at an end.

When I embarked on my research into *Bel-Ami*, it seemed that no copy of this film remained in existence. I searched all film library and archive catalogues possible. Imagine my excitement, then, when I finally managed to locate a copy at the CNC archives out in Bois d'Arcy – thanks, it has to be said, to the assiduous search made on my behalf by Daniel

Brémaud of the CNC. It then transpired that the only copy they had was the '*version russe*'. At first I was dismayed, but upon seeing it I realized I had a jewel before my eyes: Louis Daquin's much-censored film available in its original version, albeit dubbed into Russian. Finally, posthumously, Daquin had his revenge on the censoriousness of the 1950s, thanks to the French Communist Party restoring the film in 1985 for presentation in the former Soviet Union. Somehow it had ended up in the CNC's film archives. Thankfully Daquin had logged all the cuts and amendments upon which the board of censors had insisted so I could hear and see that they had been returned to this version of the film (Daquin 1960: 274–85).

In all, twenty minutes of cuts were imposed by the French board of censors before its visa was finally signed off in 1957 (Daquin 1970: 68). The original film was 106 minutes long; the greatly reduced French version was a mere 86 minutes. The Russian version I saw was 109 minutes long because of some extra inter-titles.[6] Apart from the cut of the opening fourteen shots showing Georges Duroy as a hussard in Algeria, all the excisions had been restored and the dialogue rewrites replaced with the original lines. In the original film, the opening fourteen-shot sequence illustrates the brutal treatment meted out by Duroy and his fellow soldiers to the Arabs, including holding them to ransom and murdering them for their livestock. We also see Duroy stealing a necklace from an indigenous woman.[7] The board of censors demanded it be cut in its entirety. Daquin replaced it with a written text: 'Paris 1885, Georges Duroy, recently returned from Algeria, where he served two years in the *Chasseurs d'Afrique*, reminisces about his exotic conquests with his new Parisian conquest.'[8] The new conquest is Rachel, the young woman who hangs out at the Folies-Bergère. However, the board of censors was not satisfied, and demanded a further cut as follows: 'Georges Duroy recently returned to France, after serving two years in the regiment, reminisces about his exotic conquests with his new Parisian conquest.' In the Russian version of the film, it is the first text that is retained. So, although the written text replaces the brutality of the fourteen-shot sequence, at least it refers to the country 'Algeria' and the idea of conquest. As such, the opening retains more of the film's original intent than the one finally approved by the French board of censors. Furthermore, in this Russian version, during this opening sequence – set in the café area of the Folies-Bergère – Duroy talks away to his mistress about the appeal of North Africa in general and ends by saying: 'You see there is a lot to be had in Morocco' – whereas for the French version this was yet a further line that the censors demanded be diluted (to 'There's a lot to be had in those countries').

Most significantly, in relation to this Russian version, two sequences that were entirely cut are reinserted, giving a much greater sense to the film.[9] The first occurs quite early in the film. It is an exchange between Duroy and Walter and his senior political correspondent and deputy at the Assemblée, Laroche-Mathieu, whom Walter is trying to get into government as minister of foreign affairs (to grease his own palm, of course, by fostering his commercial interests in North Africa). In this sequence, Laroche-Mathieu endeavours to get Duroy to confirm (by showing him on the map of North Africa) that the Moroccans have illegally invaded Algeria at Azilal. This incursion is tantamount to an invasion of

French territory, argues Laroche-Mathieu, who can now accuse the present minister of foreign affairs of ineptitude or concealment, thus getting him sacked and himself appointed foreign minister. Duroy, who still has some sense of integrity, insists that the Moroccans are nowhere near the border (as he points out, Azilal is in fact 300 kilometres inside Morocco, and therefore far away from the Algerian border). Laroche-Mathieu refuses to be swayed by this, and the story is published with the following headlines: 'Laroche-Mathieu challenges the government over the Azilal scandal'. In the paper, he argues that France must take action against Morocco and annex it. The coup works: the government falls and Laroche-Mathieu is appointed minister. In the belief that Morocco will be annexed, parliament votes in favour of credits (incurring debt) to finance the counter-attack. M. Walter becomes a major investor; so too does Duroy, who also invests (his briefly experienced integrity being rapidly overcome by his cupidity).

The second restored sequence takes this story further and occurs some months later. Duroy (now Du Roy du Cantel) has married the recently widowed Madeleine Forestier and is spending his honeymoon in a hotel at the spa town of Bagnoles-de-l'Orne in Normandy.[10] He is visited by Walter and Laroche-Mathieu. In this sequence, Duroy is more or less told to publish a story to the effect that the annexation of Morocco will now *not* take place. The impact of this news on the Bourse (French stock exchange) will be to cause a huge crash. However, unbeknown to Duroy, the play is double: first, to publish that the annexation *will not* take place, thus engineering a crash and allowing Walter to buy back government debt very cheaply; second, to confirm that the annexation *will* take place and see stocks soar again, at which point Walter can sell at top price (in short, an insider dealing scam).

Neither of these two sequences is an invention on Daquin's part. They are clearly to be read in Maupassant's novel (Maupassant 1999: 237–39, 264, 284–87, 294–96, 299–300, 315, 366).[11] Indeed, Maupassant had transposed over into Morocco events actually taking place in Tunisia (Daquin 1960: 268–69). In 1881, the then prime minister Jules Ferry broadcast the story (very similar to the one proposed by Laroche-Mathieu) that tribes of Tunisian brigands (the Khoumirs) had illegally invaded Algeria. This allowed Ferry to get funding from the government to counter-attack the invasion, sending an army of 30,000 men into Tunisia and annex the country as a French Protectorate. This in turn created tensions with Italy over railway development rights in that country, which the French now controlled: Tunisia was rife for financial speculation (Maupassant 1999: 148, n 1). As we know from Maupassant's novel, Walter had all sorts of business interests in 'Morocco', in particular copper mines (Maupassant 1999: 285). We can also see that Daquin, in his endeavours to placate the censors, had set his film four years later than the original text (1885 instead of 1881); however, as we know, this was still not enough: to pacify Morice, the date and the word Morocco had to be excised from the film – hence the cutting of these two crucial sequences and thereby any notion of a financial scam.

As Bazin asserts, to accuse Daquin of misrepresenting the novel is quite false: 'Daquin is guilty only of fidelity to himself and to Maupassant' (Bazin, in Daquin 1960: 269). On this point, let us leave the final word to Daquin:

I do not feel that I violated Maupassant. I feel if he had been writing now, he would probably have emphasised the influence of society more. All the same, Vailland, Pozner and myself studied the book thoroughly and I don't think we added anything. When you read it carefully, you realise that it is, in fact, the first anti-colonialist novel. (Daquin, in Berthomé 1976: 8)

Bel-Ami – a film in four parts

A film in four parts, the narrative of *Bel-Ami* unravels much like the quadrille that is danced at the Walter's ball towards the end of the third section. Each of the four parts is clearly demarcated by Duroy's next ascension on the social ladder he climbs thanks to his exploitation of women, as the table on the next page makes clear.

We can see from the timing of the sequences in the table that the film speeds up in the second half of the film. Parts I (3 minutes per sequence) and II (3.5 minutes per sequence) mark the complex ascendancy of Duroy to middle-class respectability in the form of his marriage to Madeleine. Parts III and IV (both at 2.5 minutes per sequence) indicate the rapidity with which Duroy has gained mastery of the game of social climbing. Indeed, the word 'game' is a key word to unravelling this film, beginning with the quadrille (in Part III). Just prior to this dance, Duroy had been perched on a balcony overlooking people waltzing. Madame Walter approaches him, lays her hand on his and arranges a rendezvous with him, for she has important pieces of information for him (as we later discover, when he meets her at the Trinité church, these are his wife's infidelity and the fact that Monsieur Walter has used him over the Moroccan incident). As we adopt his point of view over the dancers, we observe – as does Duroy – his previous conquests: Clothilde and Madeleine dancing (the latter with Laroche-Mathieu). His sly smirk hints that he has other conquests to make, at which point the camera cuts and we rejoin Duroy downstairs participating in the quadrille. This dance becomes an excellent metaphor for the game he is playing. All along, Duroy has thought of nothing but conquest: his whole ambitious purpose has been conducted like a campaign.

The quadrille itself is a term of military origin, and refers to an equestrian performance: a military parade within which horses make square-shaped formations, criss-crossing through the centre. As a dance, the quadrille became extremely popular during the nineteenth century. It is an intricate dance, usually with four couples lined up in columns and dancing either opposite each other or at a diagonal. They meet up moving forward or across, the man enlaces the woman, they twirl around in the middle, either return together on the same line or separate and cross over to the other side. The interesting thing for us, in this film, is that the quadrille is executed by a crossing over on the diagonal to join the partner, rather than dancing forward to the person directly opposite. Duroy first engages with Clothilde. They talk, she is quite cross with him and he puts on the charm. The next crossing over brings him to Madame Walter, who smiles radiantly as he enlaces her (no need for talk here!). Back

Bel Ami structure.

Part I => *from Rachel to Clothilde de Marelle*	Part II => *from Clothilde to Madeleine Forestier*	Part III => *from Madeleine Forestier to Mme Walter*	Part IV => *from Mme Walter to Suzanne Walter*
a) Folies-Bergère • Duroy is penniless. • Meets Rachel, his first mistress.	*a) 127 Rue de Constantinople* (Clothilde and Duroy's little hideaway) • Duroy begins affair with Clothilde.	*a) Spa hotel Bagnoles-de-l'Orne* • Duroy's hand forced by Walter and Laroche-Mathieu; to write that Morocco won't be invaded. • Mme Walter and Suzanne also at Spa hotel – brief exchange with Duroy (both clearly rather smitten by him).	*a) Hotel particulier* • Duroy bursts in on his wife and Laroche-Mathieu; instigates divorce.
b) Bois de Boulogne • Meets Forestier, who invites him to dinner. • Introduced to Mme Clothilde de Marelle (on horseback).	*b) Newspaper offices* • Duroy's hand is forced by Walter and Laroche-Mathieu over invasion of Algeria by Morocco. • Duroy is furious at humiliation; Forestier laughs at him.	*b) Walter's mansion: reception/ball* • Mme Walter shows interest in Duroy; sets rendezvous at La Madeleine. • Quadrille dance.	*b) Newspaper offices* • Walter symbolically washes hands of Duroy; tells him Morocco will be invaded. • Duroy, humiliated, plans revenge (Suzanne as his trophy).
c) Forestier's apartment • Meets Walter, who offers him a chance. • Meets Clothilde (again), Madeleine, Mme Walter, Suzanne.	*c) Folies-Bergère* • Takes Clothilde to Folies-Bergère. • Rachel sees them both as they go through the *promenoir* to their *loge*. • Humiliating showdown between Rachel and Clothilde.	*c) Church of la Trinité* • Mme Walter hints that Madeleine is having an affair with Laroche-Mathieu and exposes Moroccan scam. • Duroy puts move on Mme Walter; she 'resists'; he takes her off in carriage.	*c) 127 Rue de Constantinople* • Dumps Mme Walter. • Clothilde comes by for assignation.
d) Newspaper offices • Publishes his first article, thanks to Madeleine Forestier's dictation.			*d) Newspaper offices* • Walter fires Duroy.
			e) Quai de la Seine • Rendezvous with Suzanne; they take off in a carriage.

d) Newspaper offices
- Newspaper article on Azilal scandal printed.
- Duroy prepares to make his move on Madeleine.

e) Forestier's apartment
- Duroy visits Madeleine.

f) Newspaper offices
- Article produces results; government resigns; Laroche-Mathieu made minister; champagne celebrations.

g) Forestier's apartment
- Forestier dies.
- Duroy marries Madeleine.

d) 127 Rue de Constantinople
- Seduction of Mme Walter completed.

f) Church of la Madeleine
- Duroy marries Suzanne.
- Duroy is rich; he has the world at his feet; even Clothilde serves him a knowing wink.

26 minutes/ 9 sequences	32 minutes/ 9 sequences	21 minutes/ 8 sequences	30 minutes/ 12 sequences

to their lines, and a third crossing brings Duroy back to Clothilde. She teasingly reproaches him for abandoning her (it is clear from this interaction that he will soon resume his liaison with her). The fourth engagement brings Duroy to Madame Walter once more, and at this point they affirm their assignation at the Trinité (Madame Walter remains radiant). Now back on their lines, Duroy moves forward and this time it is Madeleine he encounters – almost as if she is there as an afterthought. They pull back to the lines and Duroy's final encounter is with Madame Walter once more. The sequence fades out on the couple as they twirl in the middle.

The dance and the crossing over are key to our understanding of Duroy's duplicity, as indeed Daquin himself asserted.[12] The military connection and the idea of performance are also key. In his campaign, Duroy performs the exquisite lover. He plays and toys with his women, twirls them around, uses them and double-crosses them. Furthermore, in this dance, only three couplings have been engaged. So the question becomes: where is the fourth (victim/conquest)? She is yet to come, and immediately upon the fade-out on this dance, Duroy is seen with Suzanne (the Walters' daughter) in the humid conservatory full of tropical plants. Small wonder the valet comes looking for her and, casting a filthy look at Duroy, takes her back to her fiancé!

Of course, Duroy is not the only one to play at double-crossing: both Walter and Laroche-Mathieu do it, arguably at a more lethal level since their practice takes place in the domain of finance and politics. However, Duroy is not far behind, representing as he does the press; and we know of his political ambitions. Just as he replaced one man, Forestier, so we can see that soon he will replace Laroche-Mathieu. Dead man's shoes indeed! Walter will not be able to wash his hands as easily of Duroy as he believes: his fortune will be next in line. There is a capital scene in Part IV that makes this clear. The sequence opens with a close-up on Walter's hands playing cards: a game of patience (in French known as '*une réussite*'). As Walter and Duroy talk, Walter moves over to a wash-stand cabinet and opens the lid, in which there is a mirror; as he washes his hands, we see Duroy's smug reflection in the mirror: he is asking Walter to back him now Laroche-Mathieu is out of the political frame (thanks to the divorce scandal). Walter dries his hands, closes up the cabinet, clearly angry at having lost a valuable asset in government thanks to Duroy. He cuts the conversation short by refusing to help; Duroy storms out, furious. Walter leaves an unsealed letter on Duroy's desk in the adjoining office, sacking him. One of Duroy's colleagues reads it before he comes back to his desk, adding to Duroy's sense of humiliation. Walter believes he has sealed Duroy's fate. No such thing, however. Duroy sits at his desk, immediately plotting his revenge, the next move on his campaign: to humiliate Walter in turn by eloping with Suzanne.

Ruthless as he is, not all the women are entirely his 'victims' – more his 'game' in the sense of the hunt – and not all succumb or fully submit. It is only Madame Walter who really suffers (and later, we assume, her daughter Suzanne). Rachel stands up to Duroy and Clothilde at the Folies-Bergère (see the table on page 302, Part Two, Section c). Madeleine is no mean challenge either. It is she who dictates to him the first article he writes for *La Vie française* (and she continues to do so once they are married). It is she who refuses to be his mistress

The quadrille dance.

and who marries on her own terms (of equality and non-possessiveness). It is she who first suggests that Duroy 'entertain' Clothilde, and that he make a friend of Mme Walter so he can get close to her husband and advance his career prospects (as we know, Georges takes this further than she intended). In essence, she has shown him the way forward (even to the point of suggesting he ennoble his name to Du Roy). When Madeleine is exposed as an adulteress, she says nothing during the entire scene; merely the most delicate smile of irony adorns her lips. We sense her distaste for Duroy's jealousy, coupled with an indifference to his vulgarity by bringing the police and the notary into the adulterous bedroom to immediately write out the divorce writ – he is not classy enough to challenge Laroche-Mathieu to a duel. She is as much in charge of her game as he is in charge of his. Clothilde never fully disappears from his amorous life, either. She is willing to accept the ups and downs of her relationship with the elegant young man.

As we have seen, then, class and political ambition drive Duroy. The dance is one metaphor, but so too is his free movement over the various geographical locations in Paris – a movement, incidentally, that is matched by Clothilde, whose main ambition appears to be to hold on to Duroy as a lover. Both Duroy and Clothilde are in a sense the outsiders trying to penetrate into the domain of the well-heeled Parisian domains inhabited by the Walters and the Forestiers, who occupy sumptuous apartments in the 8th and 9th districts (rue du Faubourg Saint-Honoré and rue Fontaine respectively). Duroy lives in the rather insalubrious 17th just above the boulevard des Batignolles in a shabby attic room. Clothilde has rooms in the 7th, on the fourth floor (a small apartment therefore) on the other side of the Seine in a narrow street off the rue des Saints Pères (rue Verneuil). However, despite their lesser means, both have the greatest mobility, suggesting amongst other things their mutual ambition and suitability in terms of each other. In their movements around the city, they mirror each other. They visit all the points on the map as it were, criss-crossing Paris: the 17th, 7th, 8th and 9th districts, the Folies-Bergère in the 9th, the newspaper offices just off boulevard Haussmann (near the Bourse in the 2nd), very much as if in a quadrille of social mobility. Moreover, it is not long before Duroy takes up residence on rue Constantinople, within the prestigious domain of the 8th, albeit in a small two-room suite more reminiscent of a lovers' nest than an exclusive bachelor's pad. It is instructive that it is Clothilde who first sets him up there when he is penniless, rather than go to his scrubby rooms in the 17th. As soon as he has the means, however, he takes it on as his own to tryst with more than just Clothilde. Mme Walter's movements take her to churches, her husband's newspaper offices, the Forestiers and, fatally, to Duroy's place on rue Constantinople. Intriguingly, the woman who moves around the least is Madeleine. Consistent with her standing as a woman of political culture, people mostly come to visit her – as if her place were a *salon*; she is then at the centre. This also suggests that she may well be another kind of *meneur du jeu* and that Duroy has, in the ultimate analysis, profoundly misunderstood her significance. If we return to the metaphor of the quadrille, we recall that she appeared to figure as an afterthought – in Duroy's mind certainly. But this criss-crossing of the city in which both he and Clothilde participate suggests an instability and therefore insecurity of position as opposed to the established certainty of Madeleine Forestier/Du Roy. Perhaps his future is less assured than he believes.

In an interview in 1979, Daquin makes an interesting comment in relation to the supposedly uninventive cinema of quality of the 1950s. He talks about how, in terms of a film aesthetic, during the 1930s he, Grémillon, Becker and Renoir were quite taken with the Hollywood filming technique. He explains how the Occupation period contributed to a detoxification from the American system. Thus, for many, the '*qualité française*' that came into being in 1950s was a manifestation of that rejection – an affirmation that there was a French film aesthetics – a point Truffaut seems to completely overlook in his diatribe. Daquin supplies two examples in his own film, which broke with the American system: the fact that he stopped using the shot/counter-shot; and that he very rarely used music, which to his mind is mostly unmotivated yet hugely manipulative (Gévaudan 1979: 34).[13] In light of the above comments, it would seem timely to suggest that Truffaut significantly misrepresented France's 1950s cinema of quality and that we should endeavour to move away from the virtual self-imposed censorship in French film studies that has been so coloured by Truffaut's sweeping generalizations and largely unfounded attack on quality cinema.

Daquin's film remains an important one on a number of fronts, all of them political in some way. It is a film made by a Frenchman who wanted to celebrate, in his work, the *oeuvre* of a great narrative master, Maupassant. In his efforts to adapt to screen a French classic, he was thwarted at all stages of the process. Yet he made a film that he readily labels as French and qualifies as an exemplar of the much maligned '*cinéma de qualité française*'. He showed great fidelity to the original text and was heavily censored for it. Crucially and sadly, because of the political furore caused by this most French of texts and because the film itself was confounded with the politics of the man behind the film, *Bel-Ami* – a very good film and fine costume drama, in my view – has to all intents and purposes disappeared from the French film heritage, remaining only in the form of a 16mm '*version russe*'.[14]

Notes

1. A longer version of this chapter appears in my book, *French Costume Drama of the 1950s: Fashioning Politics in Film*, published by Intellect (2010). My thanks also go to the British Academy for the research grant that made it possible for me to visit the CNC Bois d'Arcy archives where *Bel-Ami* is held.

2. In Maupassant's novel, Madeleine spells it out very clearly: 'I mean to be free … I will not tolerate being controlled, any jealousy or any discussion of my behaviour' (Maupassant, 1999: 208–9, my translation).

3. Something of a paradox, Morice came from a stalwart left-wing background. In 1940, he was taken as a prisoner of war (he was released in 1943). However, during the Occupation his company (l'Entreprise nantaise des travaux publics et paysagers) continued to supply equipment to the Germans, making him a tidy profit. Following the war, Morice was exonerated of any wrong-doing and went on to have a very successful political career, adhering to a right-wing

political culture (Assemblée nationale, n.d.). He was a fierce proponent of French Algeria (hence, doubtless, his ferocity with Daquin's film). He even designed the so-named Ligne Morice, a barrage that was both mined and electrified, to separate French Algeria from its neighbours and prevent the infiltration of the National Liberation Army (described on Wikipedia n.d.).

4. The signatories include Claude Autant-Lara, Pierre Billon, Pierre Bost, Yves Ciampi, René Clair, Marcel Carné, Henri-Georges Clouzot, Jean Cocteau, Jean Dréville, Abel Gance, Jean Grémillon, Henri Jeanson, Jean-Paul Le Chanois, Max Ophuls, Jean Painlevé and Jacques Prévert.

5. The nine films are: *Nous les gosses* (1941); *Madame et le mort* (1942); *Le Voyage de la Toussaint* (1943); *Premier de cordée* (1944); *Patrie* (1946); *Les Frères Bouqinquant* (1947); *Le Point du jour* (1948); *Le Parfum de la dame en noir* (1949); and *Maître après dieu* (1951).

6. In their 1957 production and review notices on the film, both *Le Film français* and *La Cinématographie française* give the film's 'nationality' as Austrian and its length as 85 minutes.

7. See Daquin (1960: 155 and 274 respectively), where he supplies these details. *Monthly Film Bulletin* has it at 100 minutes (so clearly the original uncut version was the one screened – minus the fourteen opening shots). The Austrian production company, Projektograph films, lists it at 106 minutes. The version I saw was 109 minutes – the three minutes or so being due to the inserts of explanatory shots of various letters and printed articles in Russian script. These extra shots would have been made in 1985. It is noticeable that, when no cut-away to a close-up on the written word alone can be made, the newspaper remains in French. Thus these inserts add a few minutes to the running length.

8. This text corresponds fully to Maupassant's own words (1999: 48). Further reading around this interesting case of censorship took me to Daquin's book *Le Cinéma, notre métier*, in which he acknowledges that the cut was a good thing, because to have kept it would have 'skewed the film and taken the spectator down a different path' (1960: 155, my translation).

9. When this latest request was made in 1956, Daquin agreed to them but didn't have the heart to do them himself (Daquin 1960: 273).

10. The nineteenth century witnessed a growth in leisure retreats outside Paris, including spas. Bagnoles-sur-l'Orne was well known for its thermal sources and curative waters, and the Grand Hotel is exemplary of late nineteenth century architectural elegance (doubtless the model for the Duroys' honeymoon).

11. In particular, on p. 284 Maupassant makes an almost direct reference to Jules Ferry.

12. 'We can regret that, in certain scenes, Bel-Ami's duplicity as lover and ambitious gets lost in favour of the lover. However, the scene of the quadrille, completely invented, serves precisely to redress this and to show this side of Bel-Ami' (Daquin 1960: 164, my translation).

13. Indeed, on the few occasions it is used in *Bel-Ami* it is primarily diegetic (Folies-Bergère; the ball at the Walters', the wedding organ). The one non-diegetic moment of music occurs right at the end, in the trumpet fanfare outside the church – surely an ironic comment on Duroy's ambitions?

14. Special thanks to Will Higbee and Sarah Leahy for their attentive reading and useful suggestions in drafting this chapter.

Chapter 22

Raymond Bernard's *Les Misérables* (1933)

Keith Reader

The goal of this chapter is a fairly modest one. It aims to (re)introduce Raymond Bernard's four-and-a-half-hour 1933 epic to a UK audience and to examine the reasons why the film has languished in obscurity for so long. Before doing this, however, I should like to say a few words about the reasons for my interest in this film, which are closely connected with the remarkable changes that have taken place in the field of French studies in the 40 and more years since my undergraduate days. Most significant among these is clearly the range of different types of texts that have found their way on to the syllabus, the once sacrosanct duo of language-and-literature having been supplemented by courses on critical theory, postcolonial studies, *bande dessinée*, gender studies in its multitudinous avatars and – conceivably *primus inter pares* – cinema.

My own work remains firmly anchored within the area of French cultural history and theory, with a strong but emphatically not exclusive cinematic component – something that is illustrated by my current research project, a history of the Bastille/Faubourg-Saint-Antoine area of Paris, which falls within the area (I am not sure whether it can or should be called a discipline) of cultural topography. Representations of the changing modern and post-modern city provide important common ground for those working in French and other modern language sections to dialogue with colleagues in history, sociology and urban studies, as well as with our more traditional interlocutors in the fields of literature and cinema. Andrew Hussey's (2007) *Paris: The Secret History* and Andrew Webber's (2008) *Berlin in the Twentieth Century: A Cultural Topography* provide striking book-length examples of this. Cultural topography provides by its very nature a fruitful terrain to consider a plethora of different types of text side by side, thus providing one way of keeping alive the study of a broad spectrum of texts at a time of contracting resources, and suggesting a valuable way of fostering research into works of literature and cinema that may otherwise find themselves neglected. Victor Hugo's *Les Misérables* may be among the most famous of French novels, but it rarely appears on university syllabuses, for reasons undoubtedly connected with its length and Hugo's status as *monstre sacré*, too demotic perhaps to merit the Bourdieusian distinction unproblematically accorded to a Stendhal or a Flaubert. Work in French cinema has burgeoned over the past three decades, in a manner quite literally unimaginable to those of us who tentatively introduced it on to French degree programmes in those days, but there has been a tendency – in keeping with the growing propensity to favour the defiantly contemporary in syllabus design and increasingly in the promotion of research – for it to concentrate on more recent periods. The cinema of the 1930s thus comes to occupy in many a curriculum an analogous position to medieval poetry or seventeenth-century tragedy –

recognized as extremely important, but increasingly playing a subaltern role to more modern texts. My work, as teacher and as researcher, has in large part been devoted to extending that role, which was a key factor in my decision to concentrate here on Bernard's film rather than on any of the other 25 (at the last count) adaptations of Hugo's magnificent text.

Les Misérables is the most often-filmed of canonical French novels, whose cinematic adaptations include two made in Japan and one in Egypt. Christophe Gautier suggests an explanation for this when he describes Hugo as 'the only figure to meet the demands of the middle-class public the cinema was trying to recruit along with those of the masses who knew all about the spiritual father of the Third Republic whose texts they had studied at school and those of producers eager to make their industry more profitable while conferring upon it as much legitimacy as possible' (Gautier 2005: 22). Bernard's version of the novel is described by Jean-Pierre Jeancolas as 'the most satisfying the cinema has given us', notwithstanding his criticism of 'the angled framing that became something of a signature for Raymond Bernard' (Jeancolas 1983: 162). Often adduced in praise of Bernard's film is its fidelity to the source-text – a common criterion in assessing cinematic adaptations of literature but, as Robert Stam has pointed out, a perilous one in that it implicitly subordinates the adaptation to the 'original', whereas 'a filmic adaptation is *automatically* different and original due to the change of medium' (Stam 2005: 17). A critical evaluation of the concept of fidelity in adaptation and its avatars, pointing out its persistence in the face of would-be theoretical rebuttals, is provided by J.D. Connor in *M/C Journal* (Connor 2007). In dealing with a film whose interest resides largely in its status as the 'best and most faithful' adaptation of France's most often-adapted novel, fidelity will be an inescapable issue, certainly to the extent that the extraordinary length of Bernard's film is a corollary of that of the source novel. Jean-Paul Le Chanois's 1958 adaptation, with Jean Gabin, Bernard Blier, Bourvil and Danièle Delorme, weighs in at 'only' three-and-a-half hours by contrast. Stam's call for consideration of filmic adaptations to broaden its focus 'from fidelity to intertextuality' (Stam 2005: 24) suggests a productive direction for adaptation studies to take, which will lead my comments on the film to gesture – space precludes more – towards the work of directors such as Eisenstein and Renoir, inscribing it in a context that asserts the cinematic specificity which much earlier work on adaptation might implicitly have denied it.

That said, there is no escaping the colossal cultural and textual presence of Hugo's novel; the Boublil and Schönberg musical led to a fleeting London re-release of the Le Chanois film in the late 1980s, whereas the Bernard version remained inaccessible until very recently. It was issued on DVD in 2008, along with the director's 1931 adaptation of Raymond Dorgelès' 1919 anti-war novel *Les Croix de bois/Wooden Crosses*, by the US-based Criterion Collection's 'no-frills' offshoot Eclipse – a striking proof, if proof were needed, that the preservation and reproduction of French culture are too important to be left to the French. It is intriguing to observe that three of French cinema's most prominent icons of masculinity, albeit in varyingly troubled and problematic ways, have taken the role of Jean Valjean: Gabin, seen by Ginette Vincendeau as 'an ideal hero who valorizes both masculine and feminine values' (Vincendeau 2000a: 76); Jean-Paul Belmondo in Lelouch's Occupation-set adaptation of 1995; and the 'suffering macho' (Vincendeau 2000a: 225) Gérard Depardieu in a 2000 TV mini-series directed by Josée Dayan and inexpensively available on DVD. Jean Valjean's masculinity is nothing if not ambiguous; endowed with colossal physical strength, he is also connoted as being – like his alter ego Javert – bereft of sexual experience, first through lengthy imprisonment and then due to an altruistic projection of his desires on to his adoptive 'daughter' and unconsummated *grand amour* Cosette. Bernard's Valjean, Harry Baur, is – like Gabin and Depardieu (I am less sure about Belmondo) – far from uncomplicatedly masculine.

Bernard's film has, I would argue, been subject to a fourfold exclusion that has caused it to be perceived, however unwittingly, as lacking in what Pierre Bourdieu terms 'distinction' – that quality which bespeaks cultural capital and enables texts possessing it to be regarded as worthy of serious attention (Bourdieu 1979). That exclusion pertains all at once to the film's genre, its source text, its auteur and its star. In the first place, *Les Misérables* is a precursor of what Truffaut famously reviled as the *cinéma de papa* or *cinéma de qualité*, with its stress on literary adaptation and scripting along with (by the standards of its time) lavish production values. Such a cinema has, over the past twenty or so years, acquired a measure of distinction through its reinvention as 'heritage cinema' – a term originally used in an Anglophone context – but that has not on the whole been backdated to its more modest, often black-and-white precursors, as witnessed by the fact that far more work has been done on Claude Berri's *Jean de Florette* and *Manon des sources* (both 1986) or Olivier Assayas's *Les Destinées sentimentales* (2001) than on Bernard or Fourth Republic film-makers such as Christian-Jaque, who directed adaptations of, *inter alia*, Maupassant's *Boule de suif* (1945) and Stendhal's *La Chartreuse de Parme/The Charterhouse of Parma* (1948). Not (as even his most ardent admirers would concede) on a par with Renoir, Carné or even Jean Grémillon – by comparison with whom he is too easily dismissed as an old-fashioned journeyman – Bernard clearly occupies a subaltern position in French film history, but that is not to say that his work deserves the neglect that has befallen it.

Second, while *Les Misérables* is among the best-known French nineteenth century novels, it is also among the least read and studied. Hugo figures on university French fiction syllabuses far less frequently than Balzac or Zola, a result partly of the length at which he wrote (*Les Misérables* spans some 1500 pages), but also of his 'man-of-the-people' reputation and supposedly overblown style. It is as if his status as French national treasure absolved scholars from the need to read his work seriously, a paradox encapsulated in André Gide's notorious reply to the question of who was France's greatest poet: 'Victor Hugo, hélas!' or Jean Cocteau's 'Victor Hugo was a madman who believed he was Victor Hugo.' Hugo's motto 'Ego Hugo' encapsulates the colossal egotism that laid him open to such aphoristic mockery – from, ironically and I suspect far from coincidentally, two of the biggest French literary egos of the twentieth century. The prodigious richness of *Les Misérables*, its adventurous use of digression, its creative treatment of slang, and the bravura of its urban and historical sweep remain cruelly under-rated, almost in inverse proportion to its notional renown. The third reason for the marginalization of Bernard's film is a more directly cinematic one, which is that on the totem-pole of 1930s French directors he ranks well below not only Renoir or Carné but even such figures as Julien Duvivier or Pierre Chenal. Bernard specialized in the literary adaptation of novels by writers generally nowadays regarded as minor, such as his 1953 version of Alexandre Dumas *fils' La Dame aux camélias* – the source for Verdi's opera *La Traviata* – doubtless one reason for the neglect into which his work has fallen. Symptomatically, Rémi Fournier Lanzoni's *French Cinema from the Beginnings to the Present* (Lanzoni 2002) makes no reference whatsoever to him, though for Alan Williams *Les Misérables* is 'one of the few truly great adaptations of a nineteenth-century novel to the cinematic screen' (Williams 1992: 186). Pierre Billard devotes part of a chapter of his monumental *L'Age classique du cinéma français* to Bernard's work, notably *Les Croix de bois* and *Les Misérables*. Billard praises *Les Misérables* for the 'measure and restraint' with which the more emotional scenes are shot and 'the big action scenes which he [Bernard] raises to a lyrical dimension' (Billard 1995: 75), but there is no monograph on his work, to which by and large little serious critical attention has been paid. This is despite the fact that, on its release, *Les Misérables* tapped into the volatile social and political climate of 1934 France, for it was premiered on the very day (4 February) that the head of the Comédie Française, Émile Fabré, was ousted for political reasons. Fabré had mounted a production of Shakespeare's *Coriolanus* that was taken as an affront by the Radical government, then mired in the corruption revealed by the Stavisky affair.[1] His appearance at the premiere of Bernard's film ensured that: 'Cheers broke out during the screening whenever the dialogue veered towards political or social issues', while: 'A line referring to "the sickness of the Republic" almost brought the house down' (Andrew and Ungar 2005: 35).

Billard stresses that *Les Misérables* was a team effort, in which the designer Jean Perrier, the cameraman Jules Kruger, the sound engineer Antoine Archimbaud and the composer Arthur Honegger all played their part (Billard 1995: 75). Noteworthy among the actors are Charles Vanel – later to become known for his roles for Duvivier in *La Belle Équipe/They were Five* (1936), Grémillon in *Le Ciel est à vous/The Woman Who Dared* (1944), and Clouzot in *Le Salaire de la peur/Wages of Fear* (1953) and *Les Diaboliques* (1955) – as the sombrely obsessive detective Javert, and Florelle – Valentine in Renoir's *Le Crime de Monsieur Lange/ The Crime of Monsieur Lange* (1936) – as Fantine. A somewhat saddening note is provided by Bernard in his memoirs, where he recounts that he had made nearly 150 attempts at finding the right actor to play Gavroche before happpening upon Émile Genevoix, a concierge's son who delivered a parcel to him and who would later feature in Becker's *Casque d'or/Golden Helmet* (1952) as le petit Billy, a member of the gang headed by Félix Leca (Claude Dauphin). Alas, his admirable performance for Bernard was not to prevent him from scratching a living opening car doors (Bernard 1980: 37), just as Legrand (Michel Simon) does at the end of Renoir's *La Chienne/The Bitch* (1931). The fourth major reason for the film's neglect, and perhaps the most interesting in the context of French cinematic history, is the neglect into which the film's star has fallen. Pierre Billard praises Harry Baur's performance in *Les Misérables* for the manner in which 'his strength (physical, moral and professional) … serves as a solid foundation for this passionate, moving monument' (Billard 1995: 75), while Noël

Les Misérables – Harry Baur, acting 'with all his soul'.

Burch and Geneviève Sellier analyze his performances for Duvivier in *David Golder* (1931) – the most celebrated of his Jewish roles and described as the 'first striking representation in sound cinema of the figure of a sacrificed Father' (Burch and Sellier 1996: 33) – and for André Hugon in the Algiers-set *Sarati le terrible/Sarati the Terrible* (1937), where his earring 'is evidence of his "half- caste" origins' (Burch and Sellier 1996: 41). However, they make no reference to *Les Misérables*, doubtless because the concept of the 'battle of the sexes' is scarcely relevant to that film. Throughout the 1930s, Harry Baur was a name to conjure with among French actors, often bracketed with Raimu as the leading figure of his generation. Raimu – whose real name incidentally was Jules Muraire, though nobody has yet suggested that he invented *verlan* – is nowadays a far better-known figure, thanks largely to his roles as César in the Pagnol trilogy (*Marius* 1931, directed by Alexander Korda: *Fanny* 1932, directed by Marc Allégret: and *César* 1936, directed by Pagnol himself). Baur, as his name suggests, was of Alsatian extraction, though born in Paris, and a more sombre, less ebullient performer despite his mountainous bulk than the unmistakably Provençal Raimu. He has been compared to Charles Laughton and Emil Jannings for the intensity of his performances, floridly characterized in Jean-Loup Passek's *Dictionnaire du cinéma français*:

> He acts with all his soul, but also with all his tics, too clearly in evidence in close-up: his wrinkles become deeper, his cheeks tremble; and then his voice becomes insinuating, hissing, shouting and thunderous to break down into sobs as the action requires. (Passek 1987: 31)

So heavy-duty a style, probably carried over from a highly successful stage career in the 1920s, suggests one reason why Baur is nowadays largely forgotten, for all the ambiguous masculinity suggested in his performances and by Martin O'Shaughnessy in Chapter 18 of this volume, where he observes that: 'One way to read the Baur persona ... would be to underscore its capacity to resolve social tensions through its ability to be both proletarian and bourgeois ... masculine and feminine (competitively strong yet sensitively vulnerable).' O'Shaughnessy is referring to Baur's performance for Marcel L'Herbier in *Les Hommes nouveaux* (1936), but his remarks are pertinent to *Les Misérables* too, particularly given Jean Valjean's fluctuating class status – successively convict engaged in heavy manual work, respected tradesman and citizen, and fugitive from the law – if not from justice in any true sense of the word.

In a gender context, the comparison with Charles Laughton may seem particularly apposite here, though Laughton's stock is higher, thanks in part to his status as tragic gay icon and in part to his only film as director, the masterly *The Night of the Hunter* (1955). Yet the two actors have in common a perhaps paradoxical combination of physical solidity and – as suggested by O'Shaughnessy – sensitive vulnerability, strikingly instanced in Baur's performance in the final scene of *Les Misérables*. Valjean/Baur's mountainous frame, which we have seen undertaking almost superhuman feats of strength earlier in the film, is immobilized on his deathbed, while his eyes are all but closed as he reassures the grief-

Baur as Valjean on his deathbed.

stricken Marius and Cosette: 'It's nothing to die … What's terrible is never to have lived.' The potentially sugary sententiousness of this is undercut, I would argue, by on the one hand the gentleness of Baur's voice – paternal without being excessively masculine – and on the other the stricken strength of his dying frame. There is perhaps also a tragically ironic on- /off-screen contrast between this seraphically peaceful demise and the hideous circumstances of Baur's own death, to be discussed shortly.

Another factor militating against Baur's more widespread recognition is that he never worked for any of the directors, such as Renoir or Carné, whose 1930s films are most widely available. It was for Julien Duvivier that he produced much of his best-known screen work: in addition to *David Golder*, he appeared notably in *Poil de carotte/The Red Head* (1932), *La Tête d'un homme/A Man's Neck* (1933) – where he is one of the great cinema Maigrets – and *Un carnet de bal/Christine* (1937), as a suitor of Christine (Marie Bell) turned priest out of frustrated love. Yet Renoir praised his work in an interview for *Le Travailleur du film* in 1936 – the year in which Baur was the most successful actor at the French box-office, but also that of *Le Crime de Monsieur Lange*, in which Florelle has her best-known role and which alludes to a (fictional) detective-story magazine entitled *Javert*. This may of course be only a coincidence, but it is at least an appealing one.

Another important reason for Baur's neglect is the manner of his death, one of the only partially elucidated cinematic mysteries of *les années noires*. He had been, to quote his biographer Hervé Le Boterf, 'to all intents and purposes labelled the Jew of French cinema' (Le Boterf 1995: 13) because of his roles for Duvivier in *David Golder* and Maurice Tourneur in *Volpone* (1940), in the latter of which he even sported a false nose. Le Boterf may be suspected of *parti pris* here, since he was a right-wing Breton nationalist active in Nantes under the Occupation, and was subsequently active in associations championing the two most prominent collaborationist French authors, Brasillach and Céline. It seems clear that under the Occupation Baur bent over backwards to prove himself a Gentile, declaring himself 'as much of an old Aryan as anybody' (Barrot and Chirat 2000: 60), getting a certificate of Aryanness from the Propaganda Staffel – the German censorship authority – and attending numerous collaborationist receptions. Raymond Aron was to claim that he was covertly involved with the Resistance, but no concrete evidence for this appears to have been produced. He starred in Christian-Jaque's *L'Assassinat du Père Noël/The Killing of Santa Claus* (1941), the first French film to be financed by the German-funded and run production company Continental, set up by Goebbels in September 1940 as a means of asserting control over the potentially subversive French industry. In 1942 he set off for Berlin amid much publicity to star in Hans Bertram's *Symphonie eines Lebens/Symphony of a Life* (1943), in a further attempt at self-ingratiation that was to prove quite literally fatal. On 20 May 1942, after he had returned to Paris, he and his wife, the actress Rika Radifé, were arrested by the Gestapo. She was freed after 115 days, but Baur was to remain a prisoner until 19 September, when he was released in a dreadful state, having lost 77 pounds and allegedly been kept throughout his captivity with no change of clothing. He died in his Paris home some six months later, just short of his sixty-third birthday. Though there seems to be no record of the precise circumstances of his imprisonment, it appears all but certain that he was tortured. The parallel between his treatment and, on an admittedly less homicidal scale, that of Jean Valjean and his fellow convicts is a tragically ironic one.

Harry Baur can thus be described as suffering from a twofold exclusion: too much of a bygone era on the one hand; too uncomfortably close to what is still a deeply traumatic period of French history on the other. It is thus not surprising that that has combined with the other factors mentioned above to relegate Bernard's *Les Misérables* to the status of period piece.

Bernard's film is, I would submit, worthy of renewed consideration for reasons other than Baur's performance. Its epic visual style – the only one appropriate to dealing with so quintessentially epic a text – looks at once back to the great classics of the silent era and forward to the canonical films of the 1930s and later, drawing upon a visual repertoire that spans the two. Sequences such as those involving the dastardly Thénardier couple are shot in a chiaroscuro evocative of the German Expressionists, while inventive use is made of cuts (as from Valjean's shredded convict's passport to Paris ball invitations blowing away in the breeze), wipes and the occasional iris. The sentimentalization of childhood and the melodramatic treatment of the death first of Fantine, then of Jean Valjean recall, not always felicitously, the work of D.W. Griffith, while the film's opening shot, suggesting Valjean's superhuman strength, recalls the montage of Eisenstein, with a strong allegorical component since the stone heads seen in close-up refer back to the title of the section, in the film as in the novel, 'A storm beneath a skull'. At the same time, the Paris ball sequence in which we first encounter Fantine evokes similar scenes in Carné's *Les Enfants du paradis/Children of Paradise* (1945) and Becker's *Casque d'or* (1952), while as Valjean dies, the placing beside his bed of the candlesticks given to him by the saintly bishop – in the film as in the novel – may seem to prefigure the glass dome beside the dying Kane at the opening of Orson Welles' *Citizen Kane* (1941). That comparison may seem a hyperbole too far, but the two death scenes derive their potency in large part from the sense that a complex and variegated biography – a novelistic 'life' of a kind the cinema gives us less often than we might perhaps expect – can be 'explained' by a single founding episode, in its turn materialized in the presence of an everyday but affectively and biographically charged object, or what Lacanians might call the *objet a*. Hugo, in a master-stroke of simultaneous assertion and questioning of the bishop's invisible presence beside Valjean's death-bed, has it that: 'It is probable that the bishop was witnessing this agony' (Hugo 1967: vol. III, 487). The candlesticks stand in for the bishop's absent presence more fully in the film than in the novel – an inevitable shortfall (the textual economy of adaptation, certainly if fidelity is a major criterion, is generally one of loss) but one handled by Baur and Bernard with skill, sensitivity and a lack of the over-statement to which this sequence could all too readily have lent itself.

A masterwork Bernard's *Les Misérables* probably is not – certainly by the empyrean standards of a Carné or a Welles. It does, however, deserve better than the neglect into which it has long since fallen; and the reasons for that neglect, which I have tried to analyze here, say much about how limited our knowledge of important French cinematic texts in particular is. That knowledge, to be sure, is immeasurably wider – thanks to video and DVD – than when I began teaching French cinema almost 35 years ago, yet there are still far too many films viewable only with great difficulty or not at all. Jean Eustache's 1973 masterpiece *La Maman et la putain/The Mother and the Whore* can (unless you have access to a long-ago UK VHS tape or a now-vanished Japanese DVD) quite literally be viewed nowhere – the result, by all accounts, of a seemingly interminable rights imbroglio – while with the exception of *Remorques/Stormy Waters* (1941), Grémillon's work is available only in libraries and via the occasional DVD or video copy for sale online. Likewise, that of Pierre Kast, whose *La Morte-Saison des amours/The Season for Love* (1960) I saw recently at the National Film Theatre in London after quite literally years of waiting, is largely unviewable even at the Bibliothèque nationale or other Paris archives. These examples show how the absence until recently of a legal deposit system for films in France comparable with that for books, and the inevitable backlog of older films awaiting release on DVD – frequently with copyright complications – tends to skew the balance still further towards more contemporary works. It seems to me vital that this should be redressed. Allan Bloom's view that '[t]he distance from the contemporary and its high seriousness that most students need in order not to indulge their petty desires and to discover what is most serious about themselves cannot be found in the cinema, which now knows only the present' (Bloom 1987: 64) will appear ludicrous to most readers of this chapter, but encapsulates a view of cinema as evanescent and lacking in gravitas that long militated against its acceptance as an object of serious intellectual reflection and academic study: a view that has perhaps not entirely gone away.

Part of the task of the film scholar is thus to give cinema (back) its history – textual and contextual – as the work of French writers such as Jean-Pierre Jeancolas and their Anglophone counterparts such as Colin Crisp (see Crisp 1993, 2002) has done over the past few decades. Textual availability is clearly a key factor here, and while I am under no illusion that a society and a journal such as *Studies in French Cinema* can work miracles in this respect, they can certainly play an important role in keeping little-known and/because inaccessible works before a scholarly public. Bernard's *Les Misérables* is important not only in its own right, as an exemplar of a kind of 1930s cinema generally upstaged by more canonical, yet in their day more inventive, works; it is also significant as a precursor of the heritage film and as a significant contribution to an understanding of the colossal intertextual phenomenon that is Victor Hugo. For film scholars, cultural historians and aficionados of French literature and cinema, its renewed availability is welcome indeed.

Note

1. Alexandre Stavisky, a fraudster intimately involved with the municipal finances of the south-western town of Bayonne, and almost certainly with shady dealings in the highest echelons of the French political establishment, was found shot on 8 January 1934, and shortly afterwards died of his wounds. The dubious circumstances of his death flushed out the extent of high-level corruption in France, and were to lead to the toppling of Camille Chautemps' Radical government within a month.

Chapter 23

Jewish-Arab Relations in French, Franco-Maghrebi and Maghrebi Cinemas

Carrie Tarr

E arly analyses of ethnic difference and identity in French cinema have focused primarily on representations of and by France's most visible, and most visibly discriminated against, ethnic minority, first- and second-generation Arab-Muslim migrants from France's former colonies in the Maghreb (Tarr 2005). In the 2000s, however, the 'war of memories' (Savarese 2007) has highlighted the plurality of histories and memories of the effects of colonization and decolonization, both in France and in the countries of the Maghreb.[1] Representations of and by Arab-Muslim Maghrebis in French cinema have challenged lingering imperial notions of a homogenous, monocultural 'Frenchness'. Yet the limitations of cinematic constructions of Maghrebi identities have as yet been less subject to scrutiny, even though they too need to be understood in relation to the region's multiple, intersecting, often conflictual histories and cultures, which have been erased or marginalized by Arab-Muslim reactions to the former colonial relationship in the post-independence construction of national identity. This chapter draws on a cluster of feature films produced in the mid- to late 2000s in France, Morocco, Tunisia and Algeria, which focus in particular on representations of the historically entwined relationship between francophone Jewish and Arab-Muslim Maghrebi communities, and to varying degrees evoke what Lincoln Shlensky refers to as 'the still unspoken history of shattered relationships between Jews and Muslims' in the colonial context (Shlensky 2009: 102). It argues that their emergence at this particular juncture also needs to be addressed in relation to the wider transnational context, more specifically Zionism and the escalating Israeli–Palestinian conflict on the one hand, and 9/11 and increasing Islamophobia on the other.[2]

The term 'Maghrebi' has often been used as a shorthand descriptor for the ethnic origins and cultural identity of Arab-Muslims from the former French colonies of Algeria, Morocco and Tunisia. Yet the area has historically been home not only to the Berbers, the recognition of whom is a relatively recent phenomenon, but also to pre-Arab Jewish communities, and to Christians and Jews of later European – primarily Mediterranean – origin. Indeed, as Winifred Woodhull notes, many francophone writers have testified to its 'long history of linguistic, religious, cultural and political diversity and to the futility – as well as the depravity – of attempting to eradicate it' (Woodhull 2003: 215). In terms of the Sephardic (Maghrebi) Jewish population, however, turbulent periods of anti-Semitism, provoked for example by the creation of Israel (1948), national independence (1956 for Tunisia and Morocco, 1962 for Algeria), the post-independence period of political nationalism and Arabization, and the Six-Day War (1967), drove many to migrate to France (as well as Israel and elsewhere). Their migration has arguably been a source of suffering and loss on both sides of the Mediterranean since, as Ella Shohat (2006: 224) suggests, Sephardic Jews may have more in common culturally with Arabs than with European Jews. The nostalgia of diasporic Sephardic Jews for their lost homeland, like the '*nostalgérie*' of *pieds-noirs* more generally, has been well documented (Roze 1995: 348–75).

In cinema, however, representations of Sephardic Jews and the causes and effects of their exodus from the Maghreb have to date been few and far between. In post-independence Maghrebi cinema(s), the representation of Jews as part of the region's cultural mosaic has been a taboo topic, evident in the controversy provoked by Nouri Bouzid's evocation of an Arab Muslim youth's relationship with his Jewish Tunisian mentor, a master carpenter and musician, in *L'Homme de cendres/Rih essed/Man of Ashes* (1986), and further challenged in Férid Boughedir's multi-ethnic comedy *Un été à La Goulette/Halk-el-wad/A Summer in La Goulette* (1995).[3] In French cinema, in contrast, Sephardic Jews have figured prominently in crime dramas such as *Le Grand pardon/Grand Pardon* (Arcady 1982), in comedies such as *La Vérité si je mens!/Would I Lie to You?* (Gilou 1997) that rely on larger-than-life stereotypes rather than reflecting on their characters' troubled Maghrebi past,[4] and in sentimental, semi-autobiographical films evoking pre-exilic Jewish *pied-noir* childhoods in Algeria, such as Alexandre Arcady's *Le Coup de sirocco* (1979) and Roger Hanin's *Soleil* (1997).[5] In general, however, the work of Sephardic Jewish actors and film-makers in France, many of whom are extremely well known,[6] has not been analyzed for its ethnic specificity, presumably because their integration into French culture has been assumed to be less problematic than that of Arab-Muslim migrants.

In metropolitan France in the 2000s, the increase in anti-Semitism following the initiation of the second Palestinian Intifada in the autumn of 2000, together with the increasing demonization of Islam and fear of Arab terrorism following 9/11 and 'the War on Terror', has resulted in a destabilization of both Jewish and Arab-Muslim diasporic communities, increased inter-community hostility and the development of a new sense of diasporic nationalism.[7] As Esther Benbassa points out:

> Maghrebian Jews, who live close to Arabs, are … getting themselves caught up in [a] spiral of resentment not only because of the trauma of their departure from North Africa, but also because they project their own past experience, that they interpret as 'expulsion', on what is happening in the Middle East … imagining that their co-religionists in Israel are threatened by a similar fate. (Benbassa 2007: 190)

The emergence of French, Franco-Maghrebi and Maghrebi films that draw on the conflictual present and the intersecting histories and memories of Jews and Arabs from the Maghreb thus arguably signals a move to confront not only the damage done by French colonialism and decolonization, but also the antagonism, distrust, fear and distress that increasingly divide Arabs and pro-Zionist Jews over the fate of Palestine.

The films I have identified consist of two films that directly address Jewish–Arab relations in contemporary metropolitan France, *La Petite Jérusalem/Little Jerusalem* (Albou 2005) and *Dans la vie/Two Ladies* (Faucon 2008) and six films that indirectly address present-day concerns through their reconstruction of past Jewish–Arab relations in Morocco, Tunisia and Algeria. *Marock* (Marrackchi 2006) is set in Casablanca in 1997; the others are located during more obviously traumatic moments in Maghrebi history – the German Occupation of Tunis in *Le Chant des mariées/The Wedding Song* (Albou 2008) and the French TV film *Villa Jasmin* (Boughedir 2008), the end of the Algerian war of independence in *Cartouches gauloises/Summer of '62* (Charef 2007) and the Jews' exodus from post-independence Morocco in *Où vas-tu, Moshé?/Finemachiyamoché/Where are You Going Moshé?* (Benjelloun 2007) and *Adieu, mères/Goodbye Mothers* (Ismail 2008). The male film-makers in question – Férid Boughedir (born 1944 in Tunisia), Hassan Benjelloun (born 1950 in Morocco), Mohamed Ismail (born 1951 in Morocco), France-based Medhi Charef (born 1954 in Algeria) and even France-based Philippe Faucon (born 1958 in Morocco, the son of an Algerian *pied-noir* mother and a French soldier, and himself married to an Arab-Muslim) – belong to the generation of children who witnessed the trauma and loss brought about by the breakdown in inter-faith relations following the struggle for independence. The two women film-makers – Karin Albou (born 1975 in France, the daughter of an Algerian Jewish *pied-noir* father and a French mother, and married to an Israeli) and France-based Leila Marrackchi (born 1975 in Morocco, and married to film-maker Alexandre Aja, son of Algerian *pied-noir* film-maker Alexandre Arcady) – belong to a later generation, which is committed to 'performing the transnational as a cinematic space of exchange and collaboration' (Portuges 2009: 63). In each case, then, their narratives of Jewish-Arab friends, lovers and communities whose relationships are at risk from repressive social and political discourses and practices are signs of their directors' personal investment.

By bringing together French films, Franco-Maghrebi co-productions and Maghrebi films, and locating them within both a national and a more global context (events in the Middle East and the effects of 9/11), I aim to chart a course that 'carries reflection beyond the quest for national identity' (Woodhull 2003: 213), recognizes the heterogeneity of both French and Maghrebi cultures, and does not confine consideration of the productions of minority film-makers to a centre–periphery model, but rather takes account of the impact of transnational flows on the production, distribution and reception of film. My analysis draws on Mary Louise Pratt's notion of the 'contact zone' as a space where 'cultures meet, clash, and grapple with each other, often in contexts of highly asymmetrical relations of power' (Pratt 1991: 34) and from Paul Gilroy's more positive notion of the achievability of a contemporary, convivial postcolonial 'multiculture' (Gilroy 2004: 5), in order to assess how successfully the co-presence of Sephardic Jews and Arab-Muslims in these films addresses the injustices, silences and traumas of the past, and leads to the possibility of understanding, respect and cooperation in the present.

Confronting the present

In response to the hardening of community partisanship following perceived Israeli aggression in the Middle East and increasing anti-Semitism attributed to the Arab-Muslim population, a number of metropolitan French films have offered alternative, more positive models of relationships between Jews and Arabs, notably François Dupeyron's *Monsieur Ibrahim et les fleurs du Coran/Monsieur Ibrahim* (2003) and Roschdy Zem's *Mauvaise foi/Bad Faith* (2006).[8] However, only *La Petite Jérusalem* (2005) and *Dans la vie* (2008) highlight relations between Jews and Arabs of Maghrebi origin. Significantly, both are located in areas of high levels of immigration, where Jewish and Arab-Muslim populations often live in close proximity, as in the former colonies of the Maghreb – *La Petite Jérusalem* in Sarcelles, a 'new town' north of Paris; *Dans la vie* in Toulon, a Mediterranean port city run by the Front National between 1995 and 2001. Nevertheless, they propose very different perspectives on the possibility of achieving a convivial postcolonial multiculture.

La Petite Jérusalem centres on two sisters of Tunisian Jewish heritage born in Djerba, Laura and Mathilde, who live with their widowed mother and Mathilde's orthodox Jewish family in a flat in 'Little Jerusalem', the constraints of which are evident in the film's dark palette of colours and light-blocking images of walls and windows. Punctuated with orthodox Jewish rituals, the film constructs a self-contained diasporic Jewish community that is given a particular Maghrebi inflection by the mother's superstitious practices (which contrast with the religious correctness of her son-in-law, Ariel), and her transmission of occasional memories of pre-exilic life in Tunisia, figured nostalgically in family photographs. However, the meagre details of her personal history, including her account of successfully hiding a valuable ring on leaving the country, are not embedded in a wider socio-political context that might shed light on Jewish migration from Tunisia.

The film introduces the theme of contemporary Jewish–Arab relationships first through Laura's attraction to an illegal Arab-Muslim immigrant, then through acts of anti-Semitic violence imputed to local *banlieue* youths. Laura, a philosophy student who seeks to escape the strictures of Jewish life through devotion to the rationalism of Immanuel Kant, finds herself attracted to Djamel, a fellow cleaner at the local primary school, whose body is scarred by his suffering as a journalist during the civil war in Algeria. However, their brief, passionate affair demonstrates the ongoing unacceptability of serious inter-faith relationships in both Jewish and Arab-Muslim communities through the negative reactions of Ariel and of Djamel's traditional diasporic Arab-Muslim family, whose judgement Djamel unwillingly accepts, causing Laura to attempt suicide. Ariel's defensive, inward-looking attitude is explained to some extent by scenes evoking the torching of the local synagogue and the mugging he suffers during an informal football match, events that finally lead him to decide to emigrate with his family to Israel.[9] The move reflects the panic felt in Jewish milieux in contemporary France, fed by 'the attitude and discourse of community leaders and the Jewish press, the interventionism of Israel in favour of emigration, and the alarmism of some intellectuals' (Benbassa 2007: 192), and is not necessarily constructed here as a positive choice (the toy

Dans la vie – Esther and Halima.

Israeli house constructed by Mathilde's children gets destroyed in play). Laura's decision to make a life for herself in the indifferent, multicultural spaces of Paris, enabled by the gift of her mother's ring, is equally problematic: in the film's final shot, she is standing alone on a travelator in the metro, the fate of her former lover unknown. Rather than foregrounding a shared Maghrebi heritage or suggesting that love can overcome difference within a tolerant multicultural France, then, *La Petite Jérusalem* emphasizes the suffering and isolation produced by events in the Maghrebi past (Jewish migration from Tunisia, Arab-Muslim flight from the Algerian civil war) as well as by the contemporary polarization of Jewish and Arab-Muslim diasporic Maghrebi communities.

In contrast, *Dans la vie*, a low-budget film co-authored by Faucon's producer wife, Yasmina Nini-Faucon, envisions the possibility of overcoming both anti-Arab and anti-Semitic discourses through its representation of the developing friendship between Jewish Esther, a well-to-do, elderly, irascible, wheelchair-bound *pied-noir* widow, and Arab-Muslim Halima, a similarly-aged retired cleaner and housewife.

The film begins by focusing on the contemporary climate of race hatred in France, as Halima's daughter, Selima, a visiting nurse, faces the anti-Arab racism of a Franco-French client who declares, 'I don't like people like you'. Shortly afterwards, Esther listens to a friend telling her how the Israeli–Palestinian conflict is causing Jewish children to suffer from anti-Semitism at school. Indeed, the film is set, significantly, in the summer of 2006, at the height of the tensions provoked by Israeli attacks on Hezbollah in the Lebanon (following the capture of two Israeli soldiers), the dramatic consequences of which are periodically relayed on Halima's television. However, when Selima first visits Esther's home, she is well received by Esther's successful doctor son, Elie (played by Faucon himself), and Esther is pleased to discover that Selima, too, is of Algerian origin. Selima, a modern young woman secretly living with a black boyfriend, subsequently suggests that her mother might replace the paid companion Esther summarily dismisses. Despite differences of class, wealth, religion and physical health, the two elderly women – both of whom were born in or around Oran (Algeria) – then proceed to negotiate a relationship based on shared experiences of exile and increasing trust and pleasure in each other's company, to the point where they can describe themselves as 'sisters'.

Their sisterhood, however, is not achieved without moments of hurt and disagreement. For if Esther has to learn that she cannot always treat others as servants (especially when she accepts Halima's invitation to stay with her during her son's absence rather than go into a home), Halima has to overcome her own suspicion of Jews, expressed not only in her distrust of Selima's new employer but also in an anti-Israeli outburst, 'I don't like those people', which echoes the anti-Arab racism expressed in the opening scene. Persuaded that Elie has defended her daughter from racism, however, she does her best to make Esther comfortable, learning to cook kosher food and taking her to the beach; and when Esther is staying with her, she sensitively switches off the TV news, organizes a trip to the *hammam*, and generally renews Esther's zest for life. Despite the hostility of a neighbour and some of her own (grown-up) children because she is working for a Jewish employer, Halima, a devout Muslim, maintains her ground and obtains reassurances from the local *imam* that she can legitimately use her earnings to pay for her pilgrimage to Mecca with her husband; and Esther, eventually accepted by Halima's extended community, chooses to stay with Halima until her departure (and even read the Qur'an). In the final scene, the film cross-cuts between the two women as they sadly depart in different directions, inviting the spectator to share the depth of their mutual, intercultural friendship, while acknowledging its provisional, even utopian nature.

The intermingling of diasporic Jewish and Arab cultures, relations and identities in the 'contact zones' envisioned by these two films is clearly addressed in very different ways. In the chilly climate of *La Petite Jérusalem*, Laura and Djamel negotiate their illicit relationship in the dark, constricted space of the school locker room, whereas in the sun-drenched Mediterranean climate of *Dans la vie*, Esther and Halima consolidate their (admittedly potentially less threatening) friendship in a trip to a beach, a public multicultural space where a veiled Arab-Muslim woman carries out her prayers and which, like the *hammam*, provides a sense memory of the two women's Algerian past. In *La Petite Jérusalem*, Laura's mother's family photographs and nostalgic memories cannot be shared between Laura and Djamel, since the lovers not only belong to different waves of immigration, but come from countries with different colonial and postcolonial histories, whereas in *Dans la vie* traces of the past are shared by the Jewish and Arab-Muslim protagonists. Finally, whereas in *La Petite Jérusalem* there is no attempt to confront anti-Semitic hostilities, in *Dans la vie* prejudices are confounded as knowledge of the other's cultural differences leads to mutual tolerance and acceptance. Thus, while attempts at Jewish–Arab rapprochement in *La Petite Jérusalem* are doomed to clandestinity and heartbreak, communitarian difference in *Dans la vie* gives way to a warm-hearted vision of convivial coexistence. It may be temporary, and it does not extend to the acceptance of cross-cultural sexual relationships (Esther regrets that Selima could never be her daughter-in-law), but the film's focus on the respectful sharing of everyday life in the present offers a modicum of hope for a multicultural future.

Reconstructing the past

Though contemporary Jewish–Arab relations are still a taboo topic in Maghrebi cinema,[10] a number of recent Franco-Maghrebi co-productions and Maghrebi films make up for the absence of precise historical references in *La Petite Jérusalem* and *Dans la vie* by evoking the existence of interfaith communities in the Maghreb and the traumatic circumstances leading to the Jews' departure. However, their focus on different national histories points to the different history and status of Jews in Algeria, Tunisia and Morocco (see Debrauwere-Miller 2009). In Algeria, the Crémieux decree of 24 October 1870 gave Jews French citizenship and thereby symbolic 'whiteness'. Consequently, despite the repeal of the decree under the Vichy regime (which enabled a rapprochement with Arab-Muslims to take place), Algerian Jews – along with other *pieds-noirs* – chose overwhelmingly to be 'repatriated' to France at independence

(1962). In Tunisia and Morocco, in contrast, as Tunisian or Moroccan subjects Jews were arguably colonized both by the Arabs then by the French, leading Jewish Tunisian writer and philosopher Albert Memmi to describe Zionism as 'a national liberation movement' for Jews (Memmi 1974: 149). The 'distrust, fear and suffering' experienced by Jews within these different colonial and postcolonial contexts needs to be taken into account in any reconstruction of inter-community relations – even if, as Algerian film-maker Jean-Pierre Lledo suggests, these also involved 'mutual attraction, respect, recognition and happy memories' (Lledo 2009).

The potential ambivalence of filmic reconstructions of the past is evident in Boughedir's earlier *Un été à La Goulette* (1995), one of the first films to express anxiety about the marginalization or exclusion of other cultures as an effect of the post-independence drive towards Arab-Muslim nationalism.[11] Set near Tunis in the summer of 1966, it evokes the apparently unproblematic, harmonious, multilingual, transcultural coexistence enjoyed by a Jew, a Muslim and a (Sicilian) Catholic, which is comically threatened by their teenage daughters' vow to lose their virginity to a youth from a different religious background. The film ends with the men's reconciliation when it transpires that 'nothing' has actually happened, but the end credits announce the imminence of the Israeli defeat of the Arabs in 1967.[12] The film's imagined, sensual, nostalgic vision of a convivial multicultural community is thus destabilized not by a consideration of the effects of some of the more bitter realities of interfaith antagonisms generated during the colonial and postcolonial era (and earlier), but rather by a naturalization of the older generation's mutually intransigent fear and distrust of interfaith sexual relationships, and the polarization of Jewish-Arab relations retrospectively accredited to (or displaced on to) the Israeli–Palestinian conflict.

Like *Un été à La Goulette*, Leila Marrackchi's first feature film, *Marock* (2006), also represents Jewish–Arab inter-community relationships without addressing unspoken traumas relating to the specific histories of Jewish–Arab relations in the Maghreb. Turned down for funding in Morocco, the film is an apparently innocuous teen romance, based on Marrackchi's memories of growing up in Casablanca. However, its depiction of Moroccan teenagers' embrace of westernisation, its irreverent attitudes towards religion and the family, and above all its questioning of the taboo nature of a serious Jewish–Arab love affair, provoked a scandal at the 2003 Tangiers film festival (see Boukhari n.d.).[13] Set during Ramadan, the year the protagonists are preparing for the baccalaureate, *Marock* reconstructs the hedonistic lifestyle of the children of Casablanca's wealthy Jewish and Arab communities who, largely insulated from social pressures by their class and affluence, share a penchant for parties, fast cars, western fashions, drink, drugs, sex and rock'n'roll (an image of tolerance and inter-faith conviviality that may have been counter-productive for orthodox Moroccan audiences). It centres on Arab-Muslim Rita and the gradual development of her illicit Romeo and Juliet-style romance with Jewish Youri. But it eventually kills off the dangerous Jewish youth (Youri has a fatal car accident while drinking and driving his parents' BMW), rather than depicting the relationship as a catalyst for social change (though, surprisingly, Rita's brother Mao – who returns from London an orthodox Muslim – sympathizes with his sister's loss).

The romance nevertheless exposes the still deeply entrenched prejudices of Jews and Arabs towards inter-faith relationships, and also offers a critique of the state, whose police are employed to enforce rigid patriarchal codes of sexual behaviour, and of the hypocrisy of the bourgeois Arab-Muslim family, notably through the figure of Rita's authoritarian father, who protected Mao from the law after he killed a child in a car accident, but accepts Mao's hard-line attitude towards Rita's freedom. Furthermore, if the film fails to address events in Morocco's past that gave rise to Jewish emigration, it acknowledges the influence of events in the Middle East on contemporary Jewish aspirations to harmonious coexistence. Thus, whereas the Arab-Muslim families send their children abroad for their cosmopolitan education (after Youri's funeral, Rita leaves for Paris), Youri's Jewish parents' planned migration to the United States is explicitly ascribed to fears raised by the Gulf War (1990–91).[14]

The remaining films, three of which are considered here, address the troubled past of Jewish–Arab relationships at key moments in Maghrebi history, focusing on inter-community friendships rather than doomed love affairs. Karin Albou's second feature, *Le Chant des mariées* (2008), a Franco-Tunisian co-production, is set at the time of the German Occupation of Tunisia, from November 1942 to May 1943. It centres on the dramatic upheavals in the sensual, intimate friendship between two childhood friends who dream of marriage, Jewish Myriam and Arab-Muslim Nour, whose families share the same courtyard in Tunis. The film's initial construction of inter-community neighbourliness at the celebration of Nour's engagement to her cousin Khaled is progressively destabilized by the violence of the German Occupation and its vicious anti-Semitic propaganda, which even affects the relations between the women in the *hammam*, normally a site of social gathering and ritual cleansing. As anti-Semitic regulations cause Myriam to be expelled from school and her widowed mother (played by Albou herself) to lose her work, Nour finds herself torn between her friendship with Myriam and the anti-Semitic attitudes of Khaled, who starts working for the Nazis to earn enough money to marry her and is then swayed by their promises of Arab post-war independence. Myriam is forced to marry Raoul, a wealthy, older Jewish doctor who has returned from Occupied Paris, because her mother cannot pay the heavy fine imposed on Jews; however, Raoul nobly chooses to prove his love for his reluctant wife by accepting deportation to a labour camp instead of collaborating with the Nazis. Nour first defends Khaled, but finally elects to protect her friend: putting aside their differences, she tells the Nazi soldiers raiding the *hammam* that Myriam is her sister; and on her wedding night, having discovered that the Qur'an sanctions believers of other faiths, she openly defies her husband's injunction not to see Myriam again. The film ends with the two young women, married but alone, sheltering in each other's arms as the Allies bomb Tunis, a sign of the end of the Occupation and the renewed possibility of inter-cultural friendship.

Le Chant des mariées relocates the theme of a convivial, multicultural past to the pre-Occupation period, and then charts its demise, attributing the rise of anti-Semitism largely to the Nazis, aided and abetted by their French collaborators, and thus to an extent deproblematizing and containing the issue of indigenous Arab-Muslim anti-Semitism. Nevertheless, the film does not shy away from documenting the alacrity with which

Arabs appropriated anti-Semitic attitudes and the consequent breakdown of Jewish–Arab community relations. It thus demonstrates how the fate of Jews is inseparable from events in the wider world, and presages the future exclusion of Jews from an Arab-Muslim sense of Maghrebi (Tunisian) national identity.[15]

The only film in this corpus to be set and shot in Algeria,[16] no doubt in part because of Algeria's 'parlous' film production situation following a decade of civil war (Armes 2006: 40) is Mehdi Charef's French-funded *Cartouches gauloises* (2007), based on the director's memories of his Algerian childhood. Set in the period leading to the declaration of Algerian independence, it centres on Momo, an enterprising, streetwise eleven-year-old Arab boy who is also the son of an Algerian freedom-fighter. The film initially invokes the image of a harmonious, multi-ethnic, pre-independence Algeria through Momo's friendship with a group of boys of various (French, Italian, Jewish) origins, and his friendly relations with an elderly Jewish couple. However, as independence approaches, Momo witnesses at first hand the polarization of the various populations, whom he has got to know through his sales of the local paper, and the horrific acts of violence perpetrated both by the French army and the Algerian *fellaghas*. The film accords only a marginal role to the Jewish characters, who appear to be assimilated with other French citizens. Nevertheless, it underlines the difficulties of the Jews' decision to opt for exile in France (the Jewish couple's refusal to move means they are separated from their family) when Momo and his remaining friends react to the sudden, traumatic departure of David's family with the comment that the (metropolitan) French do not like 'les Youds'. Thus, although the struggle for independence and its tragic impact on intra- and inter-community relations is figured most intensely through Momo's friendship with non-Jewish *pied-noir* Nico, the film's evocation of the plight of other communities, even as it celebrates the achievement of independence, implicitly questions whether the hurried departure of Jews, Christians and *harkis* was to the detriment of Algeria's future.

Cartouches gauloises touches on the problematic position of the Jews as French citizens in relation to Algerian national independence, but obviates any reference to indigenous anti-Semitism. In contrast *Adieu, mères* (2008) – the only independent Maghrebi production in this corpus; *Où vas-tu Moshé?* is a Moroccan-Canadian co-production[17] – bravely dramatizes the rise in anti-Semitism in post-independence Morocco. Its period reconstruction of Casablanca in 1960 reflects both on Jewish fears of the death of King Mohammed V (1961), who was considered their protector, and on the effects of the heavy propaganda produced by Israeli Zionist activists, which led large numbers of Jewish Moroccans to leave their homeland clandestinely and seek a life elsewhere, mainly in Israel, but also in France, the United States and Canada.[18]

Adieu, mères, like the other films set in the past, initially envisions the possibility of Jewish–Arab harmony, as in shots of an Arab baking for a Jewish neighbour on the Sabbath. It centres on the friendship between Jewish Henry and his childhood Arab-Muslim friend, Brahim, who together run a sawmill inherited from their fathers,[19] and between their wives, Ruth and Fatima, who work together for the same Jewish-run insurance company. The two couples treat their religious difference as a source of communication and enrichment, not as a barrier to friendship. However, when anti-Semitism leads first to the death of Ruth's mother, then to the sawmill's loss of business, Henry succumbs to the influence of Benchétrit, a ruthless Israeli recruiter. Entrusting his family and business to Brahim, he leaves for Israel on a crowded, illegal boat, which sinks with no survivors. When Ruth subsequently dies of cancer, childless Brahim and Fatima are left to bring up their friends' two children and, as a brief epilogue indicates, do so in respect of their Jewish heritage. Their openness, tolerance and loyalty contrasts with Benchétrit's pitiless treatment of a Jewish Moroccan girl, pregnant as a result of her love affair with an Arab-Muslim neighbour (which is also rendered impossible by the intransigent attitudes of both Jewish and Arab parents). The film thus invites the spectator to mourn the loss of convivial Jewish-Arab Maghrebi multiculture exemplified by Henry and Brahim's family friendship and read the film, as Ismail suggests, as 'a message of peace, showing that cohabitation between communities is possible, independently of the political tribulations which poison human relationships' (cited in Elvagabundo 2008).[20]

The three films set in the more distant past all take pains to establish an imagined contact zone in which cohabitation between Jewish and Arab-Muslim protagonists is deemed to have been possible, at least at the level of interpersonal friendship and intercommunity cooperation, if not in terms of inter-faith love affairs. In each case, however, that cohabitation is put at risk – if not irretrievably damaged – by the national and transnational context in which such cohabitation is embedded, be it the impact of the Vichy regime and the German Occupation of Tunis during World War II (a period also informed by the struggle for Tunisian independence), the struggle for Algerian independence from French colonial rule or the mood of post-independence Morocco, which lent itself to aggressive recruitment to Israel. While such 'political tribulations' may have awakened or exacerbated more atavistic fears of otherness among Jews and Arabs, however, the films' emphasis on the ability of individuals affected by them to sustain their inter-community friendships and/or mourn their loss leaves open the possibility of a renewal of convivial multiculture in the future.

The reconstructions of Jewish–Arab relations in the past, then – particularly those set in Tunisia and Morocco – not only contribute to the 'war of memories' by exposing a hidden history that has rarely been addressed in either French or Maghrebi cinema, but to a certain extent also fill out the gaps in the historical context that characterize the films set in the present or more recent past. They thereby enable spectators to appreciate the complexity of contemporary relations between Jews and Arab-Muslims of Maghrebi origin in terms of the long-term after-effects of French colonialism, Nazi (and Vichy France) anti-Semitism, the foundation of Israel and decolonization, as well as current events in the Middle East. At the same time, with the exception of *La Petite Jérusalem*, this group of films taken together offers images of harmonious cohabitation that, though they do not include intermarriage, may serve as points of reference for envisioning present and future community relations.

Notes

1. The 'war' intensified thanks to Article 4 of the law of 23 February 2005, which controversially required history syllabuses to recognize the positive role of the French presence in France's North African colonies (and was subsequently repealed). See Benbassa (2006).

2. See Shlensky (2009) for a study of francophone films that directly evoke the Israeli–Palestinian conflict.

3. The first independent film-maker in the Maghreb, Albert Samama Chikly (1872–1934), was a Tunisian Jew (see Armes 2006: 24–25).

4. A more recent example is *Coco* (2009) by Gad Elmaleh, who is of Jewish Moroccan descent.

5. Charlotte Silvera's *Louise l'insoumise* (1984), set in 1961 in the Parisian *banlieue*, features a young girl's rebellion against the expectations of her exilic orthodox Jewish Tunisian parents.

6. They include Richard Anconina, Alexandre Arcady, Richard Berry, Simone Bitton, Michel Boujenah, Patrick Bruel, Gad Elmaleh, Roger Hanin and Ariel Zeitoun.

7. France has the largest Muslim and Jewish communities in Europe: approximately five million Muslims and 600,000 Jews, 120,000 of whom migrated from Algeria and between 40,000 and 50,000 from Tunisia (Roze 1995: 356).

8. Earlier films include Mathieu Kassovitz's *La Haine/Hate* (1995) and Djamel Bensalah's *Le Ciel, les oiseaux, ... et ta mère/Homeboys on the Beach* (1999). See Loshitzky (2010: 94–116) for a brilliant analysis of *La Haine*'s construction of the 'post-Holocaust' Jew in the postcolonial French context.

9. According to Hoffman (2006), in the period 2000–05, a total of 11,148 Jews emigrated from France to Israel, including a 35-year high of 3300 immigrants in 2005.

10. But see Jean-Pierre Lledo's documentary *Algéries, histoires à ne pas dire/Algeria, Unspoken Stories* (2008) for a lucid, non-hostile discussion of the past by four contemporary non-Arab inhabitants of Algeria, including a Jew (who chooses not to be identified). Lledo (2009) suggests that the film's very existence shows that people are beginning to leave behind a racialized and/or religious vision of present-day relationships.

11. See Hafez (2006) for a discussion of the construction of national identity in post-independence Arab cinemas.

12. In the course of rioting following the Six-Day War, many Jews were killed and the Great Synagogue in Tunis was set on fire.

13. Nevertheless, the film was distributed in Morocco uncensored.

14. The controversy provoked by the film in Morocco highlights the cultural significance of Roschdy Zem's French comedy, *Mauvaise foi* (2006), in its foregrounding of a loving Arab-Muslim and Ashkenazi Jewish couple.

15. Boughedir's *Villa Jasmin* (2008), a TV adaptation of Serge Moati's eponymous semi-auto-biographical novel (2003), is a fictionalized homage to Moati's father, a Jewish Tunisian socialist (of Italian descent) active in the resistance and the struggle for Tunisian independence. Though centred on the relationship between the French-based son and his dead father, and their Jewish Tunisian identity, the film contrasts the anti-Semitism of the Nazi occupiers and their French collaborators with the close relationship enjoyed by the journalist father and his Arab newspaper colleague.

16. Roger Hanin's earlier *Soleil* evokes the Occupation of Algeria and the implementation of anti-Semitic regulations.

17 *Où vas-tu Moshé?* mixes documentary-style footage with light-hearted comedy to reconstruct the Jewish exodus from Morocco and demonstrate the desirability of peaceful cohabitation between Jews and Arabs (Barlet 2008). Set in 1963, it interweaves the story of Arab-Muslim bar owner Mustapha and Jewish watchmaker and musician Schlomo, whose resistance to inducements from his family, Israeli recruiters and local religious fundamentalists to leave the land he loves allows Mustapha to keep his bar open.

18 There were 230,000 Jews in Morocco at the time of the French protectorate, 164,000 in 1960 and 40,000 in 1975; there are only 4000 today (Tahiri 2007: 39).

19 Anti-Semitic measures taken in Morocco after independence included the requirement that Jews could only own businesses with an Arab partner and co-shareholder (Loshitzky 2010: 183).

20 'Pour moi, c'est un message de paix qui montre que la cohabitation entre communautés est possible, indépendamment des tribulations politiques qui n'ont fait qu'envenimer les rapports humains' (Ismail, n.d.).

Chapter 24

The Frenchness of French Cinema: The Language of National Identity, from the Regional to the Trans-national

Ginette Vincendeau

A n interesting paradox informs the 'concept' of national cinema, to quote the title of Andrew Higson's famous essay (Higson 1989: 36–46), or the 'very idea' of it, to borrow the title of Jinhee Choi's more recent piece (Choi 2006: 310–19). While the notion underlines the writing of film history from the very beginning, and informs our everyday filmgoing practice, in academia it is increasingly contested. In this chapter, I explore this paradox, and argue for the need not so much to rescue the notion as to recentre it.

There are good reasons why 'national cinema' might seem a quaintly retrograde notion. The point at which it became part of the film studies agenda in the 1980s was also the moment when the nation itself became problematized under the twin pulls of localization and globalization. Scholars now privilege smaller units – the local community, the ethnic group, the city, the region – or larger ones – Europe, 'Asian' cinema, global cinema, and we have recently seen the rise of the term 'glocal' cinema, designating films that engage with the local while recognizing the impact of the global. In the process, the nation seems to become irrelevant. For instance, Elizabeth Ezra and Terry Rowden argue that: 'The impossibility of assigning a fixed national identity to much cinema reflects the dissolution of any stable connection between a film's place of production and/or setting and the nationality of its makers and performers' (Ezra and Rowden 2006: 1), while Alan Williams claims that: 'We should be wary of [concluding] that there is such a thing as "national cinema"' (Williams 2002: 5). While Jimmy Choi (2002) asks: 'Is National Cinema Mr. McGuffin?', Martine Danan (2002) speaks of 'prenational' and 'postnational' cinema, and still others of 'supra' national space (for instance Bergfelder 2006: 38). Conferences gather around themes of cinema across borders, cinema at the margins or relocating cinema, another indication that the agenda has shifted to trans-nationalism, emigration and exile, diasporas and, to borrow the title of another well-known book, 'accented cinema' (Naficy 2001). These developments mirror work on the nation in the social sciences where, according to socio-linguist Christof Demont-Heinrich, hegemonic discourse equates universal progress with the transcendance of the national (2005: 68).

Another set of issues relates to the film industry. Although 'national cinema' never unproblematically referred to the films made within the borders of a particular nation, the national identity of a film has, since the 1960s, become increasingly dislocated, in particular between finance and personnel on the one hand, and content, style and language on the other – or we could say between the production of a film and its 'image' or its 'aura'. Thus *La Marche de l'empereur/March of the Penguins* (Jacquet 2005), the most successful French film ever at the international box office, is one singularly devoid of any French aura. Made by a French team with French finance, it charts the life cycle of penguins in Antartica. Significantly, its export was greatly facilitated by the absence of dialogue, its voice-over commentary easily being translated. Conversely, in a notorious case in 2004, *Un long dimanche de fiancailles/A Very Long Engagement* (Jeunet 2004) was deemed by the French film industry to be 'American' because it was part financed by Warner Bros. It was thereby denied CNC subsidy, despite its French topic and source book set during and after World War I, French dialogue, French director and an almost entirely French cast headed by Audrey Tautou.

Are these aberrations or signs of wider trends? Certainly, for every *Marche de l'empereur* there are many *Coco avant Chanel/Coco Before Chanel* (Fontaine 2009) or *Paris* (Klapisch 2008), films that advertise their Frenchness from their very titles. In any case, despite the trend towards its erasure in academic discourse, the 'national' as a critical category has proved tenacious and is used on an everyday basis for the distribution, promotion and reviewing of films, mobilizing a set of well-worn national stereotypes. To quote a few examples: the London Film Festival every year programs a separate 'French revolutions' section; a 'guide to classic French cinema' website describes French movies as being 'known for their lack of action and abundance of intellectual meaning' (Britten n.d.); Philip French sees Olivier Assayas's *L'Heure d'été/Summer Hours* (2008) as a return to 'the subtle French film of bourgeois life' (French 2008a); Vincent Cassel is deemed to play gangster Mesrine with a 'brand of Gallic swagger' (Fauth 2009); and Stuart Jeffries describes *Le Fabuleux destin d'Amélie Poulain/Amelie* (2001) as follows: 'Here is not just a French film for French audiences but one that makes punters leave the cinema with a warm glow for all things French in general' (Jeffries 2001). The currency of such clichés is graphically illustrated by a 2008 British movie called *French Film*, in which former football icon Eric Cantona plays French film auteur Thierry Grimaldi, a character who illustrates several preconceptions about cinematic Frenchness: Cantona's Grimaldi, featured on the cover of a mock *Sight and Sound*, and interviewed on stage at BFI Southbank, is both romantic ('My films are all about love') and 'intellectual', meaning pretentious: one character says in outrage, 'What is it about French men that makes them think they're so profound?'

As illustrated by the examples above, cinematic Frenchness resides in a multitude of criteria: the auteur, the stars, iconic individuals (Chanel), the deployment of landscapes and in particular the city of Paris. More intangibly cinematic Frenchness is also located in links with history ('French revolutions') and in vague notions of French ways of life ('all things French') and of the French character ('Gallic swagger'), notably associated with romantic seduction and intellectualism. Although, as Mette Hjort reminds us, we must make a distinction between the banal deployment of these 'themes of nation' as background, and their overt thematization (Hjort 2000: 108), these parameters are repeatedly used by critics, producing a potent sense of familiarity. More concretely, cinematic Frenchness is also located in types and sources of narratives and modes of narration ('lack of action'), in formal patterns and in sets of genres or sub-genres ('films of bourgeois life'). Allen J. Scott nicely, if tautologically, sums this up when he says:

It might be said without undue circularity that the distinguishing characteristic of French film is its Frenchness. This trait is embodied in a hallmark set of resonances, attitudes and gestures rooted in the everyday fabric of French society and given distinctive form in a continually evolving tradition of cinematic art. (Scott 2000: 24)

Yet, interestingly, Scott leaves one key parameter out of his list of 'resonances, attitudes and gestures': language. In this he is not alone.

Surely the most overt marker of national identity since the coming of sound, when the industry tried to negotiate this new barrier to export through multi-language versions, dubbing and sub-titling, spoken language has nevertheless been startlingly absent from debates on national identity in the cinema – in stark contrast to work in the social sciences, where it is paramount. Routinely, conferences explicitly devoted to national cinemas contain no papers addressing language. A trawl through the literature on national cinemas shows scholars typically paying lip-service to the *importance* of language as a foundation of national identity and as an obstacle to export, before quickly moving on to something else. Hamid Naficy, for example, recognizes that 'language serves to shape not only individual identity but also regional and national identities prior to displacement' (Naficy 2001: 24), but the bulk of his analysis concerns narrative and film style. Books on French directors published by Manchester University Press, despite a policy of quoting all dialogues in French, generally pay no attention to spoken language, even in the case of directors notorious for their prominent and idiosyncratic use of it (such as Eric Rohmer).

It is not immaterial, with respect to the erasure of language, that most of the literature on national identity in the cinema emanates from English-language scholarship. Indeed, Andrew Higson's seminal (1989) article 'The Concept of National Cinema' itself remains silent on the topic. Like Scott, Higson enumerates the elements that make up the 'cultural identity of a particular national cinema', among them subject-matter, narrative discourse, source material, world-view, systems of representation, construction of space and modes of performance. Significantly, his list ends with 'types of visual pleasure, spectacle and display' and 'constructions of subjectivity (and particularly the degree to which they engage in the construction of fantasy and the regulation of audience knowledge)' (1989: 42), both emphasizing the visual over the oral, and leaving out what is surely a key constituent of audiences' construction of both fantasy and knowledge: language. But then, Higson's key exhibit is British cinema and his point of reference Hollywood, leading to this linguistic blindspot, compounded by subsequent contributors to the debate such as Scott or Choi, as discussed above.

If mainstream studies of national cinemas have more or less ignored language, the few investigations of language in/and film that exist have taken different paths. One is the 'colonial studies' model, in which the work of Ella Shohat and Robert Stam remains seminal. In 'The Cinema After Babel: Language, Difference, Power', Shohat and Stam (2006) discuss issues of linguistic imperialism. Similarly, studies of language and/in 'minority' cinemas (such as Catalan, Basque or Welsh) tend to look at their 'colonization' by other, larger nations, while others examine the power hierarchies of different languages within India and Africa. Another scholarly area relates 'film language' to 'language', but this kind of study, stemming from semiotics as in the work of Christian Metz, is interested in universal structure, as in *la grande syntagmatique* (Metz 1974) rather than the particularities of languages or their relation to national identity. Two other kinds of scholarship are worth mentioning. One is the application of film to the study of languages, in which film is instrumentalized as a pedagogical aid (see, for instance, Conditto 2007). The other is that of remakes, often from the French to the American cinema, as in the work of Lucy Mazdon (2000), Carolyn A. Durham (1998), Raphaëlle Moine (2007) and Constantine Verevis (2006). But here language tends to be subsumed under cultural transfer. Finally, it is worth pointing out that the vast majority of studies of sound in the cinema address psychoanalytical or technical issues, and what could be called 'universal' sounds, especially ambient noise and music. In all this, the poor relation remains spoken language, one notable exception being Michel Chion's 2008 book *Le Complexe de Cyrano* (2008), a series of short pieces on dialogues in individual French films, but with a few general remarks on which I will draw in this article.

Thus, guided by the paradoxical disappearance of national identity from the scholarly agenda coupled with its stubborn resistance, and the strange occultation of one of its strongest markers, language, I wish to pursue my discussion of the Frenchness of French cinema through three case studies that will serve as pointers to ways in which 'national identity' is still a valid concept, and one in which language, in its socio-linguistic and performative dimension, plays a crucial part.

La Bête humaine (1938): What's in a song?

La Bête humaine/The Human Beast, directed in 1938 by Jean Renoir and starring Jean Gabin, Simone Simon and Renoir himself, might seem hardly worth discussing in terms of Frenchness, given its canonical foregrounding of three great French icons – the writer Emile Zola, the director Jean Renoir and the star Jean Gabin – and the abundant literature to which it has given rise. Widely acknowledged, too, is its status as an expression of the era's ideological climate, and in particular the end of the Popular Front. As a film that did well at the box-office, it fits Higson's criterion of an audience-led conception of national cinema, as opposed to reducing a 'national cinema to the terms of a quality art cinema' (Higson 1989: 37). One might thus say that, in terms of cultural projection, to use Jean-Michel Frodon's expression (Frodon 1998), *La Bête humaine* is almost excessively French.

More complex is the question of language. *La Bête humaine* is the story of Jacques Lantier (Gabin), a train driver with a heavy alcoholic inheritance that provokes murderous impulses in him that he cannot repress, leading him to kill his mistress Séverine and later commit suicide. In a sequence towards the end, Renoir cuts between a warm scene set in a railwaymen's ball and Séverine's apartment, where Lantier has just killed her. The scene takes place almost without dialogue, but over the oral space of a song, 'Le P'tit cœur de Ninon', which we see being

La Bête humaine – before Séverine's murder, the dance. In the background, the band who will accompany the crooner.

performed. The alternation between the two spaces creates binary oppositions, between the workers' solidarity and the loneliness of the killer, between working-class entertainment and the petit-bourgeois flat, between the space of vaudeville and the space of melodrama, between light and dark. Since I signalled the importance of language, it may seem odd to focus on an extract almost devoid of dialogue. Yet what little language there is signifies 'Frenchness', in a performative sense, in the contrast between the comic verbal swagger of Carette (who plays one of Lantier's workmates) and Gabin's silence. In a microcosm, the two actors epitomise the two tendencies highlighted by Chion as typical of French cinema – that is, an oscillation between extreme verbosity and extreme laconicity (Chion 2008: 7).

The song as a spectacle in itself, as well as part of the narrative, is typical of the popular entertainment culture of the time; it forms part of a French tradition of self-reflexive theatricality – what I call its 'art of spectacle' (Vincendeau 2004). This is not the *chanson réaliste* favoured by Poetic Realist films, nor the comic vaudeville of Fernandel films, but a romantic ballad written in 1900[1] and sung by crooner Marcel Veyran. Nevertheless, it is as 'French' as these more famous other types. The lyrics construct a world that comments on the action of the film, but is also strikingly at odds with it: 'Ninon'/Séverine makes men suffer – and we see both Lantier and her husband distraught because of her – yet *she* is the ultimate victim of men (killed by Lantier, beaten by her husband and abused by her godfather). The register of the lyrics is also significant, refined and almost precious, thus also confirming Chion's contention about the rarity of 'neutral' French in French film, leading to characters oscillating between colloquial and hyper-refined language. Finally, the *timbre* of the singer's voice further historicizes the song, which is unmistakably of the 1930s – in particular, the rolling of the consonant 'r' and the pronunciation of certain vowels. Thus Renoir's film is as much of its time, and as much a 'French' film on account of its insertion of this sentimental ballad as it is in its representation of railway workers.

L'Ennemi public N° 1 (1953): Regional to trans-national

My second case study is *L'Ennemi public N°1/Public Enemy Number One*, a 1953 comedy directed by Henri Verneuil as a vehicle for Fernandel. This film could hardly be further removed from *La Bête humaine*. Even those familiar with François Truffaut's polemic against French mainstream cinema (Truffaut 1954) are unlikely to know it, as 1950s comedy is below the radar of writing on the period, with a few exceptions, such as Richard Kuisel's piece on 'the Fernandel factor' (Kuisel 2000). Kuisel is interested in how indigenous comedies, many of which star Fernandel, helped French cinema maintain a viable market share in the face of Hollywood in the post-war period, rather than – as the prevailing view would have it – state subsidies or anti-American communist rhetoric. Although Kuisel's argument only confirms what had been evident to ordinary French viewers for decades, he has the merit of bringing it to international attention, and thus to highlight the bedrock of Frenchness for French cinema in the post-war period, namely genre and stardom.

My interest in Fernandel takes due note of his box-office power (many of his films of the decade were in the top 10), but here I want to look at the impact of his screen persona, both as a snapshot of the early 1950s and diachronically, in the way he illustrates – in particular *orally* – a fundamental shift in the place of regional identity within the cinematic construction of Frenchness. Fernandel started out as a regional star in the early 1930s, marked as being from the *midi* by his accent and professional origins on the popular stage in Marseille. He swiftly rose to national fame in comedies such as *Ignace* (Colombier 1937), in which he perfected the regressive *comique troupier*, an accident-prone, low-class soldier who nevertheless always ended up getting the better of his social and military superiors. However, his critical reputation, such as it is, has emphasized his roles in Marcel Pagnol films, including the melodrama *Angèle* (1934), in which he plays a simple farmhand, the satirical *Le Schpountz /Heartbeat* (1938), in which he is a local boy who becomes a film star, and *La Fille du puisatier/The Well-Digger's Daughter* (1940), in which he reprises the *Angèle* farmhand in a comic mode.

Fernandel's stardom in the 1930s was characterized by his ability to play on the double register of the (class-inflected) *national* through the *comique troupier* and the *regional* through the Pagnol corpus and his prominent accent (although he could modulate it – in the *comique troupier* films he has a 'country' accent with a rolled 'r' but no particular *midi* inflection). Thanks to Pagnol's films, his fame reached outside France; however, in the process his regional and class identity were erased and he became simply 'French'. An indication of this is a book of photographs published in America in 1950 as *The Frenchman*, in which his attributes are moulded into those of a 'typical' Frenchman (lubricity, frivolity, gastronomy).

For Richard Kuisel, the 'secret' of Fernandel's extraordinary success in the 1950s was his wholesale reproduction of his pre-war image. Yet, on the contrary, Fernandel's success resided in his ability to embody change in line with his audience. The erasure of the regional dimension in Fernandel's persona from the pre-war era to the post-war period was not only linked to his American exports; it was also happening both to the star's image in his French films and to the country at large. Throughout the 1950s, against the rural exodus from the French provinces to the capital, as well as the severing of cinematic links to indigenous stage music-hall, Fernandel's films took two routes, both of which had the effect of distancing him from his southern origins. The first trend was the recycling of his regional identity in an exaggeratedly folkoric or parodic form, in films like *Le Boulanger de Valorgue/The Wild Oat* (Verneuil 1953) and *Honoré de Marseille* (Régamey 1956). The other trend, on the contrary, released him from any regional attachment and cast him in locations removed from the *midi* – for instance, as an Italian priest in the *Don Camillo* series and as a French prisoner of war in Germany in *La Vache et le prisonnier/The Cow and I* (Verneuil 1958). This latter trend is particularly in evidence in *L'Ennemi public n° 1*, which is set and partly shot in New York. In it, Fernandel plays Joe Calvet, a Frenchman who has taken American nationality. Upon losing his job, he becomes confused with a gangster on the run, and is arrested and thrown into jail as 'Public enemy n° 1', later escaping and joining the gangsters led by gangster moll Lola (Zsa-Zsa Gabor).

L'Ennemi publique nº 1 – Fernandel in prison in the United States.

L'Ennemi public nº 1 functions as an extended joke on the discrepancy between Fernandel's French star identity and his character as an 'American'. The film opens with his voice-over extolling the virtues of America (*ze* biggest houses, *ze* biggest cars *in ze world*) over glamorous Manhattan cityscapes. The star's visual entrance is delayed, but his oral presence ensures instant recognition through his accent and the rhythm of his delivery, contrasted on the soundtrack with Nino Rota's pastiche jazz score. The joke continues when we see him, dressed as a cowboy, wreaking havoc at a modern home exhibition while 'demonstrating' the latest camping car technology.

Much literature has been devoted to the notion that the identity of 1950s French cinema must be defined *against* Hollywood, in the context of the fierce struggle between the two industries and cultures (this was the era of the Blum-Byrnes agreements and ferocious battles led by communist-backed unions). Yet *L'Ennemi public nº 1* shows the Franco-American dialogue as good-natured, confirming in reverse Vanessa Schwartz's thesis in *It's So French!* (Schwartz 2007) that, *contra* the prevailing view of a 'war' between (American) imperialism and (French) protectionism, the cultural exchange between the two nations was more equal. In the same way as *Gigi* (Minnelli 1958), *Funny Face* (Donen 1957) and *An American in Paris* (Minnelli 1951) celebrate French culture, *L'Ennemi public nº 1* pays tribute, in gentle parody mode, to American gangster films. The New York gangsters and police are inept, but no more than Parisian gangsters and police in countless other French films. The cartoon-like view of American culture that the film offers is reinforced by a series of self-reflexive images of Fernandel looking at newspaper pictures of himself as 'Public enemy nº 1' – as if to reinforce further his incongruity as an American gangster. Similar parodic French 'territorialization' of American culture could be seen at the time in the equally popular French thrillers featuring American actor Eddie Constantine (a big star in France, though not in the United States). In *L'Ennemi public nº 1*, Frenchness is thematized through the star's body and, crucially, the star's *voice*, against the visual spectacle of its opposite, Americanness.

At a time of great cultural levelling through rural exodus and mass education, the toning down of Fernandel's regionality takes place through vocabulary, illustrating the larger social process: no idiomatic Provençal expressions make their way into the dialogue, only a faint trace remains in his accent. *L'Ennemi public nº 1* is also typical of French cinema in displaying both the delight in the voice and the *generic* self-conscious foregrounding of spoken language – noted by Roland Barthes in the 1950s and more recently by Chion in *Le Complexe de Cyrano*. For instance, there is a scene in which a gangster, in the middle of the jail break, compliments Fernandel on his refined use of tenses. Like the song lyrics in *La Bête humaine*, language in *L'Ennemi public nº 1* is a key element of both the 'art of spectacle' and of the construction of national identity.

La Graine et le mulet: A new 'otherness'

My last example stays within the regional/national divide, but now the relationship between the two is affected by a different third term, ethnic otherness replacing America. *La Graine et le mulet/Couscous* (Kechiche 2007) is a particularly good example of the complex relation between social, cultural and *critical* constructions of cinematic 'Frenchness'. Being set in the south of France, it also allows connections to be made with the Southern culture evoked through Fernandel – and tests Chion's suggestion that beur language (slang of Arab origins) is subject to the same 'folklorisation' as the *midi* speech was.

La Graine et le mulet, directed by Abdellatif Kechiche, who was born in 1960 in Tunisia, explicitly addresses societal changes in the French population through its representation of an extended multi-ethnic family of North African origins living in the port of Sète on the Mediterranean coast. Kechiche's ethnic identity is more than a matter of biography. Henri Verneuil, the director or *L'Ennemi public n° 1* was an Armenian immigrant, born Achod Malakian in Turkey, who changed his name to Verneuil. Later in his career, he made two autobiographical films about his childhood in Marseille, *Mayrig* (1991) and *588 rue Paradis* (1992); however, for all intents and purposes his public identity was 'French', and professionally he was part of the mainstream. Kechiche, by contrast, made his dual identity explicit from the start, keeping his name (though Abdellatif is often shortened to Abdel) and starting his career as an actor in beur films in the 1980s. So far he has worked within low- or medium-budget auteur cinema. Like Fatih Akin, he received an award for his work towards 'European integration', and is thus representative of Thomas Elsaesser's concept of 'double occupancy', the notion that all Europeans in some way already have 'hyphenated' identities (Elsaesser 2005: 108).

In Anglo-American critical terms, Kechiche's cinema falls within Naficy's 'accented cinema' (Naficy 2001). More specifically, his work can be related to *cinéma beur* – generally acknowledged, in Carrie Tarr's words, as 'the work of directors of Maghrebi descent' that shows 'a concern with the place and identity of the marginal and excluded in France' (Tarr 2005: 3). *La Graine et le mulet* does allude to racism but, in the tradition of beur cinema, it does not use it as a structuring principle or a narrative theme, one aspect of its Frenchness. The main character, 50-year-old Slimane (Habib Boufares), is made redundant; as tourism replaces fishing in Sète, his shipbuilding job is axed. The film portrays his struggle to open a couscous restaurant in a reclaimed ship, with the help of Rym (Hafsia Herzi), the daughter of his lover Latifa. The film in fact goes out of its way to show him as a victim of advanced capitalism rather than of French racism, and religion is conspicuously absent. Nevertheless, the film's critical reception outside France has focused on issues of race and ethnicity; among reviewers, Philip French called it a 'fine film of exile' (French 2008b), while Jason Solomons stated that 'Kechiche's masterly work brought to the fore a cast of characters – mostly Arab in origin – ignored by French cinema for too long' (Solomons 2008). Scholarly articles likewise are addressing these issues in various ways (see Higbee 2009). This shift is also signalled by the film's UK release title, *Couscous*.

By contrast, French critics overwhelmingly approached *La Graine et le mulet* from the point of view of auteur cinema, particularly given the film's accent on personal expression and the *intimate realism* of the everyday. In a number of scenes, such as a long family lunch and the very long concluding sequence of the opening of the restaurant, semi-improvised dialogue, the use of non-professional actors, long takes and slightly wobbly close-ups are the hallmark of auteur cinema. French cinephile critics particularly praised the film's unbalanced narrative stucture, seeing the elongation of such scenes as a mark of independence of vision, and thus of authorship (among others, Delorme 2007). With an avalanche of prizes and accolades from *Cahiers du cinéma*, *Positif*, *Les Inrockuptibles* and *Télérama*, which made comparisons with Pialat, Sautet and Cassavetes and praised the *humanity* of the film, the French critical reception is striking for its lack of references to ethnicity and concentration on style. This is clearly something the director himself endorses. In interviews, allusions to his ethnic background tend to amount to a tribute to his late father (see, for example, Delorme and Frodon 2007; Domenach and Rouyer 2007), while on the DVD of the film, interviews with the two main actresses – both of whom are of North African descent – make no mention of ethnicity and instead praise Kechiche's authorial status.

In *La Graine et le mulet*, again, language is a key ingredient of the film's complex take on national identity. For instance, during the extended family lunch, language is dramatized in the 'theatrical' exchanges across the table and thematized in the way it echoes the ethnic diversity in the family: jokes about learning to speak Arabic and speaking it poorly are exchanged, and the group includes white ethnic French people and Russian immigrants. As in the rest of the film, linguistic interaction is consensual and, in this scene in particular, humorous. Later, though, language narrativizes class and ethnic differences more sharply. A brief scene near the beginning shows Slimane and Rym going to ask the bank for a loan to turn the disused boat into a restaurant.

The scene, which stages a meeting between Slimane, Rym and a banker, offers three geo-ethnic oral spaces: Slimane's North African accent and halting, laconic delivery echo the oppressed fate of his generation; he is played by a friend of Kechiche's father. The (white, female) banker's local accent sounds genuine (she is played by an amateur actress from the area); though she is friendly at fi rst, her curt delivery and command of the jargon (e.g. 'provisional budgets') translates her social control of the situation. An encounter between only these two could have led to a straightforward ethnic and social clash or even racist encounter, but the third party, Rym, defuses things by introducing another generation and culture. The young actress is from Marseille, but her accent signals more a *beur/banlieue* and generational identity than the *midi* region; it is ironic but telling in this context that the *Positif* reviewer *compliments* the film for its avoidance of *banlieue* slang (Masson 2007), while in *Cahiers du cinéma* Jean-Michel Frodon praises the film's accurate and varied use of language (Frodon 2007). At the same time, Rym's education and confidence make her the real interlocutor – at the beginning of the extract, she rapidly takes over and replaces Slimane's poorly phrased request (*'j'suis v'nu d'mander ... un prêt'*/'I've come for a loan') by a perfectly formulated 'mon beau-père souhaite ouvrir un restaurant sur un bateau qu'il vient d'acquérir'/'My step-father wishes to open a restaurant on a boat that he has just acquired' – thus illustrating once again the tendency of spoken French to jump from the very familiar/colloquial to learned language.

Interestingly, *La Graine et le mulet* ends on the two main characters' loss of language. To stop clients leaving on the opening night because the couscous is not ready, Rym stages an impromptu belly dance, with the camera lingering on her bare midriff. Meanwhile, Slimane tries to find his son and has his motorbike stolen. In running after the young thieves, he collapses. Rym's eloquence is now replaced by a mute display of folkloric Arabness (though with music), and Slimane is tragically silenced. Rym's belly dance offers a lush visual spectacle (albeit in a gendered way), but orally it betrays a pessimistic comment on the failure of Slimane's project and thus arguably of integration. In this way, it contradicts the rest of the film – just as, for Chion, characters in *L'Esquive* are fatalistically 'locked' inside language (despite the overt play on 'escaping' through another language, that of Marivaux) (Chion 2008: 167). Attention to language in *La Graine et le mulet* thus highlights the contradictions inherent in representating multi-ethnicity, for a director who also clearly positions himself within a different kind of Frenchness – that of auteur cinema. *La Graine et le mulet*, then, is multi-accented in its content but singularly French in its form.

Conclusion: The importance of speaking in tongues

In this chapter, I have been arguing for the recentring of the category 'national identity' in the cinema, against the prevaling presumption of the loss of its validity. This is not to deny the evident geopolitical drive towards globalization, nor the importance of hybridity and diversity. On the contrary, it is in the name of diversity that we must preserve the reality and the cultural identity of national cinemas. Equally, while not denying the importance of other markers of national identity – of Frenchness – I have concentrated on language because of its surprising absence, almost denial, from studies of French – as well as other – national cinemas. Historians of national identity differ in their views, but most agree with Anthony Giddens about the importance of language in the formation of nations (Giddens 2001: 443). Yet the importance France attaches to the French language is often seen as comically reactionary, particularly the *Académie française* and its struggle against *franglais*. Although historically the origins of the country are varied (the Franks were a Germanic tribe but the language was derived from Latin), the Republican faith in a unified language mirrors the French concept of citizenship, itself under fire, which explains why as recently as 2008 there were heated parliamentary debates about the recognition of regional languages as part of the French 'heritage'.

Studying spoken language in film is difficult. Exploring the nuances of a language and its enunciation – the register of the song lyrics in *La Bête humaine*, the 'grain' of Fernandel's voice, the clash of *midi* identities in the voices heard in *La Graine et le mulet* – requires linguistic proficiency, and may be seen as a barrier (*Le Complexe de Cyrano* could be 'untranslatable'). I suspect other reasons are at work that have to do on the one hand with English speakers' notorious ambivalence towards 'foreign' languages. On the other hand, on the French side, one could point to the taint of 'theatricality' that attaches to dialogues, inherited from the debates against 'filmed theatre' at the coming of sound and the New Wave-inspired horror of the polished dialogues of the Tradition of Quality (see Vincendeau 2004). It could also be argued that the study of voice, elocution, dialogue and accents is under-developed in any language, including English. This is true, but the issue takes on a more acute political urgency in the cinema when talking of non-English languages. Ignoring language in the formation and modulations of a national cinema is both paradoxical and perverse, as it undermines a key element of the diversity that is otherwise so valued.[2]

The lexical and socio-linguistic, class and regional modulations of dialogue, its enunciation and performance have a huge impact on the identity of a film, all the way from reception back to production. Language affects vividly the reception of all films in France, and whether one watches a foreign film in subtitled or dubbed form is a highly significant indicator of cultural capital, in the cinema and on television – a phenomenon that still remains to be explored. Language changes over time, contributing to our ability to 'date' a film. It has an impact on stardom and characters – for instance, Beur stars have replaced *midi* stars as the vectors of 'otherness', and new genres or sub-genres have appeared, such as the *banlieue* film, which are predicated on space, as the name indicates, yet whose 'aura' is language-based. Similarly, the evolution of French comedy could be charted in relation to changes in accents, both class-based (compare *Ignace* to *Les Visiteurs/The Visitors* [Poiré, 1993]) and region-based. The runaway success *Bienvenue chez les Ch'tis* (Boon 2008), for example, is revealing in this respect in relation to the evolution that started with the post-war Fernandel films. The film's narrative and humour are entirely based on caricatural regional difference (north vs south), and the film has widely been accused of reactionary nostalgia for a pre-immigration Franco-French idyll. Yet language and stardom tell a more complex, and more contemporary, story. The southern hero is incarnated by a beur star (Kad Merad) without a trace of a *midi* accent, while the film's main star, Dany Boon, from the north of France and speaking its local dialect, has a French mother and an Algerian father. Both stars, then, in their careers, their bodies and their voices, are a more reliable and more revealing indicator of contemporary multi-ethnic France than the comic fable they have concocted.

In French film production, language is also an irreducible category, as enshrined in CNC and César award rules, which specify that a film must be in French (though since 1989 there have been exceptions). Like the battles of the *Académie française*, this is often ridiculed as *passé* and protectionist. Here, however, I would agree with Demont-Heinrich that there is a danger in mistaking :

> the transcendence of the national and nation state for the apparent transcendence of hierarchy, power, inequality, and hegemony. The question is not simply one of what is being transcended from (the backwards nation state) but what is being transcended into (the modern global order). (Demont-Heinrich 2005)

For it is clear that what the category national cinema would be 'transcended into' ultimately looks and *sounds* uncannily like 'Hollywood' (whatever the global origins of its finance).

The 'accented' cinemas of Europe are one of its richest cultural manifestations, but they exist through the support of the industries and policies of the larger nation-states they inhabit, such as France, not through either their local communities or 'global' cinema. If we want proof *a contrario* of the importance of supporting language as a mark of national identity, we only need to look at the way in which this gets erased on the international stage, as betrayed by the insulting category in the Oscars of the 'Best Foreign Language Film'.

Notes

1. The lyrics are by Maurice Nouhaud, aka Georges Millandy; the music is by E. Becucci (from an Italian waltz, 'Tesoro mio').
2. There is evidence, though, of a welcome turn to the study of language in contemporary French film, particularly in terms of class and ethnic variations. At the time of writing, an issue of *Studies in French Cinema* includes two pieces on the subject (see Higbee 2009; Strand 2009).

Chapter 25

Four Decades of Teaching and Research in French Cinema

Phil Powrie

W ork on French cinema has developed rapidly in a relatively short space of time since the mid- to late 1970s, when teaching was confined to the occasional course unit in a handful of universities, and research was only starting to emerge from work aimed at cinephile rather than academic readerships. The aim of this chapter is to give a broad historical account of teaching and research in French cinema in France and Anglophone countries over the last 40 years, as an academic discipline rather than as a practice-based discipline.[1]

Teaching French cinema

Research in French cinema emerged from teaching that began at the end of the 1960s in France, and in the 1970s for Anglophone countries. Film studies emerged as a fledgling discipline in all the countries I am considering towards the end of the 1960s, largely as a result of the expansion of the university system and the interrogation of the traditional disciplines. Cinephiles began to integrate the study of cinema in programmes of literature or fine art, generally as optional units within a broader curriculum.[2]

In France, the first of these was the University of Vincennes, later transferred to Saint-Denis as Paris 8 (Marie 2006: 27), with many others following suit at the end of the 1960s; Paris 3, 7 and 8, for example, all started teaching some film in 1969, according to Marie. He points out that much of the teaching in France was done by hourly-paid staff, generally people involved in the cine-clubs or cinema critics. It was only when universities began to make professorial appointments in film studies that it became possible to develop programmes in this area; the study of French cinema naturally formed an important part of such programmes. The first of these was in Paris 3 (the Sorbonne nouvelle) in 1983, but it was often later – Metz, for example, started teaching film in 1976, establishing its department in 1996; the dates for Caen are 1981 and 1992 respectively.

A similar development occurred in Anglophone countries, with Iowa and Indiana in the United States being the first to teach film in the 1960s. Departments of film studies (or film studies combined with other disciplines such as television or theatre studies) were established early on in some of the universities opened during the 1960s in the United Kingdom (such as East Anglia, Kent and Warwick), where the British Film Institute (BFI) financed three-year posts on the condition that the universities concerned subsequently funded them on a permanent basis (Vincendeau 2000b: 12). Typically, film units were introduced before film programmes, and programmes were introduced well before the establishment of a department: in Exeter, for example, film teaching began in 1996, but the department of film studies was established by Susan Hayward in 2001; in Kingston, Keith Reader began teaching French cinema in 1975, a film programme was launched in 2001, and film was incorporated in a new School of Performance and Screen Studies, which was established in 2005. The relevant dates for the introduction of units followed by departments for a selection of other Anglophone universities are: Edinburgh 1982/1996, Georgia 1975/2003, Iowa 1970s/1998, King's College London 2000/2007, Otago mid-1990s/2000, Southampton 1986/2003, Stirling 1978/1983 and Warwick 1974/1980.

Many Anglophone universities do not have departments or schools of film studies and related disciplines, but rather research-oriented groupings such as centres or institutes to which the postgraduate and often the undergraduate study of film is attached. This is the case currently, for example, in Cardiff (Institute for the Study of European Visual Cultures), Leeds (Centre for World Cinemas) and Newcastle (Centre for Research in Film and Media), amongst others. But in other universities, cinema is taught without the support of a separate department or significant research-based unit. This is the case for a range of UK universities: Bristol Polytechnic, later to become the University of the West of England, where the teaching of film began in 1986; Manchester Metropolitan, where teaching began in 1997; Cambridge, where teaching also began in the mid-1990s; and Liverpool, whose European Film Studies programme was set up in 2000. It is also the case in some US universities, such as Rutgers and Washington, whose cinema programmes began in the mid-1980s. Whether there is a school/department, a research centre or institute, or a looser programme structure, the study of film is often spread over a number of different disciplines, typically Modern Languages and English/American studies, and in some cases the history of art (for example, Birkbeck College). Even in the case of a film department – for example in Exeter or King's College London – there is a small core of film studies staff complemented by colleagues in related departments.

If we now turn to curricula, French cinema is frequently taught as part of a broader film historical, film theoretical, film analytical or thematic unit, such as 'modern European film', 'film analysis', 'film theory', 'Hollywood-Europe', 'gender in film', 'adaptations' and 'cities and film'. Sometimes there is a closer focus on French cinema relative to Hollywood in the case of remakes (Southampton, Paris 10). Appendix 27.1 lists courses specifically on French cinema offered by a wide range of universities. The bulk of the units listed are generic 'histories' of the French cinema or broad introductions, where the films studied can be very variable. From my research into detailed course descriptions, where these have been available, it would appear that the most frequent areas of study are the 1930s Poetic Realist films (with a particular emphasis on Renoir) and The New Wave (with a particular emphasis on Godard), followed by literary adaptations, gender, the relationship with Hollywood cinema, and francophone film. Indeed, Otago, for example, has replaced a course titled 'Contemporary French Cinema' with 'The French New Wave', while Paris 10 has introduced a paper on Classical French cinema, which has rarely figured in its film curriculum hitherto. Both of these changes to the curriculum confirm the centrality of the 1930s and the New Wave, something that is echoed in thesis production, as we shall see below.

Before we consider the research landscape, it is worth pointing out that the teaching of French cinema in Anglophone countries is often limited by what is available in subtitled formats, as many units on French cinema are taught to non-French language specialists. Shifting technologies have also to some extent determined what academics decide to teach. French cinema in the 1970s was typically taught using 16mm or, less frequently because of the higher rental cost, 35mm film; this was followed in the 1980s by videotape (first Betamax and later VHS), whether sold as such or recorded off air, and more recently by DVD. In all cases, there have always been constraints: the vagaries of film distribution, which limit what is available for study; the technological supports during the era of the video-cassette, when the French used SECAM ('*système électronique couleur avec mémoire*') rather than the British PAL ('Phase Alternating Line'); and the lack of English subtitles for many French films, which limits their use in non-specialist language contexts.

Researching French cinema

At the beginning of the 1960s the poet-publisher Pierre Seghers established his '*Cinéma d'aujourd'hui*' series, which ran for over a decade, and included a large number of French directors, as well as a couple of actors and scriptwriters. The authors included film-makers (Henri Chapier, René Gilson and Henri Fescourt, amongst others) and journalists (for example, Robert Chazal, the editor of the popular magazine *Cinémonde* and film reviewer for *France-Soir*), as well as the more academically minded, such as Michel Estève, who was later to direct Lettres Modernes Minard's series 'Études cinématographiques', or Claude Beylie, who taught at Paris 1 and contributed regularly to *Cinéma* from 1957 to 1991, as well as the *Cahiers du cinéma* during the heyday of the New Wave (1958–63). The most striking aspect of the series (apart from the fact that all of the subjects, and all but one of the authors, are male) is the broad range of directors and stars. The series covered silent cinema right through to what were then the very recent directors of the New Wave, the latter also receiving considerable attention from French academic writers (Borde et al. 1962) as well as journalists (Labarthe 1960; Siclier 1961). In the United Kingdom and the United States, by contrast, interest during the 1960s was focused on the New Wave almost exclusively (Durgnat 1963; Armes 1966, 1968; French 1967; Graham 1968; Roud 1968; Wood and Walker 1970). These books, whether in France or elsewhere, were principally directed at an informed cinephile readership in the absence of well-established film programmes in universities.

Such programmes began in the early 1970s, with the rapid development of research as a natural consequence. For the convenience of analysis, we can distinguish four broad periods of research in French cinema, corresponding to each decade, starting in the 1970s. This is not as arbitrary as it might seem, as there are arguably defining moments over the last

40 years anchored to each decade: the first theses on French cinema in the 1970s by American and French academics; the emergence of film departments in the 1980s, coupled with a sudden increase of theses; a significant increase in major volumes linked to the centenary of the cinema in the 1990s; and finally, the consolidation of the discipline with increasing international collaboration, both conceptually and structurally, since 2000.

1970s

The year 1972 was a key one for academic research in French cinema studies. In that year, the first American and French PhD theses on French cinema were awarded: these were by Dudley Andrew on the film criticism of Bazin (Andrew 1972), and by Alain Virmaux on the Surrealist and *avant-garde* habit of writing film scripts for films that were never made, a thesis submitted to the French bastion of academic respectability, the Sorbonne (Virmaux 1972). That year also saw the publication of Paul Schrader's *Transcendental Style in Film*, originally his dissertation for the MA in Film Studies at the UCLA Film School, now published by that university's prestigious press (Schrader 1972), and there were major books on Jean-Luc Godard (Brown 1972) and François Truffaut (Crisp 1972). The New Wave remained the most popular academic focus in the 1970s, with James Monaco's influential study, published by one of the most respected academic presses, Oxford University Press (Monaco 1976), which he quickly followed with a study of one of the Left Bank New Wave directors, Alain Resnais (Monaco 1978). The BFI collaborated in the publication of a book on Truffaut (Allen 1974), although Godard was to receive more attention, with the award of Julia Lesage's PhD thesis from Indiana (Lesage 1976), followed by her publication of academic resources on Godard (Lesage 1979) and, in the United Kingdom, the BFI's publication on Godard (MacCabe et al 1980). In a similar vein to Schrader's work, Bruce Kawin published an auteurist study of Ingmar Bergman and Godard for another prestigious academic press, this time Princeton University Press (Kawin 1978).

The 1970s were not just focused on the New Wave, however. They also saw the establishment of Jean Renoir as an important figure in French cinema for Anglophone academics, with a number of influential studies (Durgnat 1974; Braudy 1977; Faulkner 1979; Sesonske 1980). At the end of the 1970s, a United States-based series started, similar to Seghers' '*Cinéma d'aujourd'hui*' collection. Three of the first volumes of Twayne's 'theatrical arts' series were on New Wave directors (Insdorf 1978; Kreidl 1978, 1980), but it also included a range of other French directors (Higginbotham 1979; McGerr 1980; Knapp 1981). The double-headed focus on the 1930s and the New Wave is a constant in the following decades. The PhDs completed in the 1970s range beyond this, however, reflecting a wider range of interests. Of the nine French theses and the sixteen US theses, there are two on Godard and one on Truffaut (all from the United States), and four on aspects of 1930s cinema. But there are also two on Robert Bresson (both from the United States), and several on very different aspects of French cinema from American scholars who, with Dudley Andrew, were later to have considerable influence in film studies more generally: David Bordwell on Impressionist cinema (Bordwell 1974); Alan Williams on Max Ophüls (Williams 1977); and Claudia Gorbman on music and French cinema (Gorbman 1978). A major French scholar, Jean-Pierre Bertin-Maghit, was awarded his thesis on the cinema of the Occupation (Bertin-Maghit 1978, published 1980).

1980s

The number of theses awarded in the 1980s more than tripled to 80, which is a good reason for seeing the 1980s as a distinct period in the evolution of French cinema studies (see Appendix 25.2). About half of them were awarded by French universities, 28 of them by Parisian universities. While there was the usual emphasis on the New Wave, with a dozen or so theses devoted to New Wave directors and six on 1930s cinema, there were three significant new emphases: francophone cinema (six theses, four of them French-based); theory, with eight theses, all United States-based, mainly on André Bazin, but also on Christian Metz and Jacques Lacan; and an equally United States-dominated emphasis on women directors, with six theses including work on Germaine Dulac, Agnès Varda and Chantal Akerman.

The United States clearly had a head start in Anglophone French cinema studies, as only three theses were awarded in the United Kingdom, all in the mid-1980s. One of those was on Akerman, as mentioned above, another being the first UK thesis on French cinema by a scholar who has shaped the field, Ginette Vincendeau, on 1930s popular cinema (1985).[3] It is this thesis that marks the start of the UK strand of French cinema studies, immediately preceded in 1984 by the first-ever panel on French cinema at the venerable Society for French Studies conference, the professional association of the 'old' universities, hitherto largely devoted to French literature. In that session, Keith Reader presented a paper on *La Règle du jeu*, Russell Cousins on *La Bête humaine* and Jill Forbes on Jean-Louis Baudry and theory.

There were significant director studies in the decade, many of them on pre-1960 directors, such as Gance, Renoir and Carné (Gauteur 1980; Bonnaffons 1981; Berthomé 1982; Buache 1982; Jenn 1984; King 1984; Faulkner 1986; Chion 1987; Magny 1987; Sandro 1987; Crisp 1988; Guérin 1988; Sellier 1989; Turk 1989). But a feature of the decade was that French and American academics turned their attention to French cinema history, with a number of books devoted to very specific periods, especially the 1930s. Freddy Buache wrote two books on the 1960s and 1970s respectively (Buache 1987, 1990), Geneviève Guillaume-Grimaud published her 1973 thesis on the cinema of the Popular Front (Chirat and Guillaume-Grimaud 1986), Jonathan Buchsbaum published a book on politically committed cinema of the 1930s (Buchsbaum 1988) and *Positif* contributor Jean-Pierre Jeancolas published a book on the 1930s and early 1940s (Jeancolas 1983). In the United States, Richard Abel published two key works on early French cinema (Abel 1984, 1988) and in 1986 the Association Française de Recherche sur l'Histoire du Cinéma launched its journal, *1895*, with a strong (but not exclusive) focus on the French silent period. There was also a massive encyclopaedia started in the mid-1980s, running through to the early 1990s (Bessy and Chirat 1986–88; Bessy et al. 1989–92).

A final point to make about this decade is that it saw the emergence of a number of scholars who would play a significant role in the development of the discipline. Apart from Vincendeau, the following also produced theses in this decade: in the United States, Sandy Flitterman-Lewis (1982, published 1990) and in France, Geneviève Sellier (1987, published 1989) – both, with Vincendeau, committed to the emerging feminist and gender studies agenda. Sellier's later pioneering work in gender studies is unusual in the French context (Burch and Sellier 1996; Sellier 2005, translated 2008). In France, Nicole Brenez, a key figure for *avant-garde* and experimental cinema, was awarded her thesis on Godard's *Le Mépris* (Brenez 1989; see Brenez 1998 and 2006 and Brenez and Lebrat 2001 for later work).

1990s

I have chosen to see the 1990s as another step in the evolution of French cinema studies because that decade saw several major new developments.

First, there was an explosion of academic books in the first half of the 1990s, culminating in the centenary of the cinema in 1995. *Le Monde* journalist Jacques Siclier published a two-volume history of the cinema (Siclier 1990). A number of Anglophone academics published important works of history and analysis: in the United Kingdom, Susan Hayward began the series on national cinemas she edits for Routledge with an ambitious re-evaluation of the whole of French cinema (Hayward 1993), as did Alan Williams in the United States (Williams 1992). Hayward and Vincendeau co-edited a key collection, to which we shall return (Hayward and Vincendeau 1990). In that same year, T. Jefferson Kline in the United States published a new approach to the New Wave (Kline 1992), Jill Forbes in the United Kingdom released a major work on cinema since the New Wave (Forbes 1992), while Prédal in France published a 560-page volume on French cinema since 1945 (Prédal 1991). The pre-1945 period was well served by two important volumes, both with the phrase 'classic French cinema' in their title. The first was by Australian academic Colin Crisp (1993), even if the focus went beyond 1945; the second was by Dudley Andrew (1995). The year in which Andrew published his book was the centenary year, celebrated in France by a number of books, of which the most significant were the massive histories written by film journalists for Flammarion (Billard 1995; Frodon 1995); a smaller but important work was Jeancolas's (1995) short but focused history for the academic publisher Nathan.

The decade can be singled out for a second reason: there was a dramatic increase in the number of theses in French cinema, from 80 in the previous decade to 180 in the 1990s. Much of that increase occurred in the second half of the decade (see Appendix 25.2). In the period 1990–94, the average annual number of theses awarded was twelve (the average for the 1980s had been eight per annum), but this suddenly increased to 24 in 1995–99. Just over 100 of these were French, with some 65 being American. As with the 1980s, there was again a significant focus on the New Wave and its directors (just over twenty theses), as well as on Renoir and the 1930s (fourteen theses). The emerging feminist agenda grew with some ten, mostly American theses, on women directors (amongst them Akerman, Marguerite Duras, Alice Guy and Varda). While work on the silent period had been more or less evenly split between France and the United States in the 1980s, the 1990s saw more American theses on this period (five). The emphasis on Francophone/colonial cinema also grew, with sixteen theses spread evenly between France and the United States, complemented by a pioneering collection (Sherzer 1996). A new focus on the film industry emerged, mostly concentrated in France, with over twenty theses on regional or local cinema, as well as the more technical aspects of the art of film-making.

Third, the 1990s saw the strengthening of work on earlier periods. Richard Abel followed up his earlier 1980 volume on the silent cinema from 1915 with a volume focusing on the pre-1915 period (Abel 1994), and Sylvie Lindeperg published a major work on representations of World War II in the post-war period (Lindeperg 1997). The Association Française de Recherche sur l'Histoire du Cinéma began to publish monographs on earlier periods. These were often recently awarded theses (Véray 1995; Dutheil de la Rochère 1997; Gauthier 1999; Gozillon-Fronsacq 2003) or, particularly since 2000, conference collections (Herpe and Toulet 2000; Bastide and de la Bretèque 2007; Véray 2008).

Fourth, there was a critical and historical return in France to the heroic years of influential cinema periodicals, with an anthology of *La Revue du cinéma* (*Revue du cinéma* 1992) and facsimile reprints of *Positif* (*Positif* 1997 and 2000; this was followed by an anthology a couple of years later – see *Positif* 2002), as well as Antoine de Baecque's history of the *Cahiers du cinéma* (Baecque 1991), which he followed at the end of the decade with an anthology from the periodical (Baecque and Tesson 1999); he also carried on work on New Wave directors (Baecque and Toubiana 1998), still an important preoccupation given the New Wave's fortieth anniversary (Loshitzky 1995; Douchet 1998).

Finally, a new series devoted to French directors was launched in 1998, established by Diana Holmes and Robert Ingram for Manchester University Press. There are significant differences compared with the 1960s Seghers series: while there are many of the same canonical directors (Bresson, Cocteau, Franju, Godard, Malle, Méliès, Renoir, Resnais and Vigo), there are also many new ones, such as the directors of the *cinéma du look* (Luc Besson, Jean-Jacques Beineix and Léos Carax) and women directors (Catherine Breillat, Claire Denis, Diane Kurys, Varda), as well as directors who had come to prominence since the 1960s (Bertrand Blier, Mathieu Kassovitz, Patrice Leconte, François Ozon, Maurice Pialat, André Téchiné) and some who had been unjustly left aside, such as Claude Chabrol and Chris Marker. The series is considerably more academic and theoretically informed than the earlier Seghers collection, reflecting developments in film studies more generally. It is also more durable than the Bibliothèque du Film's attempt in 2000 to launch a series resembling the 1960s Seghers collection; their 'Ciné-regards' only published ten titles, of which five were on French directors (Le Roy 2000; Rodriguez-Blanco 2000; Desrichard 2001; Naumann 2001; Desrichard 2003).

Amongst the many director studies published in the 1990s was, as mentioned above, Guy Austin's study of Claude Chabrol, who – surprisingly, given that he was a key New Wave director – has over the years had very little academic work devoted to him. Manchester University Press also published Guy Austin's compact introduction to contemporary French cinema in this decade (Austin 1996), and there were several other volumes focused on particular periods (Hubert-Lacombe 1996; Powrie 1997, 1999; Wilson 1999). My volumes on the 1980s and 1990s picked up on what was increasingly a trend away from the synoptic history prevalent in the 1980s (what Michel Marie calls 'the encyclopaedic tendency' – Marie 2006: 45) towards extended essays on particular films. This had started with an important collection of essays edited by the two foremost British scholars of French cinema, Hayward and Vincendeau, right at the start of the 1990s, which went to its second edition a decade later at the start of the 2000s (Hayward and Vincendeau 1990, 2000). That volume, with essays on key films by a range of international contributors, could be said to define the 1990s, as well as foreshadowing the 2000s with their emphasis on increasing international collaboration.

2000s

Many more collections on French cinema quickly followed (Harris and Ezra 2000; Hughes and Williams 2001; Mazdon 2001; Powrie 2006; Waldron and Vanderschelden 2007).[4] The trend of extended essays, often on individual films, was strengthened by the establishment of the journal *Studies in French Cinema* in 2000, along with the Association of Studies in French Cinema and its annual conference. Work on French cinema had frequently been published in the United Kingdom in journals such as *French Cultural Studies*, and to a lesser extent *French Studies* and *Modern and Contemporary France*,[5] but the establishment of *Studies in French Cinema* gave the community the chance to engage in a more sustained debate. Moreover, the journal supported the discipline in a number of ways during its first decade. First, it promoted work by PhD students and early-career colleagues; second, it adopted a policy of focusing on less well-explored areas of French cinema, such as the 1950s and 1970s; and finally, it encouraged French colleagues to publish work in the journal.

Closer ties between French and Anglophone colleagues were a feature of the decade; a conference at the Ecole Normale Supérieure in Lyon in July 2004, 'French and Francophone Fictions: Cinema and Television', brought together a number of colleagues working on French cinema: the French Association Française des Enseignants et Chercheurs en Cinéma et Audiovisuel, the American Society for Cinema and Media Studies (especially its French Francophone Interest Group) and the Association for Studies in French Cinema. Closer ties were also evident in published work, as several French scholars turned their attention to areas of the discipline previously associated with Anglophone cinema studies. Raphaëlle Moine explored genre (Moine 2005a, 2005b) and established a seminar on '*les fictions patrimoniales*', or heritage cinema as it is known in the United Kingdom. Geneviève Sellier established a series for the French publisher L'Harmattan, 'Champs visuels étrangers', the purpose of which was to translate into French key texts in cinema studies. Amongst the first to be published was Turk's 1989 volume on Carné, followed two years later by Richard Dyer's (1979) book on stars.

Work on French stars in both the United Kingdom and France took off in the 2000s, with Vincendeau's magisterial essays on the French star system, collecting work done over the previous decade (Vincendeau 2000a; see also Chapuy 2001; Austin 2003; Nacache 2003; Brassart 2004; Hayward 2004; Harris and Downing 2007; Powrie with Rebillard 2009). Much of this work was in the broader area of gender studies, now a dominant critical paradigm in Anglophone French cinema studies, and championed in France by Sellier, as mentioned above (Burch and Sellier 1996; Sellier 2005). Gender studies informed many areas of Anglophone French cinema studies, starting early in the decade with Carrie Tarr and Brigitte Rollet's *Cinema and the Second Sex* (Tarr with Rollet 2001), and complemented by other major volumes (Beugnet 2000; Conway 2004), two of which are specifically from lesbian and gay perspectives (Cairns 2006; Rees-Roberts 2008). Not only were there many studies of individual women film-makers, such as Catherine Breillat (Clouzot 2004; Vasse 2004), Claire Denis (Beugnet 2004; Mayne 2005) and Alice Guy (McMahan 2003), but studies of male directors were increasingly from a specifically gender perspective (for example, Downing 2004; Marshall 2007).

The second growth area in French cinema studies in the 2000s was Francophone and postcolonial cinema. We have already seen how this paradigm established itself during the 1990s, principally through a number of theses. There were an increasing number of theses in this area in the 2000s, as we shall see below, but there were also a number of published volumes, with broad surveys (Spaas 2000; Armes 2006; Murphy and Williams 2007) being complemented by more focused studies (Slavin 2001; Thackway 2003; Eades 2006); in a similar vein, Tarr – like Vincendeau had done for her 2000 volume on stars – collected and reframed material she had been publishing over a long period of time, and published a definitive statement on Maghrebi-French ('beur') cinema (Tarr 2005).

Theses on French cinema increased again in this decade. Whereas there had been 180 for the whole of the 1990s, by the end of 2007 there were already 195. The number of UK theses grew in the 2000s; there had been nine in the 1990s, rising to 31 in the period 2000–07. The trends were broadly similar to those of the 1990s, with an even stronger emphasis on the New Wave directors, who had some 40 theses devoted to them, as well as a number of major volumes, the most important of which was undoubtedly Sellier's gender-based critique of the New Wave (Sellier 2005).

Fifteen of the 40 theses involved work on Godard, who was the subject of a major international conference at the Tate in London in 2001. This was organized by Michael Temple, James Williams and Michael Witt, who published collections of work on Godard before and after the conference (Temple and Williams 2001; Temple et al. 2004). Work on the New Wave was complemented by other significant publications (Marie 2000; Neupert 2002; Greene 2007), as well as two major volumes on Jacques Rivette (Deschamps

2001; Frappat 2001; Morrey and Smith 2009) and a number of volumes on Rohmer (Cleder 2007; Herpe 2007; Schilling 2007; Tester 2008), both of whom had previously been neglected.

There were six or so theses on Bresson, as in the 1990s, and again some fifteen or so on Francophone cinema and on the industry. There was a new strand emerging on comparisons between the US and French cinemas (four), corresponding to a similar focus in published work (Durham 1998; Mazdon 2000; O'Brien 2005). Work on the 1930s was considerably less extensive than in the 1990s, with barely half a dozen theses; this was to some extent compensated for by an important book on the period by Crisp (2002), as well as several volumes on Renoir (the lavishly illustrated biography by Faulkner and Duncan 2007; Davis 2008; Garson 2008). French theses were increasingly published by one of the major publishers for cinema studies, L'Harmattan (see Ionascu 2001; Provoyeur 2002; Godier 2005; Marie 2005; Jardonnet 2006; Scemama-Heard 2006).

Three new areas of interest emerged at the end of the previous decade, and during this decade, although they are as yet not reflected in significant thesis production: work on politically engaged cinema (Hayes and O'Shaughnessy 2005; Marie 2005; O'Shaughnessy 2007); *le jeune cinéma* (Marie 1998; Trémois 1998; Brenez and Lebrat 2001; Prédal 2002; Serceau 2008); and the cinema of sensation (Beugnet 2007). The emergence of work on the industry that I noted above in thesis production was complemented by a number of significant volumes, most notably Creton (2004).

In the middle of the decade, there were two major events that encapsulate the coming of age for academic work on French cinema studies. Ginette Vincendeau established the I.B. Tauris French Film Guides, reprising the single-film focus established by Nathan's 'Synopsis' collection published in the period 1989–99. This was preceded in 2004 by the BFI's *The French Cinema Book* (Temple and Witt 2004), which brought together essays by a range of international scholars. Amongst them were senior scholars whose names have figured on several occasions in this chapter (Richard Abel, Nicole Brenez, Colin Crisp, Christopher Faulkner and Ginette Vincendeau).[6]

International collaboration of this kind is increasingly a feature of work in French cinema studies. Until the turn of the century, there was a clear difference between critical approaches by French scholars on the one hand and Anglophone scholars on the other; the former could be characterized as broadly aesthetic and historical, the latter broadly as based in what David Bordwell calls Grand Theory, notably spectatorship theory and gender theory. French scholars have, since the turn of the century, moved more towards the latter paradigms, led by the work of Sellier in particular. The distinguishing feature of United Kingdom-based scholarship where contemporary French cinema is concerned has been the close attention paid to popular cinema, whether popular genres or stars. There is pioneering work on stars (Vincendeau 2000; Austin 2003; Hayward 2004; Powrie with Rebillard 2009), attention paid to directors deemed too popular for critical attention in France, such as Besson (Hayward 1999; Hayward and Powrie 2006) and analysis of the nature of the popular and its intersection with the national in the Manchester conference organized in 2006 by Isabelle Vanderschelden and Darren Waldron. This led to a publication (Waldron and Vanderschelden 2007) that exemplifies what I would like to emphasize in these concluding comments: international collaboration, with its mix of Anglophone and Francophone scholars, including leading scholars in the field (Moine, Tarr, Vincendeau); and the UK emphasis on the popular, with chapters devoted to, amongst others, the films of Jeunet, the *La Verité si je mens / Would I Lie to You?* films (Gilou 1997, 2001) and the popular comedy remake *Boudu* (Jugnot 2005).

Looking back, the specific contribution of United Kingdom-based French cinema studies has been the introduction of gender-based theory, and the focus on the popular, complementing the work of French-based scholars. It is comforting to see that these paradigms are increasingly shared by a new generation, in France as well as in the United Kingdom and the United States. The study of French cinema has never been so broad in its sweep, both in terms of its interests, and in terms of its two hundred or so researchers across the globe.

Notes

1. I will therefore not be considering the work done by film schools, such as the IDHEC/FEMIS in France. Marie (2002, 2006) and Vincendeau (2000b) offer brief surveys of film or cinema studies more generally, rather than French cinema studies.
2. This remains true today. More work – both teaching and research – is done on French cinema in departments of French and related literatures than in film studies departments.
3. There had been two theses on French cinema awarded prior to this, but by individuals who were not to pursue a career in academic environments: see Jones (1978) and Kwietniowski (1984). The latter won a prize at the Berlin Film Festival for his short film *Alfalfa* (1987) and a BAFTA for *Love and Death on Long Island* (1999).
4. Powrie (2006: 263–76) contains a very extensive bibliography for French cinema.
5. Nor should we forget the many special numbers devoted to French cinema over the years, amongst them *Nottingham French Studies* (32(1), 1993), *Screen* (32(4), 1993), *Contemporary French Civilization* (22(2), 1998), the *Historical Journal of Film, Radio and Television* (18(2), 1998), *The Australian Journal of French Studies* (36(1), 1999), *Esprit Créateur* (52(3), 2002), *Film Criticism* (27(1), 2002), *French Cultural Studies* (15(3), 2004), *French Politics, Culture and Society* (23(3), 2005), *Modern and Contemporary France*, 15(1) (2005) and *Yale French Studies* (115, 2009).
6. I am grateful to the many colleagues who provided information about the teaching of French cinema in their current and former institutions: Guy Austin, Martine Beugnet, Daniel Biltereyst, Sandy Flitterman-Lewis, Frédéric Gimello-Mesplomb, Claudia Gorbman, Susan Hayward, Greg Hainge, Nick Harrison, Leslie Hill, Diana Holmes, John Izod, Anne Jackel, Noel King, Rachael Langford, Martin Lefebvre, Christopher Lloyd, Lucy Mazdon, Raphaëlle Moine, Jacqueline Nacache, Richard Neupert, Catherine O'Brien, Tim Palmer, Alastair Phillips, Hilary Radner, Laura Rascaroli, Keith Reader, Geneviève Sellier, Alison Smith, Carrie Tarr, Steven Ungar, Isabelle Vanderschelden, Ginette Vincendeau, Emma Wilson, Mike Witt. Any inaccuracies or misrepresentations are mine alone.

Appendix 25.1: Examples of course units in French cinema

The units listed are mainly extracted from university websites, with some additional information from colleagues. Many institutions incorporate elements of French cinema in broader non-French cinema-specific units. These have not been listed here; I have only included such units if a minimum of 50 per cent of the material includes French cinema.

University	Units
Alberta	• Contemporary Cinema in French
Auckland	• France on Screen: From Lumière to Godard
	• French Cinema Since the New Wave
Australian National	• French Cinema
Bath	• Images and Identities in Flux: French Cinema and the Auteur Tradition
	• Films of the Nouvelle Vague
Berkeley	• Studies in French Film
Birmingham	• French Cinema, Visual Culture and National Identity
	• Avant-garde Currents in French Cinema
	• French Auteur Cinema
Bordeaux 3	• Nouvelle Vague
Boston	• French New Wave
	• French Cinema
Bristol	• Introduction to the French Cinema
	• Contemporary French Cinema
	• Gender and Sexuality in Contemporary Film
Caen	• Nouvelle Vague
	• Aspects du cinéma français contemporain
	• Approches socioculturelles du cinéma français
	• Histoire et cinéma
Cambridge	• French National Cinema Since 1960
Cardiff	• Francophone African Film
Chicago	• French Cinema 1920s–1930s
	• The Cinema of Max Ophüls
Concordia	• Le monde du cinéma français
Dalhousie	• From the Lumiere Brothers to the New Wave
	• From the New Wave to the New Millennium
Durham	• French Cinema: 1930s to 1990s
Edinburgh	• The Nouvelle Vague and Contemporary Trends
	• Literature and Film: The Challenge of Adaptation
	• The Cinema of Chantal Akerman: Memory, History, Desire

	• Intimate Exposures: Fifty Years of French First-Person Cinema
Exeter	• French National Cinema
	• Introduction to Postcolonial Francophone Cinema
	• 101 Nights: French Women Directors
Georgia	• French Film History
Glasgow	• Classic French Cinema
Harvard	• Women's Film and Video in France: Agnès Varda, Chantal Akerman and Claire Denis
Iowa	• Introduction to European Film [includes New Wave]
	• French Cinema
	• Gender and Sexuality in French Cinema
	• Cinema, Society, and Culture in Twentieth-Century France
	• Francophone Cinema
John Hopkins	• Bresson and Ophüls
	• French New Wave
	• Topics in French Cinema: Masculin/Féminin
Kent	• Questions of French Cinema
	• Contemporary French Cinema
	• The Shifting Gaze: Cinematic Adaptations in Modern French Culture
King's College London	• French New Wave
	• French Cinema: History, Ideology, Aesthetics
Kingston	• Introduction to French Cinema
	• French New Wave
Leeds	• The Seventh Art: Cinema in France
	• Francophone Cinema: Postcolonial Images
	• Gender, Sex and Cinema in France
Leicester	• French Cinema
Liverpool	• Introduction to French Cinema
	• Cinema and Narratives of French Society
Manchester	• From Novel to Film: French Cinema and Literary Adaptations
	• Aspects of the French *nouvelle vague*
	• France and Algeria: Film, Video and Photography
	• Gender and Sexuality in Contemporary French Cinema
Manchester Metropolitan	• Introduction to French cinema
	• French New Wave
	• Contemporary French film
Massachusetts	• Transnational French Cinemas
	• Breaking New Ground in French Cinema
	• Restlessness in French Cinema
	• African Film

Middlesex	• Film and Literature in Modern France
Newcastle	• Classic French Cinema
	• Contemporary French Cinema
	• The French Horror Film
New York	• History of French Cinema
	• Cinema Culture of France
North Carolina Wilmington	• Contemporary French Cinema
	• Introduction to French Cinema
Nottingham	• The Golden Age of French Cinema
	• Adaptations of Literature into Film
	• French Cinema: The New Wave
	• French Documentary Cinema
	• Women Directors of French Film
	• Contemporary French Cinema: Heritage and Memory
	• Contemporary French Documentary Cinema
Nottingham Trent	• Film, Novel and Social Transformation in France (1950–1980)
	• Contemporary France: Text, Film, Culture
Ohio	• Introduction to French Cinema
	• French Cinema, 1945 to Present
Otago	• Topics in French and Francophone Cinema
	• French New Wave
Ottowa	• La francophonie par les films
Oxford	• Introduction to French Film Studies
Oxford Brookes	• Cinema and Social Change in Contemporary France
Paris 3	• Les écrivains dans le cinéma français (1930–1950)
	• François Truffaut
	• Le cinéma français des années 30
	• Le documentaire en France
	• Le cinéma français muet
	• Les pionniers français du film d'exploration (1895–1930)
	• La politique publique de soutien au cinéma en France: mutations et défis à l'horizon 2010
	• Économie de la filière cinématographique française
	• L'économie du documentaire en France
	• Le cinéma direct au Québec
	• Sociologie du film
	• Le cinéma en France, films, histoire, société
Paris 7	• Histoire du cinéma
	• Etudes de textes théoriques (Bazin, Metz, Deleuze)
	• Le cinéma français des années 1940–1950
	• Le cinéma français de 1945 à 1960, dans ses rapports avec les Etats-Unis
	• Le cinéma postcolonial français

	• Economie contemporaine du cinéma français
	• Cinéma(s) de la modernité
	• Archives, recherche, et histoire du cinéma
Paris 8	• Le cinéma fantastique en France
	• Jean-Pierre Melville
	• Mouvement-monde: l'avant-garde française des années 20
	• Introduction au documentaire: Agnès Varda
	• Pourquoi le cinéma? débuts de réponse avec trois cinéastes-théoriciens (Epstein, Godard, Akerman)
	• Jean-Luc Godard: les débuts
	• Robert Bresson: cinéaste-théoricien
	• Franju, Resnais, en marge de la nouvelle vague
	• Le cinéma moderne français: de la nouvelle vague au cinéma militant
Paris 10	• Buñuel
	• Guitry
	• Les films français et leurs remakes hollywoodiens
	• La comédie dans le cinéma français
	• Les fictions patrimoniales françaises
	• Le cinéma classique français
Queen Mary London	• Contemporary French Cinema
	• French Film after Auschwitz: Testimony, Memory, Mourning
	• French New Wave
	• Screening the Past: The Contemporary French History Film
Queen's, Canada	• French Cinema
	• Introduction au cinéma francophone
Queensland	• Le cinéma en français
Reading	• French Cinema
Roehampton	• Gender, Sexuality and Ethnicity in French Literature and Cinema
	• Francophone Cinema: An Introduction to Postcolonial Cinema
	• French National Cinema
Royal Holloway London	• Cinema in France: From Modernism to Postmodernism
	• The Passion of Place: Desire and Identity in Modern Paris
	• Image, Identity and Consumer Culture in Post-war Fiction and Film
Rutgers	• The French Film
	• Topics in French Cinema
	• Advanced Topics in French Cinema
San Diego State	• Romans et leurs films
	• Africa in Literature and Film
	• French Cinema and Theory

St Andrews	• From Text to Screen: Novels and their Film Adaptations
Sheffield	• French Film Classics
Southampton	• French Cinema of the 1930s
	• Contemporary French Cinematic Cultures
Stirling	• French Cinema of the Fantastic
	• Culture and Identity in Contemporary France
	• Postcolonial France
	• Transatlantic Cinema
Swansea	• French Cinema since World War Two
	• From Page to Screen
Sydney	• Minorities in French Cinema
Toronto	• French Cinema
	• Cinema and Literature in France
	• Cinema of Jean-Luc Godard
UCLA	• French Cinema and Culture
	• Cinema and Literature in France
Ulster	• French Cinema Until the 1960s
	• French Cinema Since the 1960s
University College London	• French Film
	• French Film History
	• Screen Cities: Representing the Margins of Paris, 1830–2005
	• Jean-Luc Godard: *Histoire(s) du cinéma*
Warwick	• French New Wave
	• Jean Renoir and Max Ophuls
	• The Cinematic City (Paris)
	• Paris Hollywood: French Cinema Remade in the USA
	• French Cinema and Society 1958-1974
	• French Cinema and Society 1990-present
	• Stars and Stardom in French Cinema
Wisconsin-Madison	• Immigration and Expression
	• Visual Culture in French/Francophone Studies
	• African/Francophone Film
	• French/Francophone Film
	• French Film
Wolverhampton	• Reading French Film
	• French Cinema since the 1970s
Yale	• French Women Film-makers
	• Realist French Film: Renoir, Bazin, Rohmer
	• American-French Film Relations and the Culture of Commitment, 1930–1965

Appendix 25.2: Theses on French cinema

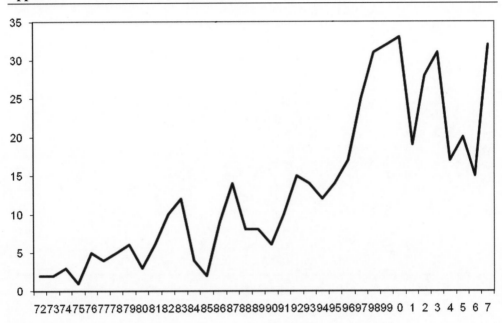

Figure 25.1: Number of theses per annum (total for France, United States and United Kingdom.

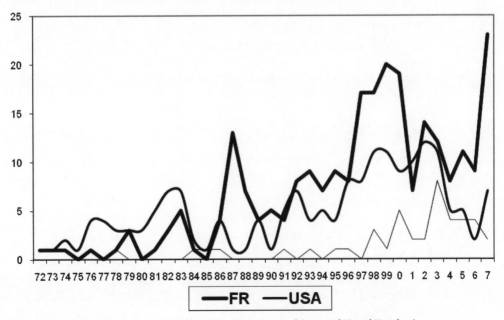

Figure 25.2: Number of theses per annum by country (France, United States and United Kingdom).

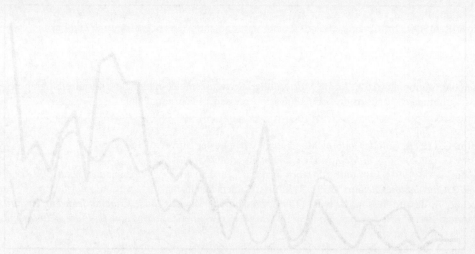

References to Part III

Abel, R. (1984), *French Cinema: The First Wave, 1915–1929*, Princeton, NJ: Princeton University Press.

Abel, R. (ed.) (1988), *French Film Theory and Criticism: A History/Anthology, 1907–1939, Vol. 1: 1907–1929*, Princeton, NJ: Princeton University Press.

Abel, R. (1994), *The Ciné Goes to Town: French Cinema, 1896–1914*, Berkeley, CA: University of California Press.

Allen, D. (1974), *François Truffaut*, London: Secker and Warburg/BFI.

Andrew, D. (1972), 'Realism and Reality in Cinema: the Film Theory of André Bazin and its Source in Recent French Thought', PhD thesis, University of Iowa.

Andrew, D. (1995), *Mists of Regret: Culture and Sensibility in Classic French Film*, Princeton, NJ: Princeton University Press.

Andrew, D. and Ungar, S. (2005), *Popular Front Paris and the Poetics of Culture*, Cambridge, MA: Harvard University Press.

Armes, R. (1966), *French Cinema Since 1946, Vol. 1: The Great Tradition; vol. 2: The Personal Style*, London and New York: Zwemmer and Barnes.

Armes, R. (1968), *The Cinema of Alain Resnais*, London and New York: Zwemmer and Barnes.

Armes, R. (2006), *African Filmmaking: North and South of the Sahara*, Edinburgh: Edinburgh University Press. Translated into French by Françoise Rippe-Lascout and Marie-Cécile Wouters, Paris: L'Harmattan.

Assemblée nationale (n.d.), 'André Morice', http://www.assemblee-nationale.fr/histoire/biographies/IVRepublique/Morice-Andre-11101900.asp. Accessed 14 February 2009.

Austin, G. (1996), *Contemporary French Cinema: An Introduction*, Manchester: Manchester University Press.

Austin, G. (1999), *Claude Chabrol*, Manchester: Manchester University Press.

Austin, G. (2003), *Stars in Modern French Film*, London: Arnold.

Baecque, A. de (1991), *Les Cahiers du cinéma: histoire d'une revue, vol. 1 À l'assaut du cinéma 1951–1959, vol. 2, Cinéma, tours détours 1959–1981*, Paris: Cahiers du cinéma.

Baecque, A. de and Tesson, C. (eds) (1999), *La Nouvelle Vague: Claude Chabrol, Jean-Luc Godard, Jacques Rivette, Eric Rohmer, François Truffaut/textes et entretiens parus dans les Cahiers du cinéma*, Paris: Cahiers du cinéma.

Baecque, A. de and Toubiana, S. (1998), *François Truffaut*, Paris: Gallimard.

Barlet, O. (2008), '*Où vas-tu Moshé? (Finemachiyamoché)* de Hassan Benjelloun'. http://www.africultures.com/php/index.php?nav= article&no=5968. Accessed 8 June 2009.

Barrot, O. and Chirat, R. (2000), *Noir et blanc: 250 acteurs du cinéma français 1930–1960*, Paris: Flammarion.

Barthes, R. (1957), *Mythologies*, Paris: Editions de Minuit.

Bastide, B. and de la Bretèque, F. (eds) (2007), *Jacques de Baroncelli*, Paris: Association Française de Recherche sur l'Histoire du Cinéma.

Benbassa, E. (2006), 'La guerre des mémoires', *Libération*, 5 January.

Benbassa, E. (2007), 'Jewish–Moslem Relations in Contemporary France', *Contemporary French and Francophone Studies*, 11(2), pp. 189–94.

Bergfelder, T. (2006), 'German Actors in Hollywood: The Long View', in A. Phillips and G. Vincendeau (eds), *Journeys of Desire: European Actors in Hollywood*, London: BFI, pp. 37–43.

Bernard, R. (1980), *Les Mémoires de Raymond Bernard*, Paris: Société des auteurs et compositeurs dramatiques.

Berthomé, J.-P. (1976), 'Interview with Louis Daquin', trans. J. Berthomé, *Film Dope*, 9, pp. 1–9.

Berthomé, J.-P. (1982), 'L'Œuvre de Jacques Demy', PhD thesis, Paris I.

Bertin-Maghit, J.-P. (1978), 'Le Cinema français: rupture et régénération 1940–1946', PhD thesis, Nice.

Bertin-Maghit, J.-P. (1980), *Le Cinéma français sous Vichy: les films français de 1940 à 1944*, Paris: Revue du Cinéma/Albatros.

Bertin-Maghit, J.-P. (1987), 'Les Films français de 1940 à 1944: signification et fonction sociale', Doctorat d'Etat, Nice.

Bessy, M. and R. Chirat (1986–88), *Histoire du cinéma français: encyclopédie des films, Vol. 1 : 1929–1934* (1988), *Vol. 2 : 1935–1939* (1987), *Vol. 3 : 1940–1950* (1986), Paris: Pygmalion.

Bessy, M., Chirat, R. and Bernard, A. (1989–92), *Histoire du cinéma français: encyclopédie des films, Vol. 4: 1951–1955* (1989), *Vol. 5: 1956–1960* (1990), *Vol. 6: 1961–1965* (1991), *Vol. 7: 1966–1970* (1992), Paris: Pygmalion.

Beugnet, M. (2000), *Marginalité, sexualité, contrôle dans le cinéma français contemporain*, Paris: L'Harmattan.

Beugnet, M. (2004), *Claire Denis*, Manchester: Manchester University Press.

Beugnet, M. (2007), *Cinema and Sensation: French Film and the Art of Transgression*, Edinburgh: Edinburgh University Press.

Billard, P. (1995), *L'Age classique du cinéma français: du cinéma parlant à la Nouvelle Vague*, Paris: Flammarion.

Bloom, A. (1987), *The Closing of the American Mind*, New York: Simon and Schuster.

Bonnaffons, E. (1981), *François Truffaut: la figure inachevée*, Lausanne: L'Âge d'homme.

Borde, R., Buache, F. and Curtelin, J. (1962), *Nouvelle Vague*, Paris: Serdoc.

Bordwell, D. (1974), 'French Impressionist Cinema: Film Culture, Film Theory, and Film Style', PhD thesis, Iowa.

Boukhari, K. (n.d.), 'Marock. Le film de tous les tabous', http://www.telquel-online.com/223/couverture _223_1.shtml. Accessed 14 July 2009.

Bourdieu, P. (1979), *La Distinction: critique sociale du jugement*, Paris: Editions de Minuit.

Brassart, A. (2004), *Les Jeunes Premiers dans le cinéma français des années soixante*, Paris: Cerf /Paris: Corlet.

Braudy, L. (1977), *Jean Renoir: The World of His Films*, London: Robson.

Brenez, N. (1989), 'Autour du *Mépris*: deux problèmes cinématographiques rapports à l'invention figurative et solutions filmiques', PhD thesis, Ecole des Hautes Etudes en Sciences Sociales.

Brenez, N. (1998), *De la figure en général et du corps en particulier: l'invention figurative au cinéma*, Paris: De Boeck Université.

Brenez, N. (2006), *Cinémas d'avant-garde*, Paris: Cahiers du cinéma/SCÉRÉN-CNDP.

Brenez, N. and Lebrat, C. (eds) (2001), *Jeune, dure et pure! Une histoire du cinéma d'avant-garde et expérimental en France*, Paris: Cinémathèque française/Mazzotta.

Britten, J. (n.d.), *French Film: A Guide to Classic French Cinema*, http://www.cinemaspot.com/features/frenchfilm.htm. Accessed July 2009.

Brown, R.S. (ed.) (1972), *Focus on Godard*, Englewood Cliffs, NJ: Prentice Hall.

Buache, F. (1982), *Claude Autant-Lara*, Lausanne: L'Âge d'homme.

Buache, F. (1987), *Le Cinéma français des années 60*, Renens: 5 Continents/Paris: Hatier.

Buache, F. (1990), *Le Cinéma français des années 70*, Renens: 5 Continents/Paris: Hatier.

Buchsbaum, J. (1988), *Cinéma Engagé: Film in the Popular Front*, Urbana, IL: University of Illinois Press.

Burch, N. (1979), *To the Distant Observer: Form and Meaning in the Japanese Cinema*, London: Scholar Press.

Burch, N. and Sellier, G. (1996), *La Drôle de guerre des sexes du cinéma français (1930–1956)*, Paris: Nathan.

Cairns, L. (2006), *Sapphism on Screen: Lesbian Desire in French and Francophone Cinema*, Edinburgh: Edinburgh University Press.

Carné, M. (1933), 'Quand le cinéma descendra-t-il dans la rue?', *Cinémagazine*, November; reprinted in R. Chazal *Marcel Carné*, Paris: Seghers, 1965.

Chapuy, A. (2001), *Martine Carol filmée par Christian-Jaque: un phénomène de cinéma populaire*, Paris L'Harmattan.

Chazal, R. (1965), *Marcel Carné*, Paris: Seghers.

Chion, M. (1987), *Jacques Tati*, Paris: Cahiers du cinéma.

Chion, M. (2008), *Le Complexe de Cyrano, la langue parlée dans les films français*, Paris: Editions Cahiers du cinéma.

Chirat, R. and Presle, M. (1985), *La IVe République et ses films*, Paris: 5 Continents: Hatier.

Choi, Jimmy (2002), 'Is National Cinema Mr. MacGuffin?', *International Films*, The Institute of Communications Studies, University of Leeds, http://ics.leeds.achttp://ics.leeds.ac.uk/papers/vp01.cfm?outfit=ifilm&folder=17&paper=22. Accessed 6 June 2009.

Choi, Jinhee (2006), 'National Cinema, the Very Idea', in N. Carroll and J. Choi (eds), *Philosophy of Film and Motion Pictures: An Anthology*, Malden, MA: Blackwell.

Cléder, J. (ed.) (2007), *Eric Rohmer: évidence et ambiguïté du cinéma*, Latresne: Le Bord de l'eau.

Clouzot, C. (2004), *Catherine Breillat: indécence et pureté*, Paris: L'Étoile/Cahiers du cinéma.

Conditto, K. (2007), *Cinephile: French Language and Culture Through Film*, Newburyport, MA: Focus.

Connor, J.D. (2007), 'The Persistence of Fidelity: Adaptation Theory Today', *M/C Journal* 10(2), http://journal.media-culture.org.au/0705/15-connor.php. Accessed 30 June 2009.

Conway, K. (2004), *Chanteuse in the City: The Realist Singer in French Film*. Berkeley, CA: University of California Press.

Creton, L. (2004), *Histoire économique du cinéma français: production et financement, 1940–1959*, Paris: Editions CNRS.

Crisp, C. (1972), *François Truffaut*, New York: Praeger.

Crisp, C. (1988), *Eric Rohmer: Realist and Moralist*, Bloomington, IN: Indiana University Press.

Crisp, C. (1993), *The Classic French Cinema: 1930–1960*, Bloomington, IN: Indiana University Press.

Crisp, C. (2002), *Genre, Myth and Convention in French Cinema, 1929–1939*, Bloomington, IN: Indiana University Press.

Danan, M. (2002), 'From a "Prenational" to a "Postnational" French Cinema', in C. Fowler (ed.), *The European Cinema Reader*, London: Routledge, pp. 232–45.

Daquin, L. (1960), *Le Cinéma, notre métier* (preface by René Clair), Paris: Les Editeurs Français.

Daquin, L. (1970), 'Louis Daquin', *Cinéma*, 151, pp. 68–9 (interviewer M.M.).

Davis, C. (2008), *Scenes of Love and Murder: Renoir, Film and Philosophy*, London: Wallflower.

Debrauwere-Miller, N. (2009), 'France and the Israeli–Palestinian Conflict', in N. Debrauwere-Miller (ed.), *The Israeli–Palestinian Conflict in the Francophone World*, New York: Routledge, pp. 1–23.

Delorme, S. (2007), 'Bateau ivre', *Cahiers du cinéma*, December, pp. 11–13.

Delorme, S. and Frodon, J.-M. (2007), 'Entretien avec Abdellatif Kechiche', *Cahiers du cinéma*, December, pp. 15–19.

Demont-Heinrich, C. (2005), 'Language and National Identity in the Era of Globalization: The Case of English in Switzerland', *Journal of Communication Inquiry*, 29(1), pp. 66–84.

Deschamps, H. (2001), *Jacques Rivette: théâtre, amour, cinéma*, Paris: L'Harmattan.

Desrichard, Y. (2001), *Julien Duvivier: cinquante ans de noirs destins*, Courbevoie: Durante/Paris: Bibliothèque du Film.

Desrichard, Y. (2003), *Henri Decoin: un artisan du cinéma populaire*, Courbevoie et Paris: Duranten et Bibliothèque du Film.

Domenach, E. and Rouyer, P. (2007), 'Entretien avec Albellatif Kechiche', *Positif* 562, pp. 13–20.

Douchet, J. (1998), *Nouvelle vague*, Paris: Cinémathèque française/Hazan.

Downing, L. (2004), *Patrice Leconte*, Manchester: Manchester University Press.

Durgnat, R. (1963), *Nouvelle Vague: The First Decade*, Loughton, Essex and New York: Motion Publications and Cinema House.

Durgnat, R. (1974), *Jean Renoir*, Berkeley, CA: University of California Press.

Durham, C.A. (1998), *Double Takes: Culture and Gender in French Films and their American Remakes*, Hanover, NH: University Press of New England.

Dutheil de la Rochère, A.-E. (1997), *Les Studios de la Victorine (1919–1929)*, Paris: Association Française de Recherche sur l'Histoire du Cinéma.

Dyer, R. (1979), *Stars*, London: British Film Institute. Translated by N. Burch, S. Meininger and J. Nacache as *Le Star-système hollywoodien suivi de Marilyn Monroe et la sexualité*, Paris: L'Harmattan, 2004.

Eades, C. (2006), *Le Cinéma postcolonial français*, Paris: Cerf.

Elsaesser, T. (2005), 'Double Occupancy and Small Adjustments: Space, Place and Policy in the New European Cinema Since the 1990s', in *European Cinema: Face to Face with Hollywood*, Amsterdam: Amsterdam University Press, pp. 108–30.

Elvagabundo (2008), '*Adieu Mères!* Un film sur l'immigration des juifs marocains', http://www.comlive. net/Adieu-Meres-Un-Film-Sur-L-Immigration-Des-Juifs-Marocains,149122.htm. Accessed 14 July 2009.

Ezra, E. and Rowden, T. (eds) (2006), *Transnational Cinema: The Reader*, New York: Routledge.

Faulkner, C. (1979), *Jean Renoir: A Guide to References and Resources*, Boston: G. K. Hall.

Faulkner, C. (1986), *The Social Cinema of Jean Renoir*, Princeton, NJ: Princeton University Press.

Faulkner, C. and Duncan, P. (eds) (2007), *Jean Renoir: A Conversation with his Films 1894–1979*, London: Taschen.

Fauth, J. (2009), 'Mesrine – L'instinct de mort and L'ennemi public n°1 – Public Enemy #1', *World/Independent Film*, http://worldfilm.about.com/od/frenchfilm/fr/mesrine.htm. Accessed 8 August 2009.

Flitterman-Lewis, S. (1982), 'Women, Representation and Cinematic Discourse: The Example of French Cinema', PhD thesis, University of California – Berkeley.

Forbes, J. (1992), *The Cinema in France after the New Wave*, Basingstoke: Macmillan.

Frappat, H. (2001), *Jacques Rivette, Secret Compris*, Paris: Cahiers du cinéma.

French, P. (2008a), 'Summer Hours', *The Observer*, 20 July.

French, P. (2008b), 'A Fine Year for War, Exile, Violence … and Old Men', *The Observer*, 14 December.

French, P. et al. (1967), *The Films of Jean-Luc Godard*, London: Studio Vista.

Frodon, J.-M. (1995), *L'Age moderne du cinéma français: de la Nouvelle Vague à nos jours*, Paris: Flammarion.

Frodon, J-M. (1998), *La Projection nationale, cinéma et nation*, Paris: Editions Odile Jacob.

Frodon, J.-M. (2007), 'La Langue d'Abdel et le pays réel', *Cahiers du cinéma*, 629, pp. 8–10.

Garson, C. (2008), *Jean Renoir*, Paris: Cahiers du cinéma/Le Monde.

Gauteur, C. (1980), *Jean Renoir: la double méprise, 1925–1939*, Paris: Les Éditeurs français réunis.

Gauthier, C. (1999), *La Passion du cinéma: cinéphiles, ciné-clubs et salles spécialisées à Paris de 1920 à 1929*, Paris: Association Française de Recherche sur l'Histoire du Cinéma.

Gauthier, C. (2005), 'La fortune critique des adaptations cinématographiques de Victor Hugo', in D. Gleizes (ed.), *L'Oeuvre de Victor Hugo à l'écran: des rayons et des ombres*, Paris: L'Harmattan, pp. 17–43.

Gévaudan, F. (1979), 'Evocation I: Louis Daquin', *Cinéma*, 241, pp. 29–40.

Giddens, A. (2001), *Sociology*, 4th ed., Cambridge: Polity.

Gilroy, P. (2004), *After Empire: Melancholia or Convivial Culture*, New York: Routledge.

Godier, R.-M. (2005), *L'Automate et le cinéma: dans* La Règle du jeu *de J. Renoir,* Le Limier *de J. L. Mankiewicz,* Pickpocket *de R. Bresson*, Paris: L'Harmattan. Thesis awarded 1999.

Gorbman, C. (1978), 'Film Music: Narrative Functions in French Films', PhD thesis, Washington.

Gozillon-Fronsacq, O. (2003), *L'Alsace et le cinéma 1896–1939*, Paris: Association Française de Recherche sur l'Histoire du Cinéma.

Graham, P.J. (1968), *The New Wave: Critical Landmarks*, Garden City, NY: Doubleday.

Greene, N. (2007), *The French New Wave: A New Look*, London: Wallflower.

Guérin, W. (1988), *Max Ophüls*, Paris: Cahiers du cinéma.

Guillaume-Grimaud, G. (1986), *Le Cinéma du Front Populaire*, Paris: Lherminier.

Hafez, S. (2006), 'The Quest for/Obsession with the National in Arabic Cinema', in V. Vitali and P. Willemen (eds), *Theorising National Cinema*, London: BFI, pp. 226–53.

Harris, S. and Ezra, E. (eds) (2000), *France in Focus: Film and National Identity*, Oxford: Berg.

Harris, S. and Downing, L. (eds) (2007), *From Perversion to Purity: The Stardom of Catherine Deneuve*, Manchester: Manchester University Press.

Hayes, G. and O'Shaughnessy, M. (eds) (2005), *Cinéma et engagement*, Paris: L'Harmattan.

Hayward, S. (1993), *French National Cinema*, London: Routledge, 2nd ed. 2005.

Hayward, S. (1999), *Luc Besson*, Manchester: Manchester University Press.

Hayward, S. (2004), *Simone Signoret: The Star as Cultural Sign*, London: Continuum.

Hayward, S. (2010), *French Costume Drama of the 1950s: Fashioning Politics in Film*, Bristol: Intellect

Hayward, S. and Powrie, P. (eds) (2006), *The Films of Luc Besson: Master of Spectacle*, Manchester: Manchester University Press.

Hayward, S. and Vincendeau, G. (eds) (1990), *French Film: Texts and Contexts*, London: Routledge (2nd ed. 2000).

Herpe, N. (ed.) (2007), *Rohmer et les autres*, Rennes: Presses Universitaires de Rennes.

Herpe, N. and Toulet, E. (eds) (2000), *René Clair ou le cinéma à la lettre*, Paris: Association Française de Recherche sur l'Histoire du Cinéma.

Higbee, W. (2009), 'Displaced Audio: Exploring Soundscapes in Maghrebi-French Film-making', *Studies in French Cinema*, 9(3), pp. 225–41.

Higginbotham, V. (1979), *Luis Buñuel*, Boston: Twayne.

Higson, A. (1989), 'The Concept of National Cinema', *Screen*, 30(4), pp. 36–46.

Hjort, M. (2000), 'Themes of Nation', in M. Hjort and S. Mackenzie (eds), *Cinema and Nation*, London: Routledge, pp. 103–17.

Hoffman, C. (2006), 'Why are French Jews leaving France?', *Jerusalem Post*, 12 September, http://www.jpost.com/servlet/Satellite?cid=1157913611906&pagename=JPost/JPArticle/ShowFull. Accessed 14 July 2009.

Hubert-Lacombe, P. (1996), *Le Cinéma français dans la guerre froide: 1946–1956*, Paris: L'Harmattan.

Hughes, A. and Williams, J. (eds) (2001), *Gender in the French Cinema*, Oxford: Berg.

Hugo, V. (1967), *Les Misérables*, Paris: Garnier-Flammarion.

Hussey, A. (2007), *Paris: The Secret History*, London: Penguin.

Insdorf, A. (1978), *François Truffaut*, Boston: Twayne.

Ionascu, M. (2001), *Cheminots et cinéma: la représentation d'un groupe social dans le cinéma et l'audiovisuel français*, Paris: L'Harmattan. Thesis awarded 1999.

Ismail, M. (n.d.), '*Adieu mères*, Mohamed Ismail', http://www.clapnoir.org/spip.php?article237. Accessed 14 July 2009.

Jardonnet, E. (2006), *Poétique de la singularité au cinéma: une lecture croisée de Jacques Rivette et de Maurice Pialat*, Paris: L'Harmattan. Thesis awarded 2003.

Jeancolas, J.-P. (1983), *Quinze ans d'années trente: le cinéma des Français, 1929–1944*, Paris: Stock.

Jeancolas, J.-P. (1995), *Histoire du cinéma français*, Paris: Nathan.

Jeffries, S. (2001), 'The French Insurrection', *The Observer*, 24 June.

Jenn, P. (1984), *Georges Méliès cinéaste: le montage cinématographique chez Georges Méliès*, Paris: Albatros.

J.G. (1956), '*Bel-Ami*', *Monthly Film Bulletin*, 23(266), p. 27.

Jones, D.W. (1978), 'Jean Cocteau's Use of the Cinema to Express the Myth of the Poet', PhD thesis, Leeds.

Kawin, B. (1978), *Mindscreen: Bergman, Godard, and First-person Film*, Princeton, NJ: Princeton University Press.

King, N. (1984), *Abel Gance: A Politics of Spectacle*, London: BFI.

Kline, T.J. (1992), *Screening the Text: Intertextuality in New Wave French Cinema*, Baltimore, MD: John Hopkins University Press.

Knapp, B. (1981), *Sacha Guitry*, Boston: Twayne.

Kramer S. and Welsh, J. (1978), *Abel Gance*, Boston: Twayne.

Kreidl, J. (1978), *Alain Resnais*, Boston: Twayne.

Kreidl, J. (1980), *Jean-Luc Godard*, Boston: Twayne.

Kuisel, R. (2000), 'The Fernandel Factor: The Rivalry Between the French and American Cinema in the 1950s', *Yale French Studies*, 98, pp. 119–34.

Kwietniowski, R. (1984), 'Chantal Akerman and the Cinema of Stories', PhD thesis, Kent.

Labarthe, A.S. (1960), *Essai sur le jeune cinéma français*, Paris: Terrain Vague.

Lanzoni, R.F. (2002), *French Cinema from the Beginnings to the Present*, London: Continuum.

Le Boterf, H. (1995), *Harry Baur*, Paris: Pygmalion/Gérard Watelet.

Le Roy, E. (2000), *Jean-Pierre Mocky*, Courbevoie and Paris: Durante and Bibliothèque du Film.

Lesage, J. (1976), 'The Films of Jean-Luc Godard and Their Use of Brechtian Dramatic Theory', PhD thesis, Indiana University.

Lesage, J. (1979), *Jean-Luc Godard: A Guide to References and Resources*, Boston, MA: G.K. Hall.

Lindeperg, S. (1997), *Les Ecrans de l'ombre: la second guerre mondiale dans le cinéma français (1944-1969)*, Paris: Editions CNRS.

Lledo, J.-P. (2009), 'Algérie, histoires à ne pas dire', *Africultures*, 2 March, http://www.africultures.com/php/index.php?nav=film&no=4943. Accessed 13 July 2009.

Loshitzky, Y. (1995), *The Radical Faces of Godard and Bertolucci*, Detroit, MI: Wayne State University Press.

Loshitzky, Y. (2010), *Screening Strangers: Migration and Diaspora in Contemporary European Cinema*, Bloomington, IN: Indiana University Press.

MacCabe, C. et al. (1980), *Godard: Images, Sounds, Politics*, London: Macmillan/BFI.

Magny, J. (1987), *Claude Chabrol*, Paris: Cahiers du cinéma.

Marie, L. (2005), *Le Cinéma est à nous: le PCF et le cinéma français de la Libération à nos jours*, Paris: L'Harmattan. Thesis awarded 2000.

Marie, M. (2000), *La Nouvelle Vague: une école artistique*, Paris: Nathan. Translated by R. Neupert as *The French New Wave: An Artistic School*, Malden: Blackwell, 2003.

Marie, M. (2002), 'Quelques réflexions sur les sujets de thèses soutenues ces cinq dernières années (1996–2000)', *Ecrans et lucarnes*, 10 September, pp. 6–7.

Marie, M. (2006), *Guide des études cinématographiques et audiovisuelles*, Paris: Armand Colin.

Marie, M. (ed.) (1998), *Le Jeune cinéma français*, Paris: Nathan.

Marshall, B. (2007), *André Téchiné*, Manchester: Manchester University Press.

Masson, A. (2007), 'Entretien avec Albellatif Kechiche', *Positif*, 562, pp. 13–20.

Maupassant, G. de (1999), *Bel-Ami*, annotated and commented by A. Wrona, Paris: Flammarion.

Mayne, J. (2005), *Claire Denis*, Urbana, IL: University of Illinois Press.

Mazdon, L. (2000), *Encore Hollywood: Remaking French Cinema*, London: BFI.

Mazdon, L. (ed.) (2001), *France on Film: Reflections on Popular French Cinema*, London: Wallflower.

McGerr, C. (1980), *René Clair*, Boston: Twayne.

McMahan, A. (2003), *Alice Guy Blaché: Lost Visionary of the Cinema*, London: Continuum.

Memmi, A. (1974), *Juifs et arabes*, Paris: Idées/Gallimard.

Metz, C. (1974), *Film Language: A Semiotics of the Cinema*, Oxford: Oxford University Press. First published in French as *Essais sur la signification au cinéma*, Paris: Klincksieck, 1971.

Moine, R. (2005a), *Les Genres du cinéma*, Paris: Armand Colin.

Moine, R. (ed.) (2005b), *Le Cinéma français face aux genres*, Paris: Association Française de Recherche sur l'Histoire du Cinéma.

Moine, R. (2007), *Remakes: Les films français à Hollywood*, Paris: CNRS Editions.

Monaco, J. (1976), *The New Wave: Truffaut, Godard, Chabrol, Rohmer, Rivette*, New York: Oxford University Press.

Monaco, J. (1978), *Alain Resnais*, New York: Oxford University Press.

Morrey, D. and Smith, A. (2009), *Jacques Rivette*, Manchester: Manchester University Press.

Murphy, D. and Williams, P. (2007), *Postcolonial African Cinema: Ten Directors*, Manchester: Manchester University Press.

Nacache J. (2003), *L'Acteur de cinéma*, Paris: Nathan.

Naficy, H. (2001), *An Accented Cinema, Exilic and Diasporic Filmmaking*, Princeton, NJ: Princeton University Press.

Naumann, C. (2001), *Jacques Becker: entre classicisme et modernité*, Courbevoie: Durante/Paris: Bibliothèque du Film.

Neupert, R. (2002), *A History of the French New Wave Cinema*, Madison, WI: University of Wisconsin Press.

O'Brien, C. (2005), *Cinema's Conversion to Sound: Technology and Film Style in France and the US*, Bloomington, IN: Indiana University Press.

O'Shaughnessy, M. (2007), *The New Face of Political Cinema: Commitment in French Film since 1995*, New York: Berghahn.

Passek, J.-L. (1987), *Dictionnaire du cinéma français*, Paris: Larousse.

Portuges, C. (2009), 'French Women Directors Negotiating Transnational Identities', *Yale French Studies*, 115, pp. 47–63.

Positif (1997), *Positif*, facsimile reprint of nos 1–15, Paris: J.-M. Place.

Positif (2000), *Positif*, facsimile reprint of nos 16–31, Paris: J.-M. Place.

Positif (2002), *L'Amour du cinéma: 50 ans de la revue Positif*, Paris: Gallimard.

Powrie, P. (1997), *French Cinema in the 1980s: Nostalgia and the Crisis of Masculinity*, Oxford: Clarendon Press.

Powrie, P. (ed.) (1999), *French Cinema in the 1990s: Continuity and Difference*, Oxford: Oxford University Press.

Powrie, P. (2002), 'Thirty Years of Doctoral Theses on French Cinema', *Studies in French Cinema*, 3(3), pp. 199–203.

Powrie, P. (2006), *The Cinema of France*, London: Wallflower Press.

Powrie, P. and Reader, K. (2004), *French Cinema: A Student's Guide*, London: Arnold.

Powrie, P. with Rebillard, E. (2009), *Pierre Batcheff and Stardom in 1920s French Cinema*, Edinburgh: Edinburgh University Press.

Pratt, M. L. (1991), 'Arts of the Contact Zone', *Profession*, 91, pp. 33-40.

Prédal, R. (1991), *Le Cinéma français depuis 1945*, Paris: Nathan.

Prédal, R. (2002), *Le Jeune cinéma français*, Paris: Nathan.

Provoyeur, J.-L. (2002), *Le Cinéma de Robert Bresson: de l'effet de réel à l'effet de sublime*, Paris: L'Harmattan. Thesis awarded 2001.

Rees-Roberts, N. (2008), *French Queer Cinema*, Edinburgh: Edinburgh University Press.

Revue du cinéma (1992), *La Revue du cinema: anthologie*, Paris: Gallimard.

Rodríguez Blanco, M. (2000), *Luis Buñuel*, Courbevoie: Durante/Paris: Bibliothèque du Film.

Roud, R. (1968), *Jean-Luc Godard*, Garden City, NY: Doubleday.

Roze, A. (1995), *La France arc-en-ciel: Les Français venus d'ailleurs*, Paris: Editions Julliard.

Sandro, P. (1987), *Diversions of Pleasure: Luis Buñuel and the Crises of Desire*, Columbus: Ohio State University Press.

Savarese, E. (2007), *Algérie, la guerre des mémoires*, Paris: Editions Non Lieu.

Scemama-Heard, C. (2006), *Histoire(s) du cinéma de Jean-Luc Godard: la force faible d'un art*, Paris: L'Harmattan. Thesis awarded 2005.

Schilling, D. (2007), *Eric Rohmer*, Manchester: Manchester University Press.

Schrader, P. (1972), *Transcendental Style in Film: Ozu, Bresson, Dreyer*, Berkeley, CA: University of California Press.

Schwartz, V. (2007), *It's So French! Hollywood, Paris, and the Making of Cosmopolitan Film Culture*, Chicago: University of Chicago Press.

Scott, A.J. (2000), 'French Cinema: Economy, Policy and Place in the Making of a Cultural-Products Industry', *Theory, Culture & Society*, 17(1), pp. 1–38.

Sellier, G. (1987), 'Les Films de Jean Grémillon: essai d'analyse narratologique', PhD thesis, Paris 3.

Sellier, G. (1989), *Jean Grémillon: le cinéma est à vous*, Paris: Méridiens Klincksieck.

Sellier, G. (2005), *La Nouvelle Vague: un cinéma au masculin singulier*, Paris: CNRS. Translated by K. Ross as *Masculine Singular: French New Wave Cinema*, Durham, NC: Duke University Press.

Serceau, D. (2008), *Symptômes du jeune cinéma français*, Paris: Cerf/Corlet.

Sesonske, A. (1980), *Jean Renoir: The French Films, 1924–1939*, Cambridge, MA: Harvard University Press.

Sherzer, D. (ed.) (1996), *Cinema, Colonialism, Postcolonialism: Perspectives from the French and Francophone World*, Austin, TX: University of Texas Press.

Shlensky, L.Z. (2009), 'Otherwise Occupied: The Israeli–Palestinian Conflict in the Francophone Cinema' in N. Debrauwere-Miller (ed.), *The Israeli–Palestinian Conflict in the Francophone World*, New York: Routledge, pp. 105–22.

Shohat, E. (2006), *Taboo Memories, Diasporic Voices*, Durham, NC: Duke University Press.

Shohat, E. and Stam, R. (2006), 'The Cinema After Babel, Language, Difference, Power', in E. Shohat (ed.), *Taboo Memories, Diasporic Voices*, Durham, NC: Duke University Press, pp. 106–38.

Siclier, J. (1961), *Nouvelle vague?*, Paris: Le Cerf.

Siclier, J. (1990), *Le Cinéma français, Vol. 1 : De La Bataille du rail à La Chinoise, 1945–1968; Vol. 2 : De Baisers volés à Cyrano de Bergerac, 1968–1990*, Paris: Editions Ramsay.

Slavin, D. (2001), *Colonial Cinema and Imperial France, 1919–1939: White Blind Spots, Male Fantasies, Settler Myths*, Baltimore, MD: Johns Hopkins University Press.

Solomons, J. (2008), 'France on the Crest of a New New Wave', *The Observer*, 16 November.

Spaas, L. (2000), *The Francophone Film: A Struggle for Identity*, Manchester: Manchester University Press.

Stam, R. (2005), 'The Theory and Practice of Adaptation', in R. Stam (ed.), *Literature and Film: A Guide to the Theory and Practice of Film Adaptation*, Malden, MA: Blackwell, pp. 1–46.

Strand, D. (2009), '*Être et parler*: Being and Speaking French in Abdellatif Kechiche's *L'Esquive* (2004) and Laurent Cantet's *Entre les murs* (2008)', *Studies in French Cinema*, 9(3), pp. 273–83.

Tahiri, F.-Z. (2007), 'Le cinéma marocain contre l'oubli', *La Tribune*, 566, 11 October.

Tarr, C. (2005), *Reframing Difference: Beur and Banlieue Filmmaking in France*, Manchester: Manchester University Press.

Tarr, C. with Rollet, B. (2001), *Cinema and the Second Sex: Women's Filmmaking in France in the 1980s and 1990s*, London: Continuum.

Temple, M. and Williams, J.S. (eds) (2001), *The Cinema Alone: Essays on the Work of Jean-Luc Godard 1985–2000*, Amsterdam: Amsterdam University Press.

Temple, M., Williams, J.S. and Witt, M. (eds) (2004), *For Ever Godard*, London: Black Dog.

Temple, M. and Witt, M. (eds) (2004), *The French Cinema Book*, London: BFI.

Tester, K. (2008), *Eric Rohmer: Film as Theology*, London: Palgrave Macmillan.

Thackway, M. (2003), *Africa Shoots Back: Alternative Perspectives in Sub-Saharan Francophone African Film*, Bloomington, IN: Indiana University Press.

Trémois, C. (1998), *Les Enfants de la liberté: le jeune cinéma français des années 90*, Paris: Seuil.

Truffaut, F. (1954), 'Une certaine tendance du cinéma français', *Cahiers du cinéma*, 31, pp. 15–29.

Turk, E.B. (1989), *Child of Paradise: Marcel Carné and the Golden Age of French Cinema*, Cambridge, MA: Harvard University Press. Translated by N. Burch as *Marcel Carné et l'âge d'or du cinéma français 1929–1945*, Paris: L'Harmattan, 2002.

Vasse, D. (2004), *Catherine Breillat, un cinéma du rite et de la transgression*, Paris: Arte/Complexe.

Véray, L. (1995), *Les Films d'actualité français de la Grande Guerre*, Paris: Association Française de Recherche sur l'Histoire du Cinéma.

Véray, L. (ed.) (2008), *Marcel L'Herbier: l'art du cinéma*, Paris: Association Française de Recherche sur l'Histoire du Cinéma.

Verevis, C. (2006), *Film Remakes*, Edinburgh: Edinburgh University Press.

Vincendeau, G. (1985), 'French Cinema in the 1930s: Social Text and Context of a Popular Entertainment Medium', PhD thesis, East Anglia.

Vincendeau, G. (2000a), *Stars and Stardom in French Cinema*, London: Continuum.

Vincendeau, G. (2000b), 'Les Etudes de cinéma et audio-visuel en Grande-Bretagne', *Ecrans et lucarnes*, 6 (May), pp. 12–14.

Vincendeau, G. (2004), 'The Art of Spectacle: The Aesthetics of Classical French Cinema', in M. Temple and M. Witt (eds), *The French Cinema Book*, London: BFI, pp. 137–52.

Virmaux, A. (1972), 'La Tentation du cinema chez les écrivains français: l'aventure du scénario', PhD thesis, Paris IV-Sorbonne.

Waldron, D. and Vanderschelden, I. (eds) (2007), *France at the Flicks: Trends in Contemporary French Popular Cinema*, Newcastle, UK: Cambridge Scholars.

Webber, A. (2008), *Berlin in the Twentieth Century: A Cultural Topography*, Cambridge: Cambridge University Press.

Wikipedia (n.d.), 'André Morice', http://fr.wikipedia.org/wiki/André_Morice. Accessed 14 February 2009.

Williams, A. (1977), 'Max Ophüls and the Cinema of Desire: Style and Spectacle in Four Films, 1948–1955', PhD thesis, New York (Buffalo).

Williams, A. (1992), *Republic of Images: A History of French Filmmaking*, Cambridge, MA: Harvard University Press.

Williams, A. (ed.) (2002), *Film and Nationalism*, New Brunswick, NJ: Rutgers University Press.

Wilson, E. (1999), *French Cinema Since 1950: Personal Histories*, London: Duckworth.

Wood, R. and Walker, M. (1970), *Claude Chabrol*, London: Studio Vista.

Woodhull, W. (2003), 'Postcolonial Thought and Culture in Francophone North Africa', in C. Forsdick and D. Murphy (eds), *Francophone Postcolonial Studies: A Critical Introduction*, London: Arnold, pp. 211–20.

Wrona, A. (1999), 'Dossier 2', in G. de Maupassant (ed.), *Bel-Ami*, Paris: Flammarion, pp. 386–400.

Index